Information Processing and Security Systems

T0189510

Information Processing and Security Systems

Edited by

Khalid Saeed
*Białystok Technical
University, POLAND*

Jerzy Pejaś
*Technical University of
Szczecin, POLAND*

 Springer

Khalid Saeed
Bialystock Technical University, POLAND

Jerzy Pejaś
Technical University of Szczecin, POLAND

Library of Congress Cataloging-in-Publication Data

Information processing and security systems / edited by Khalid Saeed, Jerzy Pejas.
   p. cm.
     ISBN-13: 978-1-4614-9810-0
     ISBN-10: 1-4614-9810-4
     ISBN-10: 0-387-26325-X (eBook)
     ISBN-13: 978-0387-26325-0 (eBook)

       1. Computer network--Security measures. 2. Information storage and
      retrieval systems--Security measures. 3. Computers-Access control. I.
      Saeed, Khalid. II. Pejas, Jerzy, 1954-

TK5105-59.I525 2005
005.8--dc22

                               2005049008

9 8 7 6 5 4 3 2 1   SPIN 11352075

springeronline.com

Table of Contents

PART II - COMPUTER SECURITY AND SAFETY

Preface

This book is based on the most recent results of collaborative research in the field of Information Processing Systems conducted by both university professors and young computer scientists. The extensive research has yielded some novel findings that might be directly employed in further technological innovations. The work reveals ground-breaking scientific achievements and indicates their practical applications.

The topics have been selected so as to cover three basic fields in Computer Science. The contents encompass three parts. Part I contains twelve chapters on Digital Image and Signal Processing. Part II consists of thirteen chapters on Computer Security and Safety. Part III includes seventeen chapters dealing with Artificial Intelligence-Oriented Trends and their Applications.

Throughout the book, a great emphasis is placed on theory as well as practice. The contributions not only reflect invaluable experience of eminent professors in relevant areas but also point out new methods and approaches developed by computer scientists and researchers. Most of the contributions are extended versions of original papers on the topics mentioned above, which were introduced at recent international conferences. These works were reviewed by two or three referees, who recommended publishing them in their modified versions.

We expect that this book will throw some new light on unresolved problems and will inspire the reader to greater challenges. Hopefully it will be an effective tool for both senior and young researchers.

Editors, K. Saeed and J. Pejaś

Foreword

This book outlines new trends that have emerged in scientific research in the field of Computer Science. It provides a forum of academic works and researches conducted by both distinguished and young computer scientists.

It is a pleasure to recognize the fact that a great number of academic teachers working for the Faculty of Engineering in Elk at the University of Finance and Management in Bialystok have appeared to be actively committed to research studies. Undoubtedly, their remarkable efforts, which are presented in this book, make a valuable contribution to science. This ascertains the fact that the newly founded academic core, which Elk became as late as the beginning of XXI century, constantly raises its educational standard.

This book is a result of a fruitful collaboration between the Department of Computer Engineering in the Faculty of Engineering in Elk and experienced Departments of Computer Science in Bialystok University of Technology and Technical University of Szczecin.

I would like to extend my sincere congratulations to the editors of the book, Dr Khalid Saeed and Dr Jerzy Pejaś, on their joint endeavor in producing a work at such a high level.

Professor Józef Szabłowski, President
University of Finance and Management in Bialystok

PART I

Digital Image and Signal Processing

Fourier Descritpor-Based Deformable Models for Segmentation of the Distal Femur in CT

Eric Berg[1], Mohamed Mahfouz[2,3], Christian Debrunner[1], Brandon Merkl[1], William Hoff[1]

[1] Colorado School of Mines

Golden, Colorado, USA, e-mail: {eberg,cdebrunn,bmerkl,whoff}@mines.edu

[2] University of Tennessee

Knoxville, Tennessee, USA, e-mail: mmahfouz@engr.utk.edu

[3] Oak Ridge National Laboratories

Oak Ridge, Tennessee, USA

Abstract:
Anatomical shapes present a unique problem in terms of accurate representation and medical image segmentation. Three-dimensional statistical shape models have been extensively researched as a means of autonomously segmenting and representing models. We present a segmentation method driven by a statistical shape model based on a priori shape information from manually segmented training image sets. Our model is comprised of a stack of two-dimensional Fourier descriptors computed from the perimeters of the segmented training image sets after a transformation into a canonical coordinate frame. Our segmentation process alternates between a local active contour process and a projection onto a global PCA basis of the statistical shape model. We apply our method to the segmentation of CT and MRI images of the distal femur and show quantitatively that it recovers bone shape more accurately from real imagery than a recently published method recovers bone shape from synthetically segmented imagery.

Keywords: *automatic 3D image segmentation, Fourier shape descriptors, principal components analysis, statistical shape model, active contours, snakes.*

1.1 Introduction

Current methods in three-dimensional image segmentation typically employ statistical shape models, first developed by Cootes and Taylor [1] as a means to incorporate *a priori* shape information. A statistical shape model is trained by a considering the canonical parameterization of a set of similar shape instances, or training shapes. Performing a principal components analysis (PCA) on the parameterized shapes highlights the statistical modes of variation in the shape, allowing for a possible reduction in the dimension of the model shape space, discussed in more detail in section 2.3. A well-constructed statistical model will provide a shape constraint on subsequent segmentations of new images.

The primary original contributions of this work are our segmentation algorithm and our statistical shape representation. The segmentation algorthm iterates two steps: a local active contour fitting of shape curves on slices through the dataset, and a global projection of the resulting shape curves onto the PCA basis of our statistical shape model. Prior methods (see e.g., [5]) simultaneously optimize for both local (image) constraints and global (statistical model) constraints. Our method allows us to include a final local (active contours) optmization step, which finds a solution close to (in the image space) but not in the model subspace determined by PCA. Our results show that this final local optimization substantially improves the accuracy of the resulting model. Our statistical shape representation is based on the principal components of the contour shape estimated on the slices, but PCA is not applied directly to the contour shape. Instead, the contour shapes are represented with Fourier descriptors and the smoothed by removing the high frequency components, and PCA is applied to the Fourier descriptors collected from the entire bone. This approach reduces the dimensionality of the PCA and restricts the statistical model to smooth bone surfaces. For the purpose of developing and testing our method, we modeled the human distal femur from 19 sets of 3D images generated by both CT and MRI image modalities (15 CT, 4 MRI); the datasets include both left and right femurs, so we mirrored the left femur across the midsagittal plane as was done in [2, 3], creating additional samples of the right femur.

1.2 Approach

In this section, we describe how the statistical models are computed from images and how these models are used in our segmentation approach.

1.2.1 Image Preprocessing

For training and evaluation purposes, each of our nineteen 3D image volumes is manually segmented to model the distal section of the femur. The resulting binary images are rigidly registered to a coordinate system defined in terms of reference points on the bone. We have built a User Interface (UI) to aid the user in both initial alignment and to visualize the segmentation process. To perform this alignment the user first loads an image data set and specifies the voxel size. The user can then visualize the image data as one or more orthogonal planes (axial, coronal, or sagittal) or as an entire volume, when used with volume visualization hardware such as VolumePro. The user then loads the appropriate mean model and using visual manipulators shown below in Fig. 1, can scale, rotate or translate the model into alignment with the image data.

1.2.2 Fourier Descriptors

Based on the manual segmentation, we compute binary images at slices of constant z-value in the registered volume. Each binary image contains at least one region representing the bone cross-section; in the case of images intersecting the condyles, two distinct regions may be present. The regions on each slice are closed contours, allowing for a Fourier descriptor (FD) [6,7] representation to be computed. A more recent application of FDs involves medical image segmentation [5], where the combined optimization approach discussed in the introduction is used.

The most significant features of the contour are captured in the lower frequency terms of the FDs, so we can produce a more concise description of the contour by eliminating the high-frequency terms. We found through experimentation that 32 coefficients sufficiently describe the shape of all distal femur cross-sections.

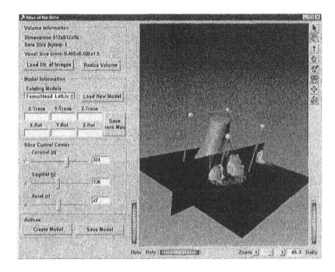

Fig. 1. Screenshot of User Interface.

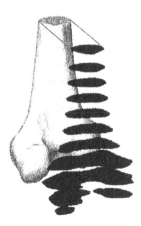

Fig. 2. Model of the distal femur demonstrating the slice structure. Note that the slices shown are a sub-sampling of the full set of slices

1.2.3 Shape Model Representation and Construction

Each femur model is composed of M contour slices parallel to the axial plane and stacked in the z-direction (Fig. 2). Each of the M contours is described by 32 FDs. A contour is represented by a single vector formed by concatenating the real and imaginary parts of the FD coefficients that represent it. The model vector m is then formed by concatenating the M contour vectors to form a vector of length $n = 64M$.

The modes of variation among the training models are captured by a PCA. Any shape instance in the training set can be represented by the mean model and a linear combination of the eigenvectors [8]. Typically, a model can be accurately approximated by $t < T$ principal components (PCs), corresponding to the t largest eigenvalues. A model is then approximated as,

$$m = \bar{m} + \sum_{i=1}^{t} b_i p_i \tag{1}$$

where b_i is the coefficient multiplying the ith PC p_i, and $\bar{m}$ is the mean of the training model vectors. The p_i form the principal basis, or shape space of the model. Thus, our representation of the statistical model consists of the mean model vector and the vectors corresponding to the first t PCs. Section 3 will provide more insight into the effects of model reduction.

1.2.4 3D Image Segmentation

A 3D image volume that is not included in the training set can be segmented by iteratively deforming the FD statistical model until it closely matches the correct features in the 3D image set. The statistical model ensures a segmentation consistent with the training models. Prior to segmentation, the new image set must be registered by hand to the coordinate frame as described in Section 2.1. A search for the optimal segmentation consists of separate local and global optimizations; a local search (unconstrained by the statistical model) is performed independently on each slice using an active contours algorithm, and a global search takes the form of a projection of the FDs of the active contours solutions onto the principal basis of the statistical model. Since the two searches are forced to intersect periodically, the constraints from both optimization functions are imposed. The approach is outlined below in Algorithm 1.

Most previous work in this area involves minimizing a single objective function that combines terms driven by the image data and terms driven by the prior shape information. This approach will often result in a solution that is not the true global minimum, but a spurious local minimum. Our algorithm also allows the final solution to lie outside the principal component space. This is important since one cannot otherwise extract new models that extend beyond the training set. By separating the local and global searches, we can find solutions that the combined optimization cannot find.

Algorithm 1. Segmentation procedure
   1) Initialize active contours (see *Local Search*) based on the mean model, $\bar{m}$
   2) Allow active contours to deform independently on each image for h iterations
   3) Convert active contours to Fourier descriptors
   4) Project FDs onto principal basis
   5) Form a new model from the projected FDs
   6) Check Equation (2) for convergence (see below)
      a) if Δ < threshold, repeat steps 2 and 3 only
      b) if Δ > threshold, repeat steps 2-6 with the new model from step 5 as the new initialization for active contours

The alternating process of active contour deformation and shape space projection continues until the following convergence function reaches some empirically determined threshold,

$$\Delta = \sum_{i=1}^{t} \left(b_{ni} - b_{(n-1)i} \right)^2 \text{ for } n > 1, \tag{2}$$

where Δ represents the change in the model parameters from one iteration to the next. When this squared sum is less than the specified threshold, the model is assumed to have converged on a shape space solution. One additional optimization of the active contours is performed after this convergence.

Local Search

The local search for a solution occurs in the individual 2D image slices using active contours. Active contours, originally developed by Kass *et al.* [4] employ an energy minimization approach to detect features in images such as lines and edges. The technique typically works best with images that have clearly defined edges with minimal noise; otherwise a good initialization is required for an active contour to converge on an acceptable solution. In the case of shape modeling, we have a good initialization provided by the model information from the previous iteration, provided by steps 1 or 6b in Algorithm 1. The active contours method minimizes an energy functional consisting of an internal energy dependent on the spacing of and bend between the contour points, and an external energy dependent on the magnitude of the image gradient under the contour. The combined internal and external energies tend to drive the contour toward the image gradients, while maintaining control over the shape of the contour.

Global Search

The global search for a solution occurs in the principal space by computing the parameters b_i in Equation (2) by projecting the FDs from step 3 in Algorithm 1 onto the principal basis. This has the effect of constraining the active contours solution to be in the shape space, thus from one iteration to the next, the local solution is projected into shape space to find a global solution. After several iterations, the parameters b_i will vary negligibly, indicating that a global solution has been found. As previously discussed, this may not represent the optimal solution since the actual solution might fall slightly outside the shape space. With this optimal global solution as an initialization for one final local optimization, ie. an additional active contours adjustment, a solution that is close to the shape space, but optimized to fit the 3D image information can be found.

1.3 Results

In order to verify the ability of our modeling and segmentation techniques to extract anatomical features from medical images, we performed experiments with the 19 CT and MRI datasets. The datasets are each segmented manually and the resulting binary images are transformed and resampled as described in section 2.1. For testing purposes we sample the image volumes to a voxel size of 0.75 x 0.75 x

3.00 mm, resulting in 40 images spanning the distal 120 mm of the femur. The original grayscale images are transformed and resampled by the same transformation as the binary images so that subsequent model-based segmentations will be performed in the model domain.

Each of the 19 image sets was autonomously segmented according to Algorithm 1 with a model defined via a leave-one-out approach (see e.g., [11]), where the remaining 18 manual segmentations are used as training shapes. To illustrate the effect of the number of principal components on model-based segmentation, each of the 19 image sets is segmented multiple times, each time with a shape model defined by the remaining 18 datasets with a varying number of PCs ($t = 1, 2, \ldots ,$ 18). This results in 19*18 = 342 total segmentations of the 19 datasets.

We compare the autonomous model-based segmentation results to the manual segmentation results to obtain a measure of the quality of the segmentation. This comparison is performed in the 3D image domain by computing the shortest 3D Euclidean distance between the two voxel "surfaces" for each voxel on the autonomously segmented set. For each of the 342 segmentations, we obtain a mean separation distance and a maximum, or worst case, distance. Ideally, these distances are zero for a perfect fit, assuming that the solution we seek is the same as the manual segmentation.

We measured the accuracy of our system both with and without the final local optimization of step 6a in Algorithm 1 to determine if this final local optimization produced a better result than a solution constrained to be fully within the shape space. Figs. 3 and 4 show, respectively, the mean and maximum distance averaged

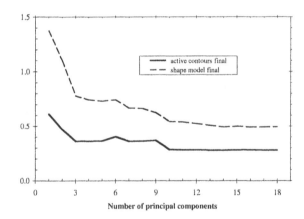

Fig. 3. Mean separation distance between autonomously segmented 3D image volumes and corresponding manually segmented volume. The solid line represents the solution where the active contours are adjusted after the final shape space projection; the dashed line is the solution resulting from the final shape space projection.

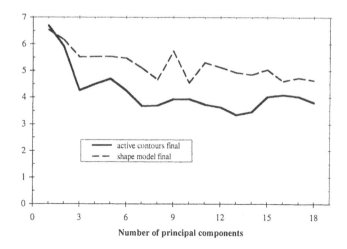

Fig. 4. Maximum separation distance between autonomously segmented 3D image volumes and corresponding manually segmented volume. The solid line represents the solution where the active contours are adjusted after the final shape space projection; the dashed line is the solution resulting from the final shape space projection.

over all segmentations as a function of the number of PCs in the statistical model. The two curves in each plot represent the solution with a final active contours optimization and the solution constrainted to lie in the shape space.

The mean separation distance shown in Fig. 3 demonstrates that an increase in the number of PCs yields a solution closer to the manual segmentation. Additionally, the final active contours adjustment pushes the mean distance between the expected surface and the actual surface to approximately half of the mean distance found by constraining the solution to be fully within the shape space. We can see the same trend for the maximum separation. Note that the mean distance levels off between 11 and 12 PCs, indicating that an increase in the number of PCs beyond 11 or 12 may not improve the segmentation. Larger training sets may of course require more PC's for accurate represntation.

Our best mean and maximum distance measures compare well to the best values presented in [3] and are summarized in Table 1. In fact, our best mean value is five times less than the best mean reported by Kaus *et al.* [3]. In this work the authors are modeling full femurs which are more variable than the distal femurs we are modeling. However we must also note that the authors of [3] are not solving the automated image segmentation problem, rather they are fitting a triangular mesh to manually segmented noiseless binary 3D images to form a surface model. We apply our method to the automated segmentation of noisy 3D medical images and evaluate our results using the 3D distances between the automatically segmented model and a manually segmented model. The authors of [3] evalute their results using the 3D deviation between the automatically computed mesh (vertices) and the manually segmented binary 3D images (voxels). Thus while our method is solving the more difficult problem of automatic image segmentation, the measures for evaluating the results are similar enough that a comparison to their results is valid.

	max Euclidean distance (mm)	mean Euclidean distance (mm)
Our results	3.35 (13)	0.28 (12)
Kaus et al.	~ 4.50 (20)	~ 1.40 (20)

Tab. 1. Comparison of results with Kaus *et al.* Value in parenthesis is the lowest number of PCs at which the value occurs

1.4 Conclusion and Future Work

The experiments have demonstrated that our model building method accurately and compactly captures the shape of the distal femur and our segmentation procedure successfully segments new datasets (Fig. 5). A comparison of our results to previously published values of Kass *et al.* [3] indicates that the accuracy of our segmentation method compares well to earlier methods. With only 12 PCs we were able to segment a 3D image volume with an average deviation of only 0.28 mm, a deviation of less than a voxel in most 3D medical images.

1.5 References

[1]   T. Cootes and C. Taylor, "Active shape models—'Smart snakes'," Proc. British Mach. Vision Conf., pp. 266-275, 1992.

[2]   C. Taylor, T. Cootes, A. Hill, and J. Haslam, "Medical Image Segmentation Using Active Shape Models," Proc. Medical Imaging Workshop, Brusseles, Belgium, pp. 121-143, 1995.

[3]   M. Kaus, V. Pekar, C. Lorenz, R. Truyen, S. Lobregt, and J. Weese, "Automated 3-D PDM Construction from Segmented Images Using Deformable Models," IEEE Transactions on Medical Imaging, Vol. 22, No. 8, pp. 1005-1013, Aug 2003.

12

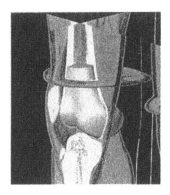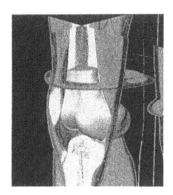

Fig. 5. Segmentation result. Initial mean model (left) and final, autonomously segmented model (right)

[4] M. Kass, A. Witkin, and D. Terzopoulos, "Snakes: Active contour models," Int. J. Comput. Vis., vol. 1, pp. 321–331, 1987.

[5] L. Staib and J. Duncan, "Boundary Finding with Parametrically Deformable Models," IEEE PAMI, Vol. 14, No. 11, pp. 1061-1075, Nov 1992.

[6] C. Zahn and R. Roskies, "Fourier Descriptors for Plane Closed Curves," IEEE Transactions on Computers, Vol. 21, No. 3, pp. 269-281, Mar 1972.

[7] E. Persoon and K. Fu, "Shape Discrimination Using Fourier Descriptors," IEEE Trans. on Sys.,Man, and Cyber., vol. SMC-7, no. 3, pp. 629-639, Mar 1977.

[8] T. Cootes, A. Hill, C. Taylor, and J. Haslam, "The Use of Active Shape Models for Locating Structures in Medical Images," Image and Vision Computing, vol. 12, no. 6, pp. 355-365, Jul 1994.

[9] T. Cootes, G. Edwards, and C. Taylor, "Active appearance models," in Proc. Eur. Conf. Computer Vision, vol. 2, H. Burkhardt and B. Neumann, Eds, pp. 484–498, 1998.

[10] T. Hutton , B. Buxton, P. Hammond, and H. Potts, "Estimating Average Growth trajectories in Shape-Space Using Kernel Smoothing," IEEE Transactions on Medical Imaging, Vol. 22, No. 6, pp. 747-753, Jun 2003.

[11] A. Kelemen, G. Székely, and G. Gerig, "Elastic Model-Based Segmentation of 3-D Neuroradiological Data Sets," IEEE Transactions on Medical Imaging, Vol. 18, No. 10, pp. 828-839, Oct 1999.

Hierarchical Segmentation of Sparse Surface Data Using Energy-Minimization Approach

Raid Al-Tahir

Centre for Caribbean Land and Environmental Appraisal Research (CLEAR)
Department of Surveying and Land Information
The University of the West Indies, Trinidad and Tobago
rtahir@eng.uwi.tt

Abstract: The main objective for this research is to develop an algorithm that produces a dense representation of a surface from a sparse set of observations and facilitates preliminary labeling of discontinuities in the surface. The solution to these issues is of a great interest to the new trends and applications in digital photogrammetry, particularly for large-scale urban imagery.

This study adopts the approach of a concurrent interpolation of the surface and detection of its discontinuities by the weak membrane. The solution was achieved through developing a multigrid implementation of the Graduate Non-Convexity (GNC) algorithm. The conducted experiments proved that the developed method is adequate and applicable for dealing with large-scale images of urban areas as it was successful in producing a realistic surface representation and fulfilling other set criteria.

Key words: Surface Reconstruction, Discontinuioty Detection, Multigrid Regularization.

1   Introduction

Surface interpolation is a common and important task for several disciplines and applications in geosciences and engineering. This topic has regain research interest with the emergence of new trends and technologies in the collection of geo-spatial data such as digital photogrammetry and lidar. Such systems provide a large amount of data in the form of discrete points of three-dimensional coordinates.

Photogrammetry is a 3-dimensional coordinate measuring technique that uses mainly aerial photographs as the fundamental medium for measurements. The basic mode of operation is based on taking photographs from at least two different view points; light rays are then traced back from each photograph to points on the object and mathematically intersected to produce the 3-dimensional coordinates for these points [1]. The advances in computer technology, digital cameras, and the increasing resolution of recorded images have allowed more optimal utilization and efficiency, as well as developing new applications [2].

The tasks of surface interpolation and surface analysis play an important role in reconstructing the surface based on photogrammetric data. Properties of visual surfaces, such as breaklines and abrupt discontinuities in surface normals, must be made explicit. They have a critical part for the success of the earlier processes of image matching and stereopsis. These processes are usually executed over a hierarchy of image resolutions (image pyramid) [3]. On another aspect, the performance of any surface interpolation method will suffer greatly without incorporating such discontinuities. The matter becomes more critical particularly for large-scale urban imagery normally associated with higher percentage of occlusion, repeated patterns, and many surface discontinuities [4].

The large quantity of data generated by a photogrammetric system makes it a challenge to deduce 3D object descriptions from such data. Visual surface discontinuities are definite indications for boundaries of objects on the topographic surface [3]. These boundaries are crucial for furnishing appropriate surface representation, and providing the means for surface segmentation and object recognition [5]. Identifying spatial discontinuities is vital in many applications such as segmentation, optical flow, stereo, image reconstruction [6], and extracting high-level cartographic features (e.g., building representations) needed in cartographic analysis and visualization [3].

Despite the significance of surface interpolation and surface analysis, not all algorithmic and implementation aspects for solving the related subtasks are fully developed. There is no straightforward choice for an optimal surface interpolation method that would accommodate the needs. Thus, the objective for this study is to develop an algorithm that produces a dense representation for a surface from a set of sparse observations and, at the same time, facilitates the preliminary labeling of discontinuities in the surface.

2 Surface Interpolation and Discontinuity Detection

Surface interpolation may be a simple and well-understood routine for some applications, or a more complicated and critical issue for others. The reason behind this is the fact that the interpolation is a prediction of what is not known that would agree with the data to some extent and behaves reasonably between data points. Based on the density and the distribution of the data points as well as the computational principle, different methods provide different interpretations of the data, and thus, different representations of the surface may result [7].

A reasonable expectation for an adapted method for surface interpolation is to construct as realistic a surface representation as possible. In addition, it should preserve essential surface characteristics implied by the observations. A violation to this condition occurs when a smooth surface is interpolated over breaklines. Preferably, the adopted algorithm should refrain from introducing new characteristics to the surface, for example, creating new maxima or minima in the surface. It should also allow incorporating and utilizing information on discontinuities whenever such information becomes available [4].

The number of methods for interpolating data over a grid is large if one considers all different variations and solution methods [8]. Several methods were reviewed, tested and evaluated according to the aforementioned criteria. The conclusion was that interpolating a surface by membrane splines fulfills the criteria above, and provides explicit information for surface analysis [4]. Depth data, in this physical/mechanical rendering, are represented by a set of vertical pins scattered within the region; the height of an individual pin is related to the elevation of the point. Fitting a surface is then analogous to constraining a membrane (thin film) to pass over the tips of the pins. Such a model would generate minimal area surface that is continuous, but need not have continuous first partial derivatives [8].

On a different aspect of the issue, and since they assume a smooth and continuous surface, the simplistic and direct implementations of conventional methods for surface interpolation may not be adequate when encountering a breakline or discontinuity in the surface. The interpolated surface will exhibit an unrealistic behavior that is manifested as oscillation and overshooting. Hence, discontinuities must be detected at a certain phase of the interpolation process.

To address the issue of detecting discontinuities in the surface, several research studies have adopted the concept of a "line process", first introduced by [9]. A line process is a set of binary variables located at the lines that connect grid cells representing the surface. The purpose of a line process is to decouple adjacent cells if the values of these cells are different. However, a penalty should be paid when a breakline is introduced. Thus, a break line will only be introduced when paying the penalty (within a cost or energy function) is less expensive than not having the break line at all. Pre-setting the line process variable associated with specific cells can accommodate available information on their boundaries.

2.1 Energy Minimization Approach

Because some information is lost in the two-dimensional photographic recording and measuring processes, reconstructing the surface from a discrete set of data is an ill-posed problem [3]. Thus, regularization is normally used for obtaining the unique solution to the problem. It involves minimizing an energy function E that essentially includes two functionals. The first functional, $D(s)$, provides a measure of the closeness of the solution (s) to the available data. It is usually taken to be the sum of the square of the differences between interpolated values and the original data. The second functional, $S(s)$, measures the extent to which the solution conforms to the underlying assumption, usually expressed by the smoothness of the solution [8].

The minimization of E is a trade-off between maintaining closeness to the original data and obtaining a smooth surface. The regularization parameter, λ^2, controls the influence of the functionals. A penalty function is added to the original energy function E. This function takes the form $P = \alpha l_i$, where α is the penalty and l_i is the line process. This produces a combination of a continuous function for the surface and a discrete one for the lines:

$$E = D(s) + \lambda^2\, S(s)\, (1-l_i) + P. \tag{1}$$

The energy functional in equation (1) prefers continuity in the surface, but allows occasional discontinuities if that make for a simpler overall description; a theme called "weak continuity constraints" [10]. This combination facilitates achieving surface reconstruction and discontinuity detection at the same time.

2.2 Graduated Nonconvexity Algorithm

The energy function E is a non-convex function that has many local minima. In such a case, variational methods are used to guarantee obtaining the global minimum. Accordingly, the solution is achieved by means of embedding the functional E into a one-parameter family of functionals $F^{(p)}$. The parameter p represents a sequence of numbers ranging from one to zero. The function F^1 is a crude, but convex, approximation to the non-convex function. However, as p goes to zero, F^p becomes closer to the original non-convex one [11].

To obtain the function sequence $F^{(p)}$, the approach of Graduate Non-Convexity (GNC) algorithm developed by [10] is adopted. Accordingly, the line process P is first merged with the interpolation function S to create the neighbor interaction function $(g_{\alpha\lambda})$ that is not continuous (Figure 1). The modified configuration is then solved by the graduated non-convexity algorithm, where the non-convex function E is gradually approximated by a convex one, F, through a family of p intermediate functions. The final solution represents a convex approximation that encompasses the original function and has only one global minimum. The neighbor interaction function is also modified accordingly and approximated with a set of splines, as shown in Figure 1, denoted as $g_{\alpha\lambda}^{(p)}(t)$, and expressed as

$$g_{\alpha\lambda}^{(p)}(t) = \begin{cases} \lambda^2 t^2 & \text{if } |t| < q \\ \alpha - c(|t|-r)^2/2 & \text{if } q \le |t| < r \\ \alpha & \text{if } |t| \ge r \end{cases} \tag{2}$$

where $c = 0.25/p$, $r = \alpha(2/c + 1/\lambda^2)$, and $q = \alpha/(\lambda^2 r)$.

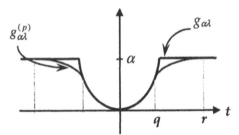

Figure 1. Approximation of the neighbor interaction function $g_{\alpha\lambda}$.

Numerical solution of the function sequence $F^{(p)}$ is achieved by implementing a relaxation algorithm, all terms of which are functions of the parameters λ and α. Beside their original connotation, the first parameter defines the distance for the interaction between discontinuities, beyond which two discontinuities do not interfere with each other. The second parameter (α) is "immunity to noise" measure that prevents generating spurious discontinuities when $\alpha > 2\sigma^2$, where σ^2 is the variance of the mean noise [10].

There are other aspects of performance that depend on these parameters in discontinuity detection. The first one is contrast sensitivity threshold ($h_o = \sqrt{2\alpha/\lambda}$), which determines the minimum contrast for detecting an isolated step edge. The other aspect is the gradient limit ($g_l = h_o/2\lambda$) that would identify a ramp as a step when its gradient exceeds g_l. These different aspects of performance in discontinuity detection provide guidelines for defining the values of λ and α. Based on the broad expectations of the surface, one may choose specific values for the parameters considering, e.g., the desired height of a step to be detected (h_o) [4].

3   Multigrid Framework Development

The Graduated Non-Convexity solution for the weak membrane has the virtue of simultaneous execution of surface interpolation and discontinuity detection. However, sparse data set poses an intricacy at deciding on the exact location of a discontinuity when it is required. This ambiguity arises from the fact that inserting a breakline anywhere between data points that are several grid nodes apart will yield the same low energy. Because of that, it was recommended that the sparse data must first be converted to a dense one using a continuous membrane [10], [4]. Thus, carrying out surface interpolation and analysis tasks would involve two main sub-tasks. The first one is surface densification that produces a preliminary dense representation of the data. The second sub-task is the actual combined process of interpolation and discontinuity detection by the weak membrane. Both sub-tasks involve applying a relaxation method.

3.1 Relaxation and Multigrid Methods

A numerical solution by relaxation techniques (e.g., Gauss-Sidel, and successive over-relaxation methods) would approximate the differential equation by finite differences (or finite elements) [12]. A grid representation of the surface is then obtained by computing its value at each node of the grid using a weighted sum of the values of the neighboring nodes. The solution is acquired through an iterative fashion, where each new iteration improves the attained surface representation.

Standard relaxation methods are inherently inefficient in propagating information over large region of no data [13]. The method of multigrid provides the remedy for dealing with low-frequency components, and speeding up the convergence. It provides two strategies; the coarse grid correction and the nested iteration. The principle of the coarse grid correction scheme is to transfer (restrict) the solution to a coarser grid when relaxation begins to stall (due to reaching smooth error modes). The low frequencies on a fine grid look less smooth (i.e., become higher ones) on a coarser grid. The process is then repeated with the possibility of transferring to yet coarser grid [13].

The other strategy in multigrid computations is the nested iteration scheme, which prescribes that the initial approximation for a fine grid is obtained by interpolating (prolonging) the solution of the coarser grid, instead of starting with any arbitrary approximation. The solution of the coarser grid, in turn, is found by the same process from even coarser grids. The solution of the coarsest level is obtained by exact, or more rigorous, solution of the problem. With such an approach, there is a smaller number of unknowns to update, smaller number of relaxation sweeps, and, thus, faster rate of convergence. Nested iteration is then a recursive application of the correction scheme [13].

3.2 Multigrid GNC for the Weak Membrane

This study opted for implementing the GNC algorithm in a multigrid scheme. As the result of pursuing the multigrid approach, gaps representing the low frequencies in the surface would be filled, and better and faster surface representation would be produced. Implementing the tasks of surface densification and the weak membrane within a multigrid scheme will therefore improve their performance.

The multigrid implementation requires defining two different structures; one is related to image pyramid and another for surface grid resolution. For every level in the image pyramid, there is a surface representation of the same resolution in the object space. However, the surface is further sampled into grids of coarser resolution to satisfy the algorithmic requirements for providing an initial approximation for the surface. This proposition is demonstrate by Figure 2.

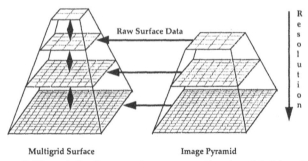

Figure 2. The relation between image pyramid and multigrid surface.

The Multigrid GNC, thus, will proceed through several phases. First of all, the original data must be preprocessed and sampled according to the definitions of the grid at each level. Secondly, a complete cycle of the multigrid membrane would be performed to obtain a dens surface at a specific level of surface representation using a prolonged solution from the previous level as well as the corresponding data. At the end of such cycle, the GNC routine would be activated as the third phase. The results of performing the GNC algorithm are a surface representation and a set of detected discontinuities at the specific level of image resolution. These results would be used to provide an approximation for the new cycle at the next finer image resolution in the pyramid.

4. Test Data and Experiments

The test data is related to a multi-story building with surrounding walkways and landscape that is visible in two consecutive aerial photographs (stereo pair). The left part of Figure 3 depicts the building in a section of one of the aerial images. The photographs were scanned at two image resolutions. The coarse resolution provides an image of a pixel size equivalent to 2 meters on the ground, while the finer resolution corresponds to 1-meter resolution.

The image-matching phase in the photogrammetric reconstruction of visible surfaces was conducted using the two image resolutions. The outcome was two sets of points, each of which represents three-dimensional points in successfully matched edge segments in the corresponding image resolution. The center and right parts of Figure 3 represent the data points obtained at the 2-meter and 1-meter image resolutions.

In order to proceed with the study, the first set (2-meter resolution) had to be sampled into three levels of cell size equals 2, 4, and 8 meters. The criterion used to determine the number of grids was the percentage of the nodes with data versus nodes without data (50% or more). Such a value was set empirically in order to promote small number of consecutive nodes of no data in a grid.

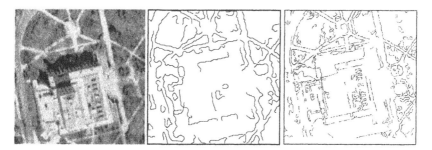

Figure 3. A section of a digital image showing the test site (left), the matched edges at 2-meter (center), and 1-meter (right) resolution.

The three-level sampled data set was then used in a full cycle of the multigrid GNC methodology (i.e., a combined implementation of the multigrid membrane followed by the weak membrane). Figure 4 represents the resulting surface in the final level after a complete multigrid cycle, as well as the detected breaklines at this level.

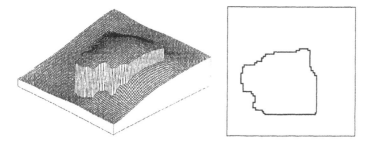

Figure 4. Surface representation for the 2-meter data resolution produced by multigrid GNC (left), and the detected discontinuities (right).

The last experiment attempted to apply the developed algorithm on multi-resolution data. Both data sets (corresponding to matched points at 2-metre and 1-meter image resolutions) were resampled to the required number of levels down to 8-meter resolution. Figure 5 shows the surface as interpolated by the multigrid implementation of the weak membrane, and the detected discontinuities.

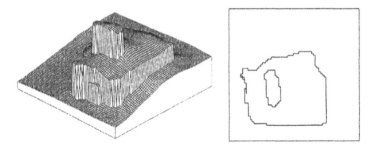

Figure 5. Surface representation for the 1-meter data resolution produced by multigrid GNC (left), and the detected discontinuities (right).

5   Concluding Remarks

The main contribution of this study was the development of a multigrid implementation of the Graduated Non-Convexity (GNC) algorithm for the weak membrane. The algorithm presented by this study offers the solution for the problems associated with the original GNC algorithm in dealing with sparse set of data. The conducted experiments proved that this algorithm is adequate and applicable for dealing with large-scale images of urban areas.

The multigrid formulation of the GNC offers an additional benefit as it lends itself to a more objective definition of the required GNC control parameters. The value of λ (the scale) can be determined in conjunction with the level of surface grid. At the lowest resolution of the grid, it is chosen a bit larger than one (e.g., 1.1) to keep the smoothing and breaking of the surface at the minimum. However, λ would be increased by one each time the algorithm progresses to the next higher level. As with respect to the contrast threshold (h_o), this study found that GNC performs better when h_o is close to twice the mean deviation from the mean of the surface. This way ho is related to the surface data and its variations.

Hierarchy is an intrinsic concept of visual surface reconstruction. Thus, multigrid scheme would provide the means for the communication between the different levels of the image pyramid and among the different phases of surface reconstruction (e.g., image matching and object recognition). In addition to dense interpolated surface, the multigrid representation of the line process serves to communicate information on detected breaklines to these components.

Besides influencing the matching process at the next level of image resolution, there are several ways to benefit from the detected discontinuities. They can be compared or incorporated with other indications. One of which is the set of building boundaries in the object-space like those inferred from lidar observations [5] or from other evidences in the aerial photos after registering and integrating both data in a fashion similar to [14]. Another way is by studying the scale-space behavior of discontinuities detected in the surface at the end of each cycle [15].

References

[1]   Mikhail E., Bethel J. and McGlone C. 2001. *Modern Photogrammetry*, John Wiley, USA.

[2]   Keating T., Garland P. and Dörstel C. 2003. 'Photogrammetry Goes Digital,. *GIS Development.*

[3]   Schenk T. 1999. *Digital Photogrammetry*, Volume 1, TerraScience, OH, USA.

[4]   Al-Tahir R. 1996. *Interpolation and Analysis in Hierarchical Surface Reconstruction*, Report 435, Department of Geodetic Science and Surveying, The Ohio State University, OH.

[5]   Al-Tahir R. 2003. 'Segmentation of Lidar surface data using energy-minimization approach'. *Conradi Research Review* 2(2), pp. 76-85.

[6]   Hewer G., Kenney C. and Manjunath B.S. 1998. 'Variational image segmentation using boundary functions'. *IEEE Transactions on Image Processing* 7(9), pp. 1269-1282.

[7]   Watson D. 1992. *Contouring: A Guide to the Analysis and Display of Spatial Data.* Pergamon Press.

[8]   Wolberg G. 1990. *Digital Image Warping*, IEEE Computer Society Press, CA.

[9]   Geman S. and Geman D. 1984. 'Stochastic relaxation, Gibbs distributions, and the Bayesian restoration of images'. *IEEE Transactions on Pattern Analysis and Machine Intelligence* 6(6), pp. 721-74.

[10]   Blake A. and Zisserman A. 1987. *Visual Reconstruction*, MIT Press, MA.

[11]   Nielsen M. 1997. 'Graduated Nonconvexity by Functional Focusing'. *IEEE Transactions on Pattern Analysis and Machine Intelligence* 19(5), pp. 521-525.

[12]   Nakamura S. 1991. *Applied Numerical Methods with Software*, Prentice Hall, NJ.

[13]   Briggs W., Henson V. and McCormick S. 2000. *A Multigrid Tutorial*, 2nd edition, Society for Industrial & Applied Mathematics, Pennsylvania.

[14]   Schenk T. and Csathó B. 2002. 'Fusion of Lidar data and aerial imagery for a more complete surface description'. *Proceedings of ISPRS Symposium Photogrammetric Computer Vision* (Austria) IAPRS 34(3A), pp 310-317.

[15]   Witkin A., Terzopoulos D. and Kass M. 1987. 'Signal matching through scale space', *International Journal of Computer Vision* 1, pp. 133-144.

Interactive Real-time Image Analysis System for Distant Operation

Mahinda P. Pathegama, Özdemir Göl

University of South Australia
School of Electrical and Information Engineering, Mawson Lakes SA 5095
Australia

Abstract: This paper reports on the development and implementation of an integrated and interactive system for cell analysis featuring remote operation and real-time analysis for generating analytical data from microscopic images. The system consists of a number of image processing modules implemented in a virtual instrumentation environment, combined with novel techniques developed for thinning and local edge-gap filling in the cell image segmentation process. These approaches, integrated with advances in networking, have been initially applied to viral feature analysis in SARS-CoV microscopy. Real-time operation through the user-interface of the proposed system generates quantitative results for remote clients. The rapidity and viability of operation permit the investigation of mutant viral agents on the basis of their morphological cell features.

Keywords: Remote analysis, cell image analysis, boundary extraction, electron microscopy

1   Introduction

Advancement of image processing techniques is a welcome adjunct in electron-microscopic cell analysis and is the object of increasing interest in research for the enhancement of accuracy in disease diagnosis. Electron microscopy is notable for its rapidity of operation and open view that permit detection and identification of emergent viral agents [1]. Electron microscopy does not require specific reagents for, or prior knowledge of, a particular agent, but can nevertheless categorise a pathogen on the basis of its morphological cell features [2] [3]. However, full exploitation of this potential requires the coordinated application of electron microscopy together with other frontline technologies [1].

The emergence and rapid spread of SARS (Severe Acute Respiratory Syndrome) has dramatically emphasised the need for both collaborative international networks [4] and linking of personnel from distant locations with laboratories monitoring and analysing test samples of the causative agent by electron microscopy. Remote monitoring and analysis is thus beneficial for the diagnosis of disease by experts in distant locations as it offers the opportunity for collaborative involvement in this type of disease surveillance.

Remote access to stored medical images in telemedicine enables the transmission of images with patient information over the Internet. Although many system developments have the ability to transmit hospital data on patients through the communication protocol TCP/IP [5], the combined facilities of real-time operation and analysis are yet to be developed for many applications. Remote users would derive considerable benefit from a system endowed with facilities enabling image acquisition, camera control, real-time monitoring, automated pattern recognition for cell feature extraction and quantitative result generation. This paper reports on the experience gained from developing and implementing an integrated and interactive system for remote cell analysis in order to produce quantitative data. System viability is demonstrated by applying it – in the first instance – to SARS-CoV identification.

2 System Features

2.1 Real-time Operation

Upon activation, the proposed system first seeks to confirm the availability of a camera coupled to the microscope and then checks the system's ability to acquire images continuously. If none is available, the program searches in image databases for any image which has been stored by the operator.

The image acquisition card used in this system is PCI-1490, which enables high-resolution, measurement-quality images to be obtained from a RS-170 standard camera. Images are acquired at double-speed with 60 frames per second for progressive scan and interlaced perception. This "frame-grabber" has three independent DMA (Data Memory Access) controllers with each controller performing scatter-gather DMA, which means that the DMA controller reconfigures on the fly, and thus performs continuous image transfers to either contiguous or fragmented buffers. Four external triggers are used for pulse generation to send commands via digital I/O lines embedded in the board for remote control of the camera connected to a frame-grabber. Additional digital outputs are used to transmit pulses for camera zooming, focusing, lighting and directional turning, so as to offer more functionality over the Internet to remote users.

The acquisition method used in this implementation utilises relatively inexpensive digitised electron microscopy instead of robotic electron microscopes having embedded acquisition devices. It is suggested [1] that diagnostic electron microscopy will be neither expensive nor difficult to perform if implemented in a diagnostic network. Machine vision utilised in the proposed system enables real-time monitoring of cell images, which are obtained from cameras coupled to electron microscope.

2.2   Vision Bias Attenuation

Medical diagnosis, based on machine vision, is becoming increasingly used in medical practice. Advantages of machine vision over human vision arise from the fact that machine vision precludes factors which can lessen diagnostic accuracy such as personal bias, physiological factors and ambient conditions. For instance, receptive cells in the human eye may respond in a particular way to the edge information of a particular image when processing image information. Direct visual inspection of medical images may result in the false interpretation of object information, if edge effects are present in the image.. An example of this situation is given in Fig. 1 which shows an edge-effect included in the image of a partly occluded cell. This type of phenomenon is referred to as the Craik-O'Brien-Cornsweet Effect [6].

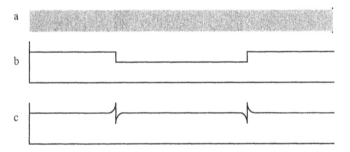

Fig. 1. (a) An example of the edge effect occurring through direct visual inspection. (b) Brain recognition of luminance distribution. (c) Actual luminance distribution.

Direct visual inspection of the cell image in Fig. 1(a) leads to the erroneous perception of a cross-sectional trough as shown in graph (b). The actual representation of the one-dimensional luminance distribution of a horizontal cross-section, correctly depicting edge effects is shown in Fig. 1(c). Somewhat stunningly, the entire image area in Fig. 1(a) can be seen as evenly bright – i.e., the cell object will disappear – when the two inner edges of the cell object are covered. Hence, some method for the observation of the actual cell luminance profile needs to be established in a user-friendly system in order to enhance the diagnostic accuracy of microscopic cell images in machine vision.

To eliminate the possibility of false interpretation of images containing edge-effects, the proposed system deploys an edge profile analysing interface as shown in Fig. 2. Real-time microscopic images and corresponding edged-images appear in a sub-window and edge profiles of images are revealed when the user draws a line across the images as demonstrated in Fig. 2.

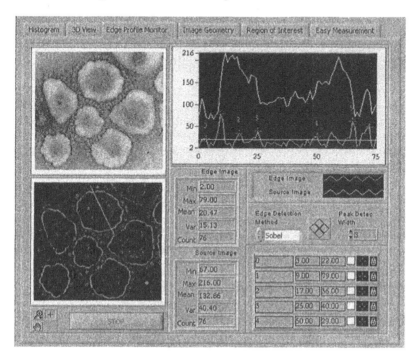

Fig. 2. Sub-window showing profiles of cell images. (The coronavirus microscopic image: Courtesy Source [7])

The proposed system implemented for remote operation performs analysis tasks, which can be controlled through graphical user interfaces (GUIs). The main GUI includes live image acquisition, image enhancing, processing and analysis based on image processing techniques including morphological transformations. The main interface programmatically links various analytical programs, which have separate control panels appearing as sub-windows within the main GUI. Various sub-windows, example of which is given in Fig. 2, are employed in the remote system to make the analysis easier, providing user-friendly interactive operation.

2.3   Client-Server Technology

The implemented system utilises client-server technology by a LabVIEW® Server [8], which enables the detection and acceptance of the network connection from the browser, the retrieval of programs and the transmission of data between the server and clients via the communication protocol TCP/IP.

Each processing step of the system - implemented with virtual instrumentation programs (VIs) - performs objective tasks, calling VIs remotely through user-interfaces and ActiveX automation. The embedded data socket technology [8] shares the live data over the Internet. The data socket delivers the data in a variety of formats, such as strings of text, arrays of data as spreadsheets and sound files. Separate data socket connections added to each required terminal in the VIs make the data available to remote locations through their own data socket connections. These connections in each VI enable remote users to manipulate the controls through the GUI and to receive new values through the data socket as they flash up on the client machine.

The server publishes GUIs as PNG formatted images as these compress graphics better than JPEG compression technique that may cause loss of detail in images. Enhanced security controls deny access to unauthorised users. In addition, the processed images and data can be stored, with later access to the database facilitating observation and further analysis by experts.

Health management services are enhanced by the availability of remote systems as they provide 24-hour access although staff may only be available during daytime. This means that at night-time in one location, the system can be operated by staff in another country where it is daytime. Operation of the system at a distance also facilitates the reduction of bio-safety risks in the case of viral disease. For instance, when a SARS case re-emerged in Singapore, investigation showed that the SARS patient had most likely acquired the infection from the laboratory where the patient had worked [11].

3   Cell Image Processing

3.1   Image Segmentation

The image processing techniques used for the remote analysis constitute the key elements of this system. A series of image processing techniques implemented in the VIs and related sub-VIs can readily be controlled from a distant location using the system. The techniques used aid in image enhancement and provide feature highlighting needed for quantitative report generation on each cell object detected in the microscopic image.

The first processing step extracts the value pane from the image displayed on the interface by effective grey-level morphological transformation. As the output images provided by each step continue into the next step, a copy of each output image is numbered and stored in temporary memory, enabling other desired actions such as subtraction, addition and comparison with other output images to be carried out.

The Gaussian filter used with a 3x3 kernel as a smoothing filter recalculates each pixel value based on the coefficients of the convolution kernel. The next step of the procedure performs edge detection using non-linear spatial filters namely, Gradient, Sobel, Prewitt, Roberts, Differentiation and Sigma operators, which can be selected from the user-interface as desired. The Sobel operator is set as default to facilitate automatic processing. Thresholding applied to the output image creates a binary image. Thresholding is always a subjective process and sometimes produces more information than is needed for the consequent binary image, leaving noisy particles or less information on edge detail than is needed. These deficiencies and the remaining superfluous incomplete cells on image corners are rectified by the following novel approaches.

3.1.1 Absolute Cell Contour Extraction

The preliminary image processing steps implemented in the VI environment employ mathematical morphology [9]. The morphological operation applied to the procedure uses structuring elements, which systematically move across the entire image, matching representative pixels with corresponding pixels, either retaining or deleting pixels to suit the application. This template acts as a criterion for removing any features that do not match the template pixels, within some tolerance. The template used to remove each small particle uses *eight-connectivity*, which specifies how the algorithm determines whether an adjacent pixel belongs to the same particle or to a different one. When the system uses the input image in Fig 3(a), the processing step provides the image as in Fig. 3(b) that include incomplete cell objects touching the image border.

a 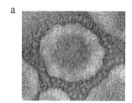 b 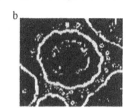 c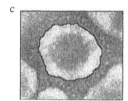

Fig. 3. (a) An electron-microscopic cell image as input [7]. (b) An image provided during image processing steps. (c) Filtering techniques producing a contiguous cell boundary.

The superfluous elements are deleted by using the structuring element in the automated process, since they will not count as cells for the final quantitative analysis. After this step and binary image inversion, the application of the thinning process converts the remaining thick boundary to a one pixel thin boundary, at the same time deleting the remaining pixels. Fig. 3(c) shows the output edged image obtained by thinning, which overlays the first copy previously created in the temporary memory.

3.1.2 Contiguous Boundary Formation

Cell images having a cluttered background usually produce open edges in the cell boundaries. When these edge-gaps are monitored, the GUI enables the user to switch on the local edge-filling process, which displays a sub-control panel. Cell boundaries with even a one-pixel open gap will not be labelled and will not be given due recognition in the analysis procedure to continue.

The process of edge-gap filling [10] creates new pixel information on corresponding empty neighbours using directional sensitivity information of edge-end pixels. This procedure searches the entire image, finding edge-end pixels row by row. The relevant direction of each of the detected pixels takes into consideration the known alignment of neighbouring pixels, setting the direction of the incomplete pixel as opposite to that of the neighbouring cell direction.

3.2 Cell Feature Analysis and Report Generation

Using the proposed system, the SARS-CoV microscopic image shown in Fig. 4(a) has been analysed from a distant location over the Internet. The image processing steps, including the edge filling, provide the required contiguous boundaries. Fig. 4(b) shows the output boundary image which overlays the base image by weighted averaging. The labelling operation, which is the next step performed by VIs, groups the same types of particles and applies colours to the objects having contiguous boundaries, as shown in Fig. 4(c).

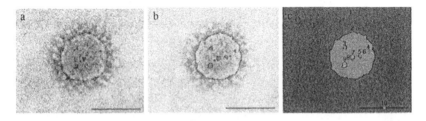

Fig. 4. Remote analysis of SARS Co-V. (a) Electron-microscopy as the input image, Source [2]. (b) Output of contiguous boundaries obtained by the system, overlaying the input image. (c) Labelling of objects to be analysed.

The VIs of the remote system detect the spatial characteristics of the labelled objects in Fig. 4(c) and measure each object. The VIs return a set of measurements as an array of coefficients recording relevant values for each object. The cell boundary (Bilayer) is detected as Object 2 with the background being detected as Object 1. The highlighted boundaries of N-protein (viral nucleocapsids) are detected as Objects 3 to 8, and their measured data are placed in a spreadsheet. Detected Object 10 is the 100nm scale given by electron microscopy and stands for the calibration of the system's units into required units; in this case in nanometres. The generated data show that the SARS-CoV (Object 2) has a longest distance of 96nm across the image and a perimeter of 314nm. A previous SARS study stated that the examination of negative-stain electron microscopy shown in Fig. 4(a) revealed that SARS-CoV has a diameter of 80nm to 140 nm [2].

The VIs embedded in the system generate multiple parameters to identify and classify the objects allowing speedier investigation of detected cell features. The system produces a variety of measurements, including shape, orientation, longest segment, movement of inertia, etc. The movement of inertia gives a representation of the distribution of the pixels in the object with respect to its centre of gravity.

For example, the VIs convert the detected object to a circle having the same perimeter and then produce a value which is half the radius of the new circle, being the hydraulic radius for the detected object. The data sheet generated on the client window shows that hydraulic radius of the bilayer in the example shown in Fig. 4(c) is 19.8nm. The Waddel disk diameter of 89.8nm given for the bilayer is derived from the diameter of the circle with the same area as the object.

4   Conclusion

The integrated system described affords the ability to perform remote analysis and report generation for cell analysis, as demonstrated in the case of a negative-stained SARS-CoV microscopic image. The system functions rapidly, producing reliable measurements followed by the cell image analysis procedures implemented on a virtual instrumentation platform. Electronic information and communication technologies embedded in the system will support collaborating healthcare professionals separated by distance.

5   References

[1]   Hazelton P.R. and Gelderblom H.R., "Electron microscopy for rapid diagnosis of infectious agents in emergent situations," Emerging Infectious Diseases 9, pp. 294-303, 2003.

[2]   Ksiazek T.G., Erdman, D. and et.al., "A novel coronavirus associated with severe acute respiratory syndrome," New England Journal of Medicine 348, pp. 1953-1966, 2003.

[3]   Murray K., Selleck P. and et.al., "A morbillivirus that caused fatal disease in horses and humans," Science 268, pp. 94-97, 1995.

[4]   World Health Organization, "Severe Acute Respiratory Syndrome (SARS)," [online] Last accessed 12.07.2003, URL: http://www.who.int/csr/sars/en/index.html.

[5]   Pereira J., Castro A., Castro A., Arcay B. and Pazos A., "Construction of a system for the access, storage and exploitation of data and medical images generated in radiology information systems (RIS)," Medical Informatics & The Internet in Medicine 27, pp. 203-218, 2002.

[6]   Cornsweet T.N., "Visual Perception," Academic Press, New York, 1970.

[7]   Northern Michigan University, "Coronavirus," [online] Last accessed 10.06.2003, URL: http://www-instruct.nmu.edu/cls/lriipi/micro/coronavirus.jpg

[8]   National Instruments, "LabVIEW measurement manual," National Instruments, Austin, Texas, USA, 2000.

[9]   Serra J., "Image analysis and mathematical morphology," Academic Press, London, 1982.

[10]   Pathegama M.P. and Göl Ö., "An artificial neural process for edge-linking in biological cell image analysis," Proceedings of 3rd International Conference on Neural Networks and Artificial Intelligence ICNNAI'2003, Minsk, 2003.

[11]   Centers for Disease Control and Prevention (CDC), "Update: Review panel concludes that laboratory was source of SARS-CoV infection in Singapore patient," [online] Last accessed 09.10.2003, URL: http://www.cdc.gov/ncidod/sars/singapore29sep2003.htm

Analysis/Synthesis Speech Model Based on the Pitch-Tracking Periodic-Aperiodic Decomposition*

Piotr Zubrycki, Alexander A. Petrovsky

Bialystok Technical University

Wiejska 45A, Poland, e-mail: palex@it.org.by

Abstract: This paper presents a speech analysis/synthesis model based on periodic-aperiodic decomposition. In presented approach, decomposition is performed in whole speech band without making identification of voiced/unvoiced regions. Other important feature is pitch-tracking ability of decomposition algorithm. For this purpose a new pitch-tracking transformation called Time-Varying Discrete Fourier Transform (TVDFT) is employed. Periodic component is modelled as a sum of pitch harmonics with amplitudes and phases estimated with TVDFT. Aperiodic component is defined as a difference between original speech signal and synthesised periodic component. TVDFT needs accurate fundamental pitch estimation. This paper also presents a robust pitch estimation.. Experimental results showing advantages of suggested model are also given.

Keywords: speech decomposition, Time-Varying DFT

1 Introduction

High quality low bit-rate speech coders are major interest in speech research [1],[2]. Models for speech coding based on sinusoidal representation proved its ability to produce good-quality synthetic speech at low bit-rates [3],[9]. Sinusoidal speech signal representation was proposed by McAulay and Quatieri [4] and further developed by George and Smith [5]. Voiced speech in this method is modelled as set of harmonically related sinusoids with parameters obtained directly from the STFT spectrum. More accurate approach to speech modelling

---

*   This work was supported by Bialystok Technical University under the grant W/WI/2/04

based on harmonic+noise model was presented in [6]. This model assumes speech spectrum to be divided in two bands by the maximum voiced frequency. Lower band consist harmonically related sinusoids, while upper band is modulated noise. In the Multiband Excitation Vocoder [7] speech spectrum is divided into a set of bands, and for each band a binary decision voiced/unvoiced is performed. In MBE only bands declared as unvoiced, represent noise part of speech.

Speech coding models in presented approaches are clearly not valid from the speech production point of view. In general, speech production process can be viewed as consisting source component and filter component. In real speech voiced part consist of some noise. It is clear, that voiced fricatives (e.g. /n/, /z/) or breathy vowels consist noise, but in normal vowels noise component is also present due to the turbulence of air around glottal closure [8]. Thus, assumption that is more accurate is to consider voiced speech as a sum of periodic and aperiodic components without identification of voiced/unvoiced regions.

Yegnanarayana et. all [8] proposed model which considers that periodic and aperiodic components are present in whole speech band. Decomposition of speech is performed on excitation signal approximated with use of inversed linear prediction filter. Idea of algorithm is to derive a first approximation of periodic and noise components, then, an iterative algorithm based on Discrete Fourier Transform (DFT)/Inverse Discrete Fourier Transform (IDFT) pairs is employed in order to refine first approximation and reconstruct noise component. Periodic component of excitation is obtained by subtracting noise component from LP residual. Periodic and noise components are used separately to excite the time varying all-pole filter to obtain the corresponding components of speech signal. Another method of periodic-aperiodic decomposition is proposed in [9]. Speech signal is windowed and window should contain integer number of pitch periods. After windowing DFT is performed to obtain periodic and aperiodic components samples. Power interpolation algorithm is performed in order to compensate errors in aperiodic component estimate caused by fundamental frequency and harmonics amplitudes variations.

Although the methods proposed in [8] and [9] are able to perform decomposition of speech signal into periodic and noise components, they have some disadvantages. Due to the time-varying nature of speech error compensation of periodic and aperoodic estimate has to be involved, as these approaches does not take into account time-varying fundamental frequency or harmonic amplitudes. Information about amplitudes and phases of harmonics in these methods is taken directly from DFT spectrum, which can cause errors. This fact reduces usability of discussed approaches as models for speech coding applications. In this paper we present another approach to speech decomposition into periodic and noise components. As the methods presented in [8],[9] it works in whole band, without making any voiced/unvoiced decisions for spectrum regions. First step of algorithm is pitch frequency estimation. A robust pitch detection method based on tuning pitch frequency to its harmonics presented in [10],[11] is used. Having information about pitch track, amplitudes and phases of pitch harmonics are determined using pitch-tracking transformation we have called Time-Varying Discrete Fourier Transform (TVDFT) [12]. This transformation provides estimation with respect to time-varying pitch frequency. Next, using a number of sinusoidal generators, periodic component is generated with time-varying pitch frequency, amplitudes and phases. Finally, decomposition is performed in time-domain, and the aperiodic component is defined as a difference between original speech signal and synthesised periodic component.

2   Pitch Estimation and Trace Tracking Method

Pitch tracking algorithm operates both in time and frequency domain. Preliminary pitch estimation is taken using autocorrelation vector, then this estimate is used to refine pitch frequency using algorithm working in spectral domain similar to the one proposed in [11]. In order to prevent Grose Pitch Errors (GPE) and pitch track distortions a tracking algorithm is used. Scheme of pitch estimation and tracking algorithm is shown on fig. 1.

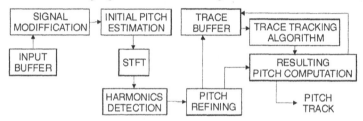

Figure 1. Pitch estimation and tracking algorithm.

First, the input speech signal is weighted in 256-point time window (sampling rate is 8kHz and overlapping coefficient is 75%). Then, autocorrelation vector is computed. Maximum of autocorrelation sequence in interval corresponding to possible fundamental frequency values (typical from 60 to 500Hz) is taken as initial estimation of pitch frequency. In order to improve robustness of the algorithm following pre-processing operations are performed according to Sondhi [14]. Next initial estimate ($\hat{F}_0$) of fundamental frequency is tuned to all present pitch harmonics [11]. After the pitch refining voiced/unvoiced decision is made on the basis of the following parameters: input signal energy, maximum of the autocorrelation sequence and harmonic factor computed as follows:

$$h_f = \frac{n_h}{n_{max}}, \tag{1}$$

where n_h is number of present harmonics, n_{max} – number of all possible harmonics with given pitch. In case of inability to identify at least two out of four leading pitch frequency harmonics, the segment is considered unvoiced. Refined pitch value F_r for each weighting window is identified with the harmonic factor, which can be understood as adequacy of the estimation. False pitch frequency estimations got during speech flow pauses are discarded on the base of analysis of the weighting factors of pitch frequency estimations and analysis of the values of the input signal level, of the speech and silence levels. In order to prevent grose errors and provide better quality, pitch estimation is performed with a delay of two analysis windows. Estimations of the pitch frequency are included in the current track in case the difference between neighbouring windows does not exceed the allowed one. Trace tracking estimation of pitch frequency is calculated using linear approximation of current trace according to the least-square method. The condition determining end of the trace tracking is checked by availability of preliminary estimations to the right of the window being analyzed and by harmonic factors. Resulting pitch frequency is determined as:

$$F_0 = h_f F_r + (1 - h_f) F_t , \tag{2}$$

where F_r – refined pitch; F_t – trace tracking estimation.

Robustness of the pitch track estimation algorithm is shown on fig. 2. Measurements were performed with a different additive noise level. It can be considered, that algorithm can work in presence of big noise and standard deviation is less than 1% even if SNR coefficient is 0dB.

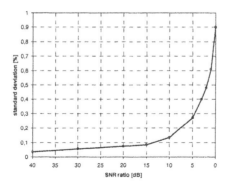

Figure 2. Pitch tracking algorithm experiments results.

3 Time-Varying Discrete Fourier Transform

It was mentioned in introduction that most important in spectral analysis of speech is determination of amplitudes and phases of harmonics. Using STFT as a spectrum analysis tool does not bring good results. Spectral lines of DFT are positioned always at the same frequency. In the Pitch-Synchronous DFT this problem is partially solved [9] by choosing length of analysis frame with respect to fundamental frequency. Spectral lines of this transformation are positioned on harmonics, but problem of time-varying pitch remains, because length of analysis frame is chosen using only one estimate of fundamental frequency within a frame. Experiments proved, that fundamental frequency changes can be even about 20% in 32ms. Without information about fundamental frequency change, it is impossible to obtain proper analysis frame length, also position of spectral lines does not match exactly harmonic frequencies. Time-Varying DFT does not have these defects. It provides spectral analysis in harmonic domain, so the fundamental frequency of analyzed signal and its harmonics are always on spectral lines [12]. This feature greatly simplifies spectral analysis of described above signals. DFT transform providind analysis in spectral domain is given by:

$$X(k) = \sum_{n=0}^{N-1} x(n)e^{-j\frac{2\pi nkF_0}{F_s}}, k = 0..K \tag{3}$$

where $X(k)$ – k-th spectral component corresponding to k-th harmonic, $x(n)$ – input signal, N – transformation length, F_s – sampling frequency, F_0 – fundamental frequency. Kernel of transformation has to be modified in case tracking analysis. Argument of exponential can be written as follows:

$$\varphi(n,k) = \begin{cases} 0 & \text{for } n = 0 \\ \sum_{i=1}^{n} \frac{2\pi k(F_0(i) - F_0(i-1))}{2F_s} & \text{otherwise} \end{cases} \tag{5}$$

where $F_0(i)$ is fundamental frequency at time specified by i. Transformation providing tracking harmonic analysis is given as follows:

$$X(k) = \sum_{n=0}^{N-1} x(n)e^{-j\varphi(n,k)}, k = 0..K \tag{6}$$

Non-orthogonal TVDFT kernel can cause energy leakage to neighbouring spectral lines. There are possible two strategies to deal with the leakage phenomenon [12]. First is to use strategy similar to the one used in PSDFT relying on choosing analysis frame length with respect to fundamental frequency changes. Second strategy is based on using pitch-tracking time windows. can be useful. Idea of this solution is to design a spectral window, which follows fundamental frequency changes. Experiments showed, that for leakage compensation good results could be achieved when Kaiser Window is used as a prototype [11]:

$$w(n) = \frac{I_0\left(\beta\sqrt{1 - \left(\frac{2x(n) - (N-1)}{(N-1)}\right)^2}\right)}{I_0(\beta)}, n=0..N-1 \tag{7}$$

where N – window length, β – window parameter, $I_0(x)$ – zero order Bessel function, $x(n)$ is a function enabling time-varying feature, given as:

$$x(n) = \frac{\varphi(n,1)}{2\pi \overline{F}_0 \frac{N}{F_s}},$$ (8)

where $\varphi(n,1)$ is computed using formula (5), $\overline{F}_0$ is average fundamental frequency in analysis frame.

4 Periodic-Aperiodic Decomposition Scheme

Speech signal decomposition is the basis in proposed coding method. Proposed method performs decomposition in whole band, which provides to more accurate representation of speech, thus synthesized signal sounds more natural. Speech signal decomposition scheme is shown on fig. 3. First step of decomposition is pitch tracking. This information is passed to Time-Varying DFT analyzer. Output of TVDFT gives information about amplitudes and initial phases of harmonics. For production of harmonic component a set of time-varying oscillators can be used using formula:

$$h(n) = \sum_{k=0}^{K} A_k(n)\cos(\varphi(n,k) + \Phi_k),$$ (9)

where phase $\varphi(n,k)$ is determined using formula (5). While TVDFT is performed every 16ms instantaneous amplitudes of harmonics have to be computed using interpolation algorithm. Piecewise cubic Hermite interpolation algorithm is used because this kind of interpolation can easily deal with large data set.

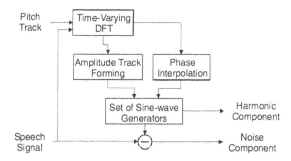

Figure 3. Speech signal decomposition scheme.

Having harmonic component, noise component is defined as a difference between input speech signal and harmonic component:

$$r(n) = s(n) - h(n)$$ (10).

In practice two possible solutions of decomposition can be implemented. First is to use overlap-add technique. Harmonic component is generated frame-by-frame with overlapping and then noise component is a difference between input frame and harmonic frame. Second solution is continue harmonic component generation. Using overlap-add method provides to less computationally efficient algorithm while continue generation introduces phase mismatches and additional phase interpolation algorithm should be involved.

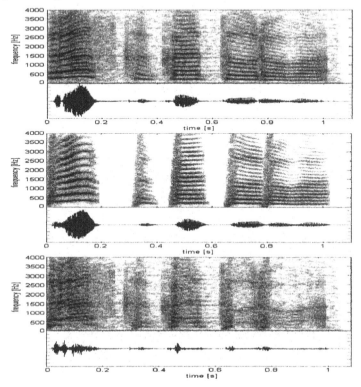

Figure 4. Example of speech signal decomposition

In order to improve decomposition an iterative algorithm can be used. After decomposition, residual signal $r(n)$ is used instead speech signal, then decomposition on this signal is provided using the same pitch track. Output harmonic component is sum of harmonic component from all iterations and noise component is residual from last iteration. Example spectrograms of harmonic and noise components are shown on fig. 4.

Important problem in almost every model for speech coding is performance loos at transient segments. Known solutions for transient speech modelling demanded special approach to speech segments considered as transient [12]. Approach presented in this paper enables using the same algorithm for all speech segments without making identifications of transient segments. Example of transient speech and corresponding harmonic component is shown on figure 5.

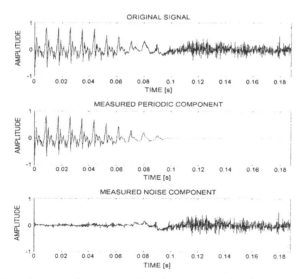

Figure 5. Transient speech segment (above), corresponding harmonic component (middle)and noise component (below)

5 Experimental Results

Set of experiments was performed in order to evaluate proposed algorithms. Listening tests showed that synthetic speech was a very good quality. There were no artefacts at transients.

Time-varying DFT algorithm experimental results are shown in table 1. The goal of this test was to deliver information about possible errors in harmonics amplitudes estimation. Synthetic harmonic signal was generated with known frequency change and harmonics amplitudes waere random in first test and the same at second test. Experiments showed, that standard deviation with time-varying window is not higher than 0,123% when harmonics with random amplitudes were generated. Experiment also showed that TVDFT with time-varying window is less sensitive to amplitude changes.

	TVDFT without compensation	TVDFT with time-varying window
	Standard deviation [%]	
Random amplitudes	16,43	0,123
Same amplitudes	2,72	0,034

Table 1. TVDFT algorithm evaluation results

Decomposition algorithm test results are shown on fig. 6. Test signal was synthetic vowel /a/ with additional white noise. Different Harmonic to Noise Ratio (HNR) coefficients were used. First test was performed with static fundamental frequency, cecond with varying fundamental frequency. Variations of pitch were not bigger than 15% during analysis frame. Performance of the algorithm without presence of noise is better, when fundamental frequency does not change during analysis frame. With presence of white noise results are almost the same for static and varying fundamental frequency.

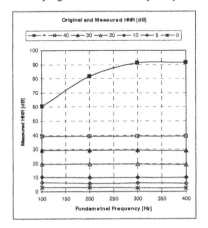 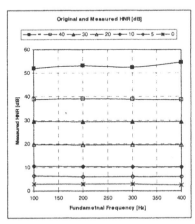

Figure 6. Decomposition algorithm results with static fundamental frequency (left) and varying fundamental frequency (right)

6   Conclusions

This paper presented a speech model that is based on decomposition of speech signal into periodic and noise components. Unlike well-known Harmonic+Noise (HNM) and MBE models of speech model presented in this paper is designed with respect to quasiperiodic speech signal nature. Decomposition into periodic and noise components is provided in whole speech band using Time-Varying DFT. Instantaneous amplitudes and phases of harmonics are modelled using cubic interpolation. Presented approach allows producing high quality synthetic speech at low bit-rates. Periodic and noise components can be coded independently. Efficient coding of model parameters involves vector quantisation both for amplitudes of harmonics and LSF's parameters (for noise component). Decomposition of speech signal allows using psychoacoustic algorithms without using any estimates of noise level, thus noise level can be easily computed.

7 References

[1] Kondoz A.M., "Digital speech: coding for low bit rate communication systems", John Wiley & Sons, Inc., New York, 1996.

[2] Spanias A.S., „Speech coding: a tutorial review", Proc. IEEE, Vol. 82, No. 10, pp. 1541-1582, 1994.

[3] Almeida L.B., Tribolet J.M., "Harmonic Coding: A Low Bit-Rate, Good Quality, Speech Coding Technique", Proc. IEEE Int. Conf. on Accoust., Speech and Signal Processing, pp. 1664-1667, 1982.

[4] McAulay R.J., Quatieri T.F., „Sinusoidal Coding" in "Speech Coding and Synthesis" (W. Klein and K. Palival, eds.), Elsevier Science Publishers, Amsterdam, 1995.

[5] George E.B., Smith M.J.T., „Speech Analysis/Synthesis and Modification Using an Analysis-by-Synthesis/Overlap-Add Sinusoidal Model", IEEE Trans. on Speech and Audio Processing, Vol5, No. 5, pp. 389-406, 1997.

[6] Stylianou Y., „Applying the Harmonic Plus Noise Mode in Concatenative Speech Synthesis" IEEE Trans. on Speech and Audio Processing, Vol. 9, No 1., pp. 21-29, 2001.

[7] Griffin D.W., Lim J.S., „Multiband Excitation Vocoder", IEEE Trans. on Acoust., Speech and Signal Processing, Vol. ASSP-36, pp. 1223-1235, 1988.

[8] B. Yegnanarayana, C. d'Alessandro, V. Darsions, "An Iterative Algorithm for Decomposiiton of Speech Signals into Periodic and Aperiodic Components", *IEEE Trans. On Speech and Audio Coding*, Vol. 6, No. 1, pp. 1-11, 1998.

[9] Jackson P.J.B., Shadle C.H., "Pitch-Scaled Estimation of Simultaneous Voiced and Turbulence-Noise Components in Speech", IEEE Trans. On Speech and Audio Processing, Vol. 9, No. 7, pp. 713-726, 2001

[10] Sercov V., Petrovsky A., „An Improved Speech Model with Allowance for Time-Varying Pitch Harmonic Amplitudes and Frequencies in Low Bit-Rate MBE Coders", Proc. of the 6ht European Conf. on Speech Communication and Technology EUROSPEECH'99, pp. 1479-1482 Budapest, Hungary, 1999.

[11] Petrovsky A., Sercov V., "Low Bit-Rate AbS Spectral Coding Based on the Harmonic Analysis of Speech Agreed Upon with Time-Varying Pitch Frequency and Psychoacoustical Optimization", Proc. of Nordic Signal Processing Symposium NORSIG2000, pp. 45-48, 2000.

[12] Petrovsky A., Zubrycki P., Sawicki A., Tonal and noise components separation based on a pitch synchronous DFT analyzer as a speech coding method // Proc. of European Conference on Circuit Theory and Devices ECCTD2003, Vol. III, pp. 169-172, 2003.

[13] Eric W. M. Yu, Cheung-Fat Chan , A harmonic+noise coder with improved transient speech performance // Proc. of European Signal Processing Conference EUSIPCO'99, Special Session "Speech Coding", 1999.

[14] Sondhi M.M., New Methods of Pitch Extraction, IEEE Trans. on Audio and Electroacoustics, Vol. AU-16, No. 2, pp. 262-266, 1968.

Bio-inspired voice activity detector based on the human speech properties in the modulation domain[1]

A.Shadevsky, A.Petrovsky

Bialystok Technical University, Belarusian State University of Informatics and Radioelectronics, Computer Engineering Department, P.Brovki 6, Minsk, Belarus, 220027, email: palex@it.org.by

Abstract:
In many conventional voice activity detection (VAD) methods, a speech signal is assumed to be acquired in high quality. This paper describes a method of robust voice activity detection, which deals with speech signal in noise environment. The proposed VAD scheme explores the properties of modulation spectrum of human speech. Speech signal is split into frequency bands and filtered in the modulation frequency domain for noise level pre-reducing. Then, spectrum energy evaluation is performed and noise threshold is calculated. The proposed method provides robust speech detection in a varying noise environment. It can be used in speech enhancement and speech coding algorithms. Characteristics of the proposed method were investigated with different types of noisy speech.

Keywords: *voice activity detector, modulation spectrum*

1 Introduction

Voice activity detector (VAD) is a vital part of multimedia systems that implement speech coding, speech recognition, speech quality improvement etc. It can imply a more significant influence on the overall performance of a system than any other component. A lot of VAD algorithms have already been developed [1-4]. Traditionally, VADs use the energy criterion, while alternative methods try to extract speech parameters (pitch frequency, formants, cepstrum, etc.) and compare them with a specific speech model. In addition, multi-channel algorithms can be used [5].

[1] This work was supported in part by Bialystok Technical University under the grant W/WI/2/04

The main goal of a voice detector is to maintain effective detection in a changing acoustic environment. In most algorithms, speech decision is based on comparison between a classification parameter and the threshold. One of the major problems in speech detection is accurate threshold determination. Threshold calculation is based on simple statistics:

$$d_{thr} = mean(d) + \lambda \cdot std(d) \tag{1}$$

where d denotes the classification parameter and λ controls the confidence bound; *mean* denotes mean value; *std* – standard deviation. The mean value and standard deviation are estimated by exponential averaging during pauses only.

This approach has a number of drawbacks. Firstly, a detection error affects the subsequent algorithm operation, as the mean value and standard deviation of the classification parameter are being estimated during pauses only. Secondly, to start working the VAD input should be receiving a speech-less signal for a certain time so the system could learn. Thirdly, such detectors fail to adjust to a rapidly changing acoustic environment.

Nowadays, one of the rapidly growing directions in engineering is the neuromorphic engineering, the essence of which consists in designing artificial neural systems, whose physical architecture and design principles are taken from biological prototypes. Neuromorphic engineering applies principles discovered in biological organisms to perform tasks that biological systems carry out without special efforts but which have been proven difficult to solve using traditional engineering techniques [6].

Recently, the analysis algorithms of speech signals that are based on human acoustic analyzer properties are being wildly spread [7-13]. Development of such class of methods is based on the assumption, that the speech analysis based on a human hearing model could be more successful, than the analysis based on rather abstract models of speech perception or statistical Markov models. In particular, it is affirmed, that systems of digital speech signals processing constructed on such principles could be more effective in preventing noise.

In this paper, the VAD exploiting the properties of human speech modulation spectrum which can be used for efficient voice activity detection in adverse acoustic environments as well as for clear speech signal is proposed.

2 Properties of human speech in modulation spectrum

Conditionally the speech human perception process consists of two stages: early and central. The early stage realizes transformation of an acoustic signal into an inner neural representation based on an auditory spectrogram [7]. The central stage analyzes the spectrogram to estimate the content of its spectral and temporal modulations.

At the early stage an acoustic signal entering the ear is transformed to mechanic oscillations by an ear-drum and stones of a middle ear. Those oscillations excite complex spatio–temporal vibration along the basilar membrane of the cochlea. The behavior of those vibrations is as follows, different tone frequencies localized at different cochlear points. Thus, the basilar membrane can be described at an electric level as the work of filters bank with a high degree of pass-bands overlapping.

The central auditory stage analyzes further the auditory spectrum into more elaborate representation, interprets them, and separates the different components and parameters, associated with different sound percepts. This stage estimates the content of the auditory spectrogram. In this process low-frequency modulation components which are the basic data carriers in a speech signal play a big role. Various scientists came to such conclusions proceeding from psychophysical, psychological, psychoacoustical and other types of research in this area. In other words, speech and other audio signals are actually low-frequency processes which modulate bearing frequencies.

As it is shown by various investigations [7-10], a major part of energy (over 95%) of clear speech signal influencing speech intelligebility and perception is concentrated in the range from 1 to 16 Hz in modulation domain, with the peak around 3–5 Hz. This corresponds to the number of syllables uttered by a human per second. Thus, the modulation components changing with frequencies outside this range can be removed by the filtration of the modulation spectrum. Thus, the partial reduction of the noise level and reverberation can be achieved. In work [8], this property of a modulation spectrum was used in the automatic speech recognition system. It allowed making the system more independent of surrounding acoustic conditions. For this purpose fixed FIR filters (1-16 Hz) with various gain-frequency characteristics were used. In [11] the modulation filter which strengthened modulation components in a range of 2-8 Hz was used, for improvement of speech intelligibility. In works [12, 13] attempts of an environment conditions estimation were made and by results of which appropriate modulation filter was selected from their set (in the first case) or it was managed (in the second case).

It is possible to perform three actions necessary for effective work of the detector in adverse acoustic conditions, using these properties of human speech in the modulation domain:

– To remove the most part of a noise energy concentrated in a frequency range 0-1 Hz. This operation makes a method invariant to dynamic background noise.

- To estimate a standard deviation of noise components in a modulation range of 1-16 Hz. The given operation allows calculating a threshold more precisely.

- To define the gains determining probability of presence of speech component in frequency bands. This action additionally weakens the noise level in a modulation range of 1-16 Hz.

3 Bio-inspired voice activity detector

In this chapter a modified method for speech detection based on the properties of modulation spectrum [14] is reviewed. Its major distinguishing feature is that the threshold is being calculated at all times regardless of the speech/pause decision, and the acoustic environment estimation is taken into account. Its block diagram is presented in figure 1. The speech signal $x(n/f_s)$ is split into M equal frequency bands using the DFT polyphase analysis filter bank. Amplitude envelopes $Y_k(nM/f_s)$ for signal $X_k(nM/f_s)$ are calculated in each frequency band. Then, they are processed by the amplitude envelope processing block. There are two signal outputs from this block: $S_k(nM/f_s)$ - amplitude envelope for speech component; $N_k(nM/f_s)$ - amplitude envelope for noise components.

The amplitude envelope processing block (fig. 2) executes three main actions. First of all, it removes the main part of noisy component energy, which is concentrated in the range of 0-1 Hz. Second, it evaluates the amplitude envelope of noisy components. Third, it determines SNR of signal and calculates gain for each frequency band.

The amplitude envelope $Y_k(nM/f_s)$ in each frequency band is transformed into nonlinear scale according to:

$$Y_k'(nM/f_s) = Y_k(nM/f_s)^{1/\gamma} \qquad (2)$$

where γ determines the compression rate. The choice of this parameter is described below.

Furthermore, the amplitude envelope $Y_k'(nM/f_s)$ is filtered by a high-pass FIR filter (1 Hz). As a result of this procedure, the noise energy is reduced. Then, signal $Y_k''(nM/f_s)$ is filtered with a low-pass FIR filter with the cutoff frequency of 16 Hz. Its operation allows removing the noisy component which is concentrated in higher frequencies (16-32 Hz) and estimating noise components by the following formula:

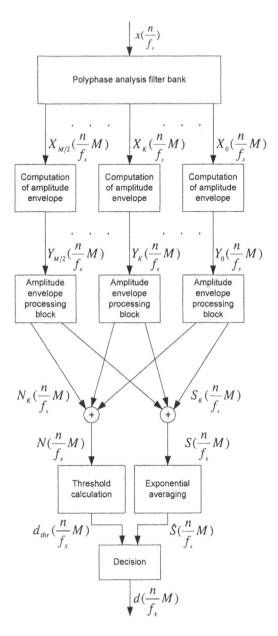

Figure 1. The voice activity detector block diagram based on the modulation spectrum processing

$$N'_K(nM/f_s) = S'_K(nM/f_s) - S''_K(nM/f_s) \tag{3}$$

Signal $N'_K(nM/f_s)$ is an approximate evaluation of the noise component in lower modulation frequencies (1-16 Hz).

Envelope processing by the high-pass FIR filter removes modulation frequencies below 1 Hz. This leads to negative values in filtered amplitude envelopes $S''_K(nM/f_s)$ and $N'_K(nM/f_s)$. Therefore, the amplitude envelopes of the speech and noise components are restored according to:

$$S'''_K(\frac{n}{f_s}M) = S''_K(\frac{n}{f_s}M) + std(S''_K(\frac{n}{f_s}M)) \tag{4}$$

$$N(\frac{n}{f_s}M) = N'_K(\frac{n}{f_s}M) + std(N'_K(\frac{n}{f_s}M)) \tag{5}$$

where std is a standard signal deviation computed on the frame with length $L = f_s/4M$. The frame length L corresponds to the modulation frequency of 4 Hz, where the energy peak of clean speech signal in modulation domain is concentrated [7].

Next, the gain in each frequency band is computed by the following formula:

$$G(\frac{n}{f_s}M) = (\hat{Y}'_K(\frac{n}{f_s}M) - \hat{S}'''_K(\frac{n}{f_s}M))/\hat{Y}'_K(\frac{n}{f_s}M) \tag{6}$$

where $\hat{S}'''_K(nM/f_s)$ and $\hat{Y}'_K(nM/f_s)$ are the smoothed values of signals $S'''_K(nM/f_s)$ and $Y'_K(nM/f_s)$ accordingly.

Multiplication of signal $S'''_K(nM/f_s)$ by the gain $G_K(nM/f_s)$ provides further noise energy reducing in the amplitude envelope (1-16Hz).

Then, amplitude envelopes $S_K(nM/f_s)$ and $N_K(nM/f_s)$ of speech and noise components (fig. 1) are summed for all frequencies. Summed speech envelope $S(nM/f_s)$ is smoothed by exponential averaging. Summed noise envelope $N_K(nM/f_s)$ is used for threshold computation. Threshold d_{thr} is computed at all times based on the noise evaluation in high frequencies of the modulation domain (above 16 Hz) $N(nM/f_s)$ by the following formula:

$$d_{thr}(\frac{n}{f_s}M) = mean(N(\frac{n}{f_s}M)) + \lambda \cdot std(N(\frac{n}{f_s}M)) \tag{7}$$

where $std(N(nM/f_s))$ is a standard deviation of signal $N(nM/f_s)$ computed on the frame with length $L = f_s/4M$; $mean(N(nM/f_s))$ is a mean value of signal $N_K(nM/f_s)$ and λ determines the confidence limit.

The speech/noise decision d is based on comparing the smoothed amplitude envelope and the threshold d_{thr} .

Amplitude envelope processing block

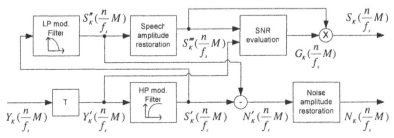

Figure 2. Amplitude envelope processing block diagram

4   Performance evaluation

The influence of such parameters, as a compression rate γ, and the maximal value of confidence limit λ on the method performance was investigated during experiments with the proposed VAD. The following objective performance evaluation criteria were used:

− $P(A)$ – correct detection rate,

− $P(B)$ – speech/non-speech resolution factor,

computed according to:

$$P(A) = P(A/S)P(S) + P(A/N)P(N) , \tag{9}$$

$$P(B) = P(A/S)P(A/N) , \tag{10}$$

where $P(S) = N_s/(N_s + N_n)$ is the speech rate, $P(N) = N_n/(N_s + N_n)$ is the non-speech rate, $P(A/S) = N'_s/N_s$ is the correct speech detection rate, $P(A/N) = N'_n/N_n$ is the correct non-speech detection rate.

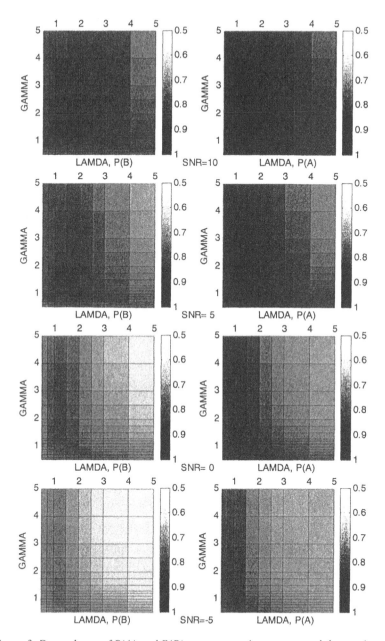

Figure 3. Dependence of P(A) and P(B) on compression rate γ *and the maximum of confidence limit* λ *for signals with SNR 10, 5, 0 and -5 dB respectively.*

The experiments with ten etalon speech signals (sample frequency 8 kHz) were made. SNR of initial signals was 30 dB. Six noisy signals with SNR 20, 15, 10, 5, 0 and -5 dB were received on the basis of each source signal by adding white noise. The influence of a compression rate γ and the maximal value of the confidence limit λ on the correct detection rate were investigated at various SNR. Parameters γ and λ were being changed from 0.5 to 5 with non-uniform steps.

The results of the experiments are submitted in figure 3. The parameters λ and γ are marked on the abscissa and ordinates axes correspondingly. Values $P(A)$ and $P(B)$ are defined by the depth of color according to the colorbar.

Based on the experimental results, it is possible to make the following conclusions:

- Changing values of the confidence limit λ and compression rate γ in the selected range does not render essential influence on the system performance for signals with SNR above 10 dB.

- The optimum value of λ corresponding to the maximal mean values of $P(A)$ and $P(B)$ for different SNR is 1. It is necessary to note, that for $\lambda = 1$, values $P(A)$ and $P(B)$ close to maximal can be always achieved, by changing compression rate γ.

- For signals with low SNR an optimum value of λ is achieved in the vicinity of value 1 (fig.4). Such results have an explanation that the maximal value of the confidence limit λ defines sensitivity of the method when SNR is low. And when the confidence limit is reduced the detector weakens threshold fluctuations, thus increasing correct speech detection rate $P(A/S)$. At the same time, it reduces the correct pauses detection rate $P(A/N)$. In case when only white noise is sent to the system input, the system performances $P(A)$ and $P(B)$ worsen.

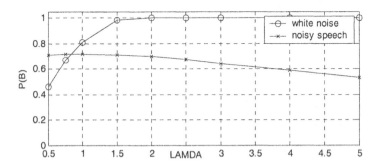

Figure 4. Dependence of speech/non-speech resolution factor P(B) on the maximum confidence limit value λ where $\gamma = 1.3$: for the white noise signal and for the noisy speech signal with SNR=-5dB.

– The compression rate γ renders significant influence on the system performance for signals with changing SNR (fig.5). An optimum value of γ for signals with SNR above 0 dB equals to 1.3. And the optimum value depends on SNR if it is below 0 dB.

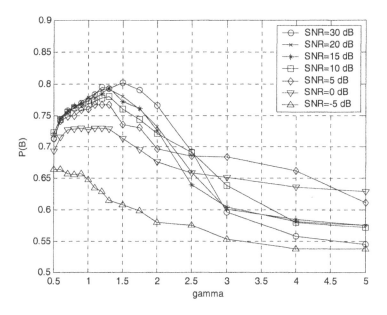

Figure 5. Dependence of speech/non-speech resolution factor P(B) on compression rate γ where $\lambda = 1$, for signals with different SNR.

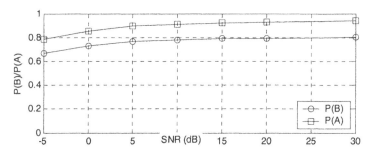

Figure 6. Dependence of speech/non-speech resolution factor P(B) and correct detection rate P(A) on signal SNR when compression rate γ is adjusted and μ equals 2.

- Managing compression rate γ with the help of SNR estimation it is possible to improve the characteristics of the offered method for signals with SNR below 0 dB (fig.6).
- The constant error detection rate on the different SNR is explained by the fact that the offered detector is sensitive enough to small intervals between syllables while the patterns are constructed word-by-word.

5   Conclusions

In this paper, we propose a biologically motivated method for a voice activity detector exploiting the properties of human speech modulation spectrum. It allows removing the main part of noise energy and making the method more invariant to dynamic background noises; accurate estimation of the noise level for threshold determination. The computation of the threshold is based on noisy components evaluation in higher frequencies of the modulation domain and signal SNR at the current frame. Because of this, the threshold is computed at all times regardless of the speech/pause decision and the proposed method does not have such drawbacks as detection errors influence and learning delays. All these features allow efficient speech detecting in signals with different SNR in different acoustic environments.

Apparently, the suggested methodology for VADs based on the human hearing model shows better results than the conventional methods. Future developments can be connected with designing the universal biologically motivated speech perception model which will allow allocating various groups of speech signal parameters. The given groups can be used in a consequence for realization of specific targets, such as automatic speech recognition, speaker identification, effective coding, speech quality and intelligibility improvement etc.

6   References

[1]   Sovka P., Polak P. The Study of Speech/Pause Detectors for Speech Enhancement Methods // Proceeding of the 4th European Conference on Speech Communication and Technology, Madrid, Spain, September 1995, pp. 1575-1578.

[2]   Borowicz A., Petrovsky A. The Comparative Study of Voice Activity Detectors // Известия Белорусской инженерной академии, №2(14)/1, 2002, c. 148-152.

[3]   Puder H., Soffke O. An Approach to an Optimized Voice-Activity Detector for Noisy Speech Signals // Proceeding of the XI European Signal Processing Conference, Toulouse, France, 03-06 September 2002, Vol I, pp 243-246.

[4] Hioka Y., Hamada N. Voice Activity Detection with Array Signal Processing in the Wavelet Domain // Proceeding of the XI European Signal Processing Conference, Toulouse, France, 03-06 September 2002, Vol. I, pp 255-258.

[5] Rosca J., Balan R., Fan N.P. and e.t. Multichannel Voice Detection in Adverse Environments // Proceeding of the XI European Signal Processing Conference, Toulouse, France, 03-06 September 2002, Vol. I, pp 251-254

[6] Special Issue "Neuromorphic Signal Processing and Implementations" edited by S.A.Shamma and A.Schaik ", EURASIP Journal on Applied Signal Processing, 7 (2003), June (2003).

[7] Elhilali M., Chi T., Shamma S. A Spectro-temporal modulation index (STMI) for assessment of speech intelligibility // Speech Communication – 2003 – 41 – pp. 331-348.

[8] Hermansky H., Morgan N. "RASTA processing of speech", IEEE Transactions on speech and audio processing 4 (2) October (1994), pp. 578-589.

[9] Drullman R., Festen J.M., Plomp R. Effect of temporal envelope smearing on speech reception // J. Acoust. Soc. Am. – 1994 – №2 (95) – pp 1053-1064.

[10] Arai T., Pavel M., Hermansky H., Avendano C. Syllable intelligibility for temporally filtered LPC cepstral trajectories // J. Acoust. Soc. Am. – 1999 – vol. 105 – pp 2783-2791.

[11] Kusumoto A., Arai T., Kitamura T., Takahashi M., Murahara Y., `Modulation enhancement of speech as a preprocessing for reverberant chambers with the hearing-impaired // Proc. of the ICASSP, Vol. 2, pp. 853-856, Istanbul, 2000.

[12] Avendano C., Temporal processing of speech in a Time-Feature Space, Ph.D. thesis, Oregon Graduate Institute, Portland, OR, Apr., 1997.

[13] Shadevsky A., Baszun J., Petrovsky A. Noise reduction based on neuromorphic speech signal processing. – Structures-waves-human health: acoustical engineering. Editor R.Panuszka. – vol. XIII, No1, Krakow 2004. – pp.115-122

[14] Shadevsky A., Petrovsky A. Voice activity detector based on human speech modulatuion spectrum exploitation // Proceeding of the 6th International Conference and Exhibition "Digital Signal Processing and its Applications", Moscow, Russia, 31 March – 2 April 2004, Vol. I, pp. 167-180, in russian.

A New Step in Arabic Speech Identification: Spoken Digit Recognition

Khalid Saeed, Mohammad K. Nammous

Faculty of Computer Science
Bialystok Technical University
Wiejska 45A, 15-351 Bialystok, Poland
http://aragorn.pb.bialystok.pl/~zspinfo/,

Abstract: This work presents a new Algorithm to recognize separate voices of some Arabic words, the digits form zero to ten. Firstly we prepare our signal by pre-processing trial. Next the speech signal is processed as an image by Power Spectrum Estimation. For feature extraction, transformation and hence recognition, the algorithm of minimal eigenvalues of Toeplitz matrices together with other methods of speech processing and recognition are used. At the stage of classification many methods are tested from classical ones, which depend on the matrix theory, to different types of neuron networks, mainly radial basis functions neural networks. The success rate obtained in the presented experiments is almost ideal and exceeded 98% for many cases. The results have shown flexibility to extend the algorithm to speaker identification.

Keywords: Speech Processing, Recognition, Burg's and Toeplitz Models, Neural Networks.

1   Introduction

This work is a continuation to the last experimental paper introduced in [1], where the speech signal is treated graphically. The application of Toeplitz forms for image description [2] are used to describe speech signal. Because this approach cannot be applied directly, for the speech complicated nature, the authors are using some other methods of speech pre-processing for better feature extract of voice image before entering Toeplitz-based algorithms. The processing methods that gave good results in most cases are *LPC* – Linear Predictive Coding coefficients [3], Discrete Fourier transform [4] and Zero-Crossing method [5]. All of them have their advantages and also disadvantages. Seeking a simple and also a more stationary way for the graphical speech description, we applied the frequency spectral estimation method based on linear prediction model introduced in [6] and will thereafter be referred to as Burg model. This method seems to be very useful for image-spectral pre-processing. The obtained signal spectrum forms the basis to further analysis for spoken-word recognition.

2   Pre-Processing Signals

The input to the system is a recorded speech waveform. Each file can contain only one voice; additionally there must be silence region before and after the right signal. The standard format used by the authors is PCM, with frequency 22050 Hz, 16-bits mono. The process of the speech preparation for feature extraction is given in **Fig. 1**.

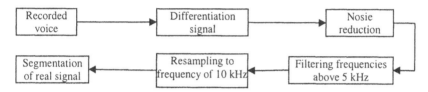

Fig. 1 The flow chart of speech signal preparation for recognition process.

More information and details about how to prepare the signals to recognition can be found in [1, 7].

Now, the new signal is ready for the next step of feature extracting.

3   Speech Signal Processing

Among many methods of Speech Signal Processing, the authors have chosen the method based on spectrum analysis. This method helps extract the speech image-features from spectral analysis in a simple way. Experiments showed that power spectrum estimation of Burg's model is one of the best for the purpose of finding a method for smoothing irregular spectral shape resulting from applying the Fast Fourier Transform. It is based on the Linear Predictive Coding approach. The theory of linear predictive coding is given in [8]. The model of Burg's method software implementation is given in [9].

Now we can use the obtained power spectrum acoustic images directly, or apply the algorithm based on minimal eigenvalues of Toeplitz matrices [2, 10] to analyze these acoustic images. When using Burg's method of estimation, however, we should notice that we need to specify the prediction order (P) and the FFT size, called the length of FFT (*NFFT*). More explanations and details about both Burg's methods and minimal eigenvalues model of image description and classification are given in [9, 11]. For convenience, a brief description of Toeplitz approach in obtaining the minimal eigenvalues as voice-image spectral-graph feature vectors carrying the main characteristics of the image is given below.

3.1 Minimal Eigenvalues Algorithm

To explain how the algorithm of minimal eigenvalues works, we first introduce the way of calculating Toeplitz-matrix determinants.

According to the method given in [2, 11], the under-test image is described by the rational function in *Eq.* (1):

$$H(s) = \frac{x_0 + x_1 s + x_2 s^2 + ... + x_n s^n}{y_0 + y_1 s + y_2 s^2 + ... + y_n s^n} \tag{1}$$

where the coefficients are the coordinates of the feature points extracted from Burg's spectral analysis graph of the voice-image (Fig.2). n is the number of feature points considered (the points marked with circles in Fig.2).

Evaluate Taylor series for *Eq.*(1) or its equivalent form $H(z)$ obtained after the bilinear transformation $s = \dfrac{1-z}{1+z}$.

$$T(z) = c_0 + c_1 z + c_2 z^2 + ... + c_n z^n + ... \tag{2}$$

From this series find Toeplitz forms and their determinants. Compute the minimal eigenvalues of the matrices:

$$\lambda_{\min}\{D_i\} = \lambda_{\min_i} = \lambda_i \ \text{ for } i = 1, 2, ..., n .$$

Hence, the following feature vector is found:

$$\Phi_i = (\lambda_0, \lambda_1, \lambda_2, ..., \lambda_n) \tag{3}$$

Eq.(3), acts as the input data to the classifying algorithms when applying the known methods of similarity and comparison for the sake of recognition. The feature vector Φ_i presents a very useful tool in describing an image within a class of similar objects. Simply, each voice-graph has its own series of minimal eigenvalues.

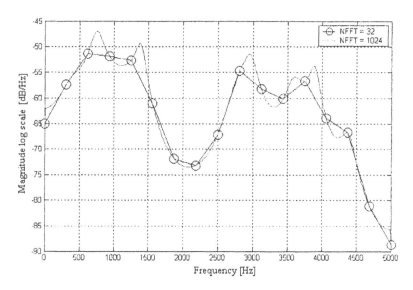

Fig. 2 Spectral analysis for Burg's method, *NFFT* = 32, 1024, *P* = 20.

Using this method with large input data increases the time and the cost of calculating, therefore in some previous works [10, 11] the selected points were limited by choosing some of them regularly, choosing for example every 10-th point or every 50-th point. Our recent experiments showed that this way was proved to be useless at least in the cases we considered because after this kind of selecting we will get the same points returned with another value of the *NFFT*, these points are marked with circles in Fig.2.

3.2 Projection Algorithm

Projection is a usual technique used in different pattern recognition tasks; it gives very good results in the handwritten recognition [12]. The first reason for using this kind of techniques in our tests is to reduce the number of essential features. Moreover, we want to find out if this method will give as good results as in other recognition fields. Projection depends on the curve obtained by Burg method, we use twelve axes and project every feature point onto the nearest one of these axes, Figure 3 explains how this is applied.

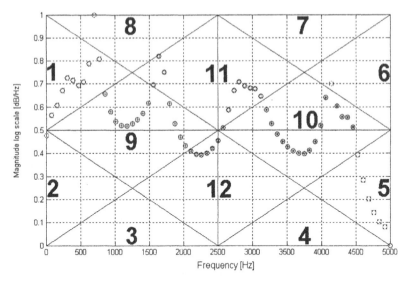

Fig. 3 Projection and spectral analysis of Burg method, voice 3, *NFFT* = 128, *P* = 20.

3.3   Base of Voices

We tried to use a regular voice-base. Therefore, in our base we have recorded voices of twenty people from six different not only Arabic speaking countries. The total number of samples is 5472 divided into two groups, for each person and voice we choose five samples to be a test set (1100 samples), while the remaining samples (4372 samples) are chosen to be the teaching set.

4   Classification

The choice of an appropriate algorithm of feature extract from the given voice data is one of the most difficult but important factors in better speech-recognition. For this purpose, the authors have chosen two simple methods, classical and neural-based ones. Five different experiments are introduced in this work to cover most of the basic results of the essential approaches. Firstly, we present the results for Burg estimation spectrum without using the minimal eigenvalues algorithm. The recognition rate is high and depends on the selected parameters. Then applications of varieties of neural networks are shown. The one we are more interested in is the Radial Network presented in Experiment 2; the one which the model of minimal eigenvalues and its modified versions work very well with.

4.1 Experiments and Results

In our experiments we tested every situation for the next values of parameters:

The length of FFT (NFFT) : 32, 64, 128, 256, 512, 1024
The prediction order (P) : 8, 10, 12, 16, 20, 24, 28, 32, 40

That means we have about 54 individual situations, but simply we will present only a few cases for every value of the first parameter (*NFFT*).

Experiment 1

Table 1 shows the results of this experiment. Through the classical method of classification, the number of wrongly recognized samples was 70 out of 1100 used samples. The recognition rate achieved by this method is 93.64% (Table 1).

Table 1 Recognition results of Experiment 1.

The length of FFT [*NFFT*]	Prediction order [*P*]	Number of wrongly-recognized in total of 1100 samples	Recognition rate %
32	8	233	78.8182
	12	141	87.1818
	20	89	91.9091
	28	110	90.00
64	12	116	89.4545
	20	76	93.0909
	24	78	92.9091
128	16	81	92.6364
	20	75	93.1818
	24	75	93.1818
256	16	84	92.3636
	20	70	93.6364
	24	72	93.4545
512	20	75	93.1818
	24	79	92.8182
	28	81	92.6364
1024	28	78	92.9091
	32	85	92.2727
	40	71	93.5455

Experiment 2

Table 2 shows the application of the Radial Basis Function RBF-type Neural Networks [13] to classify and recognize spoken Arabic digits for different parameters.

Table 2 Recognition results of Experiment 2.

The length of FFT [NFFT]	Prediction order [P]	The Spread	Radial networks	
			Number of wrongly-recognized samples out of 1100 cases	Recognition rate %
32	8	1.0	698	36.5455
	12	1.0	332	69.8182
	20	1.0	404	63.2727
	28	1.0	476	56.7273
64	12	1.0	467	57.5455
	20	0.8	71	93.5455
	20	1.0	72	93.4545
	20	1.2	69	93.7273
	24	1.0	224	79.6364
	32	1.0	229	79.1818
128	16	1.0	105	90.4545
	20	1.0	70	93.6364
	24	0.8	52	95.2727
	24	1.0	59	94.6364
	24	1.2	59	94.6364
	28	1.0	91	91.7273
256	16	1.0	93	91.5455
	20	1.0	127	88.4545
	24	0.8	94	91.4545
	24	1.0	29	97.3636
	24	1.2	28	97.4545
	32	1.0	55	95.00
512	20	1.0	254	76.9091
	24	1.0	143	87.00
	28	1.0	194	82.3636
	32	1.0	144	86.9091
1024	24	1.0	560	49.0909
	28	1.0	585	46.8182
	32	1.0	343	68.8182
	40	1.0	346	68.5455

The higher recognition rate is greater than the one obtained by classical classification method. It has achieved the value of 97.45% under the conditions highlighted in the table. Radial basis functions networks are very popular in speech and speaker recognition [14], additionally they work very well with the algorithm of minimal eigenvalues.

Experiment 3

For much better results, however, the following experiment was performed. The probabilistic networks have helped achieve this goal. We are testing the same spoken digits applying the probabilistic networks. The results are given in Table 3

Table 3 Recognition results of Experiment 3.

The length of FFT [NFFT]	Prediction order [P]	The Spread	Probabilistic networks	
			Number of wrongly-recognized samples out of 1100 cases	Recognition rate %
32	8	0.1	140	87.2727
	12	0.1	54	95.0909
	20	0.1	38	96.5455
	28	0.1	65	94.0909
64	12	0.1	44	96.00
	20	0.08	25	97.7273
	20	0.1	25	97.7273
	20	0.2	30	97.2727
	24	0.1	31	97.1818
	32	0.1	36	96.7273
128	16	0.1	26	97.6364
	20	0.1	26	97.6364
	24	0.08	21	98.0909
	24	0.1	21	98.0909
	24	0.2	22	98.00
	28	0.1	31	97.1818
256	16	0.1	26	97.6364
	20	0.08	20	98.1818
	20	0.1	20	98.1818
	20	0.2	19	98.2727
	24	0.1	23	97.9091
	32	0.1	31	97.1818
512	20	0.1	19	98.2727
	24	0.1	23	97.9091
	28	0.1	23	97.9091
	32	0.1	27	97.5455
1024	24	0.1	24	97.8182
	28	0.1	23	97.9091
	32	0.1	19	98.2727
	40	0.1	30	97.2727

This time the results are almost ideal independently of the value of spread radial function; additionally this kind of networks doesn't need any training, and the time of its creating is too short. Notice the abrupt increase in the rate of recognition and the stability of the returned results.

Experiment 4

Now we will introduce the results of the using of the Eigenvalues algorithm, Table 4 shows the results of this experiment. Through the classical method of classification the number of bad recognized samples was 149 out of 1100 used samples. The recognition rate achieved by this method is 86.45% (Table 4).

Table 4 Recognition results of Experiment 4.

The length of FFT [NFFT]	Prediction order [P]	Number of wrongly-recognized in total of 1100 samples	Recognition rate %
32	8	438	60.1818
	12	412	62.5455
	20	400	63.6364
	28	500	54.5455
64	12	255	76.8182
	20	251	77.1818
	24	280	74.5455
	32	323	70.6364
128	20	164	85.0909
	24	150	86.3636
	28	149	86.4545
256	16	237	78.4545
	20	207	81.1818
	24	177	83.9091
	32	203	81.5455
512	24	265	75.9091
	28	254	76.9091
	32	265	75.9091
1024	28	376	65.8182
	32	367	66.6364
	40	351	68.0909

Experiment 5

Consider the radial basis function networks applied to classify and recognize the spoken Arabic digits for different combinations of *NFFT*, prediction order *P*, for both radial and probabilistic networks. In this test we are using the standard values of the spread factor, for radial networks value of this parameter is 1.0, and for the probabilistic ones it is 0.1, Table 5 presents the results.

Table 5 Recognition results of Experiment 5.

The length of FFT [*NFFT*]	Prediction order [*P*]	Radial networks		Probabilistic networks	
		Number of wrongly-recognized samples out of 1100 cases	Recognition rate %	Number of wrongly-recognized samples out of 1100 cases	Recognition rate %
32	8	300	72.7273	806	26.7273
	12	226	79.4545	781	29.00
	20	213	80.6364	781	29.00
64	12	54	95.0909	734	33.2727
	20	48	95.6364	695	36.8182
	24	46	**95.8182**	685	37.7273
	32	74	93.2727	722	34.3636
128	20	52	95.2727	677	38.4545
	24	52	95.2727	673	**38.8182**
	28	58	74.7273	705	35.9091
256	16	78	82.9091	718	34.7273
	20	85	82.2727	707	35.7273
	24	77	93.00	719	34.6364
512	20	80	82.7273	707	35.7273
	24	80	82.7273	719	34.6364
	28	112	89.8182	760	30.9091
1024	24	94	91.4545	799	27.3636
	28	114	89.6364	835	24.0909
	40	258	76.5455	783	28.8182

This time the probabilistic networks return so bad results that the best recognition rate is only 38.82%, At the same time the higher recognition rate when using radial networks is greater than the one obtained by classical classification method. It has achieved the value of 95.82% under the conditions highlighted in the table.

4.2 Other Experiments

A number of other experiments were conducted with other approaches and algorithms. For comparison, we give here the results we obtained for the considered types of neural networks as the main classifying tool:

1) The first additional experiment is to input the data to the system using *Eq*.3, but with the data to *Eq*.1 being taken from reversing the coordinates of feature points. The NN used were probabilistic neural networks. Unfortunately, this type of NN showed to be impractical to use with the method of minimal eigenvalues

(the best recognition rate was 21.27%). However, using the radial basic networks gave much better results than the classical method (45.2%). For $NFFT = 256$ and $P = 16$ the efficiency of this algorithm was increased to 75.36%, but still not better than the classical eigenvalues algorithm.

2) Another modification of Eigenvalues algorithm depending on using the difference between the next points of Burg curve as coordinates put directly in $Eq.1$, the standard classification method gives 56.55% (with $NFFT = 64$, $P=24$).

3) With the same modification of Eigenvalues algorithm of the experiment in 2) we used the probabilistic networks. They showed very bad results (the best rate was 13.36%), whereas radial neural networks increased the efficiency of this method to 76.27% ($NFFT$ equals 1024, P equals 28).

4) The Recognition rate for the Projection method was low. With classical methods of classification the higher recognition rate was only 60.36%, whereas the use of radial and probabilistic networks showed even a worse rate.

5   Conclusions

Performed experiments approved that the image-based methods in speech classification have good recognition efficiencies as other known methods. In the case of individual speakers the recognition rate was almost ideal, and for a set of twenty speakers with 11 word-pattern classes the efficiency of Burg algorithm was 93.64%. Radial basis networks increased it to 97.45%, and probabilistic networks returned the best ones 98.27%.

Minimal eigenvalues algorithm when used in the same way on a written text, has not given the highest recognition rate (86.45% in best cases). However, when used with radial neural networks the rate of recognition was improved to 95.82% which is very close to the efficiency of Burg method. The system of minimal eigenvalues and neural networks seems to need more improvement.

The results obtained by the projection method were not satisfactory even when used with radial and probabilistic networks.

Finally, we must say that with this very large number of experiments, we can now test any other base of words, or do other similar tasks with only the best confirmed and established parameters, but our next goal is to test the Image-based approach in speech classification for the situation of text-dependent speaker recognition.

Acknowledgement

This work was supported by the Rector of Bialystok University of Technology (grant number W/II/3/01).

6 References

[1] K. Saeed, M. Nammous, "Experimental Image-Based Algorithm for Spoken Arabic Digits Identification," Computer Information Systems and Applications, Vol.1, pp.55-66, *WSFiZ Press*, Bialystok, Poland 2004.

[2] K. Saeed, "Computer Graphics Analysis: A Criterion for Image Feature Extraction and Recognition," Vol. 10, Issue 2, 2001, pp. 185-194, *MGV - International Journal on Machine Graphics and Vision*, Institute of Computer Science, Polish Academy of Sciences, Warsaw.

[3] R. W. Schafer, L. R. Rabiner, "System for Automatic Formant Analysis of Voiced Speech," *J. Acoust. Soc. Amer.* Vol.47, Feb. 1970.

[4] Andreas A. , "Digital Filters: Analysis and Design," McGraw-Hill, New York 1979.

[5] Cz. Basztura, "Modele analizy i procedury w komputerowym rozpoznawaniu głosów," (in Polish), *prace naukowe ITiA Politechniki Wrocławskiej*, no. 30, Wrocław 1989.

[6] L. S. Marple, "Digital Spectral Analysis," Englewood Cliffs, NJ: *Prentice Hall*, 1987.

[7] Sadaoki Furui, "Digital Speech Processing, Synthesis, and Recognition," *Marcel Dekker, Inc.* 2001.

[8] R. Tadeusiewicz, "Sygnał mowy," *WKiŁ* (in Polish), Warsaw 1988.

[9] V. K. Ingle, J. G. Proakis, "Digital Signal Processing Using MATLAB," Brooks Cole, July 1999.

[10] K. Saeed, M. Kozłowski, A. Kaczanowski, "Metoda do rozpoznawania obrazów akustycznych izolowanych liter mowy", *Zeszyty Politechniki Białostockiej* (in Polish), I-1/2002, pp.181-207, Białystok 2002.

[11] K. Saeed, M. Kozłowski, "An Image-Based System for Spoken-Letter Recognition," 10th Int. Conference CAIP'03 on Computer Analysis of Images and Patterns, August 2003, Groningen. *Proceedings published in: Lecture Notes in Computer Science*, Petkov and Westenberg (Eds.), pp. 494-502, LNCS 2756, Springer-Verlag Heidelberg: Berlin 2003.

[12] K. Saeed, M. Tabedzki, "A New Hybrid System for Recognition of Handwritten-Script," Invited for publication in International Scientific *Journal of Computing*, Institute of Computer Information Technologies, Volume 3, Issue 1, pp. 50-57, 2004, Ternopil, Ukraine 2004.

[13] Shigeru Katagiri, "Handbook of Neural Networks for Speech Processing," *Artech House*, Boston 2000.

[14] M.W. Mak, W.G. Allen and G.G.Sexton, "Speaker identification using radial basis functions", *The Third International Conference on Artifical Neural networks*, University of Northumbria at Newcastle, U.K 1998.

Split Vector Quantization of Psychoacoustical Modified LSF Coefficients in Speech Coder Based on Pitch-Tracking Periodic-Aperiodic Decomposition[*]

Alexander Petrovsky, Andrzej Sawicki, Alexander Pavlovec

Real-Time Systems Department, Bialystok Technical University
Wiejska 45A, 15-351 Bialystok, Poland,

e-mail: palex@it.org.by

Abstract: This paper presents methods of detection and quantization coefficients from speech coder based on Pitch-Tracking Periodic-Aperiodic Decomposition. Spectral envelopes of harmonic and noise components of speech are represented by linear spectral frequencies (LSF) coefficients. In this article we show new methods of quality improvement in coding signal, using perceptual properties of human ear. Spectrum envelopes of the harmonic frequencies and noise components envelopes are represented in psychoacousticaly based phon-Bark and sone-Bark scale. Line Spectral Frequencies coefficients are quantized, using methods proposed by R.M. Gray, Y. Linde and A. Buzo. For better performance, reduction of computational complexity and memory space, Split Vector Quantization methods are used. Structure of Vector Codebook is condtructed based on dependency between LSF coefficents in vectors of training sequensions. LSF vectors are patritioned into two or three sub-vectors, and each of them is coded separately. Bit realocation between sub-codebooks allow obtain improvement of codebook quality. Combination of perceptual properties and modified split vector quantization of speech signal parameters, permit achieve good quality signal in speech coder for transmission rate 2.8 kbit/s and below.

Keywords: split vector quantization, LSF quantization, psychoacoustical models of speech

---

[*] This work is supported by Bialystok Technical University under the grant W/WI/2/04

1. Introduction

In the low bit rate speech coder based on separate representation of periodic (tonal) and aperiodic (noise) components of speech signal [1] there is a necessity of quantization of its parameters. Proposed article is devoted to this problem.

Main contribution into the overall code capacity is provided by periodic and aperiodic spectral envelopes represented with line spectrum pairs (LSP or LSF). Vector quantization (VQ) is a common technique which is usually applied to the task of a bit rate reducing. In our case we need separate codebooks for quantization of tonal and noise component. Tonal component of speech is more important perceptually than noise component, thus the latter have been simply quantized with a 9-bit codebook (generalized Lloyd algorithm (GLA) [2] was used for training).

Ways of the quantization problem solving in the case of periodic part will be considered more carefully. We used two approaches for this: classical method of split vector quantization (SVQ) [3] modified with bit reallocation between codebooks and psychoacoustically motivated approach to LSF split VQ. The performance of both approaches was evaluated with an objective measure of quality.

2. Tonal Component LSF Split VQ Modified with Bit Reallocation

In this section we shall evaluate applicability of classical SVQ approach to quantization of tonal part of speech only. The main attention is paid here for searching for the best way of splitting the vector, comparing different splitting schemes and bit allocations.

The speech material used for codebook training consists of 462 files taken from TIMIT database [4]. After downsampling and lowpass filtering we applied to them coder algorithm [1] for achieving the LSF vectors of tonal part of speech. Thus we have got 33200 vectors for training. In a same manner evaluation set of LSF vectors was formed (168 files, 12182 vectors). To evaluate quantizer performance we used log spectral distortion:

$$SD = \sqrt{\frac{1}{F_S} \int_0^{F_S} [10\log_{10} S_i(f) - 10\log_{10} S_i'(f)]^2 \, df} \; , \tag{1}$$

where F_S is the sampling frequency, $S_i(f)$ and $S_i'(f)$ are the LPC power spectra of the i-th frame given by

$$S_i(f) = \frac{1}{A_i(e^{j2\pi f / F_S})} \tag{2}$$

$$S_i'(f) = \frac{1}{A_i'(e^{j2\pi f / F_S})}, \tag{3}$$

where $A_i(z)$, $A_i'(z)$ are the original and quantized LPC polynomials, respectively, for the i-th frame. There were an experimentally defined conditions in [5] for transparent quantization (no audible differences between original and quantized signals):

- The average SD is less than or equal to 1 dB;
- The percentage of outlier frames having spectral distortion in the range 2 – 4 dB should not be greater than 2%;
- There are no outlier frames having spectral distortion greater than 4 dB.

It is known that LSF parameters are correlated within a given frame. In order to find the best partitioning for LSF vector, the intraframe correlation between LSF coefficients was calculated over the whole training set. The intraframe correlation coefficients are given in table 1.

Table 1. Intraframe correlation between LSFs

LSF	1	2	3	4	5	6	7	8	9	10
1	1	0.81	0.41	0.04	-0.24	-0.32	-0.17	-0.08	-0.01	0.003
2	0.81	1	0.50	-0.03	-0.25	-0.39	-0.21	-0.09	-0.07	-0.06
3	0.41	0.50	1	0.29	-0.14	-0.15	-0.18	-0.05	0.03	-0.06
4	0.04	-0.03	0.29	1	0.51	0.14	0.07	-0.19	-0.02	-0.25
5	-0.24	-0.25	-0.14	0.51	1	0.61	0.27	0.03	-0.15	-0.32
6	-0.32	-0.39	-0.15	0.14	0.61	1	0.54	0.26	0.09	-0.17
7	-0.17	-0.21	-0.18	0.07	0.27	0.54	1	0.49	0.12	-0.12
8	-0.08	-0.09	-0.05	-0.19	0.03	0.26	0.49	1	0.39	0.12
9	-0.01	-0.07	0.03	-0.02	-0.15	0.09	0.12	0.39	1	0.37
10	0.003	-0.06	-0.06	-0.25	-0.32	-0.17	-0.12	0.12	0.37	1

We can see a strongest correlation between LSF_1 and LSF_2, the weakest between LSF_3 and LSF_4, LSF_9 and LSF_{10}. Correlation coefficients between successive LSFs from 4th to 7th are approximately of the same value. Theoretically good splitting schemes are 3-3-4 or 3-4-3. Further we shall evaluate the performance of these schemes. In addition to them we shall include 4-4-2 and 4-3-3 splittings and variants of 2-split VQ (4-6, 5-5, 6-4).

During experiments we have trained 4 kinds of codebooks for 3-split VQ (6 to 9 bit sub-codebooks) and 4 kinds of codebooks for 2-split VQ (9 to 12 bit sub-codebooks). Firstly we shall consider uniform bit allocation between codebooks.

To obtain an initial codebook we have used algorithm similar to [6]. The main idea of it is that vectors that are far apart from each other are more likely to belong to different classes. Generalized Lloyd algorithm with weighted Euclidean distance [5] as a minimization parameter was used for training.

$$d(f, \hat{f}) = \sum_{i=1}^{p} (c_i w_i (f_i - \hat{f}_i))^2 , \qquad (4)$$

where c_i and w_i are fixed and variable weights respectively. For the 10-th order LP-filter the following values of the fixed weights c_i are found to be satisfactory [5]:

$$c_i = \begin{cases} 1.0, & 1 \le i \le 8 \\ 0.8, & i = 9 \\ 0.4, & i = 10 \end{cases} \qquad (5)$$

Simple and computationally efficient scheme for variable weights calculation was proposed in [7]:

$$w_i = \frac{1}{f_i - f_{i-1}} + \frac{1}{f_{i+1} - f_i} , \qquad (6)$$

where f_i – LSF-coefficients (in radians), $f_0=0$, $f_{p+1}=\pi$. The purpose of weights using is that they allow in some way to take into consideration the human ear properties.

Evaluation results are given in Table 2 (results presented only for bit rates 21 – 27 bit/vector as they have provided better quantization quality).

Table 2. Performance evaluation for different schemes of LSF-vector splitting

Bit/vector	Splitting	Average SD (dB)	Outliers	
			2 – 4 dB, %	> 4 dB, %
21	4-3-3	1.4248	8.2335	0.057462
21	4-4-2	1.6766	20.399	0.18059
21	3-3-4	1.3172	5.7133	0.065671
21	3-4-3	1.5379	14.891	0.14776

22	4-6	1.3276	7.9462	0.0082088
22	5-5	1.2629	4.6955	0.024626
22	6-4	1.3683	7.1663	0.041044
24	4-3-3	1.1783	2.6761	0.016418
24	4-4-2	1.4353	9.4648	0.041044
24	3-3-4	1.0941	2.2738	0.016418
24	3-4-3	1.305	6.7723	0.032835
24	4-6	1.2349	5.2783	0.016418
24	5-5	1.1731	3.0537	0.0082088
24	6-4	1.2775	5.1798	0.024626
27	4-3-3	0.99107	1.1328	0.0082088
27	4-4-2	1.2298	3.9074	0.024626
27	3-3-4	0.91127	0.98506	0.016418
27	3-4-3	1.109	3.2014	0.024626

It is obviously that near transparent quantization can be achieved at bit rates about 24 bit/vector and such variants of splitting as 3-3-4 and 4-3-3 clearly outperforms the others. Further we shall examine an influence of bit allocation between sub-codebooks on quantization quality. The same distortion measures are used for the same evaluation set, but this time we consider 3-split VQ only because of its better performance (Table 2). The best variants of bit allocation for different splitting schemes are shown in Table 3 (bit allocation variants are presented at bit rates of 23 – 24 bit/vector).

Table 3. Performance evaluation for different variants of bit allocation between sub-codebooks

Average SD (dB)	Outliers		Bit/vector	Splitting / bit allocation
	2 – 4 dB, %	> 4 dB, %		
1.0766	1.5925	0.0164	24	3-3-4 / 6-9-9
1.0954	2.0276	0.0082	24	4-3-3 / 9-9-6
1.1903	4.0305	0.0328	24	3-4-3 / 8-9-7
1.2432	4.0716	0.0328	24	4-4-2 / 9-9-6
1.1543	2.2164	0.0164	23	3-3-4 / 6-8-9
1.1746	2.7828	0.0082	23	4-3-3 / 8-9-6
1.235	4.4246	0.0328	23	3-4-3 / 7-9-7
1.315	5.2044	0.0164	23	4-4-2 / 8-9-6

Here we can see that bit reallocation between codebooks has clearly improved quantizer performance for all splitting schemes considered. The most promising variant for practical applications is the splitting scheme 3-3-4 with bit allocation 6-8-9, totally 23 bit/vector.

The performance of designed quantizer (SVQ with 3-3-4 splitting scheme and 6-8-9 bit allocation) is shown below (Fig. 1, 2). The spectrogram of the periodic part of original signal (Fig. 1) is almost indistinguishable from the spectrogram of the quantized one (Fig. 2)

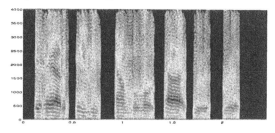

Figure 1. Spectrogram of the original periodic part of speech signal

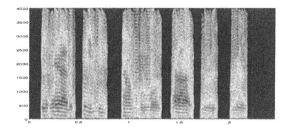

Figure 2. Spectrogram of the quantized periodic part of speech signal

3. Psychoacoustical Principles in LSF Split Vector Quantizer

3.1. Tonal spectral speech coefficients representation using psychoacoustic principles

Many researchers prove, that humans not equally perceived different frequencies [10]. Spectral component envelopes of tonal part of speech are converted using human ear properties. Human hearing system processes sound in sub-bands called critical band. One Bark corresponds to the width of one critical band. The Bark frequency scale can be approximated by the following equation, presented by Zwicker [10]:

$$z = 13 * \arctan(0.00076 * f) + 3.5 * \arctan\left(\left(\frac{f}{7500}\right)^2\right) \tag{7}$$

where f – frequency in Hz and z – frequency in Bark.

Perception of sound energy is relative to hearing frequency. Precise representation of ear energy perception at various frequencies provides Fletcher-Munson curves, presented in Figure 3. The contours of equal loudness are labeled in units of phons, which are determined by the SPL in decibels at 1000 Hz. It is relative to absolute threshold of hearing (ATH), which described area, with minimum intensity of a pure tone, which the human ear can hear in a noiseless environment.

Amplitudes of pitch frequency harmonics are modified to phons (P) scale, accordingly to formula:

$$P = D - ATH + ATH_{1kHz}, \tag{8}$$

where D is amplitude of spectral components in dB, and

$$ATH(f) = 3.64 f^{-0.8} - 6.5 e^{-0.6(f-3.3)^2} + 10^{-3} f^4 \tag{9}$$

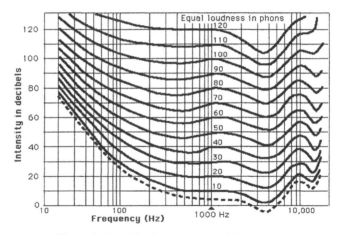

Figure 3. Equal loudness contours (phon curves)

Reference loudness, called the sone (S), is defined as the loudness of a 1000 Hz tone at a sound level of 40 dB (or a loudness of 40 phons). Phons are modified to sone (S) using equation:

$$S = \begin{cases} 2^{(P-40)/10} & \text{if } P \geq 40 \\ (P/40)^{2.642} & \text{if } P < 40 \end{cases}, \tag{10}$$

where S – loudness in sones

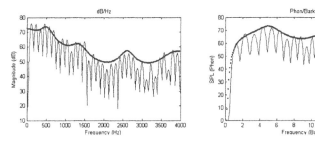

Figure 4. Spectrum envelope representation of speech in dB/Hz and Phon/Bark scale

Using psychoacoustic scales, spectral components of speech model can be better approximated at low frequencies and more hearable sounds can be better reconstructed from speech parameters.

Perceptually modified harmonics amplitudes are converted to LSF coefficients using 10-th order LPC.

3.2. LSF split quantization based on psychoacoustical models

Three kind of vector codebooks for LSF parameters were constructed, two for psychoacoustic scales: Phon/Bark and Sone/Bark and one codebook for dB/Hz scale for comparison.

To build quantizer that minimizes average spectral distortion, LBG algorithm is used [8][9]. Because of amplitude and frequency scale modification according to psychoacoustic principles, we use Euclidean distance $d(f, \hat{f})$ between LSF vectors without weighting factor.

$$d(f, \hat{f}) = \sum_{i=1}^{p} (f_i - \hat{f}_i)^2, \tag{11}$$

In view of observation dependence between LSF coefficients, we can determine, that best results are obtained, when we use codebook splitting scheme 3-3-4 or 4-3-3. Also earlier tests show, that finest performance we can get for splitting schemes 3-3-4, 4-3-3, 3-4-3, 5-5 and 4-6. For experiments we use uniform bit allocation between sub-codebooks. 24 bits are partitioned in 8-8-8 bits groups for 3 sub-codebooks split, and 12-12 bits for 2 sub-codebooks splitting schemes. 23 bits vector quantizer is partitioned using group with 8-8-7 and 12-11 bits.

Results of our research are presented in Table 4.

Table 4. Performance evaluation for perceptually based LSF-vector quantization

Scales	Bit /vector	Splitting	Average SD (dB)	Outliers	
				2 – 4 dB, %	> 4 dB, %
dB/Hz	24	4-3-3	1.434	5.234	0.082
	24	3-3-4	1.331	3.721	0.042
	24	3-4-3	1.526	7.843	0.124
	24	4-6	1.412	8.132	0.078
	24	5-5	1.362	3.923	0.061
	23	4-3-3	1.521	11.345	0.184
	23	3-3-4	1.432	10.291	0.152
Phon/ Bark	24	4-3-3	1.123	2.874	0.034
	24	3-3-4	1.081	2.127	0.012
	24	3-4-3	1.181	3.114	0.042
	24	4-6	1.172	3.451	0.034
	24	5-5	1.146	3.984	0.032
	23	4-3-3	1.321	6.291	0.092
	23	3-3-4	1.291	5.342	0.120
Sone/ Bark	24	4-3-3	1.149	3.157	0.012
	24	3-3-4	1.123	2.678	0.009
	24	3-4-3	1.231	6.132	0.018
	24	4-6	1.243	4.187	0.023
	24	5-5	1.168	2.882	0.016
	23	3-3-4	1.384	6.340	0.073
	23	3-4-3	1.332	5.842	0.098

Using Phon/Bark and Sone/Bark scales for representation of spectral components of voiced speech can enhance performance of split vector quantization. VQ with Bark/Sone and Bark/Phon scale has better average spectral distortion and less outliers than using dB/Hz scale. Experiments show (in Table 4) that for this splitting scheme 3-3-4 we have maximum performance : average spectral distortion SD is equal– 1.081 dB , about 2 % of outliers in range 2-4 % and less than 0.01 % of outliers in range upward of 4 %.

4. Conclusion

From the work performed we can make the following conclusion. Firstly, classical split vector quantization is quite applicable in case of quantizing of periodic part of speech signal providing good results.

Our experiments show that 23 and 24 bit/frame split VQ quantizes LSF coefficients of harmonic speech components with near transparent quality. Some modification of vector codebook structure allows obtain improvement of codebook quality. Perceptual principles applied to speech coefficients improve performance of standard vector quantization and provide reduction of spectral distortion and numbers of outliers, so it adjusts quality of quantised speech.

Also we have found that bit reallocation between sub-codebooks gives better performance than uniform bit allocation. The quantizer at bit rate of 23 bit/vector was designed and evaluated.

5. References

[1] Petrowsky A., Zubrycki P.,Sawicki A. Tonal and Noise Components Separation Based on a Pitch Synchronous DFT Analyzer as a Speech Coding Method , Proceedings of ECCTD, 2003, Vol. III, pp. 169-172

[2] Linde, Y., Buzo, A., and Gray, R.M. "An algorithm for vector quantizer design", IEEE Transactions on Communications, vol. COM-28, pp. 84 – 95, Jan. 1980.

[3] Gersho, A. and Gray, R. Vector quantization and signal compression. Boston, Kluwer Academic Publishers, 1992.

[4] DARPA TIMIT Acoustic-Phonetic Continuous Speech Corpus, Department of Commerce, NIST, Springfield, Virginia, Oct. 1990.

[5] Palival, K.K. and Atal, B.S. "Efficient vector quantization of LPC parameters at 24 bits/frame", IEEE Transactions on Acoustics, Speech and Signal Processing., vol.1, № 1, pp. 3 – 14, Jan. 1993.

[6] Katsavounidis, I., Kuo, C.-C.J., Zhang, Z. "A new initialization technique for Generalized Lloyd Iteration", IEEE Signal Processing Letters, vol. 1, № 10, pp. 144 – 146, Oct. 1994.

[7] Laroia, R., Phamdo, N., Farvardin, N. "Robust and efficient quantization of speech LSP parameters using structured vector quantizers", in Proceedings IEEE International Conference on Acoustics, Speech, Signal Processing, (Toronto, Canada), pp. 641 – 644, May 1991.

[8] A. H. Gray, Jr. and J. D. Markel, "Quantization and bit allocation in speech processing," IEEE Trans. Acoust., Speech, Signal Processing,vol. ASSP-24, pp. 459–473, 1976.

[9] W.R. Gardner and B. D. Rao, "Theoretical Analysis of the High Rate Vector Quantization of LPC Parameters" IEEE Trans. Speech Audio Processing,vol. 3, no. 5 pp. 367–381, 1995.

[10] E. Zwicker, H. Fastl, "Psychoacoustics: Facts and Models". Berlin: Springer-Verlag, 1990

New results in 3D views of polyhedron generation on view sphere with perspective projection

M. Frydler , W.S. Mokrzycki

Institute of Mathematical Machines, 02-798, Warsaw,Krzywickiego 34, m.frydler@imm.org.pl
Institute of Computer Science PAS, 01-237 Warsaw, Ordona 21, wmokrzyc@ipipan.waw.pl

Abstract: This article concerns generating of 3D multiview model of convex polyhedron
that are a complete representation of this polyhedron, according to viewing
sphere with perspective projection. Those models are going to be used for
visual identification based on them and a scene depth map. We give a new
concept and an algorithm for face-depended generation of multi-face views. It
does not require any preprocessing nor auxiliary mechanisms or complex
calculations connected with them.

Key words: Object visual identification, depth map, 3D multiview precise model, viewing
sphere with perspective, projection, model completion state of viewing
representation.

1. Introduction

Method of generating 3D multiview representation of polyhedron for object
visual identification described in [10] is based on the following idea: centrally
generate views relative object features chosen for identification, calculate single-
view areas on viewing sphere which correspond with earlier generated views, check
if whole viewing sphere is covered with single-view areas. If this cover is complete,
generation of viewing representation is finished. If not than generate additional
views corresponding with uncovered areas of viewing sphere and again check if this
cover is complete. Continue until complete viewing sphere cover is generated.
Complete viewing sphere cover with single-view areas means that generated
representation is complete.
Methods from [16] and [18] are better. To achieve complete representation we don't
need to act in a loop. Complete representation is obtained by strict covering viewing
sphere by single-view areas and controlling "edge" register (of no covered area).

When register is set to "empty" generation of multiview representation is done.
Generated representation is complete which follows from the generation method.
However to achieve complete representation we have to calculate one-view areas on
viewing sphere and operate them in a given order. Without their help it is not
possible to get a complete set of views of virtual polyhedron model. On the top of
that described methods are for convex polyhedron only. In this article we present a

method for generating a complete viewing representation more computational efficient then described above.

2. Research assumptions

This research focuses on developing of a method and of an algorithm for generation of multiview, polyhedron representation. For representation generation we use viewing sphere with perspective projection. For this following conditions have to be met:

1. Models are accurate - every model is equivalent to B-rep model.
2. Models are viewing models – it is possible to identify object from any view

Use of a viewing sphere with projection (Fig 1.) as a projection space allows simple view standardization.

Uses: Recognition of objects not bigger then a few meters and distant (from the system) not more then 10 – 20 meters.

Mentioned above uses allow to make certain assumptions about recognition system strategies. We assume following steps of recognition processes

1. Determining recognizable object types.
2. Definition of identification task(choose an object's shell feature used for object identification)
3. Generation of viewing models for each object system should identify
4. Creation of database containing all views of all models
5. Acquisition of scene space data and visual data
6. Isolation of scene elements and their transformation to model structures stored in the database
7. Identification of objects by comparing them with database models.

3. View generation space – viewing sphere with perspective projection. Basic concepts.

Let object be a convex, non transparent polyhedron **without holes or pits**. Let's consider its faces as features areas, those areas will be used as a foundation for accurate multiview model determining. This model is a set of accurate views, acquired through perspective projection from viewing sphere, according to the model from [10] (Fig 1). This model is best for 3D scene data acquisition and gives identification system reliability.

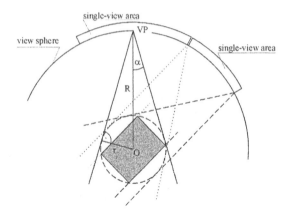

Fig. 1 Concept of view sphere and "single view" areas.

The concept from [18] of generating 3D multiview representation based on assumed generation space model is as follows:

- Circumscribe a sphere on a polyhedron. Sphere is small (radius r) and its center is at the polyhedron center.
- On this sphere place a space cone with angle of flare 2α. This is the viewing cone. Vertex of this cone is a model viewing point VP. Distance between polyhedron's center and model viewing point is R. Viewing axis always goes through the sphere's center.
- Unconstrained movement of cone vertex, where cone is tangent to the small sphere creates large sphere with radius R. This sphere is called viewing sphere (fig 1).
- Dependencies between values α , r and R and polyhedron vertices coordinates (Xvi,Yvi,Zvi) are:

$$r = \max_{i=1,\ldots,k} \sqrt{xvi^2 + yvi^2 + zvi^2}$$

$$R = \frac{r}{\sin \alpha}$$

- Generate views, taking into account only object features selected for identification i.e. faces. Faces visible in the viewing cone create a **view**, external edges from this view create **view's contour**.
- Calculate single-view areas. Those areas correspond with particular views.

  Complete set of views for a given polyhedron is obtained by covering of viewing sphere with single-view areas. Views are generated in such a way that corresponding single-view areas completely cover viewing sphere. Algorithm makes this approach complete.

Changing one view to the other is a **visual event**. This event occurs as a result of point VP movement. This event is manifested by appearance of a new feature in a view, disappearance of a feature or both.

4. Basic Definitions

Complementary viewing cone is a cone defined by current viewing axis (it's collinear with its height) and has an opposite direction of flare then the viewing cone. It intersects viewing cone with angle $\pi/2$, so its angle of flare is $\pi/2-\alpha$.

Vector Representation of polyhedron VREP is a set of polyhedron faces normals translated to point (0,0,0) Fig. 2a.

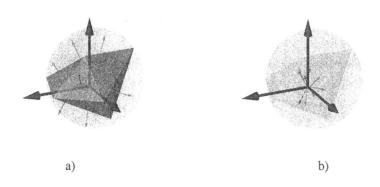

a)   b)

Fig. 2a Vector representation of polyhedron
a) Polyhedron with normals
b) Normals translated to point (0,0,0)

6 Algorithm of obtaining Views by rotating complementary cone.

For each vector v from vector representation (VREP) V of polyhedron rotate around it (vector) complementary cone and note every visual event. This event is manifested by appearance of a new versor inside complementary cone or by disappearance of versor. Result of such routine is set o vectors faces that can be seen by observer from view sphere.

If the polyhedron is convex all the faces inside view contour are visible. If it is no convex some faces can be invisible

Finally create set of different sets of vectors faces that can be seen. It is possible to achieve this by adding to set all obtained sets and by removing sets that repeats.

Representation completeness

For convex polyhedron fact that some faces normals translated to center of small view sphere contains in complementary cone mean that there are in same view. By rotating complementary cone around all normals all combination of faces normals that are in some view are obtained. That is why it is true to assume that by this algorithm all views will by collect.

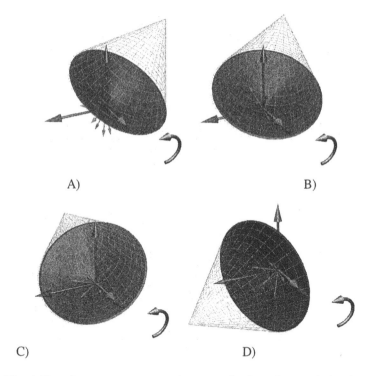

Fig. 4 Complementary cone rotation around selected normal, that is coaxial to one of main axis, perspective view

Fig. 4 is visual representation of mentioned process that is rotation of complementary cone. On this figure selected vector v is represented as blue arrow; red arrows are vectors from vector representation of polyhedron. Violet cone positioned toward observer is complementary cone which is rotated around blue vector. Green wired cone represent view cone.

Mathematical approach

At the beginning lets describe the algorithm of computing orientation of complementary cone (around vector v) in which it intersect. It is useful to use idea of coordinates transformation to simplify this task.

For vector v described in cartesian coordinates, that is in base B that contains three vectors x (1,0,0), y(0,1,0), z (0,0,1) or simply B((1,0,0), (0,1,0), (0,0,1)), designate base B'. B' is such base that can be created by multiplying B elements by (transformation) matrix [B'B]. B' is selected in such way that coordinates of vector v in this base equals v'(1,0,0)

$$v'= [B'B]*v.$$

Set of matrix's that fulfils mentioned condition is infinite. It is possible to use following approach to acquire one of them.

From base vectors (from B) select this one that angle distance between it and v is closest to 90 degrees. That is select this one that dot product is closest to 0. Mark it as t, than:

$$x'= v$$

$$y'= v^{\wedge}t$$

$$z'=v^{\wedge}(v^{\wedge}t),$$

Inversed matrix (x',y',z') fulfils our condition .

Now lets represent complementary cone that is rotated around vector v' as vector r(s) that lies in center of symmetry of cone and is function of rotation angle around v' (if consider base B'). Compute r(0) as rotation vector (1,0,0) around z' axis at $\beta/2$ angle (b is complementary cone angle), than:

$$r(s) = (r(0).x , r(0).y* \cos(s) , r(0).y* \sin(s))$$

Complementary cone intersect with h' (that is vector h transformed from base B to B') only if there is such s that:

$$r(s)*h' = \cos(\beta /2)$$

It is true because h' intersect with complementary cone only if angle distance to center of symmetry of cone equals half of cone angle.

It leads to following equation

$$r(0).x * h'.x + r(0).y * \cos(s) * h'.y + r(0).y * \sin(s) * h'.z = \cos(\beta /2)$$

If mark known values as

$$A = r(0).y * h'.y \quad B = r(0).y * h'.z \quad C = r(0).x * h'.x - \cos(\beta /2)$$

than equation simplify to "**intersection equation**"

$$A * \cos(s) + B * \sin(s) - C = 0$$

For particular data this equation can have 0 solutions when vector h' do not intersect with cone for all s, one solution when cone "touch" h' for some s and 2 solutions (s0<s1) when h' enters and leaves cone during its rotation. Only third case h is considered as to "be in one view" with vector v. Computational results achieved in base B' are also true in base B because of transformation approach .It is important to check and note if h belongs to cone if s0<s<s1 or (0<s<s1 or s2<s<2π) fulfill task conditions. Let's mark this result as Sh.

Next step consider computing set of sets of vectors that contains vectors that for some s interval lies inside complementary cone. Create set H that contains all "cone intersecting" solutions Sh{i} for all h{i} vectors from vector representation of polyhedron that are not v vector. Now by moving from 0 to 2*π check and note appearance and disappearance of previously computed solution (Sh{j}).This is equals computation of sets of vectors that are in one view. Notice, that each set contain vector v.

Below main idea of designating inclusion segments and obtaining angle ranges such that during complementary cone rotation within that range set of visible faces does not change.(on the picture first and last segment are the same)

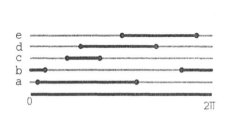 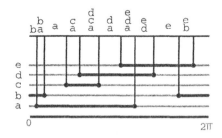

Algorithm F-M

For each vector v from object vector representation designate its transformation matrix ([B'B])

For each vector v' from object vector representation other than v

Designate its coordinates in B'

Designate and solve "intersection equation", than store solution as angle ranges (Sh)

Divide angle range (0 -2Π) by previously obtained angle ranges. **Each obtained segment represents one view.**

Remove Views that repeat itself.

7 Computational complexity

Let's assume that view cone has angle α and radius of little view sphere (which is build on polyhedron) equals r. This implicates that angle of complementary cone equals π - 2α. Surface area of small view sphere covered by rotating complementary cone equals area covered by cone that has centre in sphere centre and angle $2*(\pi - 2\alpha)$. Because surface area covered by cone that has centre in sphere centre and angle 2α equals

$$S (2\alpha,r) = 4\pi r^2 \sin^2(\alpha/2)$$

area covered by complementary cone rotation equals

$$So = 4\pi r^2 \cos^2(\alpha)$$

Let's compare it to whole sphere area $S = 4\pi r^2$

$$So/S = \cos^2(\alpha)$$

If 2α equals 30 degree So/S = 0.93...

Let's assume that computing relationship between complementary cone and faces normals is dominant operation because of it complexity. Now to obtain all views it is needed to:

- For all n faces normals of polyhedron...

- (Assuming even distribution of normals) 0.93n faces normals will be checked against complementary cone during it rotation.

At summary **computational complexity** of obtaining set that contains **ALL** views equals $0.93n^2$. This set usually has structure of set of sets of indices. Because of algorithm routine elements of this set can repeat itself. To avoid this it is needed to process this set. If set has w elements it require w^2 comparison.

Numbers of views depends on number of faces and equals [18]

$$c*n^2$$

Where value of c depends on structure of polyhedron on angle of view cone. For regular polyhedrons it is smallest and for cube and $2\alpha = 45$ degree it equals 0.72. For less regular it is close to 0.88. If we assume that than polyhedron is regular and numbers of over generated views is close to 0 than

$$w \sim m, \ w \sim n^2 \qquad (m - \text{count of targeted views})$$

and computational complexity equals $\mathbf{n^4}$

It is worth notice that cost of processing views that repeats its self shouldn't be overestimated because it is relatively low. That why overall computational complexity of this algorithm should by considered as closest to $\mathbf{n^2}$ than to n^4. Task of finding same subset of faces normal vectors could by simplify to operation performed on bits.

8 Implementation

Algorithms presented in this paper has been implemented and tested. Below screenshots from current implementation is presented. For classic, cube polyhedron 26 views have been obtained. Below 26 views are presented. Each face has different color.

8 Summary

This approach to generating 3D multiview models of polyhedron requires farther studies and researches. Result will be presented soon.

9 REFERENCES

[1] Connell J.H., Brady M. 1987: Generating and generalizing models of visual objects. AI, 31, 159-183.

[2] Bowyer K.W., Dyer Ch.R. 1990: Aspect Graphs: An Introduction and Survey of Recent Results. SPIE, 1395.

[3] Gigus Z., Canny J., Seidel R. 1991: Efficiently computing and representing aspect graph of polyhedral object.IEEE Trans. PAMI, 13(6), 542-551.

[4] Zhank S., Sullivan G.D., Baker K.D. 1993: The automatic construction of a view-independent relational modelfor 3D object recognition. IEEE Trans. PAMI, 15(6). 531-544.

[5] Leonardis A., Kovacic S., Pernus F. 1995: Recognition and pose determination of 3D objects using multiple views. Proc. CAIP'95, LNCS 970, Springer-verlag, Berlin, 778-783.

[6] Suk T., Flusser J. 1995: The projective invariants for polygon. Proc. CAIP'95, LNCS 970, Springer-Verlag,729-734.

[7] Arbel T., Ferrie F.P. 1996: Informative views and sequential recognition. Proc. ECCV'96, Cambridge, UK, April,469-481.

[8] Hlavac V., Leonardis A., Werner T. 1996: Automatic selection of reference views for image-based scene representation. Proc. ECCV'96, Cambridge, UK, April, 526-535.

[9] Arbel T., Ferrie F.P. 1997: Informative views and sequential recognition. Proc. ECCV'96, Cambridge, UK, April, 469-481.

[10] Dąbkowska M., Mokrzycki W.S. 1997: Multi-view models of convex polyhedron. MG&V, 6(4), 419-450.

[11] Madsen C.B., Christensen H.I. 1997: A viewpoint planning strategy for determining true angles on polyhedral objects by camera alignment. IEEE Trans. PAMI, 19(2), 158-163.

[12] Shimshoni I., Ponce J. 1997: Finite-resolution aspect graphs of polyhedral objects.

[13] Dąbkowska M., Mokrzycki W.S. 1998: A new view model of convex polyhedron with feature dependent view.MG&V, 7(1//2), (Proc. GKPO'98, Borki, Poland, 18-22 May), 325-334.

[14] Dąbkowska M., Mokrzycki W.S. 1998: Conditions on models for object visual identification. Proc. ACS'98, Szczecin, 19-20 Nov.,

[15] Kovacic S., Leonardis A. 1998: Planning sequences of views for 3D object recognition and pose determination.PR, 31(10), 1407- 1417.

[16]Kowalczyk M., Mokrzycki W.S. 1999 : Determining complete object's view model by joining one-view areas. Proc. ACS'99, Szczecin, 18-19 Nov., 68-72.

[17] Kowalczyk M., Mokrzycki W.S. 2002: A new method of finding one-view areas and tight view sphere covering. Proc. ICCVG'02, Zakopane, Poland, Sept. 25-29, 443-449.

[18]Kowalczyk M., Mokrzycki W.S. 2001: Obtaining complete 2 1/2D view representation of polyhedron using concept of seedling single-view area. CV &IU 91,208-301.

Gram-Schmidt Orthonormalization-Based Color Model for Object Detection

Mariusz Borawski, Paweł Forczmański

Technical University of Szczecin

71-210 Szczecin, Żołnierska Str 49, e-mail: mborawski@wi.ps.pl

Abstract: The paper presents two methods of creating custom color models used in object detection in digital images. Developed methods are based on Gram-Schmidt orthonormalization procedure and can be applied in different fields of recognition (human faces, remotely sensed images, etc.). Their main advantage over other ones is the efficient description and representation of color variations.

Keywords: Object detection, color model, orthonormalization

1 Introduction

An information concerning color is one of the most principal in the real world cognition. In long-term process of evolution many organisms have developed mechanisms that inform or warn by means of color. That is why it is so important to take into consideration the information about color when it comes to recognition of biological (or natural) structures. A good example related to this thesis are remotely sensed images (satellite or aerial) containing colors that represent different agricultural regions. Using colors we can detect them and measure their area. Another example is biometrical recognition based on face image, where the information about color is used on the first stage – face localization.

In the traditional approach to represent color image we use RGB model which utilizes vector representation of pixels colors and is rather easy to implement. This vector representation (each pixel is represented by a triple [Red, Green, Blue]) is related to the biological imaging determined by receptors in human eye. But it should be pointed out that our (humans) cognition and interpretation differs from that representation. When we name colors we never speak of each component separately, but rather we use intensity, saturation and tint.

The problem of color-based recognition can be described as operating in custom made color space aimed at certain color (or color range). In most practical cases we deal with conversion between RGB space and a custom space, because of the imaging device capabilities (in general, imaging devices work in RGB or YUV space)

2 Models Description

The main axis of color space (also called a system of color coordinates) represents the color we want to detect in analyzed image. It should be pointed out that we do not have a priori information about this particular color. Instead, we have some sample objects featuring not uniform color, which have variable (in some range) intensity, saturation and tint. The bigger the collection of template objects is, the more precisely the color range we can calculate. Based on these objects in the first step we calculate mean color value (fig. 1).

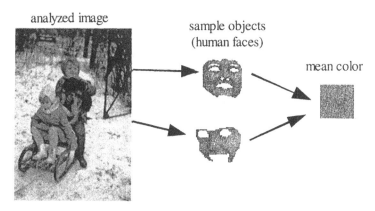

Fig. 1. Sample objects extraction and mean color calculation

Before proceeding, we should answer the question how homogeneous and compact the set of colors is? After a closer look it can turn out that this set consists of more than one subset (fig. 2).

Many subsets spreading in the color space close to each other mean that there are more colors on object's surface. Therefore all these subsets have to be extracted and considered separately. In practical approaches large color sets lead to a creation of many models (one for each subset). Small subsets (like smaller one presented in fig. 2) can be omitted without loss in representation efficiency.

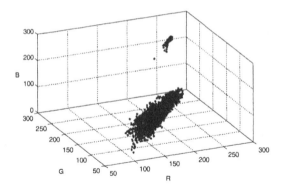

Fig. 2. Sample color set presented in RGB space

For most subsets we can calculate an axis which is interpreted as the symmetry axis:

$$\begin{cases} u_R = \dfrac{\displaystyle\sum_{i=1}^{N}\left|s_R - p_{R,i}\right|}{N} \\[3ex] u_G = \dfrac{\displaystyle\sum_{i=1}^{N}\left|s_G - p_{G,i}\right|}{N}, \\[3ex] u_B = \dfrac{\displaystyle\sum_{i=1}^{N}\left|s_B - p_{B,i}\right|}{N} \end{cases} \qquad (1)$$

where:

$p_{R,i}, p_{G,i}, p_{B,i}$ – points that belong to certain subset (R,G, B),

s_R, s_G, s_B – mean value of color component,

u_R, y_G, y_B – vector designating the main axis,

N – number of points.

The values calculated according to (1) can be interpreted as the coordinates of a vector which is parallel to the main axis of the set (fig. 3). Therefore it is taken as the first vector of a new color coordinates system (color space). We move from source color space (for example RGB) to the new one where the dominant color is related to one of the axes, which will make all calculations (e.g. description of set's boundary) easier. In the simplest case, the line $y=ax+b$ can be changed by $y=c_1$ and $x=c_2$.

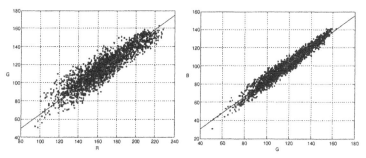

Fig. 3. Projections of sample color set onto RG and BG planes (the main axis is presented)

The color space we create is a three dimensional one, hence it is necessary to calculate two other missing axes. The most important condition to satisfy is the linear independence of all three vectors (or axes). That is why we choose these vectors as nonparallel to the main $\overline{U}$.

To simplify we can freely choose any two vectors designating RGB, but only if they are non-paralel to $\overline{U}$. In such case they will create complete system (in most cases also nonorthogonal). In that kind of system we can represent any color, but the loss of orthogonality causes the calculation to be very time-consuming.

When we take (as two additional axes) vectors related to $\overline{R}$ and $\overline{G}$ we can - utilizing orthonormalization procedure of Gram-Schimdt – transform nonorthogonal system of coordinates into orthonormal one (orthogonal and normalized). After orthonormalization the subsequent vectors of the new coordinates system will be described as following:

$$\begin{cases} \overline{W}_1 = \dfrac{\overline{U}}{\left\| \overline{U} \right\|} \\[2ex] \overline{W}_2 = \dfrac{\overline{R} - \left(\overline{W}_1, \overline{R} \right)\overline{W}_1}{\left\| \overline{R} - \left(\overline{W}_1, \overline{R} \right)\overline{W}_1 \right\|} \\[2ex] \overline{W}_2 = \dfrac{\overline{G} - \left(\overline{W}_2, \overline{G} \right)\overline{W}_2 - \left(\overline{W}_1, \overline{G} \right)\overline{W}_1}{\left\| \overline{G} - \left(\overline{W}_2, \overline{G} \right)\overline{W}_2 - \left(\overline{W}_1, \overline{G} \right)\overline{W}_{11} \right\|} \end{cases} \tag{2}$$

where

$\overline{W}_1, \overline{W}_2, \overline{W}_3$ – vectors designating the axes of new coordinates system

$(\overline{W}_1, \overline{R})$ – dot product of $\overline{W}_1$ and $\overline{R}$

In above described way we get orthogonal system of coordinates, where axis $\overline{W}_1$ is a vector normalized to one parallel to $\overline{U}$. All points can be transformed into new system by means of [2]. In our case we use the following:

$$
\begin{cases}
p_{W_1,i,j} = \dfrac{(\overline{P}_{i,j}, \overline{W}_1)}{(\overline{W}_1, \overline{W}_1)} \\[2mm]
p_{W_2,i,j} = \dfrac{(\overline{P}_{i,j}, \overline{W}_2)}{(\overline{W}_2, \overline{W}_2)}, \\[2mm]
p_{W_3,i,j} = \dfrac{(\overline{P}_{i,j}, \overline{W}_3)}{(\overline{W}_3, \overline{W}_3)}
\end{cases}
\tag{3}
$$

where

$\overline{P}_{i,j}$ - a point in RGB space

$p_{W_1,i,j}$, $p_{W_2,i,j}$, $p_{W_3,i,j}$ – new coordinates in $W_1 W_2 W_3$ space

After this transformation the new main axis is parallel to $\overline{W}_1$ (fig. 4). In the process of evaluating the similarity of analyzed color to the template one (or certain range) we omit this component because it is less important (the span along this axis is to large). The larger the distance to this axis, the less similar to the template the color is. Hence it is sufficient to introduce only two limits for each direction (dimension) $W_1 W_2 W_3$ to get good enough set boundary. It defines a range of color changes within analyzed objects. Limiting $\overline{W}_1$ is not allways necessary.

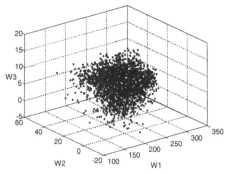

Fig. 4. Analyzed color set presented in $W_1 W_2 W_3$ space

We carried out an experiment to check, if this approach can cope with human faces detection. The results are presented in scatter plot (fig. 5). The color we have been looking for ranges from 230 to 310 for component $\overline{W}_1$, from 5 to 40 for $\overline{W}_2$ and from 0 to 16 for $\overline{W}_3$.

Additionally we can calculate an angle α between analyzed color $\overline{A}$ and axis $\overline{W}_1$, which can be taken as an extra similarity coefficient. It can be calculated as following:

$$\alpha = \arccos\left(\frac{A_{W_1}}{\|\overline{A}\|}\right), \tag{4}$$

where A_{W_1} is a projection of $\overline{A}$ onto axis $\overline{W}_1$

The angle α determines the direction of vector $\overline{A}$. If α is close to zero, then $\overline{A}$ is parallel to $\overline{W}_1$. Figure 5 presents a graphical representation of α for each pixel of sample image (intensity of pixels is related to α value – lower α is represented with darker pixels). However α can not be taken as the only one similarity factor because for color components close to zero it creates a noise ranging from 0 to 90 degrees. The length of color vector and its deviation from $\overline{W}_1$ can be used to evaluate the similarity between template color and analyzed one.

Fig. 5. Cosinus of an angle between $\overline{W}_1$ and analyzed color (left) and extracted regions (right)

It should be stressed that the operations in custom color space are not so straightforward as in classical one (RGB, CMY, YUV). Moving along each dimension changes not only the intensity but also the tint. For better usability the color model should be constructed in a way in which intensity and tint are independent. However it will lower the quality of detection, but on the other hand, it can be useful for creating more diverse models for larger class of objects with larger changes in colors.

In most cases we can assume that the main axis of a set is related to intensity changes. It means that the pixels colors change mostly in this manner. Hence, the variations in tint are smaller. Using these assumptions we define the main axis of color space as the vector $\overline{U}$ with starting point in origin of system of coordinates and ending point in the middle of the points set. The vectors defining axes of a new color space can be calculated using (3). In order to make operaions on intensity easier, we transfrom each point from $W_1 W_2 W_3$ space into destination space using the following:

$$B = \|\overline{C}\|, \quad \alpha = \arccos\left(\frac{C_{W_1}}{\|\overline{C}\|}\right), \quad \beta = \arctan\left(\frac{C_{W_3}}{C_{W_2}}\right), \tag{4}$$

where

$\overline{C}$ – a vector representing certain color,

$\overline{C}_{W_1}, \overline{C}_{W_2}, \overline{C}_{W_3}$ – projection of onto $W_1 W_2 W_3$

B – length of $\overline{C}$, intensity component

α – an angle between $\overline{C}$ and $\overline{W}_1$, related to similarity between sample color and template one.

β – an angle between projection of $\overline{C}$ on to plane $\overline{W}_2$, $\overline{W}_3$ and $\overline{W}_2$ related to tint similarity of template anf sample colors

Figure 6 shows two more examples of applying custom color model ($B\alpha\beta$) for detecting certain color regions. In each case separate color model has been created.

3 Summary

Presented custom color models can be applied in many practical tasks not restricted to human faces detection and remotely sensed images processing only. Their main advantage over other "classical" methods [4,5,6] is the precision of setting the limits of colors. It is no longer needed to calculate complicated boundaries for color sets. Instead we have only parameters describing the simple boundaries (box) or intensity and deviation of analyzed color from the template one.

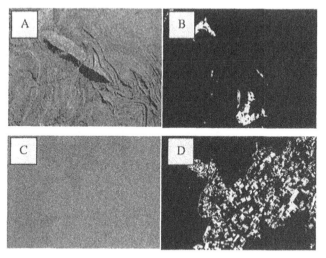

Fig. 6. Examples of locating certain areas (B,D) in satellite images (A, C) [3]

4   References

[1]   Białasiewicz J. T. „Falki i aproksymacje" Warszawa 2000 [in Polish]

[2]   Lathi B. P. „Teoria sygnałów i układów telekomunikacyjnych" Warszawa 1970 [in Polish]

[3]   Earth Sciences and Image Analysis, NASA-Johnson Space Center. „The Gateway to Astronaut Photography of Earth." <http://eol.jsc.nasa.gov/>

[4]   Arbib M. A. and Uchiyama T. „'Color image segmentation using competitive   learning". IEEE Transactions on Pattern Analysis and Machine Intelligence, vol 16, 1994

[5]   Yang Ming-Hsuan and Ahuja Narendra. „Detecting Human Faces in Color Images". International Conference on Image Processing . Vol. 1. 1998

[6]   Garcia C. , Tziritas G., „Face Detection Using Quantized Skin Color Regions Merging and Wavelet Packet Analysis", IEEE Transactions on Multimedia, 1(3) 1999

Eyes detection with motion interpretation

Arkadiusz Kogut

Wolinska 43, 72-100 Goleniów, Polska, e-mail: arkomp@poczta.onet.pl

Abstract:
The paper presents two methods of eyes detection in digital colour images with using template matching and projection method. It present a way of using results of the algorithms as a motion interpretation system.

Keywords: *Object detection, eyes detection, video sequence analysis*

1   Introduction

The most applications created for the eyes detection are concentrated on the result and they does not show how easy creation of the detection system can be. It makes the biometrics more inaccessible for common people. Closing the science for people can slow down the progress of it. The system presented in this article is an example of full accessible and intuitive application, which allows for the user to test and make his own conclusion based on various materials and conditions including graphical representation of the result.

2   The system basics

The application is based on simple rules of HSV analysis in detecting faces regions at colour images [1], projection and template matching method for detection eyes position [1]. The system was written in Borland Delphi 5.0, which allows for easy connection with video source – internal and external. Using this kind of software, preparing of the application can concentrate on content-related part of the problem.

On the picture 1 is shown the main form of the system, which lets to learn the results of all particular steps of the algorithm. At the right side of the window can be found all main parameters important for the results. There is possibility of changing the analysed materials, analogous parts of the algorithm, templates and their coefficient of size, and others.

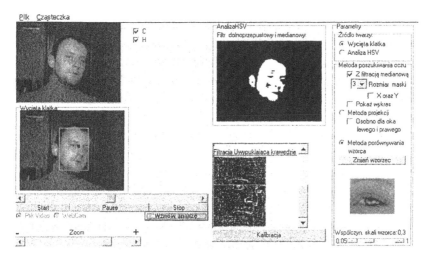

Fig. 1. The main form of the application

Every frame depends of the set values in parameters area in main window of the application. HSV analysis is the first step of the algorithm [1]. It is the method which determines the ranges for Hue, Saturation and Values typical for skin colour. The ranges are presented in picture number 2.

The source image is analysed pixel by pixel and every of them is checked if it is in the range of skin-colour or not. According to those information is created the binary map of the regions with skin-colour. The binary map is decreased six or eight times so the small noise is removed from the image. To support this process the binary image is median filtered with the mask size 3x3. All that process is illustrated frame, by frame during the action of the program. The biggest areas with skin-colour are treated as a face, and they are put to the dynamic array of the TImage objects, and all analysis is taken on that array which is showed at the bottom frame of the main window (fig. 1.).

2.1 Eyes detection methods

The next step is actual eyes detection. The applications offers two kind of solution of this problem:

- the Projection Method [1] with median filtering of the added values,

- the Template Matching Method, with searching for minimum deviation [1].

2.1.1 Projection method

First of them is very simple method based on adding the white pixels in every line and searching for the maximum which determines the position of the eyes. As it can be noticed at the picture number 3 the gradient image has the biggest concentration of edges at the eyes areas, so adding the values of the pixels can detect the line where the maximum (and the eyes line) is.

	Component	Range	Area
1	Hue	$H \leq 25.5$ or $H \geq 242.25$	
2	Saturation	$58,65 \leq S \leq 173,4$	Whole face
3	Value	$153 \leq V \leq 255$	

Fig. 2. Ranges for H, S i V to find the skin-colour areas [2].

This method is very easy to implement, but has one very weak point. During the adding the pixel values in the line it can treat the mouth line as a eyes line because when lips are opened, they can create maximum which is bigger than local maximum at the real eyes line. There are ways to remove this problem. The newest of them, detected during the application creation, is using the median filtering for removing narrow strip of local maximum created on the mouth line, because the strip of local maximum at the eyes line is more wide. The process of implementing the median filtering needs to use sorting algorithm. It is not important what kind of solution is used, because in the worst situation, it has nine values to sort, so the economy of the sorting method has low meaning. The efficacy of the method groves about 80%. The results of the method with, and without are showed at picture number 3. The fourth column shows the graph of the added values in line array. It is easy to notice the big difference with second column, where the maximum located at mouth line determines the error of detecting eyes line.

	Without median filtering		With median filtering	
Input image	The graph of values line adding of pixels	Horizontal eyes line	Median filtering of array of added values in line	Horizontal eyes line

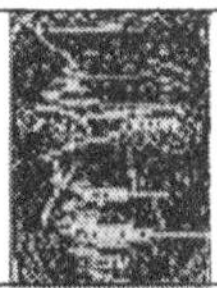

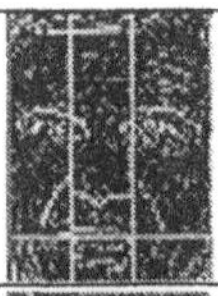

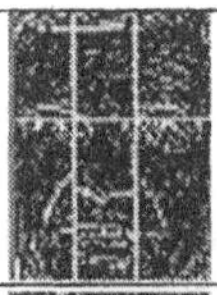

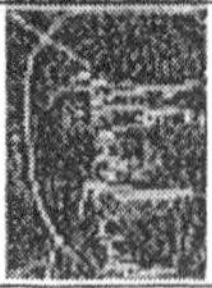

Fig. 3. The way the Projection Method works [3]

According to guidelines of this article, user can determine the source of image for analysis, size of the mask for median filtering, chose the way of filtering and detecting eyes (the same eyes line for both or separately), etc.

2.1.2 Template matching method

The other implemented method is based on searching for minimum deviation between source image and template. The program compares the part of the image (same size as template) and calculates the deviation coefficient. The lowest value of the deviation coefficient is treated by the application as the eye region, and the middle of compared area is taken as the centre of the eye.

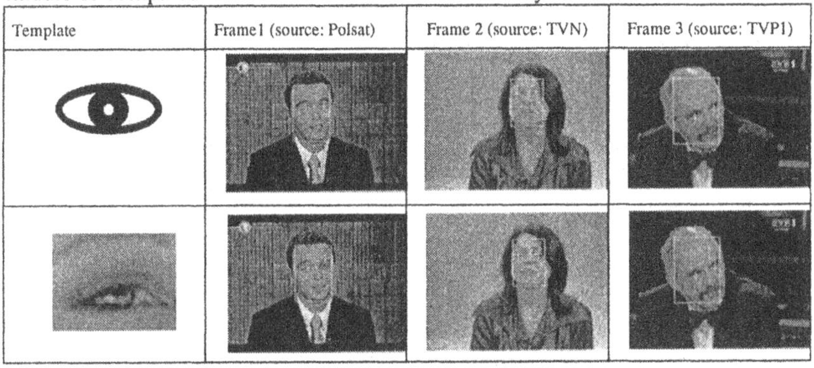

Fig. 4. The results of template matching algorithm [3]

The user can decide what kind of template the application use, can determine the size coefficient of the template (there is possibility of using every bitmap file – the size will always be change to needed). The template size coefficient is set as one third and it is used to set the height and width of the template. The width of the template is set as one third of the width of the face and height changes proportional to the width. There is possibility to change the size coefficient in range 0.05÷1 for checking different types of templates. The sample of results are presented at picture number 6. Template matching is very efficient method. Almost every analysed frame have good results if the quality of source is good also.

2.2 Results representation

The results representation and the way the system can be used is motion detection of the user working with the system. It takes a system as a way of 3D objects manipulation. For understanding it we have to concentrate a little at human anatomy.

2.2.1 Human skull

Taking the way the head is moving we have to concern the move in two axis. For simplification of calculation I have neglected the rotation in the plane of the screen. For calculation unification the normalisation of a and b (fig. 5.) distance needs to be done. That will help in finding the angle of face rotation.

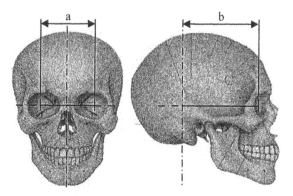

Fig. 5. Human sculpture. Distance between eyes (a) and the
axis of occiput knuckle (b) [5]

By the measuring the distances between eyes and the distance between eyes line and axis of occiput knuckle we can assume that a : b is like 1 : 1,384. After normalisation of that data we can universally use it to all sizes of detected faces.

2.2.2 Face direction analysis

For calculating the face direction method, we have to reverse the 3D images generation method. The image of the face is the result of generated 3D model. The distance between the eyes we take for calculation of distance between the object and projection surface of the screen. The angle of head rotation is very easy to find the rotation angle using trigonometric functions – that describes fig. 6. Horizontal rotation can be calculated in similar way.

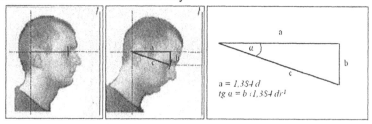

Fig. 6. The angle of head rotation, d – distance between eyes, 1 – screen surface, b
– distance between zero eyes position and real eyes position

After image processing the face direction is represented by two angles of rotation in horizontal and vertical position. The size of the angle can be used as a energy of motion. The last problem is to define if the angle means that object should be rotated left or right, but that can be determinate by comparison with zero position of eyes. The start position of eyes can be marked in calibration process similar to manual manipulators.

3   The system description

The system is a very clear structure basing on the rules presented in point two. The first point is calibration of the input image. The person using it should determine the region that will be used for calculations. That can reduce number of operation for finding face and eyes position During the calibration there is also the zero are pointed. This is the region which we can take as a straight looking to the camera. Next it is normal analysis process. Every frame got from the video stream is analysed by HSV algorithm, then by the template matching algorithm too. There is possibility of using various types of templates, which can be changed during the work of application. In every frame the middle point of the segment between the eyes is pointed and this is the most important for comparing with zero point. The distance is changed to angles described in point 2.2.2. The use of that information depends of the user. Here it is presented by 3D model written in OpenGL for Delphi.

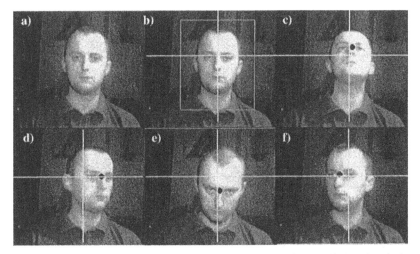

Fig. 7. Representation of application processing: a) input image, b) green frame of analysis area got in calibration process with the yellow cross of zero point, c) to f) the middle point at the segment between eyes marked by blue dot.

The main problem is the light conditions. In daily light there are no problem with HSV analysis, because the light is distracted and not distort the colours value. In artificial light there is a need to calibrate the camera to get higher efficiency of the algorithm. There is no problem with template matching when the faces areas are located in correct way (fig. 7).

During the processing application takes the difference between the blue point (fig. 7) and the zero point to find the direction of rotation, because during common calculation we get the angle but we do not have which direction we should rotate. That situation is made because of trigonometric functions used during the calculation gives only the measure of the angle. This is realized before calculating the angle. The difference value is taken to find b-value (fig. 6) so it is very easy to connect.

Final information as a result of processing are two angles which are necessary to use in OpenGL part of application.

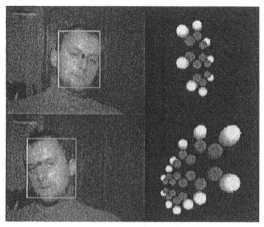

Fig. 8. The example of 3D chemical compound model rotation by implemented motion interpretation system

4   Summary

Presented solutions are examples of simple analysis of existing solution with a small innovations like median filtering used in projection method. The biggest advantage of presented application is simple and intuitive interface with very suggestive way of results representation. It is difficult to find new revolutionary solution, but the newest discoveries based on linking two tapes (or more) of algorithms to fill in disadvantages of one of them by the advantages of another gives a filling that there has not been said the last word in this subject.

The most interesting point is that α and β angles can be used in many different situations. They can be used as a typical manipulator which change the position of mouse cursor – what can help invalid persons to work with computer. That also can be new attractive way of piloting the computer games without touching the keyboard, mouse, joystick or any other well known manipulators (fig. 8).

5   Acknowledgements

The author would like to thank Georgy Kukharev dr hab. inż. prof. PS for giving the basics of biometrics systems and for showing that life is more interesting when there is a passion in it.

6   References

[1]   Kukharev Georgy, Kuźmiński Adam, Wydział Informatyki, Politechnika Szczecińska 2003. 'Techniki Biometryczne - Część 1 – Metody Rozpoznawania Twarzy.'

[2]   G. Kuchariew, Politechnika Szczecińska Wydział Informatyki, Szczecin, Informa 2001 'Detekcja obrazów twarzy w zadaniach "Name-it"', 'Materiały VI Sesji Naukowej Informatyki.'

[3]   Arkadiusz Kogut Szczecin 2003, Politechnika Szczecińska "Obliczanie współrzędnych oczu na twarzy w sekwencjach obrazów wideo."

[4]   Baza obrazów badawczych PS http://gpro.wi.ps.pl/

[5]   Wydawnicwo LibraMed http://www.libramed.com.pl/b2b/LWW.htm

Financial Distress Prediction Using Different Pattern Recognition Methods

Wiesław Pietruszkiewicz, Leonard Rozenberg

Technical University of Szczecin Faculty of Computer Science

ul. Żołnierska 49 71-210 Szczecin POLAND

e-mail:{ wpietruszkiewicz, lrozenberg }@wi.ps.pl

Abstract:
Prediction of possible financial distress is one of the most important tasks in business. This paper presents application of several pattern recognition methods in the field of financial distress prediction. All experiments were performed in troublesome Polish environment

Keywords: Pattern recognition, financial distress, crisis, memory based methods, neural networks, Discriminate Analysis

1   Forecast of financial distress

Prediction of financial distress is one of the most important tasks in business. It is a must for many groups e.g. capital donors need to protect themselves against possible loss of credits or firm's managers try to forecast crisis, which can drag enterprise into state of insolvency. The most widely used method of firm's condition evaluation is financial analysis. However its simplicity and usefulness is limited by its ambiguity e.g. firm's with good liquidity may be heading for a fall if its debts are above some dangerous limit. In such case financial analysis won't give clear signals. That shortcoming constrains developing of model combining several measures into one meaningful output indicating if firm shows any signs of possible insolvency.

There are many factors that can cause crisis. Whatever causes are, one can notice that in each firm there are a few common crisis' stages and events (Fig.1). The schema presents on Fig.1 concentrates on crisis' progress, while factors causing it can be found in appropriate positions of literature [8] or [2] and therefore they won't be explained herein.

104

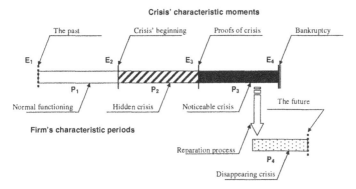

Fig. 1. The stages of crisis

Analyzing crisis progress it can be noticed that it starts in a hidden form (point E_2). It's an unnoticeable stage of the crisis i.e. cannot be noticed without any deeper analysis of firm's finance. Thus even if crisis hides and isn't obviously visible at this stage, this moment must be considered as a beginning of period where firm's condition is in great danger.

The literature mentions about many signals which can be regarded as proofs of a coming insolvency. According to Rozenberg [8] all signals can be divided into 2 groups:

– financial signals: this groups contains such effects as a increasing net loss or decreasing net profit, loss of liquidity or demand for new sources of capital used not to develop firm but to keep it running,

– non-financial signals: in this group such signals can be mentioned as ascending amount of capital locked-up in investments, lack of plans and frequent change of the managers.

Such signals often cannot be identified by a non-skilled person, thus for workers or business partners, it may seems that nothing shows any signs of crisis. Clear proofs of crisis' existence start in point E_3, where even non-skilled person can recognize that bankruptcy is closer each day. In period P_3 crisis can be noticed:

– inside firm, where occur frequent problems with liabilities like late salaries, lack of materials used in production, thus problems with keeping production running,

– outside the firm, where exists non paid liabilities or lack of power enough to fulfill placed orders on demanded goods.

Firm being at the stage P_3, where proofs of crisis are obvious, must take immediate reparation steps. Unfortunately process of reparation is very difficult at this stage and often does not protect against insolvency. Thus the aim is not identify signals in stage P_3 but to forecast coming crisis in stage P_2 i.e. where are signals of possible disaster but thy are well hidden, also where still is a hope [7].

2 Pattern recognition as a solution

The most useful and widely used attempt to problem of financial distress prediction is pattern recognition. It assumes that there must exists some similarities between failed firms and companies failed in the past can be used to estimate some pattern useful in others firms' condition evaluation.

The first used method of financial distress prediction and the most frequently used (even nowadays) is Discriminant Analysis (DA in abbreviation). It may be said that DA aims to find a projection vector (called discriminating vector), that allow to project points from N-dimensional space into new space with M-dimensions (M<N). This projection may be written as [5]:

$$y_i = w^T x_i \tag{1}$$

The choice of proper projection influences a possibility of point's separation after it. In case of wrong chosen w vector, it is not possible to distinguish samples from each group. If discriminating vector was chosen properly, dimensionality reduction allows to easily separate points.

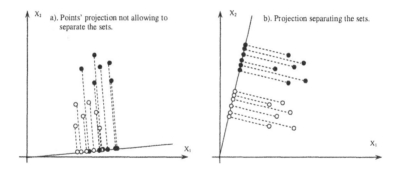

Fig. 2. Influence of disciminant projection on a possibility of class separation

The projection vector is chosen to ensure two criterions of discrimination [5]:
- points from different groups must be widely spread - between-class variance must be large,
- points belonging to the same group must lay close one to another, within-class scatter matrix must be small.

LDA maximises ratio that contains both of previously mentioned features [5]:

$$J(w) = \frac{\left| \tilde{\mu}_1 - \tilde{\mu}_2 \right|^2}{\tilde{s}_1^2 + \tilde{s}_2^2} \tag{2}$$

First quantitative model, estimating financial distress probability, was model constructed by E.I.Altman [1] or [2] in 1968. Using LDA (Linear Discriminant Analysis) Altman created a model, which even now is a point of reference for most of researchers.

However LDA usage is problematical because of the requirements of variable's normal distribution, which has not the confirmation in reality. This as well as others limitations (e.g. the linear character of division of multidimensional space) forced to develop alternative methods of the crisis's prediction. Other popular method used since eighties is logit analysis, which was first deployed by J. Ohlson [8].

The nineties began neural network usage in systems forecasting enterprise crisis. Among many works from this period Cheng [9] or Atiya [3] may be mentioned. Most of researches based on a Multilayered Perceptron, in which signals can be evaluated according to one general equation:

$$
\begin{aligned}
y &= N\{u\} \\
&= F_{wyj}\left\{W^{wyj}F\left\{W^{h}F\left\{W^{h-1}\dots F\left\{W^{1}u\right\}\dots\right\}\right\}\right\} \\
&= N_{wyj}N_{H}N_{H-1}\dots N_{1}\{u\}
\end{aligned}
\tag{3}
$$

where:

N_i	–	computing operator of i-th layer,
y	–	output vector,
u	–	input vector,
W^h	–	matrix of weights of connection between layers h-th and (h-1)-th,
F_h	–	activation operator of neurons form h-th layer.

Pattern recognition does not always require mathematical modeling. Classification can be also performed with help of algorithms called 'memory based' or 'experience based'. They assume that there exists visible similarity between samples from each class, so new coming sample may be classified by direct comparison of its attributes values with values of previously observed samples. The most frequently used methods form this group are kNN (k Nearest Neighbours) and NM (Nearest Mean). The kNN compares sample with k closest samples and NM uses means of groups in comparison. Both of these methods are very simple, however surprisingly effective. It must be mentioned, that such methods do not result in form of any models, which can be used not only to classify samples, but to gain knowledge about particular domain.

3   The dataset and crisis indicators

The dataset used in experiments contained 202 financial statements, 100 from bankrupt firms and 102 from existing (at least in the moment of database construction). A set of 30 financial ratios was calculated using financial analysis.

That set consisted of the most frequently citied and widely used in practice financial ratios. They were starting set of variables that was used as a set of possible crisis indicators. Using ANOVA (Analysis of Variance) F-tests were performed to measure differenced between means of ratios in both groups of firms (failed and non-failed). Existing differences between two group in case of all 30 variables shows if they might become handy in classification.

Due to some strong correlations between variables, it was necessary to choose a subset of variables that had biggest statistical significance but do not depend one on another. To ensure this, F-test ratios were sequentially weighted by a correlation coefficient between variable chosen lately to a subset and other variables. At each step remaining variables were sorted according to new calculated values of significance-and-independence. Finally a subset of 8 variables was used in experiments Tab. 1.

Indicator	Indicator's name
I_1	EBIT / Total Assets
I_2	Cash / Total Assets
I_3	Total Liabilities / Total Assets
I_4	Net Profit / Total Assets
I_5	Net Profit / Current Liabilities
I_6	Gross Profit / Net Sales
I_7	Net Profit / Net Sales
I_8	Net Profit / Long Term Capital

Tab. 1. Subset of variables chosen as crisis indicators (in descending level of significance)

4   The Results of experiments

In case of crisis forecasting two types of error exists. First type is a case when failed firm is classified as a non-failed firm. Such error is being called as a 'capital risk' i.e. risk avoided by a capital donors, who in this case are losing capital. Second type of error, when non-failed firm is being classified as a failed is called 'commercial risk' i.e. resulting in loss of capital sources and partners to a non-failed due to its classification as a possible bankrupt. Both types of risk are unwanted, although each of them influences different groups of subjects (internal or external).

Four methods of pattern analysis were used in the experiments: Nearest Neighbour, Nearest Mean, Neural Networks and Discriminant Analysis. Whole dataset was randomly divided onto two parts – training and validating. To estimate accuracy of prognosis hold-out method was used. Moreover, to ensure that dataset divide did not have any effect on methods' performance this process was repeated 20 times. At each step dataset was again divided into two parts.

Due to flexible architecture of ANN (Artificial Neural Networks) all experiments were performed on 5 ANNs that differ in number of neurons in a hidden layer. Results of ANN classification with different number of neurons is showed in Table 2.

No. of neurons	Prognosis accuracy %	Type I errors %	Type II errors %
4	72.6	10.6	16.8
5	72.45	11.15	16.4
6	71.3	12.45	16.25
7	71.75	12.6	15.65
8	72.6	11.8	15.6

Tab. 2. Accuracy of Neural Network classification (depending on no. of neurons in a hidden layer)

The results of other methods: NN, NM and DA are showed on Fig.3-5. Each figure represents accurate and no accurate prognosis in both cases of failed and non-failed firms.

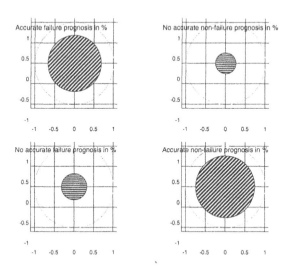

Fig. 3. The results of classification based on Nearest Neighbor method

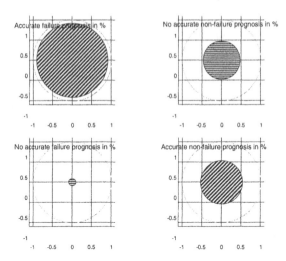

Fig. 4. The results of classification based on Nearest Mean method

Comparing in to other methods Nearest Mean had the best accuracy in failure prognosis. However it was also the weakest algorithm in case of non-failed firms. It leads to conclusion that many non-failed firms show bigger similarity to failed mean than to nonfailed.

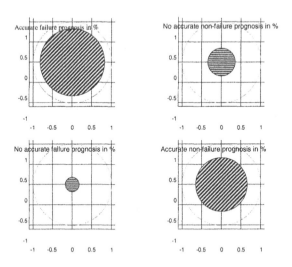

Fig. 5. The results of classification based on Linear Discriminant Analysis

Discriminant analysis had the greatest overall accuracy of prediction. To check what effect had number of ratios on its accuracy additional experiments were performed (Tab.3).

No. of ratios	Prognosis accuracy %	Type I errors %	Type II errors %
1	69.80	16.55	13.65
2	73.10	8.30	18.60
3	72.25	11.15	16.60
4	74.25	9	17.00
5	73.10	7.10	19.80
6	72.90	10.70	16.40
7	71.60	14.95	13.45
8	70.70	11.50	17.80

Tab. 3. Dependency of no. financial ratios used as crisis indicators on DA'a accuracy

As it can be noticed in Tab. 3 optimal number of ratios is 4. Fewer ratios do not carry enough of information to distinguish firms. More ratios also decrease classification accuracy.

5   Summary

The presented results of experiments proof that pattern recognition can be used in field of financial distress prediction. However these results, achieved in experiments in polish environment, differs from similar experiments performed in countries with stable economies [2], [6] or [9]. It is being caused by several reasons. First of all, bankruptcy in stable countries is regarded as a process that 'sweeps out' weak firms from a market. In Poland bankruptcy is rather considered as a disaster, resulting in unemployment. Thus polish courts often do not decide about firm's bankruptcy until it's really too late. Even if it seems as a positive market protection, in a matter of fact it is a market fixing. Too many bankrupt firms exist and when they fall, they finally drag to insolvency other companies (domino effect). Second important reason of slightly ambiguity between failed and non-failed firms are faults in management, in case when many polish managers' lack of proper knowledge and practice. Running on external capital such firms lengthen their vegetation. Howoever, even in case of nontransparent and not flexible polish economy pattern recognition can be useful tool in crisis prediction.

6 References

[1] Altman E.I. 1968 'Financial Ratio, Discriminant Analysis and Prediction of Corporate Bankruptcy'. The Journal of Finance, September, pp.589-609.

[2] Altman E.I. 2000 'Prediction Financial Distress of Companies: Revisiting the Z-SCORE and ZETA Models'. Working Paper, Stern School of Business, New York University.

[3] Atiya A. F. 2001 'Bankruptcy Prediction for Credit Risk Using Neural Networks: A Survey and New Results'. IEEE Transactions on Neural Networks Vol. 12 No. 4, pp.929-935.

[4] Fulmer J.G., Moon J.E., Gavin T.A., Erwin M.J. 1984 'A Bankruptcy Classification Model for Small Firms'. Journal of Commercial Bank Lending, pp.25-37.

[5] Michie D., Spiegelhalter D.J., Taylor C.C. 1994 'Machine Learning, Neural and Statistical Classification'. Ellis Horwood, New York.

[6] Ohlson, J. 1980 'Financial ratios and the probabilistic prediction of bankruptcy'. Journal of Accounting Research, pp.109-131.

[7] Pietruszkiewicz W. 2003 'An Application of the Discrete Dynamical System models in an Early Warning System Forecasting Financial Distress', 'International Workshop Control and Information Technology IWCIT'03'. Silesian University of Technology, Gliwice, pp.26-30.

[8] Rozenberg L. 2002 'Sanacja finansowa – metody poprawy kondycji finansowej przedsiębiorstwa', 'Praktyka zarządzania kryzysem w przedsiębiorstwie' (ed. Kozyra B., Zelek A.). Wydawnictwo Zachodniopomorskiej Szkoły Biznesu, Szczecin, pp. 167-186 (in polish).

[9] Tyree E. K., Long J. A. 1994 'Assessing Financial Distress with Probabilistic Neural Networks'. Working Paper, City University of London.

[10] Wilson R.L., Sharda R. 1994 'Bankruptcy Prediction Using Neural Networks'. Decision Support Systems No 11, pp.545-557.

Genetic algorithms applied to optimal arrangement of collocation points in 3D potential boundary-value problems

Eugeniusz Zieniuk, Krzysztof Szerszeń, Agnieszka Bołtuć
University of Bialystok, Faculty of Mathematics and Physics
Institute of Computer Science, Sosnowa 64, 15-887 Bialystok, Poland
e-mail: ezieniuk@ii.uwb.edu.pl, kszerszen@ii.uwb.edu.pl, aboltuc@ii.uwb.edu.pl

Abstract: Laplace's equation with any boundary conditions can be solved by means of the Parametric Integral Equation System (PIES). For modelling of the boundary geometry in 3D problems Bézier and Coons surfaces are used. A numerical solution of the PIES requires no boundary discretization and is reduced only to the approximation of boundary functions. For its solving a collocation method with Chebyshev polynomials was used. An arrangement of collocation points has high influence on the accuracy of obtained results. Genetic algorithms are applied for searching most optimal arrangement of collocation points.

Key words: Boundary integral equation, Parametric Integral Equation System (PIES), Bézier surfaces, Coons surfaces, collocation method, genetic algorithms

1   Introduction

Solving technical problems often leads to solving boundary-value problems. Currently, for a numerical solution of those problems two methods are particularly used. One of them is the Finite Element Method (FEM) and the other, dynamically developing in recent times, Boundary Element Method (BEM) [1].

In the FEM, the whole domain of the problem is discretized by finite elements, whereas in the BEM, only boundary is discretized by boundary elements.

Modelling of the domain in discrete way lead to use large numbers of input data and solve large numbers of algebraic equations. This is a very significant disadvantage of these methods, especially in the case of solving 3D boundary-value problems.

a)   b)   c)

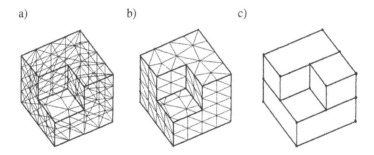

Fig. 1. 3D geometry describing in FEM, BEM and PIES:
discretization of the boundary in FEM *(a)* and BEM method *(b)*,
modelling of the boundary by Coons surfaces in the PIES method (c)

We propose a new way of defining boundary geometry using Coons linear surfaces and non-linear Bézier surfaces of the third degree. This method is used in the PIES for solving the 3D boundary-values problems.

The PIES is an analytical modification of traditional Boundary Integral Equations (BIE). The main advantage of the PIES is the fact, that during its numerical solving smaller number of input data (needed for boundary geometry defining), than in BIE, is required. The boundary geometry describing reduces only to set of corner points of used surfaces and smaller equation system is solved.

A numerical solution of the PIES requires no boundary discretization and is reduced only to the approximation of boundary functions. The separation of the boundary approximation from boundary functions makes the modification of boundary geometry easier. It also enables us to use more effective methods for the approximation of boundary functions.

In this paper for solving the PIES a collocation method [4] is used. The influence of the arrangement of collocation nodes on the accuracy of the obtained results has been studied. In order to find most optimal arrangement genetic algorithm was applied. As base functions Chebychev polynomials were used. Finally the obtained results – for 3D potential problems - have been compared with the ones obtained by the analytical method.

2   Modelling and modification of 3D boundary by means of Coons and Bézier surfaces

To define surface of polygonal boundary geometry only corner points of 3D geometry are used. The linear part the 3D boundary geometry in the PIES is built with Coons surfaces. Each of them is defined by only 4 corner points and is described using following formula [3]

$$P(w, v) = [1 - w, v] \begin{bmatrix} P_1 & P_2 \\ P_3 & P_4 \end{bmatrix} \begin{bmatrix} 1 - v \\ v \end{bmatrix} \tag{1}$$

after the multiplication of (1) following expression was obtained

$$P(w, v) = \varphi_1(w, v)P_1 + \varphi_2(w, v)P_2 + \varphi_3(w, v)P_3 + \varphi_4(w, v)P_4 \tag{2}$$

where

$$\varphi_1 = (1 - w)(1 - v), \quad \varphi_2 = w(1 - v), \quad \varphi_3 = wv, \quad \varphi_4 = (1 - w)v$$

$$\varphi_i, \ i = 1,2,3,4 \quad \text{are base functions.}$$

Bézier surface patches are used for defining non-linear parts of the boundary geometry in the PIES. Each Bézier surface is defined by grid of 16 control points in the following way

$$P(v, w) = v M_{\text{Bézier}} \begin{bmatrix} P_{1,1} & P_{1,2} & P_{1,3} & P_{1,4} \\ P_{2,1} & P_{2,2} & P_{2,3} & P_{2,4} \\ P_{3,1} & P_{3,2} & P_{3,3} & P_{3,4} \\ P_{4,1} & P_{4,2} & P_{4,3} & P_{4,4} \end{bmatrix} M_{\text{Bézier}}^{T} w \tag{3}$$

$$M_{\text{Bézier}} = \begin{bmatrix} -1 & 3 & -3 & 1 \\ 3 & -6 & 3 & 0 \\ -3 & 3 & 0 & 0 \\ 1 & 0 & 0 & 0 \end{bmatrix}$$

In the case of using **Bézier surfaces** of the zero degree it is easy to modelling any domains by only corner points. In the case of using **Bézier** surfaces of the third degree it is easy to modelling the boundary geometry in continuous solution with addition c^2 continuity with the help of a small number of Bézier control points. A smaller number of input data required for the definition of the domain as well as a smaller system of algebraic equations to be solved. Modelling and modification of the boundary geometry by means of Bézier and Coons surfaces is shown in the appendix.

3   The Parametric Integral Equation System (PIES)

Instead of the BIE we can use the PIES for an effective search of solutions on the boundary for Laplace'a equation. The PIES is obtained as a result of an analytical modification of BIE. The PIES method for the 2D boundary-value problems [6,7] after generalization to 3D boundary-value problems is presented by the following formula [6,7]

$$0.5u_i(v,w) = \sum_{j=1}^{n} \int_{v_{j-1}}^{v_j} \int_{w_{j-1}}^{w_j} \left\{ \overline{U}_{ij}^{\bullet}(v_1,w_1,v,w) p_j(v,w) - \overline{P}_{ij}^{\bullet}(v_1,w_1,v,w) u_j(v,w) \right\} J_j(v,w) dv dw \quad (4)$$

Information about 3D boundary (Coons surfaces or Bézier surfaces) is included in the kernels $\overline{U}_{ij}^{\bullet}(s_1,s)$, $\overline{P}_{ij}^{\bullet}(s_1,s)$ in the following form

$$\overline{U}_{ij}^{\bullet}(v_1,w_1,v,w) = \frac{1}{4\pi}\frac{1}{[\eta_1^2 + \eta_2^2 + \eta_3^2]^{0.5}}, \quad (5)$$

$$\overline{P}_{ij}^{\bullet}(v_1,w_1,w_1,v,w) = \frac{1}{4\pi}\frac{\eta_1 n_1^{(j)}(v,w) + \eta_2 n_2^{(j)}(v,w) + \eta_3 n_3^{(j)}(v,w)}{[\eta_1^2 + \eta_2^2 + \eta_3^2]^{1.5}}, \quad (6)$$

where

$$\eta_1 = P_i^{(1)}(v_1,w_1) - P_j^{(1)}(v,w), \eta_2 = P_i^{(2)}(v_1,w_1) - P_j^{(2)}(v,w)$$
$$\eta_3 = P_i^{(3)}(v_1,w_1) - P_j^{(3)}(v,w).$$

Function (5) is called the fundamental boundary solution and (6) is the singular boundary solution. These solutions constitute kernels in the PIES (4) and in their mathematical formalism, in contrast to traditional kernels, take into account the boundary geometry defined by means of parametric linear functions.

4 Numerical solving of the PIES aided by genetic algorithm

The separation of the boundary approximation from boundary functions enables us to use various, more effective methods for the numerical solving of the PIES. To solve the PIES well known collocation method [4] - a specific variant of the spectral method - is used. It is very effective as it requires only a single integration.

The solution of the PIES represented by formula (4) is reduced to finding the unknowns functions $u_j(v,w)$ or $p_j(v,w)$ on each of the boundary segments of the considered problem. Boundary functions are approximated by means of the following approximating expressions

$$u_j(v,w) = \sum_{p=0}^{N}\sum_{r=0}^{M} u_j^{(pr)} T_j^{(p)}(v) T_j^{(r)}(w), , \quad p_j(v,w) = \sum_{p=0}^{N}\sum_{r=0}^{M} p_j^{(pr)} T_j^{(p)}(v) T_j^{(r)}(w), \quad (7)$$

where $u_j^{(pr)}, p_j^{(pr)}$ are unknown coefficients, $n = N \times M$ — is the number of the coefficients on each segment, whereas $T_j^{(p)}(v)$ $T_j^{(r)}(w)$ are global base functions – Chebyshev polynomials described by the following recurrent formula

$$T''(x) = 2xT^{n-1}(x) - T^{n-2}(x) \qquad T^0(x) = 1, \qquad T^1(x) = x \qquad n = 2,3,.... \qquad (8)$$

Having considered (7) in the integral equations system (4) we obtain the following form of the equation

$$0.5u_i(v,w) = \sum_{j=1}^{n} \sum_{p=0}^{N} \sum_{r=0}^{M} \left\{ p_j^{(pr)} \int_{v_{j-1}}^{v_j} \int_{w_{j-1}}^{w_j} \overline{U}_{ij}^* (v_1, w_1, v, w) - \right.$$
$$\left. - u_j^{(pr)} \int_{v_{j-1}}^{v_j} \int_{w_{j-1}}^{w_j} \overline{P}_{ij}^* (v_1, w_1, v, w) \right\} T_j^{(p)}(v) T_j^{(r)}(w) J_j(v,w) dv dw. \qquad (9)$$

Equation (9) written down for all the collocation points [5] takes the following matrix form

$$[H]\{\overline{u}_j\} = [G]\{\overline{p}_j\}. \qquad (10)$$

Unknown coefficients $u_j^{(pr)}, p_j^{(pr)}$ are solution of algebraic equation system (10). Multiplication coefficients with base functions, like in (7), leads to continuous solution on each segment.

The optimal arrangement of the collocation points is important problem and is directly connected with accuracy of numerical solutions of the PIES.

4.1   Genetic algorithm used to study on optimal collocation points arrangement

The genetic algorithm (GA) is used to search an optimal arrangement of colloca-tion points in numerical solving of the PIES. Sample 3D boundary geometry with 4 collocation points on each of six surfaces is presented in Fig. 2. The GA imple-mented in this case has a continuous representation of possible optimal arrange-ments of collocations points (v,w) on the 3D boundary surface with values reduced to (0,1) for its chromosomes.

a)   b)

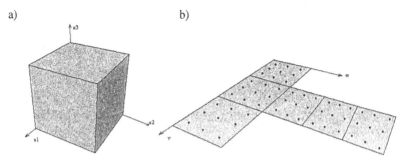

Fig. 2. 3D boundary geometry (a) with collocation points on each surface (b)

118

The GA optimization process begins by setting a random set of possible solutions, called the populations [2]. Each individual is defined by optimization variables and represents a chromosome. In each iteration of the GA, the process of selection, cross-over, and mutation operators are used to update the population of design. Each generation involves selecting the best members, performing crossover and mutation and then evaluating resultant population, until the final condition is satisfied. The fitness function applied to the GA is the average mean square error computed by comparison the PIES solutions on the boundary (for each chromosome) with analytical solutions. Optimal solution given by the PIES is the pattern of the collocations points placement, the same for each surface of 3D boundary geometry.

5   Testing example

Various configurations of optimal arrangements of collocation points, given by implemented GA, were studied. In the considered example each chromosome contains coordinates of 9 collocation points. The boundary geometry is presented in Fig. 1. The following parameters of the genetic algorithm are chosen: the population size is 50 with probability of crossover - 80 percent and probability of mutation - 15 percent. The number of GA iterations is 600. The analytical solution on the boundary is described by equation:

$$F(x_1, x_2, x_3) = e^{-\pi x_1} \sin(\pi x_2) + x_3 . \tag{11}$$

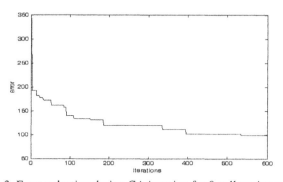

Fig. 3. Error reduction during GA iteration for 9 collocation points

The calculations carried out by genetic algorithm show the possibility of noticeable reduce of the total error (Fig. 3.). Chromosomes from each population relatively quickly locate analyzed collocation points in the centres of surfaces (Fig. 4.).

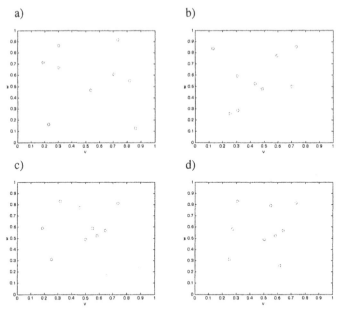

Fig. 4. Arrangement of 9 collocation points during GA iterations:
a) initial arrangement, *b)* 200 iterations, *c)* 400 iterations,
d) resultant arrangement (600 iteration)

Numerical studies confirm the trend that collocation points are located in the centres of the segments in the first iteration and then GA spends the rest of the iterations adjusting better solutions without better performance. The optimal placement of collocation points is around 0.2 from the boundary of considered surface.

6 Conclusions

The paper shows the tool for optimisation of the collocation points arrangement in the PIES based on genetic algorithms. Using the calculations from the numerical examples analysed by the authors, it appears that the arrangement of the collocation points has influence on the accuracy of the results. Most accurate results are obtained when collocation points are placed in some interval from boundary.

Appendix

Effective boundary geometries modification

The proposed algorithm for describing 3D boundary geometry was successfully tested on relatively simple and more complicated models as it is presented in Fig. 5. The developed technique is automated and applicable to most geometry [5].

a)   b)

c)   d)

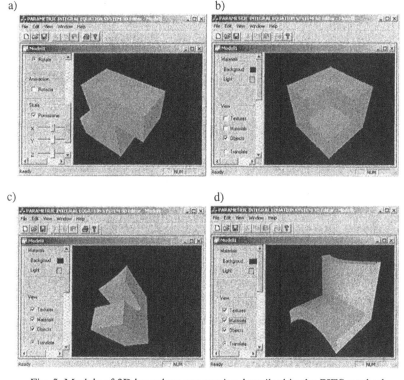

Fig. 5. Models of 3D boundary geometries described in the PIES method

Fig. 5a. presents the boundary built with the 12 Coons surfaces. In Fig. 5b. is presented model described by 14 Coons surfaces. It is possible to define non-linear shapes of the boundary by Coons and Bézier surfaces together like shown in Fig. 5c. (5 Coons and 6 Bézier segments) and in Fig. 5d. (7 Coons and 6 Bézier parts).

Fig. 6. shows a 3D view of a modification of a sample model. The original boundary is shown in Fig. 6a. Six Coons surfaces are used to describe that geometry. In

Fig. 6b for non-linear modification of the original 3D boundary six Bézier surfaces was introduced to the model instead of Coons linear surfaces.

a)   b)

c)   d)

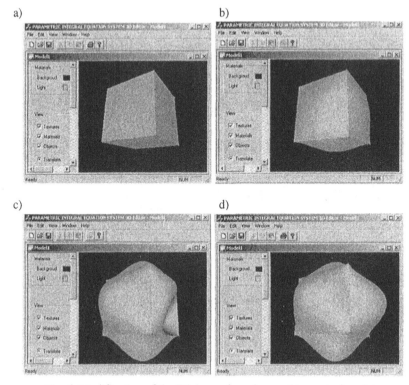

Fig. 6. Modification of the Bézier surfaces by moving controls points

The shape of the boundary of this model is manipulated according to a set of control points. Fig. 6c. and Fig. 6d. present the modification of Bézier surfaces by moving only four of sixteen control points for each surface.

References

[1]   Brebbia C.A., Telles J.C.F., Wrobel, L.C., "Boundary element techniques, theory and applications in engineering", Springer, New York, 1984.

[2]   Goldberg, David E. "Genetic Algorithms in Search, Optimization and Machine Learning", Addison-Wesley Pub. Co., 1989.

[3]   Foley J. D., van Dam A., Feiner S. K., Hughes J. F., Phillips R.L., "Introduction to Computer Graphics", Addison-Wesley, 1994.

[4]   Gottlieb D., Orszag S.A., "Numerical analysis of spectral methods", SIAM, Philadelphia, 1997.

[5]   Kiciak P., "Podstawy modelowania krzywych i powierzchni", WNT, Warszawa, 2000 (in polish).

[6]   Zieniuk E., Szerszeń K., Bołtuć A., "Płaty powierzchniowe Conssa w modelowaniu trójwymiarowej geometrii brzegu w zagadnieniach brzegowych dla równania Laplace'a", PTSK Symulacja w badaniach i rozwoju, pp. 447-454, Zakopane, 2003 (in polish).

[7]   Zieniuk E., "A new integral identity for potential polygonal domain problems described by parametric linear functions", Engineering Analysis with Boundary Elements, Volume 26/10, pp. 897-904, 2002.

[8]   Zieniuk E., "Bézier curves in the modification of boundary integral equations (BIE) for potential boundary-value problems", International Journal of Solids and Structures, Volume 40/9, pp. 2301-2320, 2003.

PART II

Computer Security and Safety

Fast Computation of Approximation Tables

Krzysztof Chmiel

Poznań University of Technology,
pl. Skłodowskiej-Curie 5, 60-965 Poznań, Poland,
e-mail:Chmiel@sk-kari.put.poznan.pl.

Abstract:
In the paper are presented results, concerning the linear approximation of arbitrary function f with n binary inputs and m binary outputs. The based on the definition of linear approximation algorithm to compute a single value of the approximation table, is of exponential complexity $O((n+m) \cdot 2^n)$. The presented in the paper fast algorithm computes the whole approximation table, in linear time $O(n+m)$ for a single value.

Keywords: *Cryptanalysis, linear approximation, approximation table.*

1   Introduction

Linear approximation of a cipher algorithm constitutes a basic concept of linear cryptanalysis – one of the most important, general methods of cryptanalysis [2, 4, 5, 6, 7, 8, 9, 10, 11, 12, 13]. By a linear approximation we mean a linear equation, relating input bits to output bits of an algorithm. The equation is satisfied with some probability p for randomly chosen input and corresponding output. The magnitude of $|\Delta p| = |p - 1/2|$ represents the *effectiveness* of the approximation. Approximations with nonzero value of the effectiveness measure are said to be effective.

In the case of iterative block ciphers, the calculation of the most effective linear approximations is carried out typically in two main steps. First, as a result of composition of approximations of component functions, the effective approximations of a single iteration are calculated. Next, as a result of composition of approximations of consecutive iterations, the linear approximation of the entire algorithm is obtained.

Approximation of an algorithm, enables the identification of the key bits, for sufficiently large family of known pairs: plaintext – ciphertext. Unlike the differential cryptanalysis, which is essentially a chosen-plaintext attack [1, 3, 10], the linear cryptanalysis is essentially a known-plaintext attack and moreover is applicable to an only-ciphertext attack under some circumstances [11, 12].

In general, the *linear approximation* of function $Y = f(X)$: $\{0,1\}^n \to \{0,1\}^m$ is defined as an arbitrary equation of the form:

$$\bigoplus_{i \in Y'} y_i = \bigoplus_{j \in X'} x_j,$$

satisfied with approximation probability $p = N(X',Y') / 2^n$, where $Y' \subseteq \{1,..,m\}$, $X' \subseteq \{1,..,n\}$ while $N(X',Y')$ denotes the number of pairs (X, Y) for which the equation holds. For simplicity the above equation is written in the following form:

$$Y[Y'] = X[X'].$$

The sets of indexes X', Y' are called input and output *mask* respectively and the function $N(X',Y')$ is called the *counting function* of the approximation.

The linear approximation *characteristic* is defined as a sequence $(X', Y', \Delta p)$, where X', Y' are masks or sequences of input and output masks and p is the approximation probability. Among characteristics we distinguish the *zero-characteristic* (Φ, Φ, 1/2), corresponding to the *zero linear approximation*, which probability is equal to 1 for arbitrary function f.

Composing linear approximations, it is necessary to formulate so called *approximation conditions* and to calculate the approximation probability of the composition. The approximation conditions eliminate the bits of the internal variables from the resultant equation. The probability Δp of the composition of n approximations with probabilities Δp_i, is calculated as follows:

$$\Delta p = 2^{n-1} \prod_{i=1}^{n} \Delta p_i.$$

2 Approximation Tables

The general form $Y[Y'] = X[X']$ of the linear approximation of function $Y = f(X)$, is illustrated in figure 1.

Fig. 1. Linear approximation of function f

Linear approximations of function f can be described in the form of the *approximation table TAf*. The element $TAf[X', Y']$ of the table, is defined as the number of pairs (X, Y) satisfying equation $Y[Y'] = X[X']$, decreased by the half of all the pairs. Thus, it can be calculated by the formula:

$$TAf[X', Y'] = \Delta N(X', Y') = N(X', Y') - 2^{n-1}.$$

Approximation table *TAf* is obtained by examination, for each mask pair (X', Y'), of all input pairs (X, Y) and contains the complete description of linear approximations of function f. In other words, table *TAf* represents all the characteristics $(X', Y', \Delta p)$ of function f, where probability Δp can be calculated as follows:

$$\Delta p = TAf[X', Y'] / 2^{n}.$$

X	$Y = f(X)$	X'	Y' 0	1	2	3
0	0	0	8	0	0	0
1	1	1	0	0	0	0
2	2	2	0	0	0	0
3	3	3	0	0	0	0
4	1	4	0	0	0	0
5	2	5	0	8	0	0
6	3	6	0	0	0	0
7	0	7	0	0	0	0
8	2	8	0	0	0	0
9	3	9	0	0	0	0
10	0	10	0	0	4	-4
11	1	11	0	0	4	4
12	3	12	0	0	0	0
13	0	13	0	0	0	0
14	1	14	0	0	4	4
15	2	15	0	0	-4	4

Fig. 2. Approximation table *TAf* of an example function f

The approximation table of an example function f is presented in figure 2. There exist 10 effective approximations of the function: 2 approximations with probability $\Delta p = 1/2$ and 8 approximations with probability $|\Delta p| = 1/4$.

For clarity, in figure 3 is presented the basic algorithm computing a single value of the approximation table of function f. Auxiliary function BIT-XOR(...) computes the XOR of the n least significant bits of parameter X. Function N(...) is the counting function of the approximation. The main function TA-F(...) returns the value $N(X', Y', n, m) - 2^{n-1}$. The time complexity of the algorithm is $O((n+m) \cdot 2^{n})$.

TA-F(X', Y', n, m)
    1. BIT-XOR(X, n)
    2. $w \leftarrow 0$
    3.   **for** $i \leftarrow 0$ **to** $n - 1$ **do** $w \leftarrow w \oplus X_i$
    4.   **return** w
    5. N(X', Y', n, m)
    6. $w \leftarrow 0$
    7.   **for** $X \leftarrow 0$ **to** $2^n - 1$ **do**
    8. $Y \leftarrow f(X)$
    9.   **if** BIT-XOR(X and X', n) = BIT-XOR(Y and Y', m)
    10.   **then** $w \leftarrow w + 1$
    11.   **return** w
    12. **return** N(X', Y', n, m) $- 2^{n-1}$

Fig. 3. Basic algorithm, computing a single value of the approximation table of f

The size of the approximation table of function f is equal to 2^{n+m} and based on the definition, calculation of a single value of the table requires $O(2^n)$ operations. The presented in the paper method, enables to calculate the approximation table in time linear for a single value.

3   Theorem

The fast computation of approximation tables method is based on the theorem formulated in this chapter. Let TAf be the approximation table of function $Y = f(X)$: $\{0,1\}^n \rightarrow \{0,1\}^m$ and let TAf_0 and TAf_1 be the approximation tables of *residual functions*:

$$f_0 = f(X_{n-1} = 0) = f(0, X_{n-2}, ..., X_0) \text{ and } f_1 = f(X_{n-1} = 1) = f(1, X_{n-2}, ..., X_0).$$

Furthermore let TAf^0 and TAf^1 denote the halves of TAf for $X_{n-1}' = 0$ and $X_{n-1}' = 1$, respectively (fig. 4).

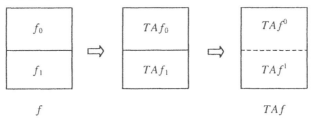

f TAf

Fig. 4. Illustration to theorem 1

Theorem 1.

For arbitrary function $f: \{0,1\}^n \rightarrow \{0,1\}^m$, where $n > 1$ and $m \geq 1$, holds:

$$TAf^0 = TAf_0 + TAf_1 \text{ and } TAf^1 = TAf_0 - TAf_1.$$

Proof.

The linear approximation of function f can be written in the following form:

$$Y[Y'] = X[X'] = X_{n-1}' \cdot X_{n-1} \oplus X_r[X_r'],$$

where $X_r = (X_{n-2}, ..., X_0)$. Let N be the counting function of the approximation of function f and let N_0 and N_1 be the counting functions of the approximations of functions f_0 and f_1, respectively. Furthermore let N_α^β denotes the counting function of the approximation of function f for $X_{n-1} = \alpha$ and $X_{n-1}' = \beta$, where $\alpha, \beta \in \{0,1\}$. For $X_{n-1}' = 0$ we have:

$$N = N_0^0 + N_1^0 = N_0 + N_1, \text{ and}$$
$$\Delta N = (N_0 + N_1) - 2^{n-1} = (N_0 - 2^{n-2}) + (N_0 - 2^{n-2}) = \Delta N_0 + \Delta N_1.$$

We have obtained that $TAf^0 = TAf_0 + TAf_1$. For $X_{n-1}' = 1$ we have:

$$N = N_0^1 + N_1^1 = N_0^0 + (2^{n-1} - N_1^0) = N_0 + (2^{n-1} - N_1), \text{ and}$$
$$\Delta N = (N_0 + (2^{n-1} - N_1)) - 2^{n-1} = N_0 - N_1 = (N_0 - 2^{n-2}) - (N_1 - 2^{n-2}) = \Delta N_0 - \Delta N_1.$$

We have obtained that $TAf^1 = TAf_0 - TAf_1$.   ∎

In figure 5 are presented four elementary approximation tables of Boolean functions of one variable. The tables can be used to compute approximation tables of Boolean functions of more variables as well as in general, of functions $f: \{0,1\}^n \rightarrow \{0,1\}^m$, where $n, m \geq 1$.

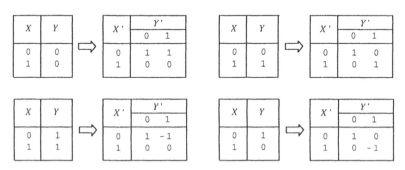

Fig. 5. Approximation tables of Boolean functions of 1 variable

The case of Boolean function of two variables is illustrated for function XOR, in figure 6. To compute the approximation table $TAXOR$ we use elementary approximation tables from figure 5, for one-variable functions $XOR(0, X_0)$ and $XOR(1, X_0)$. The upper half of $TAXOR$ is obtained as a result of addition and the lower half as a result of subtraction of the two elementary tables.

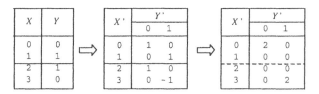

Fig. 6. Computation of the approximation table of function XOR

4   Algorithm

The fast algorithm computing the approximation table of an arbitrary function $Y = f(X)$: $\{0,1\}^n \rightarrow \{0,1\}^m$, where $n, m \geq 1$, is composed of two main steps. In the first step the initial value of TAf is computed. The initial TAf contains approximation tables of all residual functions of f, dependent of one variable X_0. In the second step the final value of TAf is computed, by applying theorem 1 to consecutive variables.

INI-TA(TAf, n, m, f, TP)
1. **for** $X' \leftarrow 0$ **to** 2^n-1 **do**
2.   **for** $Y' \leftarrow 0$ **to** 2^m-1 **do**
3. $TAf[X', Y'] \leftarrow$ BIT-XOR($f[X']$ and Y', m)
4. **for** $X' \leftarrow 0$ **to** 2^n-2 **step** 2 **do**
5.   **for** $Y' \leftarrow 0$ **to** 2^m-1 **do**
6. $(TAf[X', Y'], TAf[X'+1, Y']) \leftarrow TP[TAf[X', Y'], TAf[X'+1, Y']]$
7. **return**

Fig. 7. Procedure computing the initial value of TAf

The initial value of TAf is computed by procedure INI-TA(...) presented in figure 7. First, in steps 1-3, for each masks X', Y' is calculated the value $Y[Y']$ with use of auxiliary function BIT-XOR(...) from figure 3. Then, in steps 4-6, each pair of values, adjacent in columns and corresponding to the value 0 and 1 of variable X_0, is replaced by a pair stored in so called table of pairs TP.

v_0, v_1	$TP[v_0, v_1]$
0 , 0	(1 , 0)
0 , 1	(0 , 1)
1 , 0	(0 , -1)
1 , 1	(-1 , 0)

Fig. 8. Table *TP* of pairs

Table *TP* of pairs is presented in figure 8. For each function of one variable, defined by the values of v_0 and v_1, it contains a pair of values from the right column of the appropriate elementary approximation table (fig. 5).

CALC-TA(*TAf*, i, j, m)
1. **if** $j - i > 2$ **then**
2. $k \leftarrow (i + j)$ **div** 2
3. CALC-TA(*TAf*, i, k, m)
4. CALC-TA(*TAf*, $k{+}1, j, m$)
5. SUMSUB-TA(*TAf*, $i, k, k{+}1, j, m$)
6. **return**

Fig. 9. Procedure computing the approximation table *TAf*,
first call: CALC-TA(*TAf*, $0, 2^n{-}1, m$)

The final value of *TAf* is computed by recursive procedure CALC-TA(...) presented in figure 9. In the first call of the procedure the initial *TAf* must be used and the range of rows is from $i = 0$ to $j = 2^n{-}1$. For the range greater than 2, the problem is solved by solution of two half-sub-problems. Having computed approximation tables for the sub-problems, the approximation table of the problem is computed by the auxiliary procedure SUMSUB-TA(...) from figure 10.

SUMSUB-TA(*TAf*, i_1, j_1, i_2, j_2, m)
1. **for** $i \leftarrow 0$ **to** $j_1 - i_1$ **do**
2. **for** $Y' \leftarrow 0$ **to** $2^m{-}1$ **do**
3. $(TAf[i_1 + i, Y'], TAf[i_2 + i, Y']) \leftarrow (TAf[i_1 + i, Y'] + TAf[i_2 + i, Y'],$
4. $\qquad\qquad\qquad\qquad\qquad\qquad TAf[i_1 + i, Y'] - TAf[i_2 + i, Y'])$
5. **return**

Fig. 10. Procedure SUMSUB-TA(...)

Procedure SUMSUB-TA(...), for two approximation tables of the same size, replaces first of them by their sum and the second by their difference, according to theorem 1.

Computation of the initial *TAf* is illustrated in figure 11. Table (a) contains the example function, table (b) the result of steps 1-3 of procedure INI-TA(...), and table (c) the initial *TAf*, composed of 8 approximation tables for residual functions of one variable X_0.

	$Y = f(X)$		X'	Y'					X'	Y'			
				0	1	2	3			0	1	2	3
0	0		0	0	0	0	0		0	1	0	1	0
1	1		1	0	1	0	1		1	0	1	0	1
2	2		2	0	0	1	1		2	1	0	-1	0
3	3		3	0	1	1	0		3	0	1	0	-1
4	1		4	0	1	0	1		4	1	0	0	-1
5	2		5	0	0	1	1		5	0	-1	1	0
6	3		6	0	1	1	0		6	1	0	0	1
7	0		7	0	0	0	0		7	0	-1	-1	0
8	2		8	0	0	1	1		8	1	0	-1	0
9	3		9	0	1	1	0		9	0	1	0	-1
10	0		10	0	0	0	0		10	1	0	1	0
11	1		11	0	1	0	1		11	0	1	0	1
12	3		12	0	1	1	0		12	1	0	0	1
13	0		13	0	0	0	0		13	0	-1	-1	0
14	1		14	0	1	0	1		14	1	0	0	-1
15	2		15	0	0	1	1		15	0	-1	1	0
(a)			(b)						(c)				

Fig. 11. Computation of initial value of *TAf* for example function $Y = f(X)$

Computation of the final *TAf*, by procedure CALC-TA(...), is shown in figure 12. Table (a) contains 4 approximation tables obtained from the initial *TAf*, table (b) contains 2 approximation tables obtained from table (a), and table (c) contains the final *TAf*. The sequence in which approximation tables are computed is determined by the construction of procedure CALC-TA(...). After the first two approximation tables from table (a) are computed, is computed the first approximation table from table (b).

The computational complexity of the procedure INI-TA(...) is $O(m \cdot 2^{n+m})$. For procedure CALC-TA(...) the time needed to compute the approximation table with w rows can be described by the following recursive equation:

$$T(w) = \begin{cases} 0 & for \quad w = 2 \\ 2 \cdot T(w/2) + w & for \quad w > 2. \end{cases}$$

The solution to this equation is $T(w) = w(\log w - 1)$. Taking into account that in the first call of procedure CALC-TA(...) the number of rows $w = 2^n$, and that procedure SUMSUB-TA(...) computes in each row a new value for all of the 2^m columns of *TAf* we have, that the complexity of procedure CALC-TA(...) is $O(n \cdot 2^{n+m})$. Therefore the complexity of the fast algorithm, composed of procedures INI-TA(...) and CALC-TA(...), is $O((n + m) \cdot 2^{n+m})$. Considering the size 2^{n+m} of TAf we obtain the linear time complexity $O(n + m)$ for a single element of TAf.

(a)

X'	Y' 0	1	2	3
0	2	0	0	0
1	0	2	0	0
2	0	0	2	0
3	0	0	0	2
4	2	0	0	0
5	0	-2	0	0
6	0	0	0	-2
7	0	0	2	0
8	2	0	0	0
9	0	2	0	0
10	0	0	-2	0
11	0	0	0	-2
12	2	0	0	0
13	0	-2	0	0
14	0	0	0	2
15	0	0	-2	0

(b)

X'	Y' 0	1	2	3
0	4	0	0	0
1	0	0	0	0
2	0	0	2	-2
3	0	0	2	2
4	0	0	0	0
5	0	4	0	0
6	0	0	2	2
7	0	0	-2	2
8	4	0	0	0
9	0	0	0	0
10	0	0	-2	2
11	0	0	-2	-2
12	0	0	0	0
13	0	4	0	0
14	0	0	-2	-2
15	0	0	2	-2

(c)

X'	Y' 0	1	2	3
0	8	0	0	0
1	0	0	0	0
2	0	0	0	0
3	0	0	0	0
4	0	0	0	0
5	0	8	0	0
6	0	0	0	0
7	0	0	0	0
8	0	0	0	0
9	0	0	0	0
10	0	0	4	-4
11	0	0	4	4
12	0	0	0	0
13	0	0	0	0
14	0	0	4	4
15	0	0	-4	4

Fig. 12. Computation of TAf for example function $Y = f(X)$

5   Conclusion

The basic algorithm to compute a single value of the approximation table for arbitrary function f with n binary inputs and m binary outputs, is of exponential complexity $O((n+m) \cdot 2^n)$. The presented in the paper fast algorithm computes the whole approximation table, in linear time $O(n+m)$ for a single value. The fast algorithm is based on a general result, formulated in theorem 1, that affects the structure of the approximation table and probably has many other applications.

6   References

[1]   Biham E., Shamir A., "Differential Cryptanalysis of the Data Encryption Standard" , Springer-Verlag, New York 1993.

[2]   Chmiel K., "Linear Cryptanalysis of the Reduced *DES* Algorithms", *Proceedings of the Regional Conference on Military Communication and*

134

Information Systems'2000 (Zegrze , Oct. 4-6), WIŁ, vol. 1, pp. 111-118, Zegrze 2000.

[3]   Chmiel K., "Differential Cryptanalysis of the Reduced *DES* Algorithms", (In Polish), Studia z Automatyki i Informatyki, vol. 25, pp. 127-146, Poznań 2000.

[4]   Chmiel K., "Linear Approximation of some S-box Functions", *Proceedings of the Regional Conference on Military Communication and Information Systems 2001* (Zegrze, Oct. 10-12), WIŁ, vol. 1, pp. 211-218, Zegrze 2001.

[5]   Chmiel K., "On Some Models of Arithmetic Sum Function Linear Approximation", *Proceedings of NATO Regional Conference on Military Communications and Information Systems 2002* (Zegrze, Oct. 9-11), WIŁ, vol. 2, pp. 199-204, Zegrze 2002.

[6]   Chmiel K., "Linear Approximation of Arithmetic Sum Function", *Proceedings of the 9-th International Conference on Advanced Computer Systems ACS'2002* (Międzyzdroje, Oct. 23-25), vol. 2, pp. 19-28, Szczecin 2002.

[7]   Chmiel K., "Linear Approximation of Arithmetic Subtraction Function", *Proceedings of NATO Regional Conference on Military Communications and Information Systems 2003* (Zegrze, Oct. 8-10), WIŁ, Zegrze 2003.

[8]   Chmiel K, "On Arithmetic Subtraction Linear Approximation", *Proceedings of the 10-th International Multi-Conference on Advanced Computer Systems ACS'2003* (Międzyzdroje, Oct. 22-24), Szczecin 2003.

[9]   Chmiel K., "Linear Approximation of Arithmetic Sum Function", In Sołdek J. Drobiazgiewicz L. (Eds) Artificial Intelligence and Security in Computing Systems, *9-th International Conference ACS'2002 Międzyzdroje, Poland October 23-25, 2002 Proceedings*, Kluwer Academic Publishers, pp. 293-302, Boston/Dordrecht/London 2003.

[10]   Górska A., Górski K., Kotulski Z., Paszkiewicz A., Szczepański J., "New Experimental Results in Differential – Linear Cryptanalysis of Reduced Variants of DES", *Proceedings of the 8-th International Conference on Advanced Computer Systems ACS'2001*, (Mielno), vol. 1, pp. 333-346, Szczecin 2001.

[11]   Matsui M, "Linear Cryptanalysis Method for DES Cipher", *Advances in Cryptology Eurocrypt'93*, 1993.

[12]   Matsui M., "Linear Cryptanalysis Method for DES Cipher". *Springer-Verlag*, New York 1998.

[13]   Zugaj A., Górski K., Kotulski Z., Szczepański J., Paszkiewicz A., "Extending Linear Cryptanalysis - Theory and Experiments", *Proceedings of the Regional Conference on Military Communication and Information Systems'99* (Zegrze , Oct. 6-8) WIŁ, vol. 2, pp.77-84, Zegrze 1999.

Cryptographic Properties of Some Cryptosystem with Modulation of the Chaotic Sequence Parameters

Stefan Berczyński[1], Yury A. Kravtsov[2], Jerzy Pejaś[1], Adrian Skrobek[1]

[1] Technical University of Szczecin, Poland, e-mails: *stefan.berczynski@ps.pl*, {*jpejas, askrobek*}*@wi.ps.pl*
[2] Maritime University of Szczecin, Poland. e-mail: *kravtsov@wsm.szczecin.pl*

Abstract: This paper discusses mixing of some non-linear chaotic maps, e.g. a logistic equation and a tent mapping, as simplified method for information encryption and decryption. A ciphertext is obtained by the iteration of defined mixing chaotic maps from an initial state. Because the secure control parameters of these chaotic mappings are modulated according to currently encrypted plaintext, the proposed cipher algorithm can be treated as some homophonic substitution cipher with encryption key defined by initial state of build-in chaotic maps and some additional parameters. The resulting cipher algorithm is investigated against typical attacks on classical encryption schemes. The objective of these attacks is to recover plaintext from ciphertext or to deduce the decryption key. In this paper we study the exhaustive key search attack and find that this attack is not efficient as a practical attack on proposed cipher. Similar conclusion concerns some classical attacks, e.g.: ciphertext-only attacks and a known-plaintext attacks.

Keywords: chaotic signals and sequence, stream ciphers, logistic equation, secure data transmission; chaotic cryptosystems, cryptoanalysis.

1 Introduction

In recent years extensive studies have been done in the theory of chaos in different fields of physics, mathematics, engineering, biology, chemistry, economics and atmospheric sciences. Only at the start of last decade continuous and discrete chaotic dynamical systems has been used for development of cryptosystems (see e.g., N.K. Pareek, et al. [15] and R. Schmitz [1]). The chaotic systems are characterized by the sensitivity on initial conditions, system parameters and long time unpredictability of evolution of its orbits. These properties make the chaotic systems considerable as an alternative for cryptosystems construction.

In this paper we are presenting a cryptosystem based on one-dimensional non-linear chaotic map

$$x_{n+1} = F(x_n; \mathbf{a}),\qquad(1)$$

and sequences of consecutive applications of a finite set of maps as well

$$x_{n+1} = F_m \circ \cdots F_1 \circ F_0(x_n; \mathbf{a}),\qquad(2)$$

which generates the sequence $\{x_n, x_{n+1}, \ldots\}$, depending on a set of parameters $\mathbf{a} = \{a_0, a_1, \ldots, a_k, \ldots, a_S\}$ and $x_0 \in I$, where I is the unit interval. The equation (1) or (2) represents some discrete dynamic system naturally described by repeated applications of the same map $F: I \to I$ or sequences of consecutive applications of a finite set of maps $\{F_m, \cdots, F_1, F_0\}: I \to I$.

As writing out explicitly formulas involving repeated applications of a set of maps can be awkward, we streamline the notation by denoting a map composition by "∘".

$$G(x_n; m, \mathbf{a}) = F_m(\cdots F_1(F_0(x_n; \mathbf{a}))) = F_m \circ \cdots F_1 \circ F_0(x_n; \mathbf{a})\qquad(3)$$

Then the nth iteration of map (1) and (2) is as follows:

$$R^n(x_n; \mathbf{a}) = \begin{cases} F^n(x_n; \mathbf{a}), & R^0(x_0; \mathbf{a}) = F(x_0; \mathbf{a}) & \text{for the map (1)} \\ G^n(x_n; m, \mathbf{a}), & R^0(x_0; \mathbf{a}) = G(x_0; \mathbf{a}) & \text{for the map (2)} \end{cases}\qquad(4)$$

where

$$F^n(x_n; \mathbf{a}) = F \circ F^{n-1}(x_n; \mathbf{a}) = F(F^{n-1}(x_n; \mathbf{a}))$$
$$G^n(x_n; m, \mathbf{a}) = G \circ G^{n-1}(x_n; m, \mathbf{a}) = G(G^{n-1}(x_n; m, \mathbf{a}))$$

The *trajectories* (known also as *orbits*) on $\{x_n, x_{n+1}\}$ plane belong to one of the following three types (R.L. Devaney [3], E. Ott [8], see also S. Berczyński, et al. [14]). First of all, there exist trajectories, tending to the stable points, which satisfy the equation $\bar{x}_F = F(\bar{x}_F; \mathbf{a})$ in the case (1) and $\bar{x}_G = G(\bar{x}_G; m, \mathbf{a})$ in the case (2). Secondly, some trajectories approach to the periodic orbits, what is characteristic, for instance, for period doubling bifurcations. At last in definite areas of parameter $\{a_k\}$ space the non-linear map (1) of the set of maps (2) generates chaotic sequences $\{x_n\}$, which look quite similar to random sequences and are of primarily interest for secure data transmission. The chaotic sequences with modulated parameters were used for the purposes of hidden information transmission firstly by Anishchenko et al. [16, 17]. Different aspects of this method were studied also in the papers S. Berczyński, et al. [14] and S. G. Bilchinskaya, et el. [18].

2   A new synchronous stream encryption algorithm

A *synchronous stream cipher* is a cipher where a keystream is generated separately from the plaintext and is then combined with the plaintext to form the ciphertext. A synchronous stream cipher can be described by the equations (A.J. Menezes, et al. [4]):

$$\sigma_{i+1} = f(\sigma_i, k)$$
$$z_i = g(\sigma_i, k) \tag{7}$$
$$c_i = h(z_i, m_i, k)$$

where σ_0 is the *initial state* and may be determined from the key k, f is the *next state function*, g is the keystream output function, and h is the function that combines the plaintext m_i with the keystream z_i to produce the ciphertext c_i. Note that decryption only requires inverting the h function. The two functions f and g in equation (7) are together known as the *keystream generator*. The output of these two functions, the sequence of z_i values, is known as the *keystream*.

A classical synchronous stream cipher does not propagate the errors, i.e. a ciphertext digit that is modified (but not deleted) during transmission does not affect the decryption of other ciphertext digits. As a consequence of this, an active adversary might possibly be able to make changes to selected ciphertext digits, and know exactly what affect these changes have on the plaintext.

Our new encryption scheme has not such a weakness: the forgery (a modification or removing) on even single bit leads to the total loss of the synchronization between the sender and the recipient; from that moment decryption of received message is impossible.

2.1   From chaotic maps to stream encryption scheme

Chaotic maps are primarily characterized by an exponential sensitivity to small perturbations causing iterates of such maps to seem random and long-time unpredictable. Their sensitivity to initial conditions and their spreading out of trajectories over the whole interval seems to be a model for the classic Shannon requirements of confusion and diffusion (A.J. Menezes, et al. [4]).

If the set of chaotic systems is restricted to systems whose output coincides with the whole phase space I (see section 1), then we are working with a subset that takes the name of *ergodic systems*. The ergodicity implies the state space cannot be nontrivially divided into several parts. Therefore if some trajectory starts from any point then it never localises in a smaller region (Z. Kotulski, et al. [6]). It means the plain-text space that can correspond to a given cipher cannot be restricted to a "smaller" subspace. Thus, for the ciphertext the corresponding plaintext (during brute attack) must be searched for over all the state space.

At a higher level of the hierarchy there exists another class of chaotic systems with a new property called *mixing* property. This name refers to the particular characteristic that some ergodic systems show to have. Exploiting a simple comparison to clear the idea, it can be said that a system is mixing when it spreads out into ever finer fibres until it covers the entire phase space such as a drop of ink spreads out chaotically in water (cf. L. Cappelletti [5]). This behaviour is due to the fact that trajectories diverge from each other exponentially fast.

2.2 A new stream encryption scheme based on permuted chaotic equations (PCE scheme)

First step in a block encryption algorithm design is to choose a chaotic map. Choosing maps for encryption algorithms is not an easy task and one should consider only maps with following properties: *mixing property*, *robust chaos* and *large parameter set* (L. Kocarev, G. Jakimoski [7], cf. e.g. T.L. Carrol, L.M. Pecora [9]). Such properties ensure, among other things, that if one were to choose an initial condition x_0 at random in the domain I of F or G, then the probability that x_0 lies on a periodic point of the map is zero (E. Ott [8], see also S. Papadimitriou, et al. [2]).

In the paper mixing property of chaotic maps was achieving due to any number (depending on guaranteed level of security) of associated together dynamical chaotic equations (cf. (8)). This sequence of randomly ordered (premuted) equations is defined with accuracy to their parameters, which compose the part of whole cryptographic key. Thus the mixing is equivalent to a continuous perturbation on a chaotic system causing the system to jump from one unstable trajectory to another in accordance with the perturbation. To study the effect of mixing, let us assume that these permuted equations are in the following form (comapre S. Papadimitriou, et al. [2], T. Guoning, et al. [13]):

$$
\begin{aligned}
&y_{n+1}^{e(1)} = f_{e(1)}\left(y_n^{e(1)}, b^{e(1)}\right) \quad y_0^{e(1)} = k_1 \\
&y_n^{e(2)} = \left(y_{n+1}^{e(1)} + k_2\right) \bmod R_{e(2)} + L_{e(2)} \\
&y_{n+1}^{e(2)} = f_{e(2)}\left(y_n^{e(2)}, b^{e(2)}\right)
\end{aligned}
\tag{8}
$$

$$
\cdots\cdots\cdots\cdots\cdots\cdots
$$

$$
\begin{aligned}
&y_n^{e(m)} = \left(y_{n+1}^{e(m-1)} + k_m\right) \bmod R_{e(m)} + L_{e(m)} \\
&y_{n+1}^{e(m)} = f_{e(m)}\left(y_n^{e(m)}, b^{e(m)}\right)
\end{aligned}
$$

where $e(i)$ means the permutation on the numbers 1 through m, $f_{e(i)}$ is the $e(i)$-*th* chaotic equation (a *next state function* of a synchronous stream cipher as was defined above), *mod* – a modulo operator, $R_i = U_i - L_i$, such that $<U_i, L_i>$ is the domain of the function f_i definition. The effect of this rule is the limitation of the evolution for each function within its predefined domain.

The value m defines the number of chaotic maps used in the equation (8) and the number of scalar and vector parameters, k_i and b^i ($i=1, ..., m$) respectively. The nature of vector parameter b^i and its dimension depends on the structure of chosen chaotic maps. All enumerated parameters, i.e. $e=(e(1), ..., e(m))$, k_i and b^i are the part of the cryptographic key. First of all, more important is the parameter e, which is called below as the *permutation of chaotic equations*. We are sure, that unawareness of the permutation e increases the cryptoanalysis difficulty of proposed permuted chaotic equations (PCE) algorithm. However, we assume all maps of permuted chaotic equations belong to well-known set of chaotic maps.

The next set of equations contains the keystream output functions that produce the keystream z_n used in encryption or decryption process:

$$z_n = \left(\sum\nolimits_i^m y_{n+1}^{e(i)} + k_{m+1} \right) mod \ R_{m+1} + L_{m+1}$$

$$z_{n+S} = g^{S-1}\left(z_n, \overline{a} \right) \qquad (9)$$

$$y_n^{e(1)} = z_{n+S}$$

where $g^{S-1}(...)$ means the nth iteration of the chaotic map $g(...)$. Parameters set $\overline{a} = V_A \setminus a_i$ depends on the set V_A, which contains significantly different real values being the mapping of all symbols from some alphabet of definition, excluding the value a_i, which maps the currently encrypted plain text symbol m_k. Each value $a_j \in V_A$ is set to make the map $g(...)$ to have chaotic behaviour.

To define symbols set of an alphabet A let us assume plain messages are composed by S different symbols $\alpha_1, \alpha_2, ..., \alpha_S$ and use a bijective map

$$f_S : V_A = \{a_1, a_2, ..., a_S\} \rightarrow A = \{\alpha_1, \alpha_2, ..., \alpha_S\} \qquad (10)$$

to associate the different parameter values with different alphabet symbols. All values $a_j \in V_A$ ($j=1, 2, ..., S$) of mapping (10) are generated randomly and form another part of the PCE scheme cryptographic key.

A keystream z_n is generated in accordance with (9) and then combined with plaintext m_n to produce the ciphertext c_n :

$$c_n = \left((z_n + k_{m+2}) \ mod \ R_{m+2} + L_{m+2} \right) \oplus \lambda_n \qquad (11)$$

where the value λ_n depends on a symbol m_n and is calculated according to the following formula:

$$\lambda_n = \left(\sum\nolimits_i^S a_i \right) \oplus \left(\bigoplus_{i=1}^S a_i \right) \oplus f_S^{-1}(\alpha_k); \quad \alpha_k = m_n \qquad (12)$$

Note, that an operator $\oplus$ used in equations (11) and (12) means a bitwise XOR.

2.3 Implementation

Below we present the detailed description of proposed encryption and decryption algorithm PCE. This description is obvious for two reasons: (1) implementation details are important for cryptoanalysts to judge whether or not there exist security defects, and (2) the encryption speed and the implementation cost depend on such details.

Algorithm PCE-KC: Key generation for PCE stream encryption scheme

---

SUMMARY: Each entity A creates a symmetric key and sends it to B securely. Entity A should do the following:

1. Choose any integer m, being the number of chaotic equations and define the permutation $e=(e(1), ..., e(m))$.

2. For j from 1 to m do the following:

   2.1 Define the type of chaotic map T_i (e.g. 0 – a logistic map, 1 – a tent map, etc.) and generate its vector parameter b^i randomly, which should be set to make the map f_i to have chaotic behaviour:

      (a)   its orbits was not asymptotically periodic,

      (b)   no Lyapunov exponent is exactly zero, and

      (c)   the largest Lyapunov exponent is positive.

   2.2 Generate random any real number $k_i \in R$.

3. Define the type of chaotic map T_g for a keystream output function g. Generate random parameters k_{m+1} and k_{m+2} (any real number).

4. Define the alphabet A of the language to be used such that $|A| = S$, where S means the number of alphabet symbols; all symbols from alphabet A specify the message space.

5. Choose one of control parameter of chaotic map of type T_g and for j from 1 to S do the following:

   5.1 Generate random value a_j, meeting goals as discussed in the step 2.1.

   5.2 Assign value a_j to the symbol α_j from an alphabet A (in increasing order), i.e. define the map $f_s(a_j) = \alpha_j$.

6. The symmetric key (called secret key) of both entity A and B is the vector $K = (e, (T_1, k_1, b^1), ..., (T_m, k_m, b^m), k_{m+1}, k_{m+2}, (T_g, a_1, ..., a_S))$.

End of **PCE-KG**

A fundamental aspect of every cryptosystem is the key. An algorithm is as secure as its key. The key shall belong to well-defined *key space* V_K, i.e. such space, which does not contain the weak and degenerated keys. From a cryptographic point of view, the secret parameter should be sensitive enough to guarantee the so-called avalanche property: even when the smallest change occurs for the parameter, the ciphertext will change dramatically (G. Álvarez, Shujun Li [12]). The key space for PCE scheme and the PCE key generation are compliant with **Algorithm PCE-KC**.

The size of the key space is the number of encryption/decryption key pairs that are available in the cipher system and in the case of PCE scheme strongly depends on the number of chaotic maps and symbols from alphabet A of definition.

Given a plain-message $M = \{m_1, m_2, ..., m_r\}$ ($m_i \in A$), chaotic maps $f_1, f_2, ..., f_m$, g with different control parameters, the function f_S as in the equation (10) and a cryptographic key K, the proposed encryption and decryption schemes have the form of **Algorithm PCE-ENC** and **Algorithm PCE-DEC**, respectively (written in C pseudocode).

Algorithm PCE-Enc: PCE symmetric key K encryption

INPUT: secret cryptographic key K, a plaintext M that contains r symbols.
SUMMARY: entity A encrypts a plaintext M for B, which B decrypts. Entity A should do the following:

1. Generate random real number $RND \in R$.

2. Calculate the initialisation value IV and set the initial state of the first equation from the set of permuted chaotic equations

$$IV = RND \oplus k_1$$
$$z_0 = y_0^{e(1)} = (RND + k_1) \bmod R_{e(1)} + L_{e(1)}$$

3. Do the following calculation:

```
alpha = (∑ᵢˢ aᵢ);

for (n=0; n<r; n++) {
    for (i=1; i<=m;i++) {
```
$$y_{n+1}^{e(i)} = f_{e(i)}\left(y_n^{e(i)}, b^{e(i)}\right); \quad z_n = z_n + y_{n+1}^{e(i)};$$
```
        if (i < m)
```
$$y_n^{e(i+1)} = \left(y_{n+1}^{e(i)} + k_{i+1}\right) \bmod R_{e(i+1)} + L_{e(i+1)};$$
```
    }
    aᵢ = f⁻¹s(mₙ);  // n-th message symbols being encrypted
                    // and mapped to i-th value of a
```
$$z_n = \left(z_n + k_{m+1}\right) \bmod R_{m+1} + L_{m+1};$$
```
    k = 0;
    for (j=0; j<S; j++) {
        if (i == j) {
            k++;
```
$$z_{n+k} = g\left(z_{n+k-1}, \overline{a}(a_j)\right);$$
```
            alpha = alpha ⊕ aⱼ;
        }
```

$$c_n = \left(\left(z_n + k_{m+2}\right) mod\ R_{m+2} + L_{m+2}\right) \oplus alpha; \quad y_n^{e(1)} = z_{n+k};$$

}

4. Send the initialisation value IV and the ciphertext $C = (c_1, c_2, ..., c_r)$ to B.

End of **PCE-Enc**

Algorithm PCE-Dec: PCE symmetric key K decryption

INPUT: secret cryptographic key K, an initialisation value IV and the ciphertext C that contains r symbols

SUMMARY: Entity B decrypts a ciphertext C from entity A. To recover plaintext M from C, entity B should do the following:

1. Set the initial state of the first equation from the set of permuted chaotic equations:

$$z_0 = y_0^{e(1)} = \left(IV \oplus k_1 + k_1\right)\ mod\ R_{e(1)} + L_{e(1)}$$

2. Do the following calculation:

$$\mathtt{alpha} = \left(\sum_i^S a_i\right) \oplus \left(\bigoplus_{i=1}^S a_i\right);$$

```
for (n=0; n<r; n++) {
    for (i=1; i<=m; i++) {
```
$$y_{n+1}^{e(i)} = f_{e(i)}\left(y_n^{e(i)}, b^{e(i)}\right); \quad z_n = z_n + y_{n+1}^{e(i)};$$
```
        if (i < m)
```
$$y_n^{e(i+1)} = \left(y_{n+1}^{e(i)} + k_{i+1}\right)\ mod\ R_{e(i+1)} + L_{e(i+1)};$$
```
    }
```
$$z_n = \left(z_n + k_{m+1}\right)\ mod\ R_{m+1} + L_{m+1};$$
$$a_i = c_n \oplus \left(\left(z_n + k_{m+2}\right) mod\ R_{m+2} + L_{m+2}\right) \oplus alpha;$$
```
    // i-th value of the parameter a, f_s(a_i) = α_i = m_n
    k = 0;
    for (j=0; j<S; j++) {
        if (i == j) {
```
$$k{+}{+}; \quad z_{n+k} = g\left(z_{n+k-1}, \overline{a}\!\left(a_j\right)\right);$$
```
        }
    }
```
$$y_n^{e(1)} = z_{n+k};$$
```
}
```

3. The recovered message M has the form $M = (m_1, m_2, ..., m_r)$.

End of **PCE-Dec**

The notation $z_{n+k} = g\left(z_{n+k-1}, \overline{a}(a_j)\right)$ used in **Algorithm PCE-Enc** and **Algorithm PCE-Dec** means the making one iteration of the chaotic function g for some set of control parameters and where one of them (i.e. a parameter a_p) maps all symbols from the alphabet A. Above recurrence equation is not iterated for this value of parameter a_j, which corresponds to the currently encrypted or decrypted symbol of the alphabet A. The ranges (R_i, L_i) for $i = 1, .., m+1$ should be chosen in such way, that ones define the domain of the functions f_i and g; the range (R_{m+2}, L_{m+2}) can be selected in any way.

3 Experiments

Below we assume, that in PCE stream encryption scheme the set of chaotic maps contains one element only: a logistic function. It means, that all functions $f_1, f_2, ...,$ f_m and g are the same logistic functions with accuracy to control parameters, respectively $b^1, b^2, ..., b^m$ and a. The parameter a is a vector, which dimension $\dim(a) = S$ is equal to the number of the number of elements in the alphabet A, called the *cardinality* of A.

Assuming $m = 2$, the computational experiments have been done for two different sets of ASCII character sequences. In the first round of tests, the sequences consisted of each with randomly generated ASCII big letters repeated many times (*RandomData*). In the second round of tests, we used as plain text sequences of Polish prose of equal length (*RegularData*).

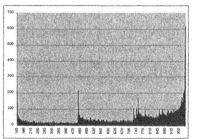 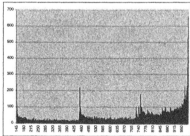

Figure 1 Frequency distributions of the keystream z_n for *RandomData* and *RegularData*

Some results of experiments are shown on Figure 1 and Figure 2. They present the cryptographic properties of the keystream z_n used in encryption or decryption process. These properties confirm good mixing property of proposed system and means that the sequence of iterative permuted chaotic equations makes the generated sequence appear as random to the intruder.

Particularly this is illustrated on Figure 2, where instead of the attractors (typical for logistic functions) we have a space filling noise like pattern in the phase space. Furthermore, the keystream z_n and the plaintext seem to be statistically independent, although the generation of keystream value depends on currently encrypted or decrypted plaintext (see equation (9)). Thus we can conclude, that proposed PCE algorithm fulfils the classic Shannon's requirements of confusion and diffusion which should be added to ciphertext and we can say that encrypted information is masked by the cipher well, because it is not possible to identify any specific trend in the cipher corresponding to the distribution in the plain text.

 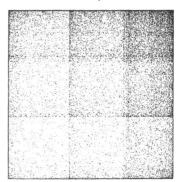

Figure 2 The attractors of the keystream z_n for *RandomData* and *RegularData*

3.1   Exhaustive key search attack

The straightforward attack on any cipher is the exhaustive key search attack. Except for the computational intensity, this is as simple as trying all the possible keys of the cipher scheme.

Generally, in the PCE scheme each key $K(m) = (m, (T_1, k_1, b^1), ..., (T_m, k_m, b^m), k_{m+1}, k_{m+2}, (T_g, a_1, ..., a_S))$ belongs to non-linear key space V_K, which dimension depends, among other things, on the number m of chaotic equations and their types. It is evident, that exhaustive key search attack needs in the worst-case searching of all possible key values, i.e. $K(1), ..., K(m)$.

Assume that the scalar values of k_i ($i=1, ..., m+2$), b^j ($j=1, ..., m$) and a_{pt} ($t=1, ..., S$) have, respectively, up to $|k_i|$, $|b^j|$ and $|a_t|$ significant bits[1]. Thus for exhaustive key search attack, the hacker requires a following maximum attempts to break the key K:

---

[1]   We say that a bit is significant if the system has a different evolution when the bit flips its value.

$$N_{Total} = \sum_{i=1}^{m} i! * 2^{\left(\sum_{j=1}^{i+2} |k_j| + \sum_{j=1}^{i} \left[b^j \left[+ \sum_{j=1}^{S} |a_{pj}| \right] \right] \right)} \tag{13}$$

Assuming that $|k_j| = |b^j| = |a_j| = 16$ bits, Tab.1 contains (as a function of some value m) the evaluation of *worst-case* complexity of an exhaustive key search attack for PCE scheme.

$O(N_{total})$	Number of chaotic equations - m			
	1	**2**	**3**	**4**
$O(N_{total})$	$O(2^{480})$	$O(2^{512})$	$O(2^{544})$	$O(2^{576})$

Tab. 1. Algorithm PCE - stream encryption scheme

The PCE algorithm with a running time $O(..)$ as is shown in Table 1 is called the *exponential-time algorithm* and is strongly resistant against the exhaustive key search attack. Note, that due to special method used for the coefficient λ_n counting (see equation (12)) it is not possible to estimate the values a_t ($t=1, ..., S$) successively: these values must be estimated simultaneously.

3.2   More complex crypotanalysis

It is possible to differentiate between different levels of attacks on cryptosystems (see G. Álvarez, et al. [12]). Below, we give some theoretical results with goal to verify the PCE resistance on the known-plaintext and chosen-plaintext attacks.

Assume an opponent is able to construct a chosen plain text attack. Because of used construction technique, the PCE encryption algorithm needs only the symbol m_i of a plaintext M that belongs to well-defined symbols of some alphabet A. It means that an opponent may not free choose an input plaintext (e.g. as any sequence of 0 bits). However, the opponent can try to construct, for example, the plaintext that contains the same multiple repeated symbol $\alpha_i \in A$ (the symbol that is reversed mapping of a control parameter, i.e. $\alpha_i = f^{-1}{}_S(a_i)$).

Under these assumptions, in a chosen plain text attack scenario we request the ciphertext of the following plain text: $M = m_0 \, m_1 \, m_2 \, ... = \alpha_i \, \alpha_i \, \alpha_i \, \alpha_i \, \alpha_i \, ...$ Then encrypted symbol for the first symbol m_0 has form (cf. equations (11) and (12)):

$$c_0^i = \left((z_0 + k_{m+2}) \bmod R_{m+2} + L_{m+2} \right) \oplus \lambda^i = C_0^i \oplus \lambda^i$$
$$c_0^i = c_0; \quad \lambda^i = \lambda_0; \tag{14}$$

Based on equation (14) we may try to guess the value λ_0. For each symbol $\alpha_i \in A$ ($i=1, .., S$) it requires the following number of operations:

$$N_{\alpha_i} = 2^{|c_0^i|} \tag{15}$$

From (15) it follows that for a single symbol $\alpha_i \in A$ exist N_{α_i} possible values λ^i (we should note that $\lambda^i \neq \lambda^j$ for each $i \neq j$). If we assume $|C_0^i| \cong const$, then further encryption of the same symbol will not change this estimation significantly. For any plaintext containing N different alphabet symbols decryption of the ciphertext may require $N_M = 2^{N*|C_0^i|}$ operations, what for large N means that this attack is more difficult to realize than an exhaustive key search attack.

Encryption of two different, multiple repeated alphabet symbols, i.e. a plaintext of the form $M = m_0\ m_1\ m_2\ ... = \alpha_i\ \alpha_j\ \alpha_i\ \alpha_j\ ...$, gives two first encrypted symbols as following:

$$c_0^i = \left((z_0 + k_{m+2})\ mod\ R_{m+2} + L_{m+2}\right) \oplus \lambda^i = C_0^i \oplus \lambda^i$$
$$c_1^j = \left((z_1 + k_{m+2})\ mod\ R_{m+2} + L_{m+2}\right) \oplus \lambda^j = C_1^j \oplus \lambda^j \tag{16}$$

Hence, and from the equation (12), we obtain:

$$c_0^i \oplus c_1^j = C_0^i \oplus \lambda^i \oplus C_1^j \oplus \lambda^j = \left((z_0 + k_{m+2})\ mod\ R_{m+2}\right) \oplus$$
$$\left((z_1 + k_{m+2})\ mod\ R_{m+2}\right) \oplus a_{pi} \oplus a_{pj} \tag{17}$$

An attempt to recover the template for any pair of two different symbols requires the following number of operations:

$$N_{\alpha_i,\alpha_j} = 2^{|C_0^i|+|C_0^j|} \tag{18}$$

In the case of any plaintext M a chosen pair symbols attack does not decrease the general number of required trails (i.e. $N_M = 2^{\lfloor N/2 \rfloor \cdot \left(|C_0^i|+|C_0^j|\right)}$), but can allow to estimate probability of guessing the bitwise exclusive-OR value ($a_{pi} \oplus a_{pj}$), corresponding to the pair of symbols (α_i, α_j):

$$Prob\left(a_{pi} \oplus a_{pj}\right) = \frac{1}{2^{|C_0^i|+|C_0^j|}} \tag{19}$$

Obviously, the probability of guessing the exact values (a_{pi}, a_{pj}) is significantly smaller (on the level of the exhaustive key search attack).

Now let us assume that an opponent has possibility to construct a chosen cipher text attack. Hence he can choose a cipher text string $C = c_0\ c_1\ c_2\ ...$ and construct the corresponding plain text string $M = m_0\ m_1\ ....$ This design rests on matching symbol $\alpha_j \in A$ of the same encrypted value as the ciphertext c_i. Complexity of this attack increases together with the ciphertext length. If this length is equal N, then attack complexity is $O(S^N)$, what makes this attack inefficient for sufficiently large N (even if S is relatively small).

Construction of two other attacks, i.e. a cipher text only attack and known plain text attack is more difficult. However, initial estimations show that it complexity is on the level of estimation for exhaustive key search attack (see Table 1).

4   Conclusions and further works

In this paper we present a new encryption scheme (PCE) that are based on the idea of permuted chaotic equations. With these equations the plain text strings are mixed and chaotically modulated. The system is easy to implement but the encryption and decryption processes of a message need synchronization.

The PCE scheme appears to be resistant to exhaustive key search and classical attacks on cryptosystems. Furthermore, attacks presented in this paper do not allow to identify whole mapping $f_S(a_{pi}) = \alpha_i$. That is why we believe our PCE scheme is practically one-time pad cryptosystem if its secret key can be well procected and the encryption time is much shorter than the period of computer realization of chaos.

There are some open problems that we believe are of importance for the future research of our PCE scheme. First, a further step of work would be now to perform a more complete cryptanalytic study to test cipher security, and to relate the performances of the system both to the types of chaos used and to the number of the chaotic equations applied to generate the keystream sequences. The PCE algorithm resistance against error function attack (EFA), when the intruder may try to extract the secret key and then unmask all future plaintext, requires more detailed analysis. Since EFA utilizes all information available for the legal receiver except the secret key only, it can be regarded as a very effective attack (see T. Guoning, et al. [13]).

All calculations of currently implemented algorithm are based on floating point arithmetic. In next versions we are going to either use discretized form of chaotic equations or realize some calculations in the domain of integers, like a keystream or a ciphertext generation. In last case the calculation in the domain of integers should effectively enhance the robustness of the communication against the round-off errors of both sender and recipient computers.

Proposed stream encryption scheme can also affect the features of block cipher with cryptographic block chaining. This modification should improve definitely the encryption speed of this new cryptoscheme.

Also, we intend to study other maps and their discretized forms. The main of this future effort is establishing a connection between discretized chaotic systems and encryption schemes.

5 References

[1] R. Schmitz *Use of chaotic dynamical systems in cryptography*, Journal of the Franklin Institute 338 (2001), pp.429 –441

[2] S. Papadimitriou, A. Bezerianos, T. Bountis, G. Pavlides *Secure communication protocols with discrete nonlinear chaotic maps*, Journal of Systems Architecture, 47 (2001), pp.61-72

[3] R.L. Devaney *An Introduction to Chaotic Dynamical Systems*, 2nd Edition, Addison-Wesley Publishing Company, Reading, MA, 1989

[4] A.J. Menezes, P.C. van Oorschot, S.A. Vanstone *Handbook of Applied Cryptography*, CRC Press (1997)

[5] L. Cappelletti *An FPGA Implementation of a Chaotic Encryption Algorithm*, Thesis, Università Degli Studi Di Padova, 2000

[6] Z. Kotulski, J. Szczepński *On the application of discrete chaotic dynamical systems to cryptography. DCC method*, Biuletyn WAT, Rok XLVIII, Nr 1 0(566), pp.111-123, 1999

[7] L. Kocarev, G. Jakimoski *Logistic map as a block encryption algorithm*, Physics Letters A 289 (2001), pp.199–206

[8] E. Ott *Chaos in Dynamical Systems*, Cambridge University Press, Cambridge, MA, 1993

[9] T.L. Carrol, L.M. Pecora *Cascading synchronized chaotic systems*, Physica D 67 (1993), pp.126-140.

[10] G. Álvarez, Shujun Li *Cryptographic requirements for chaotic secure communications*, eprint arXiv:nlin/0311039, November 2003, 13 pages, http://adsabs.harvard.edu/cgi-bin/nph-bib_query?2003nlin.....11039A

[11] Ninan Sajeeth Philip, K. Babu Joseph *Chaos for Stream Cipher*, in Proceedings of ADCOM 2000, Tata McGraw Hill 2001

[12] G. Álvarez, F. Montoya, M. Romera, G. Pastor *Cryptanalysis of dynamic look-up table based chaotic cryptosystems*, arXiv: nlin. CD/ 0311043 v1 20 Nov 2003

[13] T. Guoning, W. Tang, W. Shihong, L. Huaping, H. Gang *Chaos-based cryptograph incorporated with S-box algebraic operation*, Physics Letters A, Vol.318, Issues 4-5, pp. 388-398, 17 November 2003

[14] S. Berczyński, Yu. A. Kravtsov, J. Pejaś, E. D. Surovyatkina *Secure Data Transmission via Modulation of the Chaotic Sequence Parameters*, 10th Multi-Conference On Advanced Computer Systems. 22-24 October 2003, Międzyzdroje, Poland

[15] N.K. Pareek, Vinod Patidar, K.K. Sud *Discrete chaotic cryptography using external key*, Physics Letters A 309 (2003), pp.75–82

[16] V.S. Anishchenko and A.N. Pavlov, Phys. Rev., 57 (1998), pp. 2455-2461.

[17] V.S. Anishchenko, V.V. Astakhov, A.B. Neiman, T.E. Vadivasova and L. Schimansky-Geier *Nonlinear Dynamics of Chaotic and Stochastic Systems. Tutorial and Modern Development*, Springer, Berlin, Heidelberg, 2002.

[18] S. G. Bilchinskaya, O. Ya. Butkovskii, M. V. Kapranov, Yu. A. Kravtsov, A. G. Morozov, E. D. Surovyatkina *Signal reconstruction errors in data transmission using modulation of the parameters of chaotic sequences*, J. Comm.Technol.Electron.,48 (2003), pp.284-292.

Keys distribution for asymmetric cryptographic systems

Eugeniusz Kuriata

University of Zielona Góra
Institute of Control and Computation Engineering
ul. Podgórna 50
65-552 Zielona Góra
e-mail: E.Kuriata@issi.uz.zgora.pl

Abstract:
The article discusses issues related to security policies which can emerge in the process of generating qualified certificates. There is presented a system enabling generation of qualified keys for asymmetric cryptographic system without the necessity of appearing in person of the person or body applying for the certificate at the seat of certification authority.

Keywords: *Cryptography, security, e-document.*

1 Keys obtaining conditions for asymmetric cryptographic systems

Electronic signature act [1] determines legal effects of its application, principles of rendering certification services, conditions of use of electronic signature, and principles of supervising the certification service providers. A certificate will be called an electronic certificate containing, among others, the public key of the person or body applying for the certificate, which can be used for verification of the person or body signing a given document. It is assumed that to provide such services it is not required to possess licence for rendering them, with a restriction, that such bodies cannot issue qualified certificates. Qualified certificates are issued by a qualified certification authority, which fulfil all the requirements of the electronic signature act, and they are also entered in the register of qualified certification service providers. Possessing a qualified certificate one can place a safe electronic signature, and the digital data signed with a safe electronic signature hold the same importance as to the legal consequences as documents provided with a hand-written signature.

The person or body applying for qualified certificate is obliged to provide the certification authority with documents testifying to its identity in person or through a legal representative. In the case of false information contained in the certificate, the certification authority is not deemed responsible for eventual losses or damages connected with these data. Currently the persons or bodies interested in acquisition of a qualified certificate are forced to appear in person (or through a legal representative) in the place stipulated by the certification authority to apply for a certificate, with prior confirmation of their identity on the basis of the supplied documents. Those obstacles greatly restrict the process of implementation of electronic documentation circulation technology.

There is a group of people in the society (a small one yet existing), a criminal group, for whom obtaining identity documents at any name and of any personal information is of no problem. The practice indicates that spotting forgery in such documents is very difficult, and sometimes, for a non-expert, utterly impossible; it is easy to imagine a situation when such persons in PKI infrastructure could function as any citizen, providing that the "real" one does not have their classified certificates yet. What happen if the "forged" certificate and the proper one are issued by two different certification authorities? This "collision" can appear at the moment when the person whose identity has been used by the "intruder" and the intruder would want to obtain certificates from the same certification authority. In such a case the person applying at later time will be notified that the certificate has already been provided to them. For the certification authority both clients, the one who has already been issued with a certificate and the one just applying for it, are equally credible, one them being false. How to distinguish between them? Most probably the real one will try and clear up the matter to the end; and the other, the false one, will never show up again and will not try and prove their truthfulness. There can be presented more scenarios with a similar end result.

How serious a problem authentication of a user (client) [6] is could be shown in the wording of the confidential information act [2] declaring that when verifying personal identity information in the process of security certification there is required that the person applying for such certification should provide three persons who could confirm the applicant's identity.

Considering the above one can state that possession of certain documents does not necessarily mean that the person who produced them is the person whose data are in the documents. This means that presently having a qualified certificate and using it does not have to testify to the correspondence of identity provided by the certificate with the actual identity of the certificate holder. Such a state allows to declare that in a critical situation application for a certificate in an appointed place by an intruder using forged documents could be compared to application for a certificate by phone: it is equally risky, the price being the only difference. The main problem for a client using qualified certificate is obtaining a safe, not discredited private key, for which there has been generated a public key placed in the certificate together with other data.

This shows that there is an urgent need to develop a system in which the certification authorities could generate, for example, "a temporary qualified certificate" requiring confirmation by other authorised institutions that the applicant who already possesses a private key and "temporary qualified certificate" is indeed that one it claims to be.

The electronic signature act [1] reads that "the certificate issued by a certification authority not having its seat in the Republic of Poland and not providing services on its territory is held equal in law with qualified certificates issued by a qualified body providing certification services having its seat or providing its services on the territory of the Republic of Poland," should certain conditions be fulfilled. For many potential users of safe information exchange that would like to use PKI infrastructure to appear in person in the seat of the body providing qualified certification services, having its seat in Poland or abroad, should not constitute a problem. Majority of such users, despite many obstacles, will be forced to comply with that, whereas some part of the society, due to certain difficulties, will give up communicating in this way altogether.

On the occasion of a common access to PKI infrastructure it would be possible to greatly simplify, and thus decrease costs of many undertakings, which in some way paralyse functioning of a state: for example carrying out various elections, referenda and polls or replacing electronic documents [3].

A client applying for a qualified certificate is forced to trust in honesty of the certification authority (it is obliged to that by the act), on the other hand there are known incidences were the authorities obliged to confidentiality do not satisfy those obligations. Considering the above a client can proceed according to the principle of "limited trust." Then how and from where one can obtain keys for asymmetric cryptographic systems?

There are known studies of generating qualified keys for asymmetric cryptographic systems at a client's [4] as well as at a qualified certification service provider's [5]. In the case of generating keys at the client's the system ensures that the keys generated in this way can be recognised by a qualified certification service provider as qualified keys generated at its site.

Below there is presented a way of safe data transmission necessary to generation of certificates on the server and keys for asymmetric cryptographic systems, with employment of electronic information transmission media. The system does not require appearance in person at the certification services provider's [5] to place an application for a qualified certificate.

2 Generation of keys to asymmetric cryptographic systems

As a result of cryptographic hash function on a given file one can obtain a unique sequence, which will be called a file-hash value. The sequence is characterised by that that being in its possession we are unable to determine the file to which the hash value was assigned. The value was used for generation of keys in symmetric cryptographic system during generation of electronic documents [3].

In the below-presented algorithm, a client sends e-mails an application to certification services provider (called also server) for generation of qualified certificate and private key. Responding to the application server sends a special form to the client for filling-up. The data entered in the form's fields are later placed in the certificate by certification services provider.

In the form received from the server the client, after filling up all the obligatory data fields D, enters into a special field a random sequence of characters X in which there must be placed characters required in correctly created cryptographic keys. This produces file A being data file D extended with a random sequence X.

$$A = D \| X.$$

A client does not have to remember the random sequence X, as the data from this field are not used for generation of the certificate. The field with the random sequence X is used to prevent an intruder from determination of the hash value of the data sent by a client. This means that if an intruder knows the data D contained in a form (this being possible), the random sequence of characters X prevents determination of hash value of the filled-up file #A.

Figure 1 shows a diagram of document generation, which will be sent to certification services provider (server).

At the moment of engaging in sending the data, a client enters random data ID (this also does not have to be remembered), which are accumulated in adder with the file hash value #A

$$K = \#A \oplus ID.$$

Parameter K is used as an encoding key of symmetrical cryptographic system.

Filled-up form, called data file A (data and sequence of random characters), is expanded with client's identification number ID

$$M = A \| ID$$

then the expanded file M is encoded in symmetric cryptographic system with key K, being the same of file hash value #A and client's identification number ID

$$C = K(M) = (\#A \oplus ID)\{A \parallel ID\}.$$

Encoded expended file C and encoded key L is sent to server, where it is divided into two parts (Fig. 2).

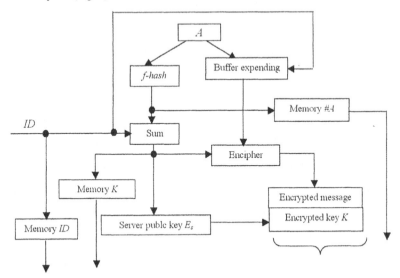

Fig. 1. Algorithm of client's certificate application generation

Encoding key of symmetric cryptographic system is encoded with open server key

$$L = E_s(K)$$

and is added to encoded expanded file M.

Expanded file M is decoded in encoder of symmetric cryptographic system with a key being a decoded total of values of hash $\#A$ and client's ID – previously encoded by a client with open key of server E_s – with secret key of server D_s.

$$K = D_s(L) = D_s(E_s(K)) = \#A \oplus ID.$$

From the decoded expanded file M client's ID is separated in a separating buffer, then the ID is sent to adder in which it is accumulated with key K of symmetric cryptographic system being a sum of file hash value $\#A$ and client's identification number ID. The sum of client's identification number ID and key K of symmetric cryptographic system

$$G = K \oplus ID$$

is compared with the value of decoded file hash $\#A$. If values of the quantities are identical, $G = \#A$, it is assumed that file hash value $\#A$ defined by the client is identical with the file hash value $\#A$ decoded by server. On that basis server, after

154

separation of data D from file A, generates a certificate and its public key E_k and private key D_k.

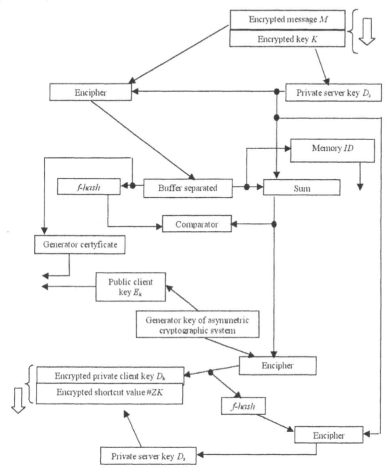

Fig. 2. Generation of certificate and client's private key on a server side

If $G = \#A$, then client's private key is encoded in symmetric cryptographic system with key G being a sum of client's ID value and key K of symmetric cryptographic system $G = K \oplus ID$

$$ZK = G\,(D_k).$$

Value of client's encoded private key hash $\#ZK$ – encoded in symmetric cryptographic system with key K being a sum of file hash value $\#A$ and client's identification number ID, and then encoded in asymmetric cryptographic system with secret server key D – is added to client's encoded private key $\#ZK$.

$$U = D_s \, (\, K \, (\, \#ZK \,)).$$

Encoded client's private key ZK with the added encoded hash value $\#ZK$ server sends to the client.

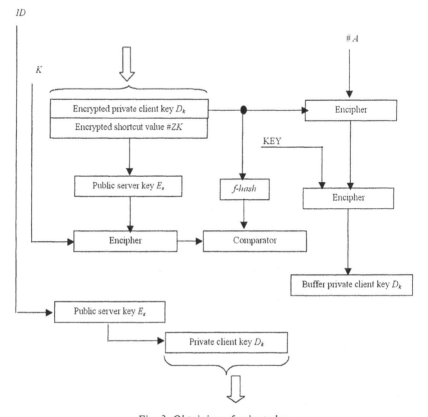

Fig. 3. Obtaining of private key

Client's private key D_k is encoded in symmetric cryptographic system to which key KEY is entered by the client.

Hash value – encoded by server in symmetric cryptographic system – of client's encoded private key $\#ZK$, whose key is the sum of encoded file's hash $\#A$ and client's identification number ID, and in asymmetric cryptographic system with private key of server D_s,

$$U = D_s \, (\, K \, (\, \#ZK \,))$$

client decodes in asymmetric cryptographic system with public key of server E_s and then in symmetric cryptographic system with key K

$$H = K(\, E_s \, (U)).$$

The encoded private key ZK received by client and extended with encoded hash value of encoded private key U is divided into two parts (Fig.3).

Encoded client's private key $ZK = G (D_k)$ is decoded in encoder of symmetric cryptographic system, to which the key is obtained from memory #A

$$T = \#A (G (D_k))$$

and if $\#A = G$ it is assumed that $T = D_k$.

For client's private key encoded in symmetric cryptographic system, there is defined value of encoded client's private key $\#ZK$, the value of which is compared in comparator with value H being hash value of client's private key $\#ZK$ encoded by server after performance of decoding.

If $H = \#ZK$ then client's private key, received by the client, is identical with the private key sent by server.

Client, after receiving their private key D_k, sends identifier ID having been encoded in asymmetric cryptographic system with server public key E_s, and then their own private key D_k.

$$R = D_k (E_s (ID)).$$

Server, having received client's identifier ID encoded in asymmetric cryptographic system, decodes it, first with public key E_k, then with its own private key D_s (Fig. 4).

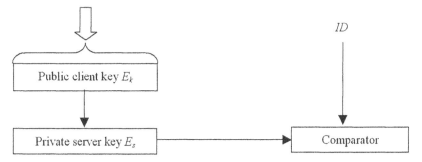

Fig. 4. Client's confirmation of reception of private key

If after decoding identifier ID obtained from the client is identical with the ID memorised by server and obtained from the separating buffer as a result of its separation from expanded file M, it is assumed then that client's private key has been delivered to the user who placed an application for the certificate. Server places the certificate with client's public key in commonly accessible database.

3   Conclusion

Presented above way of distribution of keys for asymmetric cryptographic system ensures safety of their distribution provided that the applying person or body is reliable and the data provided for this purpose are true. In the case of fraudulent purposes of the applying person or body, the above presented way of certificates distribution is not effective, although if there would be a system developed requiring confirmation of the applicant's identity this could prove satisfactory.

The analysis of the presented system as to its safety and preservation of confidentiality of the transmitted private key has been proved safe and reliable. This means that a person or body applying for qualified certificate would obtain it with adherence to all the rules required on this occasion. A different matter is whether the data reflected in the certificate are real data of the person of body applying for the certificate. The problem can cause many troubles to PKI service providers, especially to those PKI service providers distributing keys for asymmetric cryptographic systems. In the case of authorities providing qualified certification services, certificate issuance will be connected with increase of certain costs, connected for example with insurance of the key, etc. This aspect can present some sort of limitation in abuse of PKI due to use of false identity. Presently there are quite a few PKI service providers not charging fees for such services. Here we can see a great number of applications, many of them aiming at hindering the process of obtaining keys for asymmetric cryptographic systems, but only hindering.

The proposed system is simple and does not require that the applying person or body should possess knowledge in the area of system safety. Preparation of an application does not require that the person or body should remember any passwords or keys.

An idea of issuance of "temporary certificates" seems essential in this article. There should be developed a suitable protocol of actions, and also be determined who could authorise such certificates.

In the presented above way of distribution of keys, after introduction of client identification mechanisms, there exists a possibility of provision of certificates by foreign centres of qualified certification services. Here the crucial problem lies in searching for such certificates.

4   References

[1]   *Act of 18 September 2001 r. on electronic signature*, The Journal of Laws 2001, No 130, item 1450, Poland

[2] *Act of 22 January 1999 r. on protection of confidential information*, The Journal of Laws 1999, No 11, item 95, Poland

[3] *The way of generation of electronic documents with time marker*, Patent application P 366965 of 05.04.2004, The Patent Office of the Republic of Poland

[4] *The way of generation of keys to asymmetric cryptographic systems at the client's*, Patent application P368491 of 14.06.2004, The Patent Office of the Republic of Poland

[5] *The way of obtaining keys to asymmetric cryptographic systems*, patent application P 367587 of 28.04.2004, The Patent Office of the Republic of Poland

[6] M. Bellare and P. Rogaway *Entity Authentication and key distribution*, Advances in Cryptology - Crypto 93 Proceedings, Lecture Notes in Computer Science Vol. 773, D. Stinson ed., Springer-Verlag, 1994

Two-pattern test generation with low power consumption based on LFSR

M. PUCZKO, V.N. YARMOLIK

Bialystok University of Technology
15-950 Bialystok, Wiejska 45A
mpuczko@ii.pb.bialystok.pl, yarmolik@ii.pb.bialystok.pl

Abstract: A method of logic synthesis for low-power design for two-patterns test
              sequence is presented in this paper. The idea of power consumption
              minimization by modifying the structure of LFSR (Linear Feedback
              Shift Register) have been proposed. In this paper some examples are
              included.

Key words: low power design, two-test pattern, built-in self-test, switching activity, Test
              Pattern Generator

1 Introduction

The increasing prominence of portable systems and the need to limit power
consumption (and hence, heat dissipation) in very-high density VLSI (Very Large
Scale of Integration) chips have led to rapid and innovative developments in low-
power design during the recent years. The driving forces behind these developments
are portable applications requiring low power dissipation, such as notebook
computers, portable communication devices and personal digital assistants. In most
of these cases, the requirements of low power consumption must be met along with
demanding goals of high chip density. Hence, low-power design of digital circuits
has emerged as a very active and developing field of CMOS design.

With the ever increasing complexity and density of today's VLSI circuits
that makes external testing more and more difficult, BIST (Built-In Self-testing) has
emerged as a promising solution to the VLSI testing problems. BIST needs Test
Pattern Generators on-chip. They can be classified in two families: scan-based TPG
(test-per-scan technique) and at-clock speed TPG (test-per-clock technique). The
main goal of scan based TPGs is loading serially vector tests into scan chains.
Usually, the TPG is an LFSR. At-clock speed TPGs do not need serial loading since
they provide test patterns directly at the inputs of each Circuit Under Test (CUT).
Several approaches of low power BIST have been proposed. In [1], the author
presents a test scheduling approach that takes into consideration the power
consumption. For general BIST structure a new test pattern generator is proposed
[2] to reduce the circuit inputs activity without affecting test efficiency, thus
reducing power consumption. As have been shown in previous publications [3] more
commonly used self-test technique is 'test-per-scan'.

The approaches presented above address the detection of stuck-at faults. But to assure high quality parts it should be performed to find delay and stuck-open faults. Testing for these models generally requires a two-pattern test. The first pattern sensitize a path in the login and the second pattern stimulates any delay fault [4]. Because of the dependencies between flip-flops, applying two-pattern tests to sequential logic is more complicated that applying the single pattern tests necessary for detecting single-stuck faults. Two delay faults models are proposed in the literature. The gate fault model considers a single failure at a faulty gate [5] while the path delay fault models considers that the failure caused by process variations is distributed over a path [6]. Similar to stuck-at faults, the simplest approach to detect delay faults is an exhaustive two-pattern test. For an n-input CUT (Circuit Under Test), TPGs must run through all the $2^n x(2^n-1)$ different possible pairs of patterns. For example approach presented in [7] requires only $nx(2^n-1)$ pairs of patterns. There is presented a method based on switching of a single bit in the test pair which allows to prevent the prohibitive test time. The paper presents a method of logic synthesis for low-power design for two-patterns test sequence. There is proposed an idea of power consumption minimization by modifying the structure of LFSR (Linear Feedback Shift Register). In this paper some examples are included. The paper gives the answer on question: Which primitive polynomials should be used to obtain the lowest power consumption during generation of two-patterns test sequences.

2 low power design methodology

To reduce the power consumption the semiconductor industry has adopted multifaceted approach, attacking the problem on four fronts [8]:

- Reducing chip and package capacitance: this can be achieved through process development such as process scaling to sub-micron device sizes, and advanced interconnect substrates such as Multi-Chip Modules (MCM). This approach can be very effective, but is expensive.
- Scaling the supply voltage: this approach can be very effective in reducing the power dissipation, but often requires new IC fabrication processing. Supply voltage scaling also requires circuitry for low-voltage operation, including, level-converters and DC/DC converters, as well as detailed consideration of issues such as signal-to-noise.
- Using power management strategies: the power savings that can be achieved by various static and dynamic power management techniques are very application dependent, but can be significant.
- Employing better design techniques: this approach promises to be very successful because the investment to reduce power by design is relatively small in comparison to the another approaches.

In this paper the last approach has been investigated.

3 PSEUDORANDOM TEST PATTERN GENERATION

A linear feedback shift register (LFSR) is the heart of any digital system that relies on pseudorandom bit sequences, with applications ranging from cryptography to wireless communication systems. Each LFSR is described by its characteristic polynomial which is presented below:

$$\varphi(x)=a_0+a_1x+a_2x^2+\ldots+a_{m-1}x^{m-1}+a_mx^m; \; a_m=a_0=1; \; a_i \in \{0,1\} \quad (1)$$

where a_i are the binary coefficients. When $a_i = 1$ it implies that a connection exists. On the contrary when $a_i = 0$ it implies that no connection exists and the corresponding XOR gate can be replaced by a direct connection from its input to its output, like it is shown in Fig. 1 for polynomial $\varphi(x)=1+x+x^4$.

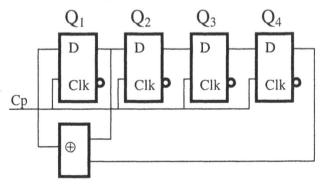

Fig. 1 Standard form of LFSR $\varphi(x)=1+x+x^4$

Q_1, Q_2, Q_3, Q_4 describes state sequences generated by LFSR shown in Fig. 1.

For the primitive polynomial $\varphi(x)=1+x+x^4$ the state sequences of LFSR can be described as:

$$\begin{aligned}
Q_1(k+1)&=Q_1(k)\oplus Q_4(k)\\
Q_2(k+1)&=Q_1(k) \qquad\qquad\qquad (2)\\
Q_3(k+1)&=Q_2(k)\\
Q_4(k+1)&=Q_3(k)
\end{aligned}$$

Next table shows all possible states for LFSR presented on Fig. 1.

State	$Q_1Q_2Q_3Q_4$	State	$Q_1Q_2Q_3Q_4$
0	1 0 0 0	8	1 1 0 1
1	1 1 0 0	9	0 1 1 0
2	1 1 1 0	10	0 0 1 1
3	1 1 1 1	11	1 0 0 1
4	0 1 1 1	12	0 1 0 0
5	1 0 1 1	13	0 0 1 0
6	0 1 0 1	14	0 0 0 1
7	1 0 1 0	15	1 0 0 0

Tab. 1 State sequences for LFSR 4th degree

Fig. 2 presents a mathematical description of LFSR, where $Q_m(k)$ are the previous states of LFSR and $Q_m(k+1)$ are the next states.

$$Q(k+1) \qquad\qquad V \qquad\qquad Q(k)$$

$$\begin{vmatrix} Q_1(k+1) \\ Q_2(k+1) \\ Q_3(k+1) \\ \cdots \\ Q_m(k+1) \end{vmatrix} = \begin{vmatrix} \alpha_1 & \alpha_1 & \alpha_1 & \cdots & \alpha_{m-1} & \alpha_m \\ 1 & 0 & 0 & \cdots & 0 & 0 \\ 0 & 1 & 0 & \cdots & 0 & 0 \\ \cdots & \cdots & \cdots & \cdots & \cdots & \cdots \\ 0 & 0 & 0 & \cdots & 1 & 0 \end{vmatrix} = \begin{vmatrix} Q_1(k) \\ Q_2(k) \\ Q_3(k) \\ \cdots \\ Q_m(k) \end{vmatrix}$$

Fig. 2 **Mathematical description of LFSR**

The next states of LFSR are generated using equation (3):

$$Q(k+1) = V \, x \, Q(k) \quad (3)$$

where $Q(k)$ is the vector of previous state. By modulo 2 multiplication $Q(k)$ and V matrix the next new states of LFSR are received as the vector $Q(k+1)$.
Adequate value in matrix $Q(k+1)$ are calculated using (4) and (5).

$$Q_1(k+1) = \sum_{i=1}^{m} \alpha_i Q_i(k) \qquad (4)$$

$$Q_j(k+1) = Q_{j-1}(k), j = \overline{2, m}, k = 0,1,2,\ldots \qquad (5)$$

Example
The matrix V for the primitive polynomial $\varphi(x) = 1 + x + x^4$ (Fig. 1) is presented below:

$$V = \begin{vmatrix} 1 & 0 & 0 & 1 \\ 1 & 0 & 0 & 0 \\ 0 & 1 & 0 & 0 \\ 0 & 0 & 1 & 0 \end{vmatrix} \qquad (6)$$

This matrix allows to design the LFSR structure presented in Fig. 1.

4 POWER CONSUMPTION BY CMOS CIRCUITS

Power dissipation in CMOS circuits can be classified into static and dynamic. As have been shown before [9], dynamic power is the dominant source of power consumption, what is due to short circuit current charging and discharging of load capacitance during output switching. The power consumed at node j per switching is $1/2 C_j V^2_{dd}$ where C_j is the equivalent output capacitance and V_{dd} is the power supply voltage. Hence, a good estimation of the energy consumed during f_j switching at node j is $1/2 f_j C_j V^2_{dd}$. Nodes connected to more than one gate are nodes with higher parasitic capacitance C_j is assumed to be proportional to the fan-out of the node v_j [10]. The resulting expression for consumed energy E_j at node j is $E_j = 0.5 v_j f_j C_0 V^2_{dd}$, where C_0 is the minimal output load capacitance for the case when $v_j = 1$. According to the last expression, the estimation of the energy consumption at the logical level requires the calculation of the fan-out v_j and the number of switching f_j on the node j.

The product v_jf_j is named Weighted Switching Activity (WSA) of node j and is used as a metric for the power consumption at the node, due to it is the only variable part in the energy consumption expression. The WSA generated in the circuit after application of one clock pulse can be expressed as:

$$WSA_{cl} = \Sigma_j \, v_jf_j \quad (7)$$

This metrics will be used to measure the power efficiency of *BIST* hardware.

5 SWITCHING ACTIVITY REDUCTION METHOD

Generally to generate two-pattern test sequence with low power consumption it is necessary to use $2*n$ degree primitive polynomial for n-bits test pattern. For example for 10-input circuit it is essential to use primitive polynomial of 20th degree.

By modifying equation (3) it is possible to obtain next N's states of LFSRs with lower power consumption.

$$Q(k+N)=V^NQ(k) \quad (8)$$

where N is a power of V matrix.

Below is presented matrix V^2 (9) and modified structure (Fig. 3) of LFSR for the polynomial $\varphi(x)=1+x+x^4$ which allows to generate 2-bits test pattern.

$$V^2 = \begin{vmatrix} 1 & 0 & 1 & 1 \\ 1 & 0 & 0 & 1 \\ 1 & 0 & 0 & 0 \\ 0 & 1 & 0 & 0 \end{vmatrix} \quad (9)$$

In the Fig. 3 the modified structure of LFSR is presented.

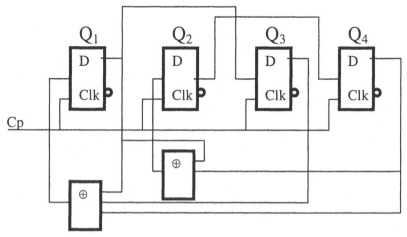

Fig. 3 Modified structure of LFSR for polynomial $\varphi(x)=1+x+x^4$

For example to generate two-test pattern sequence for 2-input sequential circuit it is necessary to calculate matrix V^2, where N=2. The example of above sequences is presented in Fig. 4. Symbol on the left describes number of pair and part of the pair. For example 2-1 means first part of the second pair.

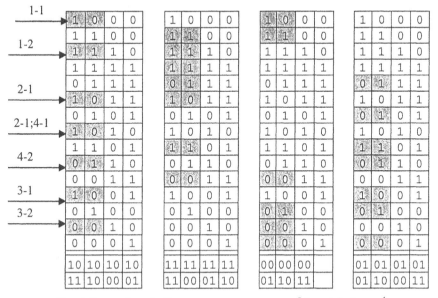

Fig. 4 Generation of all two-patterns test sequence for $\varphi(x)=1+x+x^4$

There is no pair "00 00" because it is impossible to generate this state by LFSR.

6 EXPERIMENTAL RESULTS

Weighted Switching Activity for the modified structure of LFSR was calculated for all primitive polynomials up to 20th degree. The results are shown below. Primitive polynomials with the lowest power consumption for the modified structure were selected. As it was noticed in [11] the primitive polynomials with the smallest number of XOR gates have the lowest power consumption. But taking into consideration modified structure of LFSR it is not always true what was proved by experimental results presented in Tab. 2

Calculation showed that the smallest power consumption have the primitive polynomials of 10th and 18th degree (Tab. 1). The way of calculation were presented in [12]. Tab 2. showed the power reduction for LFSR's from 4 to 20 degree. Primitive polynomial of 14th degree $\varphi(x)= 1+x^9+x^{10}+x^{11}+x^{14}$ consumed 36,13% less power than $\varphi(x)=1+x+x^2+x^4+x^8+x^{10}+x^{11}+x^{13}+x^{14}$. Analyzing power consumption polynomials of 18th $\varphi(x)= 1+x^{11}+x^{18}$ (WSA=6,5) and $\varphi(x)= 1+x+x^2+x^4+x^6+x^7+x^{10}+x^{13}+x^{15}+x^{17}+x^{18}$ (WSA=11,66) it was showed that it is possible to obtain power reduction up to 79,38%. Maximal reduction of power consumption, achieved for 20th degree, was equal 87,69%.

Polynomials of 10th degree	WSA	Polynomials of 18th degree	WSA
$1+x^7+x^{10}$	6.5	$1+x^{11}+x^{18}$	6.5
$1+x^3+x^{10}$	6.7	$1+x^7+x^{18}$	6.61
$1+x+x^2+x^3+x^4+x^5+x^6+x^7+x^{10}$	7.5	$1+x^9+x^{14}+x^{17}+x^{18}$	7.5
$1+x^6+x^7+x^9+x^{10}$	7.5	$1+x+x^2+x^3+x^4+x^5+x^6+x^7+x^8+x^9+x^{10}+x^{11}+x^{18}$	7.5
$1+x+x^2+x^3+x^4+x^5+x^6+x^9+x^{10}$	7.5	$1+x^{10}+x^{16}+x^{17}+x^{18}$	7.5

Tab. 2 WSA of polynomials of 10-th and 18th degree with the smallest WSA

degree of LFSR - n	N=n/2	WSA_{min}	Primitive polynomial for WSA_{min}	WSA_{max}	Primitive polynomial for WSA_{max}	Power reduction
4	2	6,5	$1+x^3+x^4$	6,75	$1+x+x^4$	3,84%
6	3	6,5	$1+x^5+x^6$	7,66	$1+x^2+x^3+x^5+x^6$	17,84%
8	4	7,37	$1+x+x^2+x^3+x^6+x^7+x^8$	8,37	$1+x+x^3+x^5+x^8$	13,56%
10	5	6,5	$1+x^7+x^{10}$	9	$1+x^3+x^4+x^5+x^6+x^7+x^8+x^9+x^{10}$	38,46%
12	6	7,5	$1+x^6+x^8+x^{11}+x^{12}$	9,66	$1+x+x^2+x^4+x^6+x^8+x^9+x^{11}+x^{12}$	28,8%
14	7	7,5	$1+x^9+x^{10}+x^{11}+x^{14}$	10,21	$1+x+x^2+x^4+x^8+x^{10}+x^{11}+x^{13}+x^{14}$	36,13%
16	8	7,31	$1+x^5+x^{10}+x^{11}+x^{16}$	10,75	$1+x^2+x^3+x^4+x^5+x^7+x^8+x_9+x^{11}+x^{12}+x^{13}+x^{15}+x^{16}$	47,05%
18	9	6,5	$1+x^{11}+x^{18}$	11,66	$1+x+x^2+x^4+x^6+x^7+x^{10}+x^{13}+x^{15}+x^{17}+x^{18}$	79,38%
20	10	6,5	$1+x^{17}+x^{20}$	12,2	$1+x+x^3+x^4+x^5+x^8+x^9+x^{10}+x^{11}+x^{12}+x^{15}+x^{18}+x^{20}$	87,69%

Tab. 3 Power reduction for LFSRs of 4-20 degree

The experimental results of WSA for modified structure of LFSR were presented in this section.

7 Conclusion

It have been proved that by using modified structure of LFSR it is possible to generate two-pattern test sequence with low power consumption per one new bit. By making calculations for all primitive polynomials the polynomials with the smallest power consumption have been obtained. Considered standard structure of LFSR using primitive polynomials with the minimal number of XOR gates can guarantee low power consumption. It was proved that with modified structure of linear feedback shift register it is possible to obtain very low power consumption per one new bit using primitive polynomials with non minimal of XOR gates.

ACKNOWLEDGEMENTS – The work was sponsored by a research project KBN S/WI/03, KBN S/WI/04.

8 REFERENCES

[1] Zorian Y., "A Distributed BIST Control Scheme for Complex VLSI Dissipation", Proceedings of IEEE VLSI Symposium, 1993, pp.4-9.

[2] Wang S., Gupta S., "DS-LFSR: A new BIST TPG for low Heat Dissipation", Proceeding of IEEE International Test Conference, November 1997, pp.848-857.

[3] Manich S., Garbarro A., Lopez M., Figueras J., Girard P., Guiller L., Landrault C., Pravossoudovitch S., "Low Power Bist by Filtering Non-Detecting Vectors", IEEE European Test Workshop, 1999.

[4] Lin C. J., Reddy S. M., „On delay fault testing in logic circuits", IEEE Trans. Comp. Aided, vol. 6, no.5, pp. 694-703, Sept. 1987

[5] Pramanick A. K., Reddy S. M., „On the detection of delay faults", Proc. of Int' l test Conf., pp.845-856, Oct. 1988

[6] Smith G. L., "Models for delay faults based upon paths", Proc. of Int'l Test Conf., pp.342-349, Nov. 1985.

[7] Craig G. L., Rkime C., "Pseudo-exhaustive adjacency testing: a BIST approach for stuck-open faults", Proc. of Int' l test Conf., pp.126-137, Oct. 1985.

[8] Iman S., Pedram M.,"Logic synthesis for low power designs", Kluwer Academic Publishers, 1998, pp.5-6.

[9] M.A. Cirit,"Estimating Dynamic Power Consumption of CMOS Circuits", ACM/IEEE International Conference on CAD, November 1987, pp.534-537.

[10] Girard, L. Guiller, C. Landrault, S. Pravossoudovitch, "A Test Vector Inhibiting Technique for Low Energy BIST Design", Proceedings of IEEE VLSI Test Symposium, 1999, pp.407-412.

[11] Brazzarola M., Fummi F., "Power Characterization of LFSRs", Proceedings IEEE International Symposium of Detect and Fault Tollerance in VLSI Systems, Albuquerque, New Mexico, 1-3 November, 1999, pp. 139-147

[12] Puczko M., Yarmolik V.N., "Projektowanie generatorów testów o niskim poborze mocy", RUC 2004, Szczecin

Unauthorized servers for online certificates status verification

Witold Maćków, Jerzy Pejaś

Technical University of Szczecin, Faculty of Computer Science and Informations Systems, 49 Żołnierska St, 71-210 Szczecin, e-mail: wmackow,jpejas}@wi.ps.pl

Abstract: This paper is a continuation of the proposal of the linked authenticated dictionaries usage for certificate revocation. Usage of specific data structures allows preparing online certificate status verification protocol, in which status servers are unauthorized entities. Additionally this scheme provides possibility of generating certificate status requests dependent on time and achieving responses about status of archival certificates

Keywords: certificate revocation, authenticated dictionary, dictionaries linking, online certificate status protocol

1   Introduction

There are a few propositions (including some in international standards) of online certificate verification protocols. Some of them are used for complete verification, for example: Simple Certificate Verification Protocol (SCVP) or Extended Online Certificate Status Protocol (OCSP-X). These protocols allow for verification of all certificates correctness criterions, for example validity or signature (including certification path analysis). In most cases some simple protocols should be used only for certificate status verification. The most important and well known is Online Certificate Status Protocol (OCSP) – it could be received certificate status information in current time using this protocol. The end user verifies all other elements by himself. The protocol proposed in this paper is similar to OCSP but bring in some important changes in its operation – both in front-end and back-end parts.

2 Bases of the OCSP protocol

The standard describing Online Certificate Status Protocol - OCSP – was defined by IETF (RFC 2560) in 1999 and develop till now. This protocol operates on question-answer rule – question about a certificate status cause sending an answer signed by OCSP server (OCSP responder). This answer includes information about certificate status: revoked, not revoked, unknown. For the correctness of this status verification is responsible the OCSP server.

The right to issue the certificate status evidence is delegated by Certification Authority to OCSP server. CA does it by certification of the OCSP server key, which will be used to status answers signing. This key could be used only for this kind of activity. By doing this CA declares trust to server – only in mentioned extent – but not enable end user to verify this trust. The correct sign of the OCSP server on response containing status shows only that this information wasn't modified after leaving the OCSP server but doesn't prevent some OCSP frauds. This situation limits the system scalability – each potential server has to be approved by CA. Recapitulating the user has to trust server because CA does it.

The next limitation is necessity to ask question about certificate status, which was current in the moment of the answer generating (or, because of some mechanisms limitation, in some period of time around this moment). There is no possibility of generating question about past status, especially for archival certificates.

All above OCSP protocol limitations are direct result of the mechanism used in the back-end layer. The most often mechanism in use is Certificate Revocation List CRL. There is stored information about valid certificate revocations only. The actualization is made in some constant time intervals (it is not depend on real revocation time). Additionally this data structure format – whole list signed by CA - makes impossible to detach of some piece information in authenticated manner.

So we consider OCSP protocol limitation presented below:

- impossibility of using unauthorized servers (servers are some successive points of trust apart from CA);

- impossibility of getting some information about certificate status in the moment different from the current one;

- time of updates of revocations information is not adequate to real time of revocations (actualization time of CRL).

3 Certificate status

From farther point of view certificate we can describe using five parameters: (1) *ca* – an identifier of Certification Authority which issued certificate (it may be a complex ID like in OCSP – hash of CA name and its public key, (2) *a* – certificate serial number, (3) $ti_{ca,a}$ - certificate issue time, (4) $te_{ca,a}$ - certificate expiry time, (5) $tr_{ca,a}$ - optionally certificate revocation time.

Obviously the certificate should have all remaining fields like a public key or CA signature, but these fields does not make any influence on proposed protocol activity and they will be omitted in this paper. Each certificate may have in a moment t_x some features from set presented below:

- NI - not issued, where: $t_x < ti_{ca,a}$;
- I - issued, where: $t_x \geq te_{ca,a}$;
- NE - not expired, where: $t_x < te_{ca,a}$;
- E - expired, where: $t_x \geq te_{ca,a}$;
- NR - not revoked, where: $t_x < tr_{ca,a}$;

Additionally it is obvious that for each CA authority and a certificate serial number there must be fulfilled two basic conditions:

- $\forall ca, a : ti_{ca,a} < te_{ca,a}$ - certificate expiry ($te_{ca,a}$ moment) has to be preceded by issue of certificate ($ti_{ca,a}$ moment);
- $\forall ca, a : ti_{ca,a} < tr_{ca,a} < te_{ca,a}$ - certificate revocation ($tr_{ca,a}$ moment) may (but not need to) occur only in a period from issue to expiry.

Taking it under consideration certificate may in one of the below state:

- {NI,NE,NR} - not issued (and obviously not expired and not revoked too);
- {I,NE,NR} - issued, not expired, not revoked;
- {I,NE,R} - issued, not expired, revoked;
- {I,E,NR} - issued, expired, not revoked;
- {I,E,R} - issued, expired, revoked.

For the verifier one an only correct state is {I, NE, NR}, each other disqualify certificate usage. This situation is presented on the Fig. 1 in a form of a graph. Three upper axes symbolize time flow related to issue, expiry and revocation events. Lower axes present two possible scenarios of certificate life, dependent on revocation occurrence.

If the end user/verifier collects certificate which state he want to define, he is able to check certificate issue and expiry times by himself. In situation like this the verifier is able to decide for any moment t_x if the certificate was issued or expired $(ti_{ca,a} < t_x < te_{ca,a})$. He is interested in server answer concerning only possible revocation, so for a t_x moment he could get an answer {I,NE,NR} or {I,NE,R}.

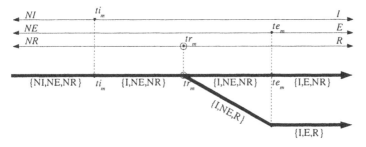

Fig. 1. Status changes during certificate lifetime

There is possibility that the verifier doesn't have demanded certificate but only signed message. We could assume that signature format allows to get certificate issuer and certificate serial number for certificate associated with key used for this signature. The verifier doesn't know either certificate issue time or expiry time – that is why when he asks about certificate state in a t_x moment, the server answer may be on of following: {NI,NE,NR}, {I,NE,NR}, {I,NE,R}, {I,E,NR} or {I,E,R}.

4 Protocol proposal

4.1 General scheme

In this scheme it was assumed existence of many independent Certification Authorities. They are publishing certificates and revocation information in common accessible directories. These directories do not need to be connected with particular CA and further on CA do not need to limit publishing to one particular directory. CA publishes authentication data with help of Trusted Publisher TP (similarly to directory, publisher is not associated with one and only CA). Unauthorized status servers USS have free access to data stored in directories and on that basis they can construct trusted answers to queries about particular certificate status. On the other side end user **R** ask question about certificate status to local certificate server. His server is responsible for local management of certificates and revocation information and for communication with directories and status servers. Following symbols for protocol sides will be used in the further part of a note:

CA – Certification Authority, generally trusted agent responsible for issue and revocation of certificates and directories updates.

D – directory, database consisting of certificates and revocation information (in a form of linked authenticated dictionaries). There are stored data actual and archival as well. The directory does not need to be associated with particular CA in one-to-one relation. In one directory could be placed some information from many different CA and one CA may publish in many directories.

TP - Trusted Publisher, an agent responsible for publication of some verification information;

USS – Unauthorized Status Server, server of online certificate status verification service. It accepts requests from LCS and on the basis of the data taken form directories it generates the answers. Revocation information is stored in directories in authenticated dictionaries, so each answer is authenticated a priori by particular CA. USS need not be trusted.

LCS – Local Certificate Server, service in **R** requestor system, responsible for local certificate management and its correctness verification. It could be a standalone server for few requestors or only service for one particular requester in his local machine.

R – Requestor, a person or a program demanding certificate status information in a one particular moment.

On the Fig. 2 is presented exemplary dependence network in described scheme.

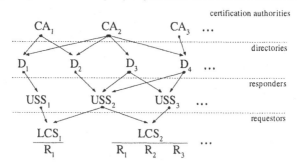

Fig. 2. Example of dependencies between protocol sides

4.2 Back-end

In all certificate status verification protocols it could be distinguished two layers. Higher one, so called front-end, defines successive protocol steps, format of sent data etc. Lower one, back-end, is a set of all mechanisms, structures and functions allowing protocol operation. For example OCSP protocol is actually only front-end. For correct working it needs back-end – usually Certificate Revocation List are used for it. It's obvious that used back-end solutions affect front-end functionality.

Back-end of a proposed protocol is based on linked authenticated dictionaries. This solution was presented in earlier note [3]. Authenticated dictionary is a dictionary, which response to *Search* command not only with *found* / *not found* information, but also adds proof of authenticity of this information. There's a new element in a scheme with authenticated dictionary – untrusted mediator placed between the trusted data holder and the requestor. The trusted data holder shouldn't serve requestors *Search* queries directly – it's responsible only for data structure updates. The holder distributes updated authenticated dictionary (or the authenticated update package) among mediators. The holder generates the authenticity proof after each update and it's the integral part of the authenticated dictionary.

Dictionaries linking allow trusted storage of archival information and prevent frauds based on revocation order changing.

4.3   Front-end

Proposed protocol is shown on Fig.3. Each step is presented as an arrow, which points out a data flow direction and it is indicated by step number. Steps number 2 and 3 are optional and they are drawn with dash-line.

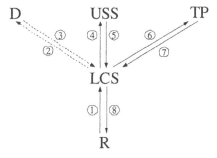

Fig. 3. Proposed protocol scheme.

Successive steps of a protocol are described below:

1) Requestor **R** sends question to his local certificate server **LCS**. This question refers to status of certificate issued by *ca* authority with serial number *a*. Status should be determined for t_x moment. If **LCS** has got this certificate in his resources the next step is 4. In other case next step is 2.

$R \rightarrow LCS : \{ca, a, t_x\}$

2) **LCS** hasn't got requested certificate in his local resources and sends request for this certificate to directory **D** (authority *ca*, serial number *a*).

$LCS \rightarrow D : \{ca, a\}$

3) Requested certificate $C_{ca,a}$ (authority *ca*, serial number *a*) is looked for in directory **D** and sent back to **LCS**.

$D \rightarrow LCS : C_{ca,a}$

4) LCS server takes issue time $ti_{ca,a}$ and expiry time $te_{ca,a}$ from certificate $C_{ca,a}$. If $t_x < ti_{ca,a}$ then LCS sets variable *status* ={NI,NE,NR} and the next step is 8. In other case **LCS** sends a request for certificate status to unauthorized status server. This request refers to status of certificate issued by *ca* authority with serial number *a* and expiry time $te_{ca,a}$.

$LCS \rightarrow USS : \{ca, a, te_{ca,a}\}$

5) **USS** server has got up-to-date linked authenticated dictionaries of *ca* authority. Dictionaries were received from **D** directory. Opening time of *j* round in *ca* authority is signed as $t_{ca,j-1}$. The requested certificate is archival if $te_{ca,a} < t_{ca,j-1}$. **USS** looks for such a closing time $t_{ca,r}$, that $t_{ca,r-1} < te_{ca,a} \le t_{ca,r}$. Archival dictionary **PAD**$_{ca,r}$ with $t_{ca,r}$ closing time is searched with key *a*. Certificate is up-to-date if $te_{ca,a} \ge t_{ca,j-1}$. In such a case, **USS** searches with key *a* archival dictionary **PAD**$_{ca,j-1}$ and temporary dictionary **TAD**$_{ca,j}$. The response consists of fields $ans_{ca,a}$ i $pr_{ca,a}$. Both fields format depends on types of used dictionaries. In the case when the certificate revocation information was found the filed $ans_{ca,a}$ should contain at least REV$_{ca,a}$={a, $te_{ca,a}$, $tr_{ca,a}$, r, s, c}=REV$_{ca,r,s,c}$, where: $tr_{ca,a}$ is a revocation time, *r* is a round, when revocation happened, *s* subround of this round and *c* number of revocation in this subround. The field $pr_{ca,a}$ contains an unambiguous proof of searched element presence or absence in analyzed dictionary. Proof may be treated as trusted only in cooperation with additional information published by **TP**.

$USS \rightarrow LCS : \{ans_{ca,a}, pr_{ca,a}\}$

6) LCS requests published intermediated proof, prepared for *ca* authority, for *r* round, *s* subround - IP$_{ca,r,s}$. The same proof may be taken from any other trusted place.

$LCS \rightarrow TP : \{ca, r, s\}$

7) Publisher sends requested proof to answer:

$TP \rightarrow LCS : IP_{ca,r,s}$

8) On the base of received proofs LCS verifies authenticity of data and it formats answer *state*. Possible answers are: {I,NE,NR}, {I,E,NR}, {I,NE,R} and {I,E,R}. Answer {NI,NE,NR} is prepared in step 4 if necessary.

$LCS \rightarrow R : state$

5 Summary

Proposal presented above help us to eliminate described OCSP protocol limitations, i.e. there's a possibility of an unauthorized status servers usage (certification authority needn't control servers) and generation of dependent on time status requests (different from current time). Back-end structure, which is a foundation of whole protocol, let us increase frequency of revocation information updates.

The choice of optimal structures for TAD and PAD dictionaries implementation is our current goal. Not only efficiency, but also protocol formal description depends mainly on this choice.

6 References

[1]   Arnes A., "Public Key Certificate Revocation Schemes". PhD thesis, 2000.

[2]   Arnes A., Just M., Knapskog S., Lloyd S., Meijer H., "Selecting Revocation Solutions for PKI", Proceedings of NORDSEC 2000 Fifth Nordic Workshop on Secure IT Systems, Reykjavik, 2000.

[3]   Maćków W., "Linked authenticated dictionaries for certificate status verification", Enhanced Methods in Computer Security, Biometric and Artificial Intelligence Systems, Springer, pp.35-46, 2005.

[4]   Chocianowicz W., Maćków W., Pejaś J., "Protocols of revocation and status verification methods for public key certificates", RSA Conference, Paris, 2002.

[5]   Myers M., et al., "X509 Internet Public Key Infrastructure Online Certificate Status Protocol – OCSP", RFC-2560, 1999.

[6]   Fox B., LaMachia B., "Online Certificate Status Checking in Financial Transactions: The Case for Re-issuance", Proceedings of the Third International Conference on Financial Cryptography, pp.104-117, 1999.

[7]   Willemson J., "Certifcate Revocation Paradigms", Technical Report, Cybernetica 1999.

Micropayments with Privacy – a New Proposal for E-commerce

Krzysztof Szczypiorski, Aneta Zwierko, Igor Margasiński

Warsaw University of Technology, Institute of Telecommunications,
ul. Nowowiejska 15/19, 00-665 Warsaw, Poland
e-mail: {K.Szczypiorski, A. Zwierko, I.Margasinski}@tele.pw.edu.pl

Abstract: This paper presents an original concept of micropayment schemes which combine both the simplicity of an electronic pre-paid card without trusted third party and user's privacy. Two protocols are proposed - the first one is based on a secure one-way hash function, the second one is based on a cryptographically secure pseudorandom bit generator. The main advantage of the proposed schemes is the ability to perform a cryptographic key distribution within the micropayment process.

Keywords: micropayments, e-commerce, privacy

1 Introduction

Micropayments (defined as electronic transactions transferring very small sums of money) are very attractive from the privacy's perspective. In this paper we propose two new micropayment schemes (MINX - **M**icropayments with Secure **N**etwork E**x**change) based on different cryptographic primitives (an one-way function and a cryptographically secure pseudorandom bit generator). They provide both the user and the vendor with reasonably fast and secure protocol for micropayments. The main idea of the proposed schemes is the ability to perform cryptographic key distribution with the micropayment process. Other advantages of the presented system include an immediate double spending detection, effective forgery prevention and confidentiality of transactions. Some of those unique properties were made possible by merging the role of a service provider (a vendor) and a broker (a guarantor of a payment) into one: an operator. This situation is typical in the telecommunications environment.

2 Related Work

The most important and known micropayment schemes are PayWord and Micromint proposed by Ronald L. Rivest and Adi Shamir in 1996 [14]. Both schemes are based on Trusted Third Party (TTP) named broker and need Public Key Infrastructure (PKI) in order to work properly [10]. In the first one, PayWord, an user utilizes a cryptographic one-way function to produce a sequence of coins. A payment is granted by the broker. Once a day vendors contact brokers and vendors' money gets transferred. The second scheme is based on a different idea – it also uses the one-way function as a method of producing coins, but the coins come from a broker and then are distributed to users. This special method makes forging coins much more difficult than producing real ones by a broker. This concept is based on the birthday-paradox for one-way functions [10]. Another micropayment scheme was proposed by Torben P. Pedersen and was named the CAFÉ project ([12], [1]). It is also based on the one-way function and it is very similar to the schemes proposed by Shamir and Rivest, but it was developed independently. The CAFÉ system is a part of the ESPIRIT project. Other schemes were proposed by Shamir (based on lottery tickets system [13], improved in [11]). A similar micropayment scheme, based on hash functions and called NetPay, was proposed by Xiaoling Dai and John Grundy [2]. Their paper also provides details of a possible architecture and an implementation of such system. The idea of combining some properties of macro- and micropayments schemes was introduced by Stanisław Jarecki and Andrew Odłyżko in [8]. Their scheme combines the simplicity of an off-line micropayment scheme with an on-line security of a transaction, which means that a vendor is consulting a broker from time to time during communication with a client. This enables the vendor to check if the client is not cheating. Many other micropayment methods are discussed in [7] and [4]. One of the commercial systems was proposed by IBM: Internet Keyed Payment Systems (*i*KP), discussed in [6].

3 Proposals of New Schemes

We propose two new schemes for micropayments. Both are pre-paid cards oriented, which means that they have almost all the advantages and disadvantages of real-life pre-paid cards. The main novel idea of the MINX system is the performing cryptographic key distribution within the micropayment process.

3.1 Properties of Pre-paid Cards

Pre-paid cards can be treated as types of micropayments. Contradictory to classic micropayment schemes, there is no TTP. When a user buys a pre-paid card the user has to trust an operator that the card is valid and ready to use. In a traditional purchase (not pre-paid), the user knows exactly how it works. That is why a trusted operator is the major factor in the schemes discussed. Another advantage of the pre-paid card is the possibility to use only a fraction of it. A partially used card is ready to be utilized at any time. The process does not require a user to provide an operator with any information during card purchase or its usage.

The proposed schemes are based on two different cryptographic primitives: the one-way hash function and the cryptographically secure pseudorandom bit generator.

A hash function h maps an input x to output $h(x)$ of a fixed length. For a given x, $h(x)$ is easy to compute. A one-way hash function (h) has the following properties [10]:

- one-way (preimage resistance) – for $y = h(x)$, computing x from y is infeasible,
- weak collision resistance (2nd preimage resistance) – for given x_1 and $h(x_1)$ it is computationally infeasible to find such x_2 that $h(x_1) = h(x_2)$,
- strong collision resistance – it is computationally infeasible to find such x_1 and x_2 that $h(x_1) = h(x_2)$.

A pseudorandom bit generator (PRBG) is a deterministic algorithm which for a given input sequence (a truly random binary sequence) outputs a different binary sequence, much longer, which "appears" to be random. The PRBG passes the *next-bit* test if there is no polynomial-time algorithm which can differentiate between this PRBG output and a truly random sequence with probability significantly greater than ½. The PRBG, which passes the *next-bit* test, even under some plausible, unproved mathematical assumptions, is called the cryptographically secure pseudorandom bit generator (CSPRBG).

3.2   MINX General Overview

Basic definitions:
- *key:* in MINX system a key means a secret key for a symmetric cipher (like Advanced Encryption Algorithm – AES, RC6),
- *impulse:* an impulse means one unit of payment which can be extracted from a pre-paid card,
- *ID:* every user who wants to use a valid card has a unique identifier – named ID assigned by an operator; the ID enables the operator to find a proper secret key for decrypting data received from each user.

Both MINX schemes are based on the same **four steps** (Fig. 1):
- **Step 1.** A user shows part of a card to an operator.

- **Step 2.** The operator sends a confirmation and an assigned ID to the user; at the same time the operator computes a current key.
- **Step 3.** The user computes a current key and an impulse, encrypts it with requested data and sends it to the operator.
- **Step 4.** The operator validates it and sends a response back to the user.

After the completion of step 4, it is possible to establish a secure communication between the user and the operator – a key (shared between the user and the operator) **is destined to be used as a session key in all secure exchanges between the parties until a new key gets established.** The last two steps are repeated until the user wants to use a service provided by the operator (with a set fee) or the user's virtual pre-paid card is used up.

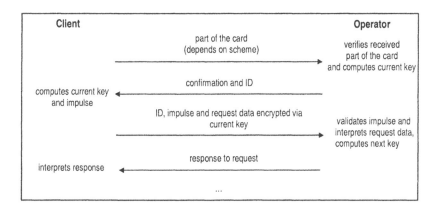

Fig. 1. MINX – four basic steps

3.3   Scheme Based on One-Way Hash Functions

A client buys a pre-paid card, which consists of 4 elements: secret initialization value (seed) – **x**, card's value, the number of hashes – z (number of impulses on card is z/2) and function for generating impulses – **h**. The card with the above parameters has to be delivered secretly and should be authorized by an operator. We do not specify a way of buying a card. This topic is not included in this paper and can be realized by a macropayment system or a physical purchase.

When a user wants to use a pre-paid card, the user sends the following values to an operator: value of the card, number of impulses and $h^z(x)$ – the zth hash of x value computed using h. This initial step of communication can be kept secret. For example, the user can encrypt the card with the operator's public key. The operator does not need to authorize this activity, because only when x is known to the user, the user can participate in the rest of the communication.

The operator, using $h^z(x)$ and other values sent by the user (step 1), can identify a pre-paid card in its own database and validate it. While using a contemporary secure hash function, $h^z(x)$ is a unique identifier for each card. The length of $h^z(x)$ should be from 160 bits (SHA-1 – Secure Hash Algorithm) up to 512 bits (SHA-512).

If the card is valid, the operator computes the first secret key $h^{z-1}(x)$ and gives the user a unique identifier (ID), so the user's messages can be distinguished from other messages. At the same time the operator sends user confirmation and ID (step 2).

The user, after having received a confirmation from the operator, also computes the first secret key: $h^{z-1}(x)$ and the first impulse: $h^{z-2}(x)$. Next the user encrypts the impulse and the information about service that the user requested with a secret key and sends it to the operator along with a unique identifier (step 3). After decryption the operator can verify the impulse value by hashing it twice and checking if it equals to what is stored in the database ($h^z(x)$). Then, the user is provided with the requested service, and the data for this card is changed in the database. The operator computes a new key and changes the value of the card from: $h^z(x)$ to $h^{z-2}(x)$ (step 4).

When the operator receives the impulse equal to x from the user, the card gets used up. The operator should hold it in its database: $h^z(x)$, x and value of the card to be able to validate incoming cards. Changing $h^z(x)$ to $h^{z-2}(x)$ (new values) enables the operator to hold current value/number of impulses in its database. The user does not have to send every impulse to the operator. The user can show the operator that the user wants to use more impulses at this time to pay for more expensive services or to use the service for a longer time.

The impulses themselves, in this scheme, are random-looking. Based on the properties of a hash function, it is not possible to compute x from $h^z(x)$. The reason for the implementation of additional secret keys, connected to impulses, is to provide the user with confidentiality of services that the user requests without the need for public key cryptography or secret-key sharing schemes.

The advantages of this scheme include:
- confidentiality of communication between the user and the operator,
- possibility of using services with different values/prices with one card,
- no need for the TTP to compute impulses prior to card usage. The user does not have to request an authorization of the card.

The disadvantages include:
- computation of impulses and keys, their validation is slower than in classical micropayment schemes,
- the operator has to be trusted just like in the real world.

3.4 Scheme Based on Pseudorandom Bit Generator

This scheme is almost the same as the previous one. The only difference is that instead of the hash function, a client uses a cryptographically secure pseudorandom number generator (CSPRBG). The CSPRBG is used for generating binary sequences in the manner described by Blum, Blum & Shub [10], which are treated as impulses or secret keys. The advantage of CSPRBG over hash function is that having x_n the user can compute x_{n-1} or x_{n+1} with the same amount of computation (if the user knows parameters of CSPRBG). If the user does not have these parameters the computation any of the values x_{n-1} or x_{n+1} is very difficult (even having x_n). This means that the generation and the verification of a key and an impulse take almost the same amount of time.

In this scheme the card consists of the following: secret seed – x, card's value, the number of products of CSPRBG – z (number of impulses on card is $z/2$) and the secret parameters of CSPRBG.

The user shows the operator x_z and hash of parameters of CSPRBG (step 1). The confidentiality of this operation can be based on the operator's public key.

The first key could be x_{z-1} and the first impulse x_{z-2}. The operator only has to compute x_z from x_{z-2} to verify the impulse (step 3). To check if the card is still valid and not used up an operator has to store x and z. The rest of the scheme is the same as in the previous one.

The advantages include:
- the same number of operations to generate key/impulse every time and to verify them,
- the same as in the previous scheme.

The disadvantages are:
- generating proper parameters of CSPRBG is quite complex,
- the computation of the CSPRBG values is not very fast, and poses almost the same problems as public-key cryptosystems.

3.5 Additional feature of schemes

Another feature of MINX, not commonly found in other micropayment systems, is the possibility to utilize more than one impulse at a time. The price of one unit of some services may be a multiple of the impulse, or a user may want to buy service for longer time / in larger amount. This kind of situation is typical in telecommunications: the user wants to be able to make both local and international calls using one phone card. Another typical situation is when the user wants to buy video-on-demand services for longer period of time (e.g. whole movie) without having to contact the operator every time the service bought for one impulse expires.

Let's assume that a user has n impulses on a card ready to utilize. Now the user wants to pay for a service that would cost him m impulses. We assume that m < n, because otherwise buying a service would be impossible. The user sends to the operator $h^{(n-m-1)*2}(x)$ ((n-m-1)*2'th hash), including in the data sent the information that the user wants to utilize m impulses. The encryption of information is done with hash $h^{(2*n-1)}(x)$, using the session key that was previously computed by both the user and the operator. To check the validity of the impulse the operator hashes 2m times the delivered impulse and compares it with the information stored in the operator's database. If the impulse is valid, the operator computes new session key: $h^{((n-m-1)*2-1)}(x)$ and sends requested service to the user.

A card based on the CSPRNG can be used in the same way (appropriate products of the generator instead of hashes should be computed).

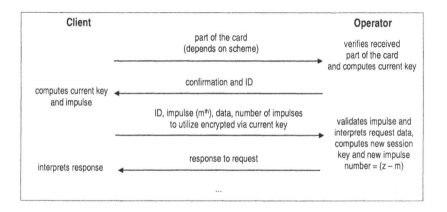

Fig. 2. Basic scenario for paying bigger amounts with MINX

This feature of the MINX gives a user a greater flexibility when using a card. Not only can the card be used at any moment, but also different amounts of impulses can be utilized at the same time. This feature makes the card suitable for a wider range of services.

4   Security

The security of both schemes is based on the same assumptions, therefore the security is analyzed for the overall scheme.

Main security assumptions are:

- the operator is trusted,
- the utilized hash function is hard to invert,
- the CSPRBG has properties as in point 3.1.

The security evaluation criteria, discussed below, are based on the proposals included in [4].

4.1 Forgery Prevention

There are two types of forgery in the proposed schemes: forgery of a card and forgery of an impulse.

In the first case, a malicious user can send a regular request for a validation of a card which is really invalid. If an operator cannot find such a card in its database, the situation is clear: the card is invalid and no validation can be made. No fraud is possible. But there can be a card with the same ID in the database. In this case, the operator computes the session key and sends validation along with ID to the malicious user. Still, the user is not able to use the card: the user is not able to invert hash function or compute following number of the CSPRBG to use it as the key. Therefore, the user cannot decrypt the data sent by the operator. The user is still also not able to compute the proper impulse value. The only situation in which the user can gain anything from guessing hash values from the card is when the user would produce all hashes or CSPRNG products (so all impulses and keys for this card), in proper amount (so their amount is the same or smaller than the operator has in its database). But this is very computationally ineffective and the probability of success is very small (when the operator uses large enough seed). It is even more ineffective for the CSPRBG than for the hash function scheme, because apart from computing impulses and keys, the user has to also find parameters of the pseudorandom generator and then try with all possible seed values. Therefore, the probability of such an attack is very small.

Another similar situation occurs when the user wants to use more impulses than the user's card poses. This is not possible since the operator stores the number of impulses in its database, and marks the card as used when this number reaches zero. At that moment the user has the same chance of deceiving the operator as in the case described earlier.

4.2 Double Spending Detection

The double spending of an impulse is almost impossible in the proposed schemes if a proper hash function or a CSPRBG is chosen (as described in section 3.1). During the transaction an operator is able to check validity of every impulse sent by a user. The operator also stores the number of impulses that the user is still able to spend. So, there is no sense in trying to spend the same impulse twice, if the user has a proper card, because the user is restricted in the number of impulses. Moreover, the possibility of having an impulse that is the same as the subsequent one is negligibly small for the proper hash functions and the CSPRBGs. As a result, in the proposed schemes, the double spending detection is immediate and double spending is not only nearly impossible but also non-profitable for the user.

4.3   Confidentiality

A third party can observe only a part of communication between a user and an operator that is not encrypted. As a result, it is only possible to misuse the information contained in the request for validation that the user sends to the operator in open-text. Only important data sent by the user is an initial impulse. If an eavesdropper could invert an impulse and generate a session key or the next impulse, this information would be very useful. However, since the hash function in the proposed scheme should be hard to invert and the generator used should be cryptographically secure, it is not possible. The rest of the communication between the operator and the user is encrypted, so it is secure and no one is able to misuse it.

4.4   Anonymity

The presented schemes also provide users with anonymity. No one observing communication between the user and the operator is able to acquire any information about a service that the user is requesting. It is also not possible to see how much money/impulses the user spent in a current transaction. Only when observing every transaction, especially every request for validity sent by the user to the operator, it is possible to identify how many impulses the user spent in the last transaction. But this problem can be eliminated by not including the number of valid impulses left on the card, in the request for validation. This data is needed only for additional validation of a card, so it is not necessary for the operator. This small change in the scheme equips a user with a complete anonymity against all observers. Unfortunately, the user is not that anonymous to the operator, who knows what services were sent and where. But this obvious disadvantage is reduced by the operator being a trusted party.

5 Applications

There are at least two versions of the potential MINX applications. The first one is based on an independent cryptosystem at the application layer where micropayments are provided. The keys placed on the pre-paid cards are utilized to provide confidentiality for users' requests or operators' responses including security of the transferred content during the payment process.

It is also possible to use the keys from pre-paid cards directly in the existing, well known security protocols like SSL/TLS (Secure Sockets Layer/Transport Layer Security – [3]). In this case (i.e. SSL/TLS), the adequate session key (SSL/TLS MasterKey) is extracted from a pre-paid card and is utilized to provide transaction security according to the admitted context (for example duration time or data volume).

The presented micropayment schemes can be useful in case where users wish to protect their privacy during small, frequent payments. Considering repeated payments via Internet, there is a serious possibility of spying, tracing and profiling users. MINX is the solution for customers who prefer to protect information about their favourite products' preferences and e-commerce habits. Therefore, MINX, as a means of a payment for anonymity, is the next important application field. Implementations of anonymity providing systems equipped with the payments for the services occur very rarely – known systems from state of the art (e.g., Freedom [5]) include payments which can compromise users' privacy. The anonymity service providers will need effective methods for generating revenue, as they would not look for profits from advertisements or user profiling attempts. The MINX micropayment schemes, which protect consumers' anonymity, can be an effective method of payment for Web anonymity service on the Internet. Association of MINX and VAST [9] (*Versatile Anonymous System for Web Users*) – which provide anonymity for individuals browsing WWW pages – seems to be a solid and practical solution for Web privacy. Combination of VAST anonymous Web browsing with MINX anonymous payments for the service is a good proposal for widespread, commercial implementations.

6 Conclusions

The proposed schemes, which are similar to the existing micropayment systems, have distinctive features including: the possibility of using some of the impulses on a card at any time, the possibility of making a payment with the same card for services with different base-unit costs. The card usage is anonymous: a user does not have any public/private key. Transactions do not require the presence of a

TTP. Another unique feature of the proposed schemes is preservation of privacy: the micropayment systems known from the e-commerce literature do not support confidentiality. MINX provides a secure communication between an operator and a user without the need for any kind of key distribution scheme. This approach creates very attractive telecommunications environment that provides the possibility of a payment for an access to resources without compromising users' privacy.

7 References

[1] Boly, J-P., Bosselaers, A., Pedersen, T. et al.: The ESPRIT Project CAFE. ESORICS 94, Springer-Verlag LNCS Vol. 875 (1994) 217-230

[2] Dai, X., Grundy, J.: Architecture of a Micro-payment System for Thinclient Web Applications. Proceedings of the 2002 International Conference on Internet Computing (2002)

[3] Dierks T., Allen C.: The TLS - Protocol Version 1.0. IETF RFC 2246 (1999)

[4] Ellis, C.: Evaluation of Micropayment Schemes. Tech Report HPL-97-14 (1997)

[5] Goldberg, I., Shostack, A. Freedom Network 1.0 Architecture and Protocols. Zero-Knowledge Systems. White Paper, 1999.

[6] Hauser, R., Steiner, M., Waidner, M.: Micro-Payments based on iKP. Research Report 2791 (# 89269), IBM Research (1996)

[7] Jakobsson, M., Hubaux, J-P., Buttyan, L.: A Micro-Payment Scheme Encouraging Collaboration in Multi-Hop Cellular Networks. Financial Cryptography'03 (2003)

[8] Jarecki, S., Odłyżko, A.: An Efficient Micropayment System Based on Probabilistic Polling. Financial Cryptography '97, Springer-Verlag LNCS Vol. 1318 (1998) 173-191

[9] Margasiński, I., Szczypiorski, K.: VAST: Versatile Anonymous System for Web Users. Enhanced Methods in Computer Security, Biometric and Artificial Intelligence Systems, Springer-Verlag (2004)

[10] Menezes, A., van Oorschot, P., Vanstone, S.: Handbook of Applied Cryptography. CRC Press, Inc. (1997)

[11] Micali, S., Rivest, R.: Micropayments Revisited. CT-RSA 2002, Springer-Verlag LNCS Vol. 2271 (2002) 149-163

[12] Pedersen, T.: Electronic Payments of Small Amounts. Technical Report IDAMI PB-495 (1995)

[13] Rivest, R.: Electronic Lottery Tickets as Micropayments. Financial Cryptography '97, Springer-Verlag LNCS Vol. 1318 (1998) 307-314

[14] Rivest, R., Shamir, A.: PayWord and MicroMint: Two simple micropayment schemes. Proceedings of 1996 International Workshop on Security Protocols, Springer-Verlag LNCS Vol. 1189 (1997) 69-87

A model-based approach to analysis of authentication protocols

Janusz Górski, Marcin Olszewski

Gdańsk University of Technology

Narutowicza 11/12, 80-952 Gdańsk, Poland

e-mail:{ jango,olszes}@eti.pg.gda.pl

The paper presents the OF-APSAF integrated framework for authention protocol analysis. The framework is built on top of a well-established formal method CSP and its supporting tools: Casper and FDR. The integral part of OF-APSAF is the object-oriented semi-formal approach to modelling of cryptographic protocols, their application context and security requirements. The modelling is based on UML and a catalogue of specialised analytical patterns. Object-orientation helps to cope with the complexity inherent to the domain of security protocols verification and formal methods in general.

Keywords: security protocols, formal methods, object-oriented modelling

1   Introduction

1.1   Motivation

Communication between remote hosts over a network is one of the main features of contemporary distributed systems. Valuable information is often transported outside the constituency controlled by its owner (e.g. LAN) and sent at considerable distances over a foreign medium (most often the global Internet). Two issues arise from this fact:

- information in transit may be intercepted with malicious intent,
- it is difficult to obtain a guarantee that the system a given host is communicating with is indeed the one it pretends to be.

The issues described above are addressed by a class of communication protocols called security, or cryptographic, protocols. Security protocols utilise tools of modern cryptography, such as symmetric and asymmetric ciphers, one-way functions and digital signatures to provide security services to applications. However, the present experience with security protocols is that they are often prone to design and implementation errors. Such errors can easily make a protocol susceptible to attacks, even if it utilises strong cryptographic tools. If such errors indeed exist, it may happen that an intruder does not have to crack the cryptographic defences on transmitted data at all, or the risk of the success of such an attack is unacceptably increased.

Therefore it is postulated that the same care must be given to the way the cryptographic primitives are combined together into the whole protocol, as to the reliability of individual cryptographic tools. Unfortunately, security protocols are usually designed and implemented by humans, and as such are very prone to errors .

There is a demand for tools and methodologies, which, if applied to a cryptographic protocol, would allow us to find all possible defects, or, if none are found, provide enough confidence that the protocol is indeed secure. Such potential can be found in formal methods, both those dedicated to the analysis of security protocols (e.g. BAN belief logic [1]), as well as those originating from other fields of high integrity systems engineering (such as CSP process algebra [2]). These methods may be used to construct a formal specification of a protocol in question and then to analyse it (preferably by means of supporting tools) in order to assess its trustworthiness.

1.2 Innovation

To facilitate analysis of security protocols (our primary focus is on those intended for authentication of remote hosts) we propose the Object-oriented Authentication Protocol Security Analysis Framework (OF-APSAF). The main incentive for defining such a framework was to provide the engineers with an analytical environment that supports shifting the analyst's attention to the issues of modelling the architecture of the protocol and its application contexts with less attention to the underpinning mathematical "machinery" employed to perform the analyses. The basic assumption was to build the framework on the top of an existing formal method, treating it as an important mean to achieve the goal, but not as the goal by itself. Our intention was to exploit the strengths of the chosen formal method, not overlooking or underestimating its weaknesses and limitations that possibly coul be effectively addressed by using other engineering techniques.

Incorporating a formal method into engineering practice is generally very challenging. One of the reasons for this is a significant gap between the abstract mathematical domain and the application domain or even technical domain. The OF-APSAF aims to "fill in" this gap by offering analytical tools to make the formalisation leap easier and more manageable. The whole process should be as transparent as possible, different steps should be traceable and all decisions well-documented (we assume that the formal specification itself is not an adequate documentation). To achieve this goal the OF-APSAF framework integrates informal and semiformal modelling and analysis of the system security context with formal protocol verification techniques.

2   Overview of the framework

OF-APSAF combines together various tools and methodologies with the intention of allowing the user to carry the protocol analysis as an engineering task with the focus on cost-effectiveness and reliability of the analytical procedure. Below we characterise the main components of the framework.

2.1   CSP for formal specification and verification

Employing CSP to security protocol analysis was addressed by many researchers, an overview can be found in [3]. The CSP process algebra can be used to model the protocol in question, the network running it and the security requirements it should satisfy. The FDR [2] model checker offers tool support – it is used to verify CSP specification, thus effectively checking whether the protocol achieves its asserted security goals. Another software tool, the Casper specification compiler [4], helps to avoid tedious and error-prone CSP coding and to focus the analyst's attention on actually modelling the protocol using a simple formal language. A description of how we apply CSP within the OF-APSAF framework is given in Section 3.

2.2   Patterns for object-oriented analysis

The OF-APSAF analysis is model driven. Object-oriented models serve as a primary tool for documenting the analysed protocol, its context (including the threat model) and the security requirements. Conversion of those models into the CSP formal domain is done as the last step, right before the actual automated verification is being performed.

However, building models each time from scratch would be too expensive and somewhat redundant, as many aspects of different security protocols are recurring. To provide for effective reuse we propose a set of analytical patterns to guide the user while developing the object oriented models related to a given protocol (we use UML as the principal modelling language). More details on how the object-oriented modelling is used in OF-APSAF are given in Section 4.

2.3 Analytical procedure

In order to employ formal verification as a part of the engineering task it should be embedded into a well-defined process context. OF-APSAF defines such a context supporting a systematic approach to the analysis of security protocols. The steps of the associated procedure include: informal analysis of the security domain the protocol runs in, semi-formal modelling, developing formal specifications, and finally, verifying them using the appropriate software tools. The OF-APSAF procedure also defines more specific tasks of each step and specifies input and output artefacts for each task. It also provides a template for the report summarising the results of the analyses. Such report, if maintained throughout the whole process, would contain information necessary to track the progress of analyses and to understand the results.

3 The formal analysis step

CSP is a general-purpose formal framework which may also be applied to security protocol analysis [2, 3]. The basic objects in CSP are abstract processes which may be combined into a larger network. They run independently in parallel and occasionally exchange messages with each other or the environment. The protocol participants are modelled as processes with patterns of communication reflecting the specification of the analysed protocol. For each process, the record of the messages it communicates is called its trace. By defining constraints on traces (e.g. which messages are allowed, or what should be their relative order) the analyst can formally express various security properties, including secrecy and authentication. The intruder can be defined as a special CSP process and its capabilities, such as initial knowledge or the extent to which he controls the communication medium can be specified explicitly. By configuring the intruder the analyst can modify the assumed threat model.

CSP has a strong tool support – the FDR model checker [2]. The tool converts the CSP model of the protocol into a state machine which represents all possible agents' behaviours. Then the state graph is traversed to check whether unsecure states (which contradict the requirements on traces defined for the model) are reachable. If the system can indeed reach an unsecure state, FDR outputs the pattern of inter-process communication leading to this situation. This helps the analyst to derive the corresponding attack scenario.

One of the main limitations of the CSP/FDR approach is that it requires the analyst to specify in advance both, the maximum number of agents which can participate in the protocol and the maximum number of sessions each of the agents can run consecutively. Consequently, the protocol is being checked for faults only with respect to a limited size of the network which uses it, and the analysis is likely to give no results about the security of larger systems. There are some techniques to overcome this problem, but they do not solve it completely. The second limitation of the method results from the complexity of the analyses – the state machines produced by FDR grow exponentially with the size of the protocol and of the network.

The advantages of the CSP/FDR framework are not to be ignored as well. First of all, the method is mature and has been used with success on many occasions, finding previously unknown faults or rediscovering classical attacks. Secondly, the FDR software is a widely recognised tool and is commercially available

3.1 CSP in the OF-APSAF framework

Modelling security protocols in low-level CSP is a tedious and error-prone task. Finding the optimal CSP implementation of a given model is not obvious and automated model checking with FDR is quite hard in terms of computational complexity. For those reasons, the task of implementing CSP scripts that model a given cryptographic protocol is an ideal candidate for automation. That led to development the Casper tool [4] which primary objective is to compile scripts that contain:

- definition of a given security protocol,

- description of the network of agents running the protocol and data objects they use,

- specification of security goals supposedly achieved by the protocol,

- description of intruder's capabilities and knowledge.

into the corresponding CSP model. Even though input files for Casper use a type of formal language, it is by far less complicated then low-level CSP. The goal of Casper is to allow the analyst to focus on the actual problem and to free him/her from implementation details, saving time and effort and reaching out to users with lesser skills in CSP or formal methods in general.

Casper was included in OF-APSAF as a primary tool to express formal specifications of protocols. Because the specifications were further subjected to the verification by FDR, to meet the restrictions of the tool and to facilitate the analyses, the standard approach of OF-APSAF is first to partition the problem into several security scenarios and then to develop a separate Casper script for each scenario (a sort of "divide and conquer" strategy). Through superposition, successful verification of all scenarios provides a convincing argument that the protocol satisfies the asserted security goals.

4 The object-oriented modelling step

In OF-APSAF, object-oriented models expressed in UML [5] form an intermediate representation of the analysed protocol and its context. The models help in crossing the gap between the informal (engineering) dmain and its formal counterpart. As shown in Figure 1, such models offer an intermediate level of abstraction and thus help both with constructing formal specifications (a transition from informal to formal) and interpreting them (a transition in the opposite direction).

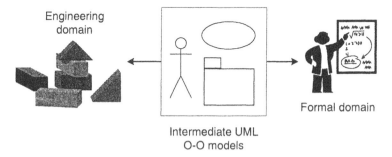

Fig. 1. Role of object-oriented models in OF-APSAF

The OF-APSAF analytical process definition refers to specific models (diagrams, perspectives) the analyst should prepare at a given step. To help the analyst, OF-APSAF defines the security protocol metamodel. Individual aspects of the metamodel can be efficiently constructed by using special OF-APSAF analytical patterns, covered in the next section.

Another way of looking at the object-oriented models in OF-APSAF is to consider them as a platform for documenting formal specifications. The latter, due to their mathematical nature may be difficult to communicate information about the protocol and the way its verification was carried out.

4.1 Analysis patterns of OF-APSAF

OF-APSAF features a catalogue of analityc patterns which guide the analyst through the process of modelling. Each pattern defines a scheme for constructing a particular aspect of the protocol model from some specific perspective. The patterns help in efficient solving of modelling problems commonly shared between different projects. By applying those patterns, the analyst is supported in constructing models which are:

- internally consistent,

- have a relevant scope,
- can be easily mapped to the domain of formal (mathematically verifiable) Casper specifications.

By defining a set of analysis patterns which the analyst is encouraged to use, OF-APSAF introduces a certain degree of formalisation into the modelling process. UML language does not guide its user and leaves much freedom to the analyst [5]. If each protocol modelling task were approached independently, the possibility for reuse would be significantly reduced and the performance of the entire process would suffer.

4.1.1 Documenting analysis patterns

Analytic patterns are described according to the following structure:

- Pattern name – a descriptive name of the pattern.
- Intent – which modelling issues are addressed by the pattern.
- Definition – UML diagram defining the pattern; description of the pattern and its elements.
- How it works – explanation of how the pattern works in practice; supported by a real example from one of the Case Studies.
- Pattern's role in the meta-model – which elements of the protocol meta-model are covered by the pattern.

4.1.2 An example pattern

a) **Pattern name:** "Agent Sessions"

b) **Intent:** Most of model checking techniques for protocol verification (including CSP/FDR) impose restrictions on the size of the model. The factors that determine the size of the resulting state machine include but are not limited to:

- number of agents participating in the protocol,
- number of sessions each agent can run concurrently or consecutively.

The Agent Sessions pattern allows representing the two above characteristics for each security scenario. Due to its dependency on the model checking paradigm, it is tailored especially for the CSP/FDR formal approach.

c) **Definition:**

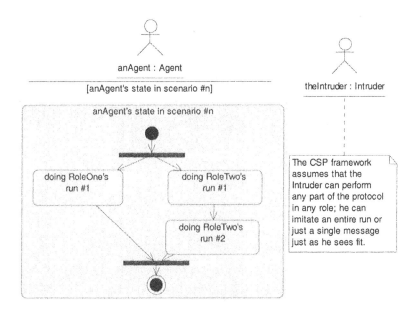

Fig. 2. A structure of the "Agent sessions " object model

The pattern (Fig. 2) uses state machines to express Agents' behaviour. Each agent is characterised by a single compound state which contains sub-states representing individual sessions the agent can run. The state model is flexible enough to express:

- the fact that a single agent can take multiple roles,
- how many runs a given agent can run taking a particular role,
- whether agent's sessions should be run concurrently or consecutively.

The intruder has been introduced to explicitly document the fact that it can run any number of sessions taking whatever role it needs.

4.2 Formalising object-oriented models

After preparing and documenting the object-oriented models, the analyst proceeds to the formalisation step. This step comprises preparation of Casper scripts that model individual security scenarios. Because the models are standardised (prepared using corresponding analytic patterns) this task can be accomplished relatively easy. The framework offers rules in a tabular form which explain how to translate given fragments of object models into Casper syntax.

5   Validating the framework

Three separate experiments were conducted to validate different aspects of the framework. During each of these experiments a different authentication protocol was analysed using some or all of the tools offered by OF-APSAF.

5.1   The HomeBanking wireless authentication protocol

The first case study was aiming at validation of the set of analytic patterns. The target of the study was a protocol for authenticating wireless handheld devices to a stationary server. The protocol is described in [6] and used in a HomeBanking application. The analysis using OF-APSAF confirmed that the protocol is secure.

5.2   The classic SPLICE/AS authentication protocol

The second experiment demonstrated that the framework is indeed capable of detecting security flaws in protocols. A classic SPLICE/AS authentication protocol [7] was analysed and as a result the well known attack [8] was rediscovered.

5.3   Authentication scheme in the DRIVE solution

Finally, the third case study focused on investigating the usefulness of OF-APSAF in analysing protocols running in a complex application and security context. The experiment also aimed at checking the applicability of OF-APSAF in supporting trust cases (a trust case is a documented body of evidence justifying trust in the considered system [9]). In this case we used OF-APSAF to produce objective and trustworthy evidence that can be referred to in the trust case.

For this purpose the authentication scheme implemented in DRIVE [10] was analysed, the identified faults were corrected, and the existing trust case for DRIVE was extended by the results of this verification.

6   Conclusions

At present, OF-APSAF can handle analysis of linear authentication and key exchange protocols. It has been confirmed by three separate case studies. They demonstrated the usefulness of OF-APSAF in both, finding security faults and positively verifying security properties. An interesting result is also the ability to use the results of OF-APSAF analyses as arguments supporting trust in the analysed systems.

Our ultimate goal is to to support analyses of practical, real-life protocols, including protocols for mobile agents. Specifications of such protocols are often very complex and lengthy). The protocols are often of a compositional design – i.e. a larger protocol uses smaller linear ones as the building blocks. Mobile agent systems themselves pose numerous new analytical challenges. The additional complexity has to be dealt with in a traceable manner before the actual automated formal verification can proceed. We believe that the model based approach of OF-APSAF involving the intermediate representations, step-by-step formalisation and well-defined documentation can help to overcome those difficulties.

7   References

[1]   Burrows M., Abadi M. 1989. 'A logic of authentication'. Technical Report 39, Digital Systems Research Center.

[2]   Roscoe A.W. 1998. 'The Theory and Practice of Concurrency'. Prentice-Hall, International Series in Computer Science, ISBN 0-13-674409-5.

[3]   Ryan P.Y.A, Schneider S.A., Goldsmith M.H., Lowe G., Roscoe A.W. 2001. 'The Modelling and Analysis of Security Protocols: the CSP Approach'. Addison-Wesley, ISBN 0-201-67471-8.

[4]   Lowe G. 1998, 'Casper: A Compiler for the Analysis of Security Protocols'. Journal of Computer Security, Volume 6, pp. 53-84.

[5]   Object Management Group 2000. 'OMG Unified Modelling Language Specification ver. 1.3'

[6]   Simoes P., Alves P., Rogado J., Ferreira P. 2000. 'An Authentication Protocol for Mobile Devices'. Advance Program for International Workshop on Internet 2000.

[7]   Yamaguchi S., Okayama K., Miyahara H. 1991. 'The design and implementation of an authentication system for the wide area distributed environment'. IEICE Transactions on Information and Systems. E74(11):3902--3909.

[8]   Hwang T., Yung-Hsiang Chen 1995. 'On the security of splice/as : The authentication system in wide internet'. Information Processing Letters 53:97--101.

[9]   Górski J., Jarzębowicz A., Leszczyna R., Miler J., Olszewski M. 2003. 'An Approach to Trust Case Development'. Lecture Notes in Computer Science 2788. Springer-Verlag.pp. 193-206.

[10]   http://www.e-mathesis.it/Drive/, IST-DRIVE project's official website.

Accessibility of information in realtime systems

Tomasz Hebisz and Eugeniusz Kuriata

University of Zielona Góra
Institute of Control and Computation Engineering
ul. Podgórna 50, 65-246 Zielona Góra,
e-mail: {T.Hebisz,E.Kuriata}@issi.uz.zgora.pl

Abstract:
In the paper the problem of information's security defined as fulfilment of confidentiality, authenticity and accessibility is presented. The accessibility, as the element of security is especially importand in realtime systems, in which the time of replying to received information is limited, while undelivering the messages right on time is unacceptable. The accessibility of information is fulfiled thought application of error control coding, in particular by using cyclic Reed-Solomon codes.

Keywords: Information's Accessibility, Security, Cryptography, Error Control Coding

1   Introduction

Generally, the security of information is defined as fulfilment for information three main properties, i.e. confidentiality, autheticity and accessibility. In currently used cryptosystems, only the confidentiality and authenticity of information is considered, while the accessibility in contemporary cryptographic systems is neglected, because there is an assumption that this part of security is achived by using of other manners application, such as improvment of communication channel's properties, etc.

In practice, as often as not one can meet with the situation, in which the direct goal of intruder isn't to possess of protected information, but to prevent the deliveration of information right on time to the declared receiver. The problem of fulfiling the accessibility is getting the great importance, especially in real-time systems, where the time of replying to the received information is limited, while the undelivering of information on time can lead to the crisis situation.

The accessibility of information can be guaranteed by redundant encoding prevously encrypted message. There are known cryptosystems based on linear error correction codes [13, 8, 15]. W McEliece's cryptosystem [13] the linear error-control codes are applied. The essence of operation of that system is based on disturbance of sended message for making it unreadable, what give us un opportunity to fulfil the confidentiality of information. Using correcting property of applied code, the recipient is able to correct this disturbances, what makes the decryption process available. Such kinds of systems fulfil the high level of confidentiality, because of their cryptographic resistance is comparable with the present asymetric cryptosystems based on complexity of large numbers factoring problem. As the matter of disadvantages of the systems based on linear error correction codes, the most important is to high complexity of decoding codes of long codewords. Such kinds of cryptosystems can fulfil just confidentiality and authenticity of information.

In [5] the cryptographic system based on systematic cyclic Reed-Solomon codes is presented. The main idea of this system is based on a fact, that the cryptogram is consisted only of the redundant part of the systematic code's codeword. That property of the system makes it unresistant to the disturptions of the signal in communication channel.

In the paper the cryptographic based on applying the cyclic Reed-Solomon codes, which give us the possibility of fulfilling the accessibility of information is presented. In the shown system, the information is coded, while the generator polynomials of used code are in fact the equivalents of cryptographic keys. By using double coding, the rate of the correct decoding procedure is achived.

2 Applying of error correction codes in cryptography

Error correction codes can be applied as an equivalent of the cipher on condition that the code generators be kept in secret, what mean that these generators be regarded as cryptographic keys. For this reason there is absolutely necessarily to make the key space as huge as posible. Thus, very specific mathematical methods of computations in finite fields have to be applied.

The cryptographic keys should fulfil the specific conditions, because in modern cryptography the security level of cryptograms depend on the key's space. In the situation, when the information is coded with redundant code, the generator determaining the code can be treated as the encryption key. This means, that the generator should have the same characteristic features, as the cryptographic key. The The problem of finding the generator polynomial $g(x)$, which determines cyclic Reed-Solomon code, can be considered in the same way, as the choice problem of encryption key in cryptographic systems.

2.1 The procedures of encryption and decryption

Presented cryptographic algorithm uses the procedures of encoding and decoding of the cyclic Reed-Solomon code. In such approach, the procedures of encryption and decryption are alse expanded of applying the key polynomial $k(x)$, what make the possible to use the CBC (cipher block chaining) mode of operationg of the cipher. Therefore the fuctions of encryption and decryption are implemented by the following equations

$$c(x) = E_{RS}(m(x) + k(x), g(x))$$

and

$$m(x) = D_{RS}(c(x) - k(x), g(x)),$$

where
        $m(x)$, $c(x)$, $g(x)$, $k(x)$ denotes, respectively, code polynomial (cryptogram polynomial), generator polynomial and key polynomial, while

E_{RS} and D_{RS} denotes, respectively, encoding and decoding procedures of nonsystematic cyclic Reed-Solomon code over $GF(q)$ field.

Thanks to applying the key polynomial $k(x)$ to the initial processing of information polynomial $m^{(i)}(x)$, there is possible to apply CBC mode, in which the encryption procedure of the first block of cryptogram $c^{(1)}(x)$ is based on the operation of addition of information polynomial $m^{(1)}(x)$ and key polynomial $k(x)$

$$m_c^{(1)}(x) = m^{(1)}(x) + k(x),$$

and as the result of this operaton one can obtain the encrypted message polynomial $m_c^{(1)}(x)$. In the next step, this polynomial is putted on the input of the coder, which transforms it into the cryptogram polynomial $c^{(1)}(x)$.

The encrytpion of i-th cryptogram polynomial $c^{(i)}(x)$, for $i = 2,3,...$, take place in the way, that the information polynomial $m^{(i)}(x)$ is added to the cryptograms' feedback polynomial $k'^{(i-1)}(x)$

$$m_c^{(i)}(x) = m^{(i)}(x) + k'^{(i-1)}(x),$$

where the degree of cryptograms' feedback polynomial $k'^{(i)}(x)$ is identical, as the degree of the information polynomial $m^{(i)}(x)$.

Cryptograms' feedback polynomial $k'^{(i)}(x)$ is defined as the result of the following steps; according to the compressing permutation, P_k the subset of cryptogram polynomial $c^{(i)}(x)$ coefficients are taked and used as the coefficients of the cryptograms' feedback polynomial (fig. 1).

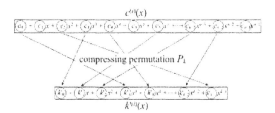

Fig. 1. The mechanism of choosing the coefficients
of cryptograms' feedback polynomial

It is important to note, that as early as the second block of cryptogram, information polynomial $m^{(i)}(x)$ is added to the cryptograms' feedback polynomial $k'^{(i-1)}(x)$ of previous cycle, instead of the key polynomial $k(x)$.

In the consecutive step of encryption procedure, the cryptograms' feedback polynomial $m_c^{(i)}(x)$, and the generator polynomial $g(x)$, are putted on the input of cyclic Reed-Solomon encoder. As the result of encoding procedure, one can obtain the code polynomial $c^{(i)}(x)$, which in case of systematic code, can be descrypted in the following form

$$c^{(i)}(x) = m_c^{(i)}(x)x^{n-k} - (m_c^{(i)}(x)x^{n-k}) \bmod g(x),$$

while in the case of non-systematic code, as follows

$$c^{(i)}(x) = m_c^{(i)}(x)g(x).$$

This mean that, the key polynomial $k(x)$ is the starting polynomial, used only in initial of encryption procedure. For this reason, this polynomial can be applied as receiver's identifier.

The fig. 2 shows an algorithm of encryption in CBC mode.

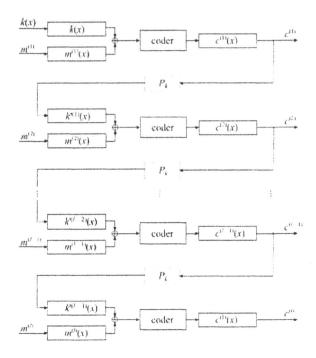

Fig. 2. An algorithm of encryption in CBC mode

3   Cryptosystem with the verification
of the communication channel noise level

Using the basis of the encrytpion and decrytpion procedures presented above, one can build the cryptosystem fulfiling the accessibility of information. The main idea of such system is based on applying two codes of different correcting properties. The first code performs the protection of the shortcut of information, which is represented as coefficients of the information shortcut polynomial. This polynomial is encrypted and concatenated to the information, what finally give the information part of the second code's codeword.

Having specified information polynomial $m^{(i)}(x)$ and defined galois field $GF(q)$, by substituting, respectively, every elements of $GF(q)$ as the arguments of information polynomial $m^{(i)}(x)$ one can obtain q values of this polynomial. If there be one element of $GF(q)$, which is known only to the valid users, the sender of the information polynomial $m^{(i)}(x)$ can compute the value $Ws_{m^{(i)}}$ of this polynomial, of which argument is that earlier established element of $GF(q)$. In the next step, the set of the shortcut values as the coefficients of the shortcut polynomial $w_s^{(i)}(x)$ is encoded using the polynomial $g_1(x)$ of systematic cyclic Reed-Solomon code. One can notice, that the shortcut polynomial do not fulfils classical function of the message diggest functions, but the only application of it is the verification of the correct decoding procedure.

Obviously, with the fixed length of the codewords, the length of the redundant part is getting smaller during the increasing of the information part. Thus, while using relatively small degrees of the shortcut polynomials, one can add the shortcut polynomial to the disturbance level key polynomial, which is known for the sender and the recipient. By coding this polynomial, we obtain the redundant polynomial, which can be regarded as encrypted shortcut polynomial $zw_s^{(i)}(x)$. Using the cyclicity of the code and from the fact, that the recipient knows the disturbance level key polynomial, there is possible to recover the structure of the whole codeword. This can be made by cyclic shift of the known codeword elements. Fig. 3 presents the structure of the codeword before and after cyclic shift of its elements.

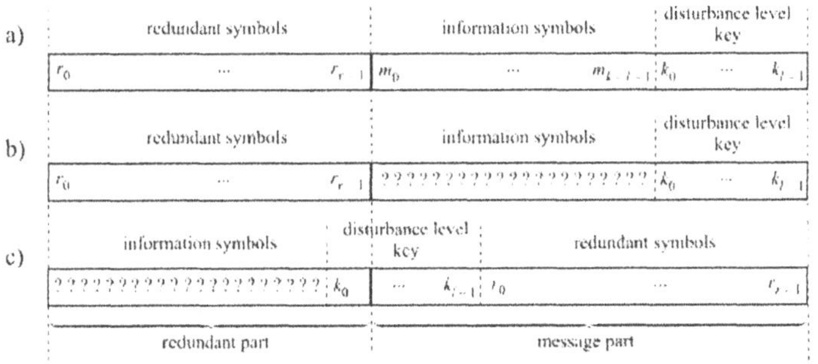

Fig. 3. Structure of the codeword a) at sender side, b) at recipient side before the cyclic shift, and c) at recipient side after cyclic shift.

Ecrypted shortcut message polynomial $z_{ws}^{(i)}(x)$ is concatenated to the information polynomial $m^{(i)}(x)$, what in result give us the information part polynomial $m_{inf}^{(i)}(x)$. This last polynmial is finally encoded using generating polynomial $g_2(x)$ of nonsystematic cyclic Reed-Solomon code, what give us the cryptogram polynomial. The algorithm of encryption is shown on fig. 4.

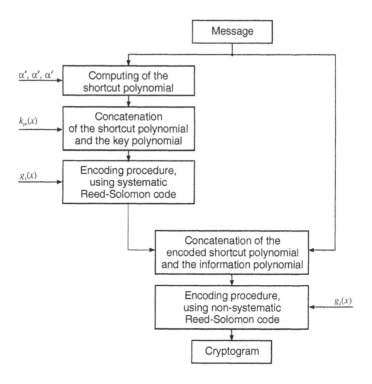

Fig. 4. The Algorithm of encryption

In the decryption procedure, the coefficients of the shortcut polynomial $w'^{(i)}_s(x)$ are recreated. Nextly, in the result of the comparison of the received and recreated polynomial $w^{(i)}_s(x)$ computed by the recipient, one can find that the form of the information polynomial $m'^{(i)}(x)$ is the same as the form of the polynomial $m^{(i)}(x)$ which is sended by the sender. The algorithm of decryption is shown on the fig. 5.

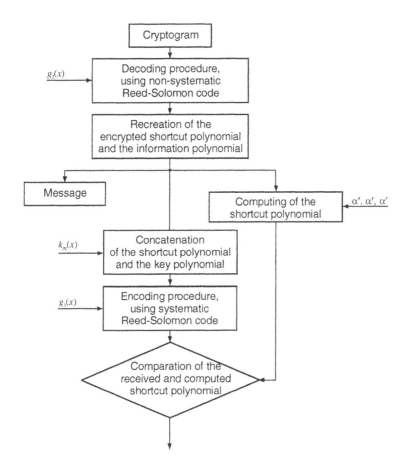

Fig. 5. The algorithm of decryption

By using of two codes, defined by the polynomials $g_1(x)$ i $g_2(x)$ there is a posibility of assertion, if the received block of cryptogram, which in fact consists of the Reed-Solomon cyclic codeword, generated with the $g_2(x)$ polynomial, is decoded correctly. However applying of two codes of high correcting properties results the decreasing of the transmission speed, because transmitted message have to be splitted to the smaller parts. This is the consequence of the fact, that the bigger correcting property requires less information symbols in the codeword.

4 Conclusions

The presented cryptosystem, by mean of using two redundant codes, allows to fulfil the confidentiality, the authentitcity and, what is the most important, also the accessibility of information. The application of error correction is the most advisable in the systems, which are used to the making of decision, i.e. systems, in which the information "life time" is not big, while the information have to be delivered to the valid user, right on time, and the information have to be credible.

Applying of two codes allows to detect the noice level of the communication channel. This means, that one can detect the wrong proceeding of the detection procedure, in which we obtain different codeword of the same code.

The providing the comuptations in isomorphic galois field $GF(q)$, by mean of using the theory of finite fields isomorphy, fulfils the high level of the confidentiality, because it allows to obtain the maximum number of the code generator polynomials $g(x)$ which determine the code over $GF(q)$. The number of the tables of arithmetic operations in isomorphic finite field $GF(q)$ is comparable with the number of operations required for key breaking in asymmetric public-key cryptosystems. Thus the generator poylomial $g(x)$ is treated as the cryptographic key, and the codeword obtained from the encoding procedure of cyclic nonsystematic Reed-Solomon code is an equivalent of cryptogram.

5 References

[1] T. Hebisz, Cz. Kościelny. *A method of constructing symmetric-key block cryptosystem resistant to manipulations on ciphertext*. Bulletin of the Polish Academy of Sciences, Technical Sciences, Vol. 50, No. 4, 2002.

[2] T. Hebisz, E. Kuriata, M. Jackiewicz. *Fulfillment of computer security and safety by using symmetric-key block cryptosystem resistant to manipulations on ciphertext*. International Conference on Computer Information Systems and Industrial Management Applications CISIM '03, 2003.

[3] A. Kiayias, M. Yung *Polynomial Reconstruction Based Cryptography*. SAC 2001. ICALP 2002. LNCS 2259. pp. 129-133. Springer-Verlag. 2002.

[4] A. Kiayias, M. Yung *Cryptographic Hardness Based on the Decoding of Reed-Solomon Codes*. Springer-Verlag. ICALP 2002. LNCS 2380. pp. 232-243. 2002.

[5] Cz. Kościelny, W. Mochnacki. *Kryptografia z zastosowaniem kodów cyklicznych*.
II Krajowa Konferencja Naukowo-Techniczna „Przetwarzanie sygnałów w telekomunikacji, sterowaniu i kontroli", Vol. 1, pp. 20-23, 1986.

[6] Cz. Kościelny. *Computing in the composite $GF(q^m)$ of characteristic 2 formed by means of an irreducible binomial*, International Journal of

Applied Mathematics and Computer Science, Vol. 8, No. 3, pp. 671-680, 1998.

[7]   Cz. Kościelny, T. Hebisz. *More secure computing in finite fields for cryptographic applications.* Mathematical Theory of Networks and Systems MTNS 2000, The fourteenth International Conference, Perpignan, 2000, CD-ROM.

[8]   E. Krouk. *A new Public Key Cryptosystem.* Proc. of Sixth Joint Swedish-Ruppian Intern. Workshop on Information Theory, 1993.

[9]   E. Kuriata. *Error correction codes in crytography.* VI Intern. conference "Wojskowa Konferencja Telekomunikacji i Informatyki", 1997 (in polish).

[10]   Y. X. Li, R. H. Deng, X. M. Wang. *On the equivalence of McEliece's and Niederreiter's public-key cryptosystems.* IEEE Trans. on Information Theory. Vol. 40. pp. 271-273. 1994

[11]   R. Lidl, H. Niederreiter. *Introduction to finite fields and their applications.* Cambridge University Prepp, 1986.

[12]   G. Marsaglia. *Statistical tests Diehard.* http://stat.fsu.edu/~geo/diehard.html.

[13]   R. J. McEliece. *A Public Key Cryptosystem Based on Algebraic Coding Theory.* JPLDSN Progrepp Rept., pp. 42-44, 1978.

[14]   A. J. Menezes, ed. *Application of Finite Fields.* Kluwer Academic Publishers, 1993.

[15]   H. Niederreiter. *Knapsak-type cryptosystems and algebraic coding theory,* Probl. Control and Inform. Theory, Vol. 15, 1986.

Protocol for Certificate Based Access Control Policies Description Language

Jerzy Pejaś, Paweł Sukiennik

Technical University of Szczecin
Faculty of Computer Science & Information Systems
ul. Żołnierska 49, 71-210 Szczecin, e-mails: {jpejas, psukiennik}@wi.ps.pl

Abstract: Access control in wide distributed networks has to be separated into domains in order to make it easily scalable and manageable. The management system also has to be automated to reduce complexity. Role based access control allows to achieve this goal, however adding public key infrastructure to RBAC approach would expand system capabilities in many ways. One of them is ability to specify certificate–based policies, which allow to access system resources by users form un-trusted sources. Adding digital signature to policies increases system security. This paper describes communication protocol in certificate based access control system, based on XACML standard described in [1].

Key words: certificate-based access control, role-based access control, domain, policy, digital signature, PKI, PMI, and XACML.

1   Introduction

Among three developed access control types: discretionary, mandatory and role–based, the last one has generated the most significant interest in recent years. The main reason for this tendency is the growth of the networks, and thus increase in complexity of these systems. Usage of RBAC can in many ways simplify security management:

- one or more roles can be assigned to one or many domains. Domain can contain one to many users. Each role specifies permissions for one or many targets,

- adding new system resources or subjects requires assigning them to existing domain or domains (scalability),

- user can delegate roles to other users if one has permission to do so (delegation of duties),

- roles and privileges are easily understandable, therefore system management is not complicated,

- support for negative or positive policy specification,

- defining role hierarchies allows implementing inheritance of the privileges.

Furthermore, many recent systems require authorization of users from un-trusted sources or users unknown to the system. Use of Public Key Infrastructure and Privilege Management Infrastructure allows extending capabilities of role based access control. PKI allows authentication of subject who has his certificate. Certificate authority service verifies trust to the holder of the certificate. Formal logic for certificate based access control has been presented in [10].

It is also essential to verify privilege attributes of the user. Even if user is authenticated he or she can still be not authorized to access specific system resources. Privilege Management Infrastructure allows verifying subject's attributes. Attribute Certificates maintain a binding between user's name and his privilege attributes. Use of X.509 Attribute Certificate in role based access control system was proposed in [3].

To extend the flexibility of the access control system the use conditions need to be specified. System resources or capabilities can vary depending on time of day or other conditions of the environment. Defined in [11] Use Condition Certificates contain digitally signed conditions that must be met by user to perform certain actions on certain targets. The stakeholder specifies the use conditions.

There are many elements, which must be included in such access-controlled system. Two main parts are: policy management system and the certificate management system. Because both of these systems need to communicate with each other communication protocol must be defined. This article in particular describes a communication protocol based on XML standard in certificate based access control system. Architecture for certificate based access control system was proposed in [8] and [9].

2 XML based access control language

XML is a platform-independent standardized markup language. It can be used in many environments. Because of this feature it is nowadays widely used in many domains of computer science, especially in that are web-based. It does not only define the format of a document but also allows validating it. Validation is achieved by parsing XML instance, which verifies if it is formatted as defined in Document Type Definition associated witch that document. XML does not only show the contents of data but also the constrains and relationship between data [6].

Described in [1] XACML is a general-purpose access control policy language. It provides syntax defined in XML for managing access to resources. There are some other languages for access control systems, but some points are in favor for XACML [2]:

- it's standard, therefore it is used by other developers and can be easily understood by them,
- it's generic, which means it is platform-independent and can be used in any environment,
- it's distributed – one policy can be referred to other policy kept in other locations,
- it's powerful, which means it can be extended for example to other standards like LDAP.

The root of all XACML policies is made of Policy or a Policy Set. Policy is a set of rules representing single access control policy. A Policy Set is constructed from other policies or policy sets. Access control system is composed of following items:

- Policy Administration Point (PAP) – unit in which policies and policy sets are created,
- Policy Decision Point (PDP) – entity that makes decision point based on evaluated policies,
- Policy Enforcement Point (PEP) – performs access control, by making decision request and authorization decisions,
- Policy Information Point (PIP) – source of attribute values.

Main elements of the XACML syntax:

- <Policy> - entity which is presented to PDP for evaluation
- <Target> - identifies set of decision requests
- <Subjects> - identifies whom requests concerns
- <Resources> - identifies resources in the system to which access is asked for
- <Rule> - identifies individual rule in the policy
- <Condition> - a boolean function over subject, resource, action, and environment attributes.
- <Actions> - identifies actions to be taken
- <Apply> - applies a function to its arguments

Figure 1 presents a sample policy written in XACML. This policy says that it only applies to requests for the resource "Printer" and it permits to access this resource only if subject does log in.

```
<Policy PolicyId="SamplePolicy">
  <Target>
    <Subject>
      <AnySubject/>
    </Subject>
    <Resources><ResourceMatch MatchId="string-equal">
      <AttributeValue>Printer</AttributeValue>
    </ResourceMatch MatchId></Resources>
  </Target>
  <Rule RuleId="LoginRule" Effect="Permit">
    <Target>
      <Subject> <AnySubject/> </Subject>
      <Resources><AnyResources/></Resources>
      <Actions><ActionMatch MatchId="string-equal">
        <AttributeValue>login</AttributeValue>
      </ActionMatch></Actions>
    </Target>
</Policy>
```

Fig.1 Sample XACML policy.

3 Certificate Based access control

It is possible to extend proposed access system with certificates, attribute certificates and use conditions. In order to assure compatibility of access control system and certificate service XML will also be used. XML Signature Standard described in [4] proposes standard for representation of X.509 based certificates and attribute certificates in XML. There is also related work concerning RBAC Policies in XML for X.509 certificates described in [3].

Certificate Based Access Control System described in [8] and [9] is made of three main units:

- policy management point,
- certificate service,
- domain server.

Simplified system architecture is shown in Figure 2. All system information are stored in LDAP service (*Lightweight Directory Access Protocol*) e.g. system structure ,domain hierarchy. The management concole is uded for assigning roles and policies or policy sets to subjects. Policies and policy sets are written in a policy editor. Policy editor and management console use domain browser to simplify system management. Policy management system uses data stored in LDAP service and Certificate service to make responses to access requests send by the subject. Policy management system uses external Certificate Authority to validate certificates of users unknown to the system.

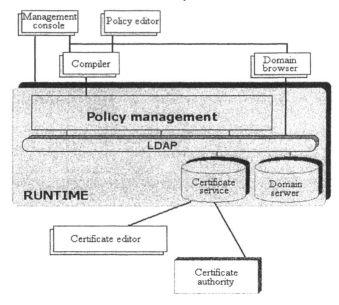

Fig.2 Certificate based access control system architecture

Policy management system is described below.

4   Communication protocol

Based on data flow diagram presented in [1] we have introduced certificates, attribute certificates and use conditions to create certificate based access control system. It allows to sing access request send by the subject, as well as policies and policies sets defined by stakeholder. Users certificates are used do verify his/her authenticity and attributes.

We have introduced Validation service, which is responsible for validation of all request (e.g. request authorization, policy authorization). It is important to ensure security for the system, therefore at the beginning of each session communication between services will be established. During this a key pair will be generated for each of the services. The mechanism is presented below.

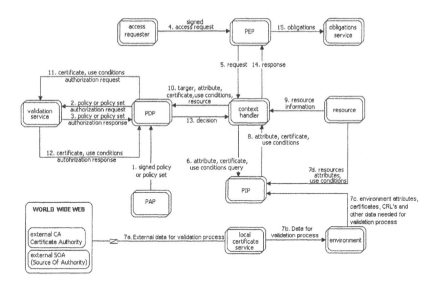

Fig.3. Modified Policy management system for Certificate based access
control

Presented in Figure 3 model operates as follows:

1. Policy Administration Point (PAP) defines policies and policy sets. These
    are signed with his private key, therefore if intruder tries to define his
    policies which would allow him to access system resources they would
    be rejected because only authorized useres can define policies or policy
    sets.

2. Policy Definition Point (PDA) sends policy or policy set authorization
    requests along with its signature to validation service, which then verifies
    if policies were issued by authorized subject. Policy authorization request
    syntax is presented in Figure 4.

```
<xs:element name="AuthRequest" type="xacml-context:RequestType"/>
<xs:complexType name="RequestType">
  <xs:sequence>
    <xs:element ref="xacml-context:PolicySet"/>
    <xs:element ref="xacml-context:Policy"/>
    <xs:element ref="xaxml-context:Signature"/>
  </xs:sequence>
</xs:complexType>
```

Fig.4 Policy authorization request syntax

3. At the begining of each session PDP and Validation service generate a
    key pair for communication. For policy or policy set received in
    authorization request, validation service creates unique MAC, which is
    then send back to PDP. MAC is generated from the validation result with

Validation serwice key. PDP generates own MAC value from its own key and then compares it with MAC received form Validation service. If they are the same, the policy or policy sets are valid and are added to policy definitions stored by PDP. Policy authorization response syntax is presented in Figure 5.

```
<xs:element name="AuthResponse" type="xacml-context:ResponseType"/>
<xs:complexType name="ResponseType">
  <xs:sequence>
    <xs:element ref="xaxml-context:MAC"/>
  </xs:sequence>
</xs:complexType>
```

Fig.5 Policy or policy set authorization response syntax

4. Access requester sends signed access request to policy enforcement point to grant an access to a specific resource. Access request contains a unique number to prevent resending authorization request by intruder. PEP stores unique numbers from each received policy, therefore, if intruder resends captured policy it will be rejected by PEP. Signed access request context syntax is presented in figure 6.

```
<xs:element name="Request" type="xacml-context:RequestType"/>
<xs:complexType name="RequestType">
  <xs:sequence>
    <xs:element ref="xacml-context:Subject" maxOccur="unbounded"/>
    <xs:element ref="xacml-context:Resource"/>
    <xs:element ref="xacml-context:Action"/>
    <xs:element ref="xacml-context:Environment" minOccurs="0"/>
    <xs:element ref="xacml-context:Signature"/>
    <xs:element ref="xacml-context:UniqueNumber"/>
  </xs:sequence>
</xs:complexType>
```

Fig.6 Singed access request context syntax

5. Policy enforcement point sends request to context holder.

6. Context holder sends query to policy information point to gather required information about surrounding, that is: the resource, environment, validation data.

7. Policy information point receives: subject's attributes and certificate from certificate service send by environment, environment attributes, resource attributes and use conditions. If subject is unknown to the system, local certificate service receives it's certificate from external Certificate Authority. Local certificate service also gathers information required for validation, e.g. CRL's.

8. Policy information point sends gathered information to context handler

9. Resource send it's information to context handler

10. Context handler sends target, subject's attribute and certificate, environment attributes, and resource use conditions, attributes and other required validation information to policy definition point

11. Policy definition point verifies received information by sending request to certificate service.

12. Validation service sends response MAC back to policy definition point.

13. If policy definition point generated MAC is the same as received from validation service it sends it's positive decision to context handler if not, negative decision is sent.

14. Context handler sends its response to policy enforcement point

15. Policy enforcement point sends its obligations to obligation service, which then grands access to subject if decision was positive, or denies to grant access for negative decision made by PDP.

Presented signed policy context syntax includes types specific for certificate based access systems, which could follow XML – signature standard.

5 Sample policy

Presented in Figure 6 sample policy example for resource 'printer'. Its target says, that the policy applies only for the server called 'printer'. The policy has a rule, which specifies, that a subject has to have valid attributes to be able to print on this target (printer).

There are many credentials that could be included in a single policy. For example it could be certain time of the day, when user can use the target. It could be use conditions (e.g. user having certain attributes can have video conference if available transfer rate is grater than 1 Mb/s).

Presented in Figure 6 samples contains specific information:

Lines 002 – 009: specifies policy target

Lines 003 – 005: specifies subject for target, any subject in this case

Lines 003 – 008: specifies resource of target, a Printer

Lines 010 – 024: specifies a rule in policy

Lines 011 – 023: specifies a target for rule

Lines 012 – 018: specifies rule's subject, in this case any subject who will give valid Attributes

Lines 019 – 019: specifies resources for role – all resources in target

Lines 020 – 022: specifies what actions shuld be taken for the role – authentication

```
001: <Policy PolicyId="SampleAuthorizationPolicy">
002:   <Target>
003:     <Subject>
004:       <AnySubject/>
005:     </Subject>
006:     <Resources><ResourceMatch MatchId="string-equal">
007:       <AttributeValue>Printer</AttributeValue>
008:     </ResourceMatch MatchId></Resources>
009:   </Target>
010:   <Rule RuleId="GetAttributes" Effect="Permit">
011:     <Target>
012:       <Subject>
013:         <SubjectMatch MatchId="GetAttributes">
014:           <Apply>
015:             <Apply FunctionId="subject-get-attributes"/>
016:           </Apply>
017:         </SubjectMatch>
018:       </Subject>
019:       <Resources><AnyResources/></Resources>
020:       <Actions><ActionMatch MatchId="string-equal">
021:         <AttributeValue>authenticate</AttributeValue>
022:       </ActionMatch></Actions>
023:     </Target>
024:   </Rule>
025: </Policy>
```

Fig. 6. Sample Authorization policy.

6 Conclusion and further work

In the paper we have shown, that combining of XACML and XML signature standard can lead to specification of high level, powerful certificate based access control language. The protocol for the communication can be very effective and errors prove. By introducing certificates to role based access control high flexibility can be achieved. Not only users known to the system can be authorized and authenticated, but also users from un-trusted sources, who are not known to the system. Public Key Infrastructure and Privileged Management Infrastructure can achieve this.

The detailed implementation of presented protocol is the next step. All certificate services will be implemented using OpenCA. Open LDAP will be used to store network information. XACML allows us to specify policy and policy sets and XML Schema for signature all required information for validation services.

7 References

[1] Simon Godik, Tim Moses. 2003. *eXtensible Access Control Markup Language (XACML) Version 1.0.* Oasis Open 2003.

[2] A Brief Introduction to XACML. Sun Microsystems 2003.

[3] D.W. Chadwick, A. Otenko RBAC Policies in XML for X.509 Based Privileges Management, University of Salford

[4] M. Bartel, J. Boyer, B. Fox, B. LaMacchia, E. Simon *XML Signature Syntax and Processing*, W3C Recommendation 2002.

[5] R. Chandramouli Specification and Validation of Enterprise Access control Data for Conformance to Model and Policy Constrains, NIST Computer Security Division

[6] X. Zhang, J. Park, R. Sandhu *Schema Based XML Security: RBAC Approach*, 17th IFIP 11.3 Working Conference on Data and Application Security, Estes Park, Colorado, USA August 4-6

[7] R. Chandramouli *Application of XML Tools for Enterprise-Wide RBAC Implementation Tasks*, NIST Computer Security Division

[8] J. Pejaś, P. Sukiennik *Access Control Description Language in Wide Distributed Systems*, VI Krajowa Konferencja Naukowo-Techniczna. Diagnostyka Procesów Przemysłowych.

[9] P. Sukiennik Framework for Certificate-Based Access Control Policies Description Language Ponder, Advanced Computer Systems 2003.

[10] M. Kurkowski, J. Pejaś *A Propositional Logic for Access Control in Distributed Systems*, in Artificial Intelligence and Security in Computing Systems, Kluwer Academic Publishers, Boston/Dordrecht/London 2003

[11] J. Pejaś *Certificate-Based Access Control Policies Description Language*, in Artificial Intelligence and Security in Computing Systems, Kluwer Academic Publishers, Boston/Dordrecht/London 2003

Impact of the address changing on the detection of pattern sensitive faults

**Bartosz Sokol[1], PhD eng Ireneusz Mrozek[2],
Prof. Dr hab Wiaczeslaw Yarmolik[3]**

[1] Bialystok Uuniversity of Technology, Wiejska 45A street, 15-351 Bialystok,
Poland, imrozek@ii.pb.bialystok.pl, bsokol@ii.pb.bialystok.pl
[2,3] The University of Finance and Management in Bialystok branch in Elk,
Grunwaldzka 1, Elk,Poland, yarmolik@gw.bsuir.unibel.by

Abstract: This paper introduces a new concept for memory testing based on transparent memory tests in terms of pattern sensitive faults detection with different address order generation technique. It is commonly known, that only march tests can be in use now to test modern memory chips. Every march test algorithm can be applied in different ways and still be effective to detect target faults. Using properties of Degrees of Freedom in march testing [6] such as address changing, we can detect Pattern Sensitive Faults (PSF). Combination of march tests with proposed technique allows us to detect all memory faults, including PSF, with a high probability. Used tests are more effective and in many cases, experimental studies even show a higher efficiency of use of simple march tests in connection with proposed technique.

Keywords:memory testing, pattern sensitive faults, march tests

1   Introduction

Testing semiconductor memories is becoming a major cost factor in the production of modern memory chips; hence the selection of the most appropriate test, technique and particular set of fault models become increasing importance. In addition, tests with high defect coverage for realistic faults and with an acceptable test length are required.

Modern computer systems typically contain a variety of embedded memory arrays like caches, branch prediction tables or priority queues for instruction execution [4]. Fault free memory operations are crucial for the correct behaviour of the complete system, and thus, efficient techniques for production testing as well as for periodic maintenance testing are mandatory to guarantee the required quality standards. However, advances in memory technology and in system design turn memory testing into more and more challenging problem.

1.1 Classification of memory faults

We can divide memory faults on the bases of a number of cells being faulty into one-cell faults (e.g. stuck-at faults, transition faults) and multiple cells faults (e.g. coupling faults), which are more difficult to detect. The general case of fault belonging to the second group is Pattern Sensitive Fault (PSF). A cell (base cell) is said to have a PSF if its value gets altered as a result of certain pattern of 0s and 1s, 0->1 transition, or 1->0 transition in a group of other cells called the cell's neighborhood. Three types of PSFs can be distinguished:

Active PSF: the base cell changes its contents due to a change in the neighborhood pattern. This change consists of a transition in one neighborhood cell, while remaining neighborhood cells and the base cell contain a certain pattern

Passive PSF: the content of the base cell cannot be changed due to a certain neighborhood pattern.

Static PSF: the content of a base cell is forced to a certain state due to a certain neighborhood pattern

Pattern Sensitive Faults arise primarily from the high component densities and the related effect of unwanted interacting signals. As a RAM density increases, the cells become physically closer, and PSFs become the predominant faults. Moreover, other faults classes such as stuck-at faults, transition faults and coupling faults can be regarded as special types of PSFs. Because of address line scrambling, done to minimize the silicon area and the critical path length, the effective detection of pattern sensitive faults depends on having scrambling information [2]. However this information may not always be available. It may not be published by producers of memory or it can undergo changes (ex. for reconfigured RAM, after reconfiguration, the logical neighborhood of the memory cells may no longer be same as physical neighborhood). That is why it is not always possible to use tests, which take advantage of scrambling information. In this paper we propose to use properties of Degrees of Freedom in march testing and march tests to detect PSF [6]. The suggested technique is based on transparent march tests with different address order based on LFSR (Linear Feedback Shift Register) generation technique. We use the most commonly applied tests in the process of memory testing. Their main advantages are as follows:

- high fault coverage;
- linear complexity – O(N), where N – memory size

Moreover these tests can be easy transformed into transparent tests according to [3]. It enables us to use them in a cyclic transparent memory test with different address order.

2   Detection of pattern sensitive faults with address changing

According to [7] it can be stated that all march tests that cover Coupling Faults cover SAFs and TFs too. It should be noticed that CFs can be regarded as special types of PSFs Therefore it can be stated that the relation (1) is true.

$$P(SAF) > P(TF) > P(CF) > PF(PSF3) > P(PSF5) > P(PSF9) \qquad (1)$$

where $P(F)$ – probability of detection of fault F, and $PSFn = minimum$ $(P(APSFn), P(SPSFn), P(PPSFn))$.

According to (1) if we say that a probability of detection of PSF3 by certain test equals P, this means that the same test detects SAFs, TFs and CFs with probability at least equal P too [8].

2.1   Generation of "orbit"

When we change a content of memory cells, the different multiple faults can be activated, and part of faults will not be activated. In such case, some multiple faults will be activated during the generation of $k+1$ states in k cells. Studying the efficiency of memory systems tests, we have to take under consideration complexity of generating all 2^k combination for k memory cells, which is an essential, and in many cases sufficient condition, which allow us to detect different multiple faults given by a parameter k. To present above mentioned statement, MATS test [1] $\{\Uparrow(ra, wa^*); \Updownarrow(ra^*)\}$ is going to be considered. Let's take four memory cells ($k=4$) with addresses λ, μ, ν, π and increasing address order. Let's mark it as: $a_\lambda, a_\mu, a_\nu, a_\pi, a_i \in \{0,1\}$, $i \in \{\lambda, \mu, \nu, \pi\}$, a_i^* is a complementary value of a_i. As a result of one–time use of MATS test, we obtain five different states in four cells:

$$
\begin{array}{cccc}
a_\lambda & a_\mu & a_\nu & a_\pi \\
a_\lambda^* & a_\mu & a_\nu & a_\pi \\
a_\lambda^* & a_\mu^* & a_\nu & a_\pi \\
a_\lambda^* & a_\mu^* & a_\nu^* & a_\pi \\
a_\lambda^* & a_\mu^* & a_\nu^* & a_\pi^*
\end{array}
$$

Fig. 1. Five different states after use of MATS test.

In case of address order changing, following example present this situation. Let's take four memory cells with addresses λ, μ, v, π (address order: $\mu \rightarrow \lambda \rightarrow \pi \rightarrow v$) and initial states a_λ, a_μ, a_v, a_π, $a_i \in \{0,1\}$, $i \in \{\lambda, \mu, v, \pi\}$, a_i^* is a complementary value of a_i. As a result of one – time use of MATS test, we get five different states in four cells:

$$
\begin{array}{cccc}
a_\lambda & a_\mu & a_v & a_\pi \\
a_\lambda & a_\mu^* & a_v & a_\pi \\
a_\lambda^* & a_\mu^* & a_v & a_\pi \\
a_\lambda^* & a_\mu^* & a_v & a_\pi^* \\
a_\lambda^* & a_\mu^* & a_v^* & a_\pi^*
\end{array}
$$

Fig. 2. Five different states after use of MATS test with different address order.

When we consider the case of memory test phase with one read operation, during one phase, k-memory cells run through k different patterns. Let's define this set of patterns as an *"orbit"*. We can get different orbits as an effect of:

- initial state changing – using 3rd Degree of Freedom (DOF): if the march test is built symmetrically, the data written to the cells can be changed completely [6];

- address order changing – using 1st and 2nd DOF: the address sequence can be freely chosen as long as all addresses occur exactly once and the sequence is reversible (1st DOF); the address sequence for initialization can be freely chosen as long as all addresses occur at least once [6];

- using more complex march tests.

The following statements are true for orbits (O).

Statement 1: There are 2^k distinct orbits for 2^k initial states in k arbitrary memory cells.

Statement 2: In one orbit O different patterns exist.

Statement 3: There are no two identical orbits O_i and O_j with the same patterns for different initial states $i \neq j$.

Statement 4: The minimum number $min_l(O)$ of orbits received as a result of background changes, essential to obtain all possible 2^k patterns should satisfy to the inequality:

$$
min_l(O) \geq \left\lfloor \frac{2^k}{k+1} \right\rfloor, \quad k = 1,2,3, \ldots \tag{2}
$$

Statement 5: There are $k!$ different orbits for k arbitrary memory cells with constant initial state and random address order.

For larger values of k, quantity of orbits generated during address order changing is significantly bigger than a quantity of orbits obtained during background changing. Except this, we should add, that in case of address order changes, in every orbit the first and the last patterns are the same.

For example for k=3 we have 6 different orbits:

$O0$ 1-2-3			$O1$ 1-3-2			$O2$ 2-1-3			$O3$ 2-3-1			$O4$ 3-1-2			$O5$ 3-2-1		
0	0	0	0	0	0	0	0	0	0	0	0	0	0	0	0	0	0
1	0	0	1	0	0	0	1	0	0	1	0	0	0	1	0	0	1
1	1	0	1	0	1	1	1	0	0	1	1	1	0	1	0	1	1
1	1	1	1	1	1	1	1	1	1	1	1	1	1	1	1	1	1

Fig. 3. Six different orbits for k=3 cells.

Statement 6: There are different patterns in specific orbit O.

Statement 7: Do not exist two orbits O_i and O_j with the same patterns.

Statement 8: The minimum number $min_2(O)$ of orbits received in result of address order changes, essential to obtain all possible 2^k patterns should satisfy to the inequality:

$$min_2(O) \geq \left\lfloor \frac{(2^k - 2)}{k - 1} \right\rfloor, k = 2,3,4, \ldots \tag{3}$$

Proofs of above mentioned statements are presented in [9].

2.2 Memory cell address generation technique

During the studies of efficiency of march test with reference to PSF, we have to consider two different ways of address changing:

- Random address order
- Address order based on LFSR.

First approach consists on use of march test 2^n times with different address order, put in random way. In the second approach, testing session consists of one-time use of march test, while each test phase was performed 2^n times longer according to addresses generated by LFSR.

Address order generation for 4 cells memory with LFSR is presented on the figure 4.

222

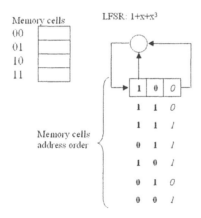

Fig. 4. Address order generation with LFSR for k = 4 memory cells.

Polynomial degree is calculated according to equation (4):

$$d = log_2N + n \tag{4}$$

where N is a memory size and n is a number, which extend the polynomial degree and allows us to generate more addresses, and repeat testing procedure in a cell, which was already checked. We can use polynomial with higher degree to generate addresses, which was already visited and check each cell again (number of repeated addresses depends on polynomial degree). When we consider the number of polynomials used to generate addresses, following situations are true.

When we use 2 polynomials with degree n, we generate twice different address order and we have to remember it. Instead of this situation, we can use one polynomial with $n+1$ degree, and generate all addresses only once. The same situation is with 4 polynomials with degree n. We have to use four different LFSR's and remember four different address orders. Otherwise we can use a polynomial with $n+2$ degree and use it only once and generate all addresses 4 times.

In our experiment we compared the efficiency of memory march testing with the first addressing technique (random address order) to the efficiency of memory march testing with the second addressing technique (with extended LFSR).

3 Experimental results

It is commonly known, that all march tests detect some percentage of complex faults. Obviously, using only one test many times with different initial conditions, we can detect all or the very high percentage of faults.

Evaluation of efficiency of multiple use of test can be checked on example of Pattern Sensitive Faults, because all simple faults can be detected with one-time use of test. In our experiment we randomly change an address order once with random generation, twice with LFSR generation.

To present above mentioned experiments, MARCH LA and MATS ++ tests [1] were considered.

Table 1 shows probability of SPSF5 detection in different iterations, depending on random address changing.

No. of iterations	Probability of SPSF5 detection		
	March LA	March C-	Mats++
1	0,269600	0,284500	0,128200
2	0,461075	0,467138	0,217100
4	0,672288	0,692788	0,316000
8	0,871575	0,873488	0,460700
10	0,919250	0,919750	0,500337
15	0,967487	0,973375	0,550275
20	0,986237	0,990200	0,569100
40	0,999587	0,999688	0,627387

Tab. 1. Probability of SPSF5 detection, depending on random address changing and the number of iterations.

Above presented results shows, that the probability of detection PSF is relative high after only a few iterations.

Next experiments based on comparison of tests with random addresses and LFSR addresses were realized. Results obtained from those experiments show growth of efficiency of tests with LFSR addressing technique. Comparison of results for MARCH LA and MATS++ is presented in table 2.

No. of iterations	Probability of SPSF5 detection			
	March LA		Mats++	
	Random addr.	LFSR addr.	Random addr.	LFSR addr.
2	0,43925	0,44443	0,22405	0,30085
4	0,65170	0,69785	0,35645	0,57005
8	0,84461	0,90065	0,54985	0,82885
16	0,96605	0,99095	0,74355	0,97483
32	0,99695	0,99975	0,85855	0,99932

| 64 | 0,99985 | 0,99998 | 0,90115 | 0,99998 |

Tab. 2. Probability of SPSF5 detection by March LA and MATS++ test using random and LFSR addressing

Figure 5 shows growth of efficiency of MATS++ test (in %) where LFSR technique was used. Similar results were obtained for other tests.

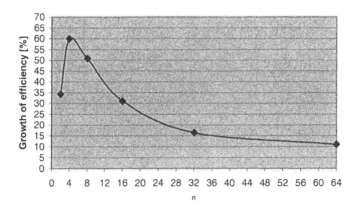

Fig. 5. Growth of efficiency of MATS++ test with LFSR address generation.

4 Conclusions and future researches

In this paper new approach to addresses generation in transparent march tests have been presented. According to obtained results it can be said that it is better to one-time use of test, while each test phase is performed 2^n times longer, then use of march test 2^n times with different address order put in random way. Moreover, with comparison to random addresses order technique schemes, presented approach can significantly reduces hardware overhead and at the same fault coverage.

The goal of future researches is to propose a new algorithms and techniques for memory addresses generation. The memory address A with the width m consist of m bits, so A=a1a2a3...am, where ai $\in$ {0,1}. According to the address algorithm we can get entire set of all 2^m addresses.

There is the strong requirement to generate all addresses in arbitrary order and the same seqence of addresses in inverse order for the memory test implementation. There are some traditional approaches such as:

1. Counter sequences

2. LFSR based sequences

3. Gray code sequences

4. Other combination of traditional solution 1,2,3.

In the future work we will investigate the problem of the different address sequences generation based on various techniques.

5 References

[1]   A.J. Van de Goor, "Testing semiconductor memories, theory and practice", John Wiley & Sons 1991, ISBN 0 471 92586 1.

[2]   K.L. Cheng., C.W. Wu, "Neighborhood Pattern-Sensitive Fault Testing for Semiconductor Memories", proc. VLSI Design/CAD Symp., Pingtung Aug. 2000, pp. 401-404.

[3]   M. Nicolaidis, "Transparent BIST for RAMs", Proc. IEEE Int. Test Conf., Baltimore, MD, Oct. 1992, pp. 598-607.

[4]   D.K. Bhavsar, J.H. Edmondson, "Alpha 21164 Testability Strategy", IEEE Design&Test, Vol. 14, No 1, January-March 1997, pp.25-33.

[6]   D. Niggemeyer, J.Otterstedt, M. Redeker, "Detection of Non classical Memory Faults using Degrees of Freedom in March Testing", Rec. 11th Workshop "Testmethods and Reliability of Circuits and Systems", Potsdam, Feb. 1999.

[7]   A.J. Van de Goor, G.N. Gaydadjiev, V.N. Yarmolik, V.G. Mikitjuk, "Memory Tests and their Fault Coverage into a New Perspective, Resulting into a New Test", SEMICON, Seul, Korea, Jan. 1996.

[8]   I. Mrozek, V.N. Yarmolik, "Detection of Pattern Sensitive Faults by Multiple Transparent March Tests", Mixed Design of Integrated Circuits and Systems, proc. 10th International Conference, Lodz 26-28 June 2003 - MIXDES'03, pp. 542-545.

[9]   B. Sokół, V.N. Yarmolik, "Wpływ zmian porządku adresów i zawartości na efektywność testów pamięci", proc. VII Krajowa Konferencja Naukowa, RUC'2004 Reprogramowalne Układy Cyfrowe", Szczecin 13-14 May 2004.

Software IP Protection Based on Watermarking Techniques

Vyacheslav Yarmolik
The University of Finance and Management in Bialystok branch in Elk
Grunwaldzka 1, Elk, Poland
e-mail: yarmolik10ru@yahoo.com

Siarhei Partsianka
Belorussian State University of Informatics and Radioelectronics
P. Brovki Str. 6, Minsk, Belarus
e-mail: sergeip@tut.by

Abstract: This paper focuses on software watermarking techniques and analysis of the executable code statistical characteristics as a mean of watermark embedding. As an application, several new approaches for executable code watermarking based on statistical characteristics variations have been proposed.

Keywords: Software watermarking, authorship, statistical characteristics

1   Introduction

The problem of protection of the software developer's right exists for many years already. First of all, this problem concerns applications available to users over the Internet. Violation of authorship may be caused by such actions as decompiling and reverse engineering. In most cases the goal of these attacks is gaining commercial edge over use of application's key algorithms in another software product. Thus, pieces of original application could be reused. In order to detect such cases of authorship violation in the field of digital images authorship protection, the technology named "digital watermarking" is used. Similar approaches haven't been achieved wide recognition in the field of software authorship protection yet, but this approach of development the software protection tools looks quite optimistic [1, 2].

2 Software statistical characteristics analysis

Main problem that appears during software watermarking is requirement to use only such transformations, which wouldn't change characteristics of original software modules such as executable code size and time of execution (time and space penalty).

The key idea of our proposal is based on statistical characteristics of executable code. In other words, watermark will be hidden as one of program statistical characteristics variations [3]. In order to estimate the capabilities of statistical characteristics to be used for watermarking we analyzed large amount of applications created for Win32 platform.

We were looking for statistical characteristics of program code, which are independent on program functionality and designated by such conditions as architecture of program execution environment, syntax correctness and performance requirements. Such characteristics are: the probability of certain instruction appearance, the probability that considered instruction will be followed by certain instruction, an average distance between the same instructions in a program code. Further we will focus on these characteristics.

The frequency of instruction was the first of program characteristic, which was taken for consideration. Fig.1 shows distribution of frequencies of appearance of 20 most often used assembler instructions obtained from 3 different DLL (Dynamic Link Library) modules.

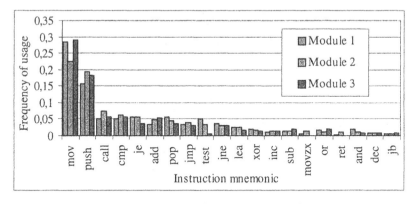

Fig. 1. Frequencies of assembler instructions

Distribution shown in Fig. 1 is strongly irregular. The most frequent operations for Intel x86 series assembler code are: data transfer commands (mov), unconditional control flow (jmp), procedure call (call), pushing values to stack (push). Experiments show, that this consistent pattern keeps constant for other analyzed programs with small deviations (Fig.1). This fact allows to make an assumption that frequencies of assembler instructions in general depend on program execution environment architecture.

We also analyzed dependence between the number of different commands and the total number of commands in program module. All modules were split on three groups: modules, which contain small number of commands; modules with intermediate number of commands; modules, containing large amount of commands. Each group was split on subgroups by such property as the number of different assembler instructions (size of alphabet). We determined that the most frequent combinations among the programs chosen for analysis were: small modules with small alphabet, modules with intermediate size and alphabet, big modules with large amount of different instructions. In all further experiments we used members from all three mentioned above sets.

We composed an alphabet containing 135 different instructions and assigned an index to each of them. Further, we calculated an average value of this index (m_x). Such calculations were performed for about 40 modules (.exe and .dll). Results are shown in Fig. 2.

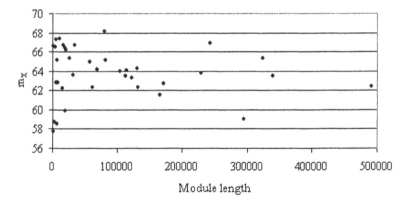

Fig. 2. Dependence between m_x and total number of commands in module

Obtained experimental data allows us to make conclusion that parameter m_x has no strong dependence on program functionality and varies in certain interval. Bounds of this interval are getting closer when the total number of instructions in program is growing. This consistent pattern related to parameter m_x is also observed when instead of analysis of the entire program (N instructions) we analyze the subset containing randomly chosen L instructions. Fig. 3 shows corresponding dependencies for $L=N$, $L=N/10$ and $L=N/100$ obtained for 18 program modules.

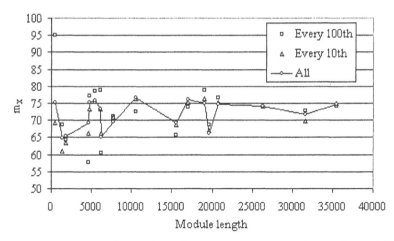

Fig. 3. Experimental dependency between m_x and program length obtained for entire program, 10% and 1% of its instructions

Experimental results let us to make conclusion that value of parameter m_x calculated for subset of program instructions also varies in certain interval. Experiments showed that for $L=N/100$ the value of m_x varies in interval 55 - 95.

Experiments showed that analysis of even 1 per cent of program instructions shows existence of consistent pattern. An important issue is determining of minimum L/N ratio when subset analysis remains reasonable. This is necessary for advisability estimation of different based on statistical characteristics watermark embedding methods. There is also an important question related to minimal size of watermarked program and minimal size of instructions alphabet used in it.

One more statistical characteristic of executable code is its autocorrelation function. Lets consider two programs: P and P'. Program P' is obtained from P by cyclical shift of its commands k times. Now if we compare P and P' and count coincidences of commands having the same positions - we will obtain certain value $S(k)$. Thus, if we will consider mentioned above instruction indices as an elements of random sequence, then $S(k)$ will describe its autocorrelation function. Fig. 4 shows an experimental dependency between shift value k and relative coincidence value $Sn(k)=S(k)/N$, where N is program length.

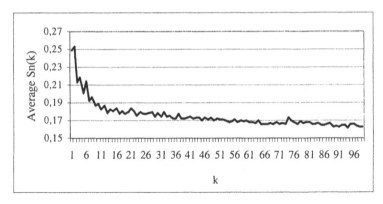

Fig. 4. Experimental dependency *Sn(k)* computed for 7 arbitrary taken programs

Experiments showed that starting with certain shift distance the percentage of coincidences remains approximately constant. For considered Win32 application we obtained the value of *Sn(k)* about 12 per cent for *k* grater than 2000.

We assumed, that such statistical characteristics as percentage of instruction coincidences calculated for certain shift value *k* also can be considered as parameter that keeps approximately constant value independently on program functionality. In order to check this assumption we analyzed over 40 Win32 program modules and calculated for each module the value *Sn(k)* for *k*=2000. Minimal size of studied module was about 700 commands and maximum – over 490.000. Obtained results shown in Fig. 5.

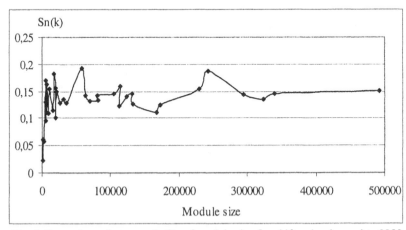

Fig. 5. Dependence between *Sn(k)* and module size for shift value *k* equal to 2000

Experimental data allows assumption that starting with program module size grater than, for example, 100.000 commands $Sn(k)$ varies in a fixed interval (0,1 – 0,2). Thus, if we analyze enough large amount of program modules, we can experimentally determine an interval of values in which parameter $Sn(k)$, calculated for arbitrary program, will be enclosed with high probability. Hence, $Sn(k)$ can be considered as one more statistical characteristic that remains approximately constant independently of analyzed program functionality.

3   Proposed watermarking algorithms

Given above results of experiments show that some statistical characteristics of program executable code have weak dependence on program functionality. This fact will be used for program watermarking. As the basis of all described below watermarking methods we propose to use the modifications of program statistical characteristics. Very similar approach is used in classical algorithm for raster images watermarking called "Patchwork" [4].

This approach is based on fact, that for any quite large number of randomly selected image pixels an average difference between the two selected in series pixels brightness (L_{ab}) is approximately equal to zero. The watermark is embedded by increment or decrement of some pixels brightness. The pixels whose brightness will be changed are selected using pseudorandom generator. The goal of these modifications is reaching of significant difference between new value of an average L_{ab} and the old one for considered set of pixels called "patch". Following steps checks the existence of certain watermark:

I. Using the secret key as initial seed for pseudorandom generator the coordinates of pixels, which belong to patch, are generated in the same way like it was done for watermark embedding;

II. For selected pixels an average L_{ab} is computed;

III. If obtained L_{ab} value is equal to zero, than the watermark is not exists, otherwise – the image contains watermark.

Use of other keys for watermark extraction will result selection of completely different pixel sets, which were not modified and has standard value of an average L_{ab}.

In order to adopt this approach for software watermarking we need to choose assembler code statistical characteristic, which can be used in the same way as L_{ab} in "Patchwork". Value of this characteristic must be constant or vary in known interval (like L_{ab} for raster images) for any arbitrary taken program [5]. Modifying this statistical characteristic we embed in a program a special sign, (watermark), which existence will in future help to prove the program ownership and determine its origin.

3.1   Use of command frequencies distribution

Experimental data reflected in Fig. 2 and Fig. 3 point to the fact, that an average instruction index (m_x), which is calculated for any quite big program, has value, which varies in certain interval. Thus, for any arbitrary selected program we can state with certain probability, that calculated for this program m_x value will be enclosed in, for example, interval equal to 60-80. Fig. 3 shows that the same consistent pattern is observed when instead of the entire program analysis we consider only certain pseudorandomly selected subset of L commands $(L<<N)$.

The key idea of proposed approach consists in modification of only such commands, which belong to L. The positions of these commands are generated by pseudorandom law using secret initial seed. Such modifications will affect instruction frequencies and therefore change m'_x (an average index of instructions, which belong to L), but m_x variations, which will be caused by them, will be undistinguishable. Watermark is embedded when absolute difference $|m_x - m'_x|$ is grater than some value ε. Hereby, because the positions of commands constituting L are computed using secret key, the watermark can be detected only by the person why knows this key.

3.2   Use of autocorrelation function

Our experiments showed, that for quite long shift distances (but less than program length divided by two) an average program has coincidences percentage about 12-15 % [6]. We propose to embed the watermark by means of program semantics-preserving transformations (instruction substitutions or instruction reordering). The goal of these modifications is to transform the program is such a way that its further pseudorandom modifications (using certain initial seed) will result extraordinary $S(k)$ values for certain shift distances. Mentioned above initial seed is kept in secret and therefore the watermark cannot be extracted without knowledge about its value.

4   Conclusions

In this paper the capabilities of statistical characteristics use for software authorship protection are shown. In particular, an implementation of adopted variant of "Patchwork" algorithm is considered. An assembler code autocorrelation function is shown as one of program statistical characteristics, which can be used for watermark embedding.

5 References

[1] Monden A., Iida H., Matsumoto K. A. 2000. 'Practical Method for Watermarking Java Programs', *The 24th Computer Software and Applications Conference (compsac2000), Taipei, Taiwan,* pp. 191-197.

[2] Collberg C., Thomborson C. 1999. 'Software Watermarking: Models and Dynamic Embeddings', *The 26th ACM SIGPLAN-SIGACT Symposium on Principles of Programming Languages,* Jan. 1999, pp. 311-324.

[3] Stern J.P., Hachez G., Koeune F., and Quisquater Jean-Jacques. 2000. 'Robust Object Watermarking: Application to Code', *In A. Pfitzmann, editor, Information Hiding '99, volume 1768 of Lectures Notes in Computer Science (LNCS), Dresden, Germany,* Springer-Verlag, pp. 368-378.

[4] Bender W., Morimoto G. N., Lu A. 1996. 'Techniques for data hiding', *IBM Syst. J.*- vol. 35, pp 313-336.

[5] Yarmolik V.N., Portyanko S.S. 2003. 'State of Art in Software Ownership Protection', *Computer Information Systems and Industrial Management Application, Editors: Khalid Saeed, Romuald Mosdorf, Olli-Pekka Hilmola. Bialystok, Poland,* pp. 188-195.

[6] Partsianka S.S., Yarmolik V.N. 2003. 'Software modules unauthorised use defense by means of watermarking', *Izvestiya Belorusskoi Inzhenernoi Akademii,* No 1(15)/3, pp. 163-165.

Probabilistic Analysis
of Operational Security for Network Systems

Jolanta Koszelew[1,2]

[1]The University of Finance and Management in Bialystok,
Faculty of Engineering

[2]Bialystok Technical University, Faculty of Computer Science,
e-mail: koszelew@pb.bialystok.pl

Abstract: Survivability is the ability of system to continue operating in the presence of failures or malicious attacks [4]. We present an original method for performing probabilistic analysis of survivability of network systems. We can simulate failures and intrusion events in our method and then observe the effects of the injected events. Our model is based on Markov Decision Processes which are generalization of Markov Chains and provides the analysis of probabilistic measures for network systems, such us: probability that a service that has been issued will be finished or the expected time it takes a service to finish. We illustrate the idea of our technigues by a simply example.

Keywords: Markov Decision Processes, Computation Tree Logic, Bayesian network.

1   Introduction

Survivability is the ability of system to continue operating in the presence of failures or malicious attacks.

Network systems, which are recently used, are exposed on a lot of accidental failures (e. g. a disk crash) and malicious attacks (e.g. denial of service attack). Disruption of services caused by such undesired events can have catastrophic effects, in particular if network system serves medical application.

A network system consists of nodes and links connecting the nodes. Communication between the nodes occurs by passing messages over the links. An event in the system can be either a user event, a communication event, or a fault. A service is associated with a given start event and an end event.

Our method can be used by the system architect to simulate the effect of a fault or to count probability that a service that has been issued will finish or expected time it takes a service to finish. With this information, the architect can weigh some decisions related to survivability of the designing system.

Survivability analysis is fundamentally different from analysis of properties found in other areas (e.g., algorithm analysis of fault-tolerant distributed systems, reliability analysis of hardware systems and security analysis of computer systems).

First, survivability analysis must handle a broader range of faults than any of these other areas; we must minimally handle both accidental and malicious attacks. Our method allows an architect to incorporate any arbitrary type of fault in the system model.

Second, events may depend on each other, especially fault events. In contrast, for ease of analysis, most work in the fault-tolerant literature makes independence assumption of events.

Third, survivability analysis should also be service dependent. The architect for a network system might choose to focus on the one select service as being critical, although the system provides other services.

Finally, survivability analysis deals with multiple dimensions. It simultaneously deals with functional correctness, fault-tolerance, security and reliability.

2 Formal Model

Model checking for our method is based on Markov Decision Processes (*MDP*) [1]. *MDP*s are a generalization of classic Markov chains, where the transition probabilities depend on the events in the history. A *MDP* is a 4-tuple $<S, A, P, c>$ where: S is a finite state space; A is a finite set of actions. P are transition probabilities, where $P_{sas'}$ is the probability of moving from state s to s' if action is chosen; $c : (S \times A) \to \Re$ is the immediate cost, i.e., $c(s,a)$ denotes the cost of choosing action a at the state s. For a state $s \in S$, $A(S) \subset A$ is the set of actions available at state s.

History at time t (denote by h_t) is the sequence of states encountered and actions taken up to time t. A policy u takes into account the history h_t and determines the next action at time t. Specifically, $u_t(a|h_t)$ is the probability of taking action a given history h_t. A policy u defines a value function $V^u : S \to \Re$, where $V^u(s)$ is the expected cost of the actions taken if the *MDP* uses policy u and starts in state s (the cost c is used to define expected cost). The technical definition of V^u can be found in [1]. Our aim is to find a policy that minimizes the value V^u.

3   Description of method

In this section we provide a detail overview of our model, illustrating it with a very simple example. We consider an abstract   model of exchange of secret information system, depicted in *Fig. 1*. There are three levels of organizations: the Agents on the bottom, the Contact Boxes and the Central Agencies at the top. If two Agents are connected to the same Central Agency, then the exchange of secret message between them are handled by the Contact Box; there is no need to go through the Central Agencies. To illustrate the architecture, suppose the Agent-*A* sends the secret message to the Agent-*C*. Because of Agents A and C have a different Contact Box, the message must be verify by the proper Central Agency.

Agent-A and Agent-C are not connected through the same Contact Box, so the message is then sent to the Contact box connected to Agent-A. In this case, let's choose Contact Box I.

1. The message is sent to the Central Agency closest to Contact Box I, in this case Central Agency II.
2. The message is then sent to the Central Agency that has jurisdiction over Agent-C, in this case Central Agency II.
3. The message finally makes it way to Agent-C through the Contact Box III.

We now present details of each step in our method illustrating them with the above example.

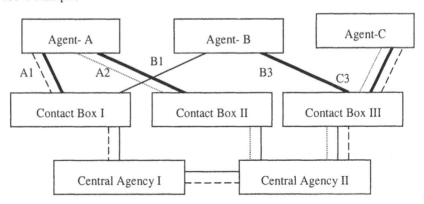

Legend:

▬▬▬   links that can be faulty,

──────   links that can not be faulty

──── ── ──   two possible tracks for message from Agent -A to Agent- C,

Xi   links between Agent-*X* and Contact Box *i* (A1, A2, B1, B3, C3).

Fig. 1 Secret Information System

3.1   Model of Network

First, the architect models a network system, which can be done using one of many formalisms. We choose to use state machines and we use them to model both network nodes and links. We use shared variables to represent communication between the state machines.

In our secret information system example, we use state machines to model the Agents, the Contact Boxes, the Central Agencies and links. We make some simplifying assumptions in the model of our system:

1. There is only one secret message active at any time.
2. The name of source and destination Agents are decided nondeterministically.

3.2   Assumptions for Faults

Both links and nodes may be faulty. With our state machine of the network system, we need not make a distinction between nodes and links when considering faults.

To represent faults in our method, for each state machine representing a node, we introduce a special variable called fault, which can range over a user-specified set of symbolic values. For example, the following declaration states that there are three modes of operation for a node, representing whether it is in the normal mode of operation, failed, or compromised by an intruder: fault ={ normal, failed, intruder}.

In our secret information system example, we inject the following faults:

1. Links between the Agents and the Contact Boxes are the only network elements that can be faulty. The Central Agencies and the Contact Boxes do not fail.
2. When a link is faulty, it blocks all messages and no message ever reaches the recipient.
3. Links may become faulty at any time. Therefore, we allow a nondeterministic transition to the state where fault is equal to failed. The intruded value is not used in this case.
4. Agents can sense a faulty link and route the message accordingly.
5. A service is associated with a *start event* (e.g. Agent sends a message to any other Agent) and an *end event* (e.g. Agent receives a message from any other Agent).

On the base of the above assumption we can conclude that the Central Agencies are impenetrable and links between them are highly reliable and secure.

Under the normal mode of operation, the Agent receives (nondeterministically) a message with its source address. Depending on the destination address of the message, the Agent either clears it locally or routes it to the appropriate Contact Box. For example, if a message from Agent-A to Agent-B is sent, then it is first sent to the Contact Box I and then sent to the Agent-B. On the other hand, the message from Agent-A to Agent-C has to clear through the Central Agency (as in *Fig. 1*). If an Agent is faulty, then message are routed arbitrarily by the intruder. Agent can then at any time nondeterministically transition from the normal mode to the intruder mode. Once the Agent is faulty it stays in that state forever.

3.3 Definition of Survivability Properties

We focus on two classes of these properties: fault and service related. We use *CTL* (Computation Tree Logic) [9] to specify survivability properties.

1. Faulty Related Properties: It is not possible for a node N to reach a certain unsafe state if the network starts from one of the initial states. The precise semantics of an unsafe state depends on the application. For example, if a node represents a computer protecting a critical resource, it could represent the fact that somebody without the appropriate authority has logged onto the computer. Let the atomic proposition unsafe state represent the property that node N is in an unsafe state. We can then express the desired property *CTL* as follows:

    $$\mathbf{AG}(\neg\text{unsafe}) \qquad (1)$$

    which says that for all states reachable from the set of initial states it is true that we never reach a state where unsafe is true. The negation of the property is

    $$\mathbf{EF}(\text{unsafe}) \qquad (2)$$

    which is true if there exists a state reachable from the initial state where unsafe is true.

2. Service Related Properties: Service issued always finishes. Let atomic proposition start express that a service was started, and finished express that the transaction is finished.

    $$\mathbf{AG}(\text{start} \rightarrow \mathbf{AF}\ (\text{finished})) \qquad (3)$$

    The above formula expresses that for all states where a service starts and all paths starting from that state there exists a state where the service always finishes. For secret information system example, we would like to verify that a message if sent is always eventually received.

The analysis of survivability properties can help identify the critical nodes in a network system. Suppose we have modeled the effect of a malicious attack on node N. Now we can check whether the desired properties are true in the modified network system. If the property turns out to be true, the network is resistant to the malicious attack on the node N.

3.4 Generate Scenario Graph

We automatically construct scenario graphs via model checking. A scenario graph is a compact representation of all traces that are counterexamples of a given property. These graphs depict ways in which a network can enter an unsafe state or ways in which a service can fail to finish. We can generate three kinds of scenario graphs: Fault Scenario Graph, Service Success Scenario Graph and Service Fail Scenario Graph.

First we describe the construction of Faulty Scenario Graph. We assume that we are trying to verify using model checker whether the specification of the network satisfies $\mathbf{AG}(\neg\text{unsafe})$. The first step in model checking is to determine the set of states S_r that are reachable from the initial state. Next, the algorithm determines the set of reachable states S_{unsafe} that have a path to an unsafe state. Then, we construct the set R_u which consists of transitions between unsafe states. Faulty Scenario Graph is $G = \langle S_{unsafe}, R_u \rangle$, where S_{unsafe} and R_u represents the nodes and edges of the graph respectively.

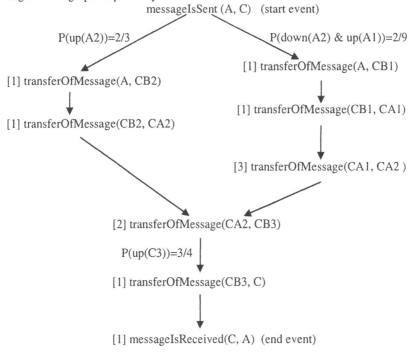

Fig. 2. A Simple Service Success Scenario Graph

For services we are interested in verifying that service started always eventually finishes. The Service Success Scenario Graph captures all the traces in which the service finishes. The Service Fail Scenario Graph captures all the traces in which the service fails to finish. These scenario graphs are constructed using a procedure similar to the one described for the Faulty Scenario Graph.

The scenario graph shown in *Fig. 2* shows the effect of link failures on the transfer of message service with source address Agent-A and destination address Agent-C. (Legend for *Fig. 2*: A, B, C – Agents; CB1, CB2, CB3 – Contact Boxes; CA1, CA2 – Central Agencies). The start event is labeled as messageIsSent(A, C) in the figure. The event corresponding to sending a message from location L1 to L2 is denoted as transferOfMessage(L1, L2). We also denote link between Agent-X and Contact Box n as Xn (A1, A2, B1, B3, C3) (*Fig. 1*). The predicates up(Xn) and down(Xn) indicates whether link Xn is up or down. Recall that we allow links to fail nondeterministically. Therefore, an event transferOfMessage(A, CB2) is performed only if A2 is up, i.e., up(A2) is the pre-condition for event transferOfMessage(A, CB2). If a pre-condition is not shown, it is assumed to be true. Note that a fault in a link can also be constructed as an intruder taking over the link and shutting it down. From the graph it is easy to see that a message is received if link A2 and link C3 are up, or if link A2 is down and link A1 and link C3 are up.

3.5   Probabilistic Properties Analysis

We have now a scenario graph and we can perform reliability and latency analysis. First, the architect specifies the probabilities of certain events of interest, such as faults, in the system. We do not assume independence of events and therefore we use formalism based on Bayesian networks [8]. Our scenario graph with probabilities produces an *MDP*. Then using *MDP* we compute reliability and latency by calculating the value function corresponding to the optimal policy.

First we calculate these properties for our example. We define probability event Xn which corresponds to link Xn being up and $\neg$Xn event which corresponds to link Xn being down. Assume that event $A2$ is dependent on $A1$ and there are no other dependencies. Let $P(A1)=2/3$ and $P(C3)=3/4$ where $P(A1)$ and $P(C3)$ are the probabilities of link A1 and link C3 being up. The probability of event $A2$ depends on the event $A1$, and we give its conditional probabilities as $P(A2|A1) = 2/3$ and $P(A2|\neg A1) = 1/3$ reflecting that if link A1 is down, it is more likely that link A2 will go down. If an event A depends on the set of two events $A1$ and $A2$, then we have to compute $P(A1|A1\cap A2)$, $P(A1|A1\cap\neg A2)$, $P(A1|\neg A1\cap A2)$ and $P(A1|\neg A1\cap\neg A2)$.

In our example, first we have to compute the probability of the two events $A2$ and $\neg A2\cap A1$. These events correspond to events up(A2) and down(A2) & up(A1).

$$P(A2) = P(A2|\neg A1) \cdot P(A2|A1) \cdot P(A1) = \frac{1}{3}\left(1 - \frac{1}{3}\right) + \frac{2}{3} \cdot \frac{2}{3} = \frac{2}{3}$$

$$P(\neg A_2 \cap A1) = P(\neg A2|A1) \cdot P(A1) = (1 - P(A2|A1)) \cdot P(A1) = \frac{2}{9}$$

(4)

We add these probabilities to the relevant edges of the scenario graph in *Fig. 2*. Since we might assign probabilities to only some events (typically faults) and not others, we obtain a structure that has a combination of purely nondeterministic and probabilistic transitions. In our example, the architect might assign probabilities only to events corresponding to faults. The user of the our example system still nondeterministically sends message.

We now explain the algorithm to compute reliability and latency by first considering a property about services. Let G be the Service Success Scenario Graph. Now, the goal of the environment is to devise an optimal policy or equivalently choose nondeterministic transitions in order to minimize reliability or maximize latency. We define a value function V assigns a value $V(s)$ for each state s in the scenario graph. Next we describe an algorithm to compute the value function V^p corresponding to this optimal policy. Later we explain how the value function can be interpreted as worst case reliability and latency.

1. Initial step: $V(s) = 1$ for each step which has the property finished and $V(s) = 0$ for others.
2. We compute $V(s)$ separately for probabilistic and nondeterministic states separately:

$$V(s) = \begin{cases} 1 & \text{if } s \text{ is finished state} \\ \min_{s' \in succ(s)} c(s \to s') + V(s') & \text{if } s \text{ is nondeterministic state} \\ \sum_{s' \in succ(s)} p(s, s')(c(s \to s') + V(s')) & \text{if } s \text{ is probabilistic state} \end{cases}$$

(5)

In definition given above, $succ(s)$ is the set of successors of state s and $p(s, s')$ is the probability of a transition from state s to s' and $c(s \to s')$ is the cost of edge $s \to s'$ in the scenario graph. Intuitively speaking, a nondeterministic move corresponds to the environment choosing an action to minimize the value. The value of a probabilistic state is the expected value of the value of its successors.

After the above algorithm converges, we end up with the desired value function V^p. Let s_0 be the initial state of the scenario graph.
- If the cost c, associated with the edges is zero, then $V^p(s_0)$ is the worst case reliability corresponding to the given property.
- If the cost c, associated with the edges corresponds to negative of the latency, then the value $-V^p(s_0)$ corresponds to the worst case latency of service.

In our example (*Fig. 2*) the worst case reliability using our algorithm is

$\left(\dfrac{3}{4}\cdot\dfrac{2}{3}\right)+\left(\dfrac{3}{4}\cdot\dfrac{2}{9}\right)=\dfrac{2}{3}$. That is, the worst case probability that a message which is sent by Agent-A is received by Agent-C is 2/3. Latency in days for all the events is shown in *Fig. 2* inside square brackets, e.g., latency of the event transferOfMessage(CA2, CB3) is 2 days. The worst case latency using our algorithm computes to be 4 days.

4   Final Remarks and Future Work

Survivability is a fairly new discipline, and viewed by many distinct from the security and faulty-tolerance areas [4]. The most famous method for analyzing the survivability of network architectures is *SNA* [4] methodology, which is recommended as the "best practices" to an organization on how to make their systems more secure or more reliable. In contrast, our method is formal, because it is based on model checking. Research on operational security by Ortolo, Deswarte, and Kaaniche [6] is closest to Step: Generate Scenario Graph of our method. Moreover, in our method a scenario graph corresponds to a particular service; in contrast their graph corresponds to a global model of the entire system. Besides, events in our model may be depend on each other, especially fault events.

There are many well known techniques which are used on verifying probabilistic systems and our algorithm for computing reliability draws on this work [3]. The novelty in our work is the systematic combination of different techniques into one method.

There are several directions for future work. First, we plan to implement the prototype tool that supports our method. We try to use *PrAl* semantics [7] in this implementation. *PrAl* is an algorithmic language special for projecting probabilistic systems. Since for real systems, scenario graph can be very large, we plan to improve the display query capabilities of our tool so architect can more easily manipulate its output. Finally, to make the fault injection process systematic, we are investigating how the best to integrate operational security analysis tools (cf. [5]) into our method.

5   References

[1]   Altman E.,"Constraint Markov Decision Processes", Champan and Hall, 1998

[2]   Clarke E. M., Grumberg O., Peled D, "Model checking", MIT Press, 2000

[3] Courcoubetis C., Yannakakis M., "The complexity of probabilistic verification", Journal of ACM, 42(4), pp. 857-907, 1995

[4] Ellison R., Fisher D., Linger R., Longstaff T., Mead N., "Survivability network system analysis: A case study", IEEE Software 16/4, pp. 307-317, 1999

[5] Farmer D., Spafford E., "The cops security checker system", Proceedings Summer Usenix Conference, 1995

[6] Ortalo R., Deswarte Y., Kaaniche M., "Experimenting with quantitative evaluation tools for monitoring operational security", IEEE Transactions on Software Engineering, 25/5, pp. 633-650, 1999

[7] Koszelew J., "Some methods for verification of probabilistic programs interpreted in finite structures", Computer information systems and industrial management applications : CISIM'03. WSFiZ, pp. 140-147, 2003

[8] Pearl J., "Probabilistic Reasoning in Intelligent Systems: Networks of Plausible Inference", Morgan Kaufmann, 1998

[9] Pnueli A., "A temporal logic of concurrent programs", Theoretical Comput. Sci., 13, pp. 45-60, 1980

Quality of Service Requirements in Computer Networks with Blocking

Walenty Oniszczuk

Bialystok University of Technology
Faculty of Computer Science
15-351 Bialystok, ul. Wiejska 45A, Poland
E-mail: walenty@ii.pb.bialystok.pl

Abstract: This paper provides an analytical study of the closed type, multi-center networks with two different blocking strategies. The measures of effectiveness related to such models, and based on Quality of Service (QoS) requirement, are studied. In finite population (closed) multi-node models, where the number of tasks is equal to the population in the network, there are service centers and source centers treated as an infinite server (IS – means, ample-server model). In the systems described here, there are a finite number of tasks cycling from one service center to the other. If the buffer at a front of the service center is full, the accumulation of new tasks by this center is temporally suspended (blocking).

Keywords: Quality of Service (QoS) requirements, Finite Source Queuing Models with Blocking, Blocking Strategies.

1 Introduction

The theory of queuing networks has been widely applied as a powerful tool for modeling of discrete flow systems, such as computer systems, computer or communication networks [2], [4], [7], [11], [14], [15], [17]. Quite often, in complex information systems composed of shared nodes, there are limitations on the capacity of buffers at the front of each operating node. When the buffer is full, the accumulation of new tasks is temporally suspended and a phenomenon called blocking occurs, until the queue empties and allows new inserts. Simply defined, blocking forces a departure from the queue or an arrival to the queue to stop temporarily due to lack of space in the queue. Queuing network models, with finite capacity queues and blocking, have been introduced and applied as more realistic models of the systems with finite capacity resources and with population constrains [1], [3], [5], [8], [12], [13], [16], [19].

Consider a computer network consisting of several service centers (or nodes). The number of tasks waiting in one or more service buffers is restricted due to finite holding space associated with these nodes. The system may be modeled as an open or closed queuing network with finite capacities [10], [20]. When modeled as a closed network, the total number of tasks waiting for service and those currently receiving service is defined by the parameter N [5], [6], [9], [13], [18].

2 Closed two-center networks with blocking

Let us consider the two-node closed network with two different blocking strategies as shown in Fig. 1 and Fig. 2. The general assumptions for these models are [13]:

- The source of tasks is finite, say of size N,
- All tasks are generated independently by a unit source (the arrival process is Poissonian with parameter $\lambda = 1/a$, where a is mean inter-arrival time),
- c number of service lines is available,
- Mean service time is identical (exponential random variables) with $s = 1/\mu$ (where, μ is mean service rate),
- Service center buffer capacity is finite, for example equal m.

2.1 Model with source blocking

In this kind of model (Fig. 1), if there are $(m+c) < N$, we have a classical system with blocking. If buffer is full, the rest of N-m-c source units cannot proceed to the service station. More precisely, any new generated tasks are forced to wait in front of the source center.

A given two-center model with source blocking has only H_k possible states ($k = 0, ..., c+m+1$). State H_0 describes the idle system (empty service lines and service buffer) and state H_{c+m+1} describes the state, where c number of tasks are being processed, m tasks are waiting in the queue (the buffer is full) and the next task is being generated but is waiting for the buffer to become available (network is blocked). The number of tasks in the network at time t is a Markovian birth and death process in which the rates are given by:

$$\lambda_0 = N \cdot \lambda, \quad \lambda_1 = (N-1) \cdot \lambda, \quad \lambda_2 = (N-2) \cdot \lambda, \quad ..., \quad \lambda_{c+m} = (N-(c+m)) \cdot \lambda$$
$$\mu_1 = \mu, \quad \mu_2 = 2 \cdot \mu, \quad ..., \quad \mu_c = c \cdot \mu, \quad ..., \quad \mu_{c+m+1} = c \cdot \mu$$

Based on the queuing theory [2], [13], [14], [15] before the evaluation the main measurements of effectiveness, must be calculated for all probabilities of states p_k ($k = 0, ..., c+m+1$) in the statistical equilibrium.

The steady-state probability p_k can be interpreted as the probability of finding k tasks in the system with blocking at any arbitrary point of time after the process has reached its statistical equilibrium. The set of equation to get the steady-state solution for p_k may be written as:

$$0 = -(\lambda_k + \mu_k) p_k + \mu_{k+1} p_{k+1} + \lambda_{k-1} p_{k-1} \qquad \text{for} \quad k = 1, 2, 3, ..., c+m+1 \quad (1)$$
$$0 = -\lambda_0 p_0 + \mu_1 p_1 \qquad \text{for} \quad k = 0$$

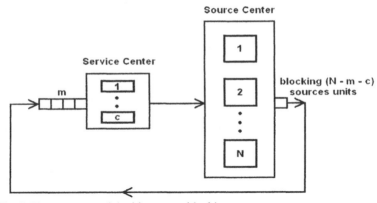

Fig. 1. Two-center model with sources blocking.

These equations may be solved recursively:

$$p_k = \frac{N\lambda \cdot (N-1)\lambda \cdots (N-k+1)\lambda}{\mu \cdot 2\mu \cdots k\mu} \cdot p_0 = \frac{N!}{(N-k)!\,k!} \rho^k \cdot p_0 \qquad \text{for } k \le c \quad (2)$$

$$p_k = \frac{N\lambda \cdot (N-1)\lambda \cdots (N-k+1)\lambda}{\mu \cdot 2\mu \cdots c\mu \cdot c\mu \cdots c\mu} \cdot p_0 = \frac{c^c N!}{(N-k)!\,c!}(\frac{\rho}{c})^k \cdot p_0 \quad \text{for } k \ge c+1 \quad (3)$$

where $\rho = \dfrac{\lambda}{\mu}$ and $p_0 = [\,N!\sum\limits_{k=0}^{c}\dfrac{\rho^k}{(N-k)!\,k!} + \dfrac{N!\,c^c}{c!}\sum\limits_{k=c+1}^{c+m+1}\dfrac{(\frac{\rho}{c})^k}{(N-k)!}\,]^{-1}$ (4)

Now, we can derive measurements of effectiveness for two-center network with source blocking using the steady-state probabilities given by Equations 1, 2 and 3 in the following manner:

1. Probability of source center blocking p_{bl}:

$$p_{bl} = p_{c+m+1} = p_0 \cdot \frac{c^c N!}{(N-c-m-1)!\,c!}(\frac{\rho}{c})^{c+m+1} \quad (5)$$

2. Idle system probability p_{idle}:

$$p_{idle} = p_0 = [\,N!\sum\limits_{k=0}^{c}\frac{\rho^k}{(N-k)!\,k!} + \frac{N!\,c^c}{c!}\sum\limits_{k=c+1}^{c+m+1}\frac{(\frac{\rho}{c})^k}{(N-k)!}\,]^{-1} \quad (6)$$

3. Waiting in the queue probability p_{wait}:

$$p_{wait} = p_{c+1} + p_{c+2} + \ldots + p_{c+m+1} = \sum\limits_{k=c+1}^{c+m+1}p_k = p_0 \cdot \sum\limits_{k=c+1}^{c+m+1}\frac{c^c N!}{(N-k)!\,c!}(\frac{\rho}{c})^k \quad (7)$$

4. Probability of immediately service p_{imm}:

$$p_{imm} = p_1 + \ldots + p_c = \sum\limits_{k=1}^{c}p_k = p_0 \cdot \sum\limits_{k=1}^{c}\frac{N!}{(N-k)!\,k!}\rho^k \quad (8)$$

5. The average number of blocked source units:

$$n_{bl} = (N - m - c) \cdot p_{c+m+1} = (N - m - c) \cdot p_0 \cdot \frac{c^c N!}{(N - c - m - 1)! \, c!} (\frac{\rho}{c})^{c+m+1} \qquad (9)$$

6. The average number of tasks in the service buffer:

$$v = \sum_{k=1}^{m} k \cdot p_{c+k} + m \cdot p_{c+m+1} =$$

$$= p_0 \cdot \frac{c^c N!}{c!} \sum_{k=1}^{m} \frac{k}{(N - c - k)!} (\frac{\rho}{c})^{c+k} + m \cdot p_0 \cdot \frac{c^c N!}{(N - c - m - 1)! \, c!} (\frac{\rho}{c})^{c+m+1} \qquad (10)$$

7. The average number of tasks in the service node:

$$n = p_0 \cdot N! \, [\sum_{k=1}^{c} \frac{\rho^k}{(N - k)! \, (k - 1)!} + \frac{c^c}{c!} \sum_{k=c+1}^{c+m} \frac{k}{(N - k)!} (\frac{\rho}{c})^k +$$

$$+ (c + m) \cdot \frac{c^c}{(N - c - m - 1)! \, c!} (\frac{\rho}{c})^{c+m+1} \,] \qquad (11)$$

8. The mean rate of task arrivals to a service station:

$$\Lambda = p_0 \cdot \sum_{k=0}^{c} \frac{N! \, \lambda}{(N - k - 1)! \, k!} \rho^k + p_0 \cdot \sum_{k=c+1}^{c+m} \frac{c^c N! \, \lambda}{(N - k - 1)! \, c!} (\frac{\rho}{c})^k \qquad (12)$$

9. The mean response time q and the mean blocking time in the source center t_{bl} are respectively:

$$q = \frac{n}{\Lambda}, \qquad\qquad t_{bl} = \frac{n_{bl}}{\Lambda} \qquad (13)$$

2.2 Model with blocking within additional source buffer

In this type of blocking strategy an additional buffer located in the front of the source center for temporary placement of new tasks is proposed (Fig. 2). This buffer collects the newly generated tasks, if the service buffer is full (blocking). When free space appears in the service buffer, the transmission process to the service center is immediately resumed.

Similarly, as in the previous model, there is a finite number $N+1$ of possible states. Here, the border states can be described as follows: H_0 – idle system (empty the service buffer and service lines), H_N – c number of tasks on the service lines, m– the number of tasks in the service buffer, $(N-c-m)$ the number of tasks in the source-waiting buffer.

This is again a Markovian birth and death process with rates:

$$\lambda_0 = N \cdot \lambda, \quad \lambda_1 = (N-1) \cdot \lambda, \quad \lambda_2 = (N-2) \cdot \lambda, \quad \dots, \quad \lambda_{N-1} = \lambda$$

$$\mu_1 = \mu, \quad \mu_2 = 2 \cdot \mu, \quad \dots, \quad \mu_c = c \cdot \mu, \quad \dots, \quad \mu_N = c \cdot \mu$$

The ergodicity condition of the birth and death process is always satisfied and the stationary solution is easily obtained:

$$p_k = \frac{N\lambda \cdot (N-1)\lambda \cdots (N-k+1)\lambda}{\mu \cdot 2\mu \cdots k\mu} \cdot p_0 = \frac{N!}{(N-k)! \, k!} \rho^k \cdot p_0 \quad \text{for} \ \ k \leq c \qquad (14)$$

$$P_k = \frac{N\lambda \cdot (N-1)\lambda \cdots (N-k+1)\lambda}{\mu \cdot 2\mu \cdots c\mu \cdot c\mu \cdots c\mu} \cdot p_0 = \frac{c^c N!}{(N-k)! \, c!} (\frac{\rho}{c})^k \cdot p_0 \text{ for } k \ge c+1 \text{ (15)}$$

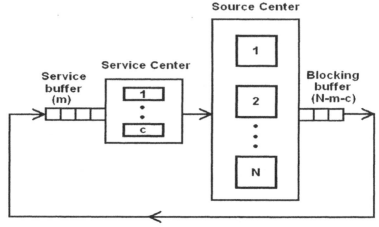

Fig. 2. Two-centre network with additional source buffer.

After that p_0 is obtained by normalization of the preceding stationary solution:

$$p_0 = \frac{1}{N! \sum_{k=0}^{c} \frac{\rho^k}{(N-k)! \, k!} + \frac{N! \, c^c}{c!} \sum_{k=c+1}^{N} \frac{(\frac{\rho}{c})^k}{(N-k)!}} \tag{16}$$

The main measurements of effectiveness are:

1. Blocking probability p_{bl} :

$$p_{bl} = p_{c+m+1} + p_{c+m+2} \cdots + p_N = p_0 \cdot \frac{c^c N!}{c!} \sum_{k=c+m+1}^{N} \frac{1}{(N-k)!} (\frac{\rho}{c})^k \tag{17}$$

2. Idle system probability:

$$p_{idle} = p_0 = \frac{1}{N! \sum_{k=0}^{c} \frac{\rho^k}{(N-k)! \, k!} + \frac{N! \, c^c}{c!} \sum_{k=c+1}^{N} \frac{(\frac{\rho}{c})^k}{(N-k)!}} \tag{18}$$

3. Waiting in the queue probability p_{wait} :

$$p_{wait} = p_{c+1} + p_{c+2} + \ldots + p_N = \sum_{k=c+1}^{N} p_k = p_0 \cdot \sum_{k=c+1}^{N} \frac{c^c N!}{(N-k)! \, c!} (\frac{\rho}{c})^k \tag{19}$$

4. Probability of immediately service p_{imm} :

$$p_{imm} = p_1 + \ldots + p_c = \sum_{k=1}^{c} p_k = p_0 \cdot \sum_{k=1}^{c} \frac{N!}{(N-k)! \, k!} \rho^k \tag{20}$$

5. The average number of blocked tasks:

$$n_{bl} = p_0 \cdot \frac{c^c N!}{c!} \sum_{k=c+m+1}^{N} \frac{(k-c-m)}{(N-k)!} (\frac{\rho}{c})^k \qquad (21)$$

6. The average number of tasks in the service buffer:

$$v = \sum_{k=c+1}^{c+m-1} (k-c) \cdot p_k + m \cdot \sum_{k=c+m}^{N} p_k =$$

$$= p_0 \cdot \frac{c^c N!}{c!} \sum_{k=c+1}^{c+m-1} \frac{(k-c)}{(N-k)!} (\frac{\rho}{c})^k + m \cdot p_0 \cdot \frac{c^c N!}{c!} \sum_{k=c+m}^{N} \frac{1}{(N-k)!} (\frac{\rho}{c})^k \qquad (22)$$

7. The average number of tasks in the service station:

$$n = p_0 \cdot N! \, [\sum_{k=1}^{c} \frac{\rho^k}{(N-k)!(k-1)!} + \frac{c^c}{c!} \sum_{k=c+1}^{c+m} \frac{k}{(N-k)!} (\frac{\rho}{c})^k +$$

$$+ \frac{c^c}{c!} \sum_{k=c+m+1}^{N} \frac{c+m}{(N-k)!} (\frac{\rho}{c})^k \,] \qquad (23)$$

8. The mean rate of arriving tasks:

$$\Lambda = p_0 \cdot \sum_{k=0}^{c} \frac{N! \, \lambda}{(N-k-1)! \, k!} \rho^k + p_0 \cdot \sum_{k=c+1}^{N-1} \frac{c^c N! \, \lambda}{(N-k-1)! \, c!} (\frac{\rho}{c})^k \qquad (24)$$

9. The mean response time q and the mean blocking time of tasks in the source center t_{bl} are respectively:

$$q = \frac{n}{\Lambda} \, , \qquad t_{bl} = \frac{n_{bl}}{\Lambda} \qquad (25)$$

3 Numerical example

In this section, the results of an investigation of two-center networks with different blocking strategies (Fig. 1 and Fig. 2) are presented. To demonstrate, the following configuration parameters are chosen: $N = 45.0$, $s = 1/\mu = 3.0$, the mean inter-arrival time within a range from 20.0 to 100.0 time units (for study models with the different coefficients of the utility - from small to high server utilization), service center with $c = 3$ parallel service lines, the buffer with finite capacity (size) $m = 10$. For models with blocking described above, the results, obtained with special consideration to Quality of Service (QoS), are presented in Fig. 3, Fig. 4, Fig. 5, Fig. 6 and Tab. 1.

4 Conclusions

In this document, two different blocking strategies in the closed type two-center computer systems are investigated. For each model, the exact steady-state solution is provided, along with the analysis based on performance measurements of quality of service requirements (QoS) such as blocking probability, mean blocking time, mean number of blocked source units, etc. Comparison of these strategies shows that in the heavy-traffic case the blocking probability grows more rapidly in the model with additional source buffer than in the model with source blocking.

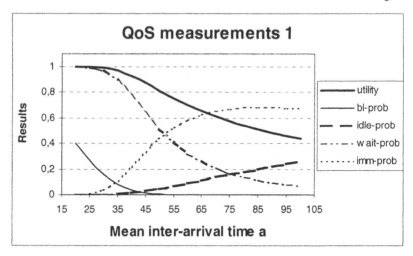

Fig. 3. QoS parameters: *utility* – utilization factor, *bl-prob* - blocking probability, *idle-prob* - idle system probability, *wait-prob* – waiting probability, *imm-prob* – immediately service probability, for model with source node blocking.

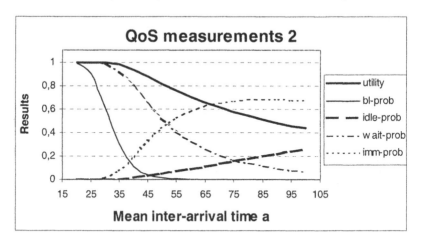

Fig. 4. QoS parameters: *utility* – utilization factor, *bl-prob* - blocking probability, *idle-prob* - idle system probability, *wait-prob* – waiting probability, *imm-prob* – immediately service probability, for model with blocking in the additional source buffer.

In both models, measurements of effectiveness presented in the Tab. 1 (for different coefficient of the utility, from small to high server utilization) are more or less similar. That means that both blocking strategies may be recommended for practical applications.

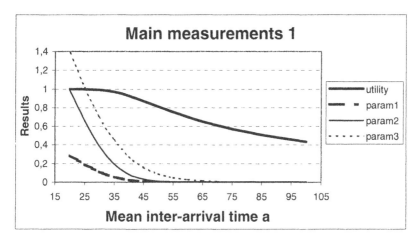

Fig. 5. The average number of blocked tasks related to source center capacity, service center capacity and mean number of tasks in the service buffer, for model with source node blocking, where *utility* – utilization factor, *param1* = n_{bl} / N, *param2* = n_{bl} / (c+m), *param3* = n_{bl} / n.

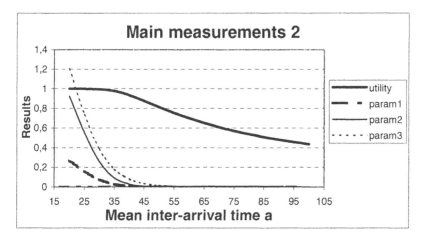

Fig. 6. The average number of blocked tasks related to source center capacity, service center capacity and mean number of tasks in the service buffer, for model with blocking in the additional source buffer, where *utility* – utilization factor, *param1* = n_{bl} / N, *param2* = n_{bl} / (c+m), *param3* = n_{bl} / n.

Table 1. Comparison of the main measurements of effectiveness in two models with different blocking strategies. Parameters with asterisk belong to model with additional source buffer (see Fig. 2), without - to source blocking (see Fig. 1), where: a – mean inter-arrival time, q – mean response time, t_{bl} – mean blocking time, n – mean number of tasks in service station, n_{bl} – mean number of blocked tasks.

a	q^*	q	t_{bl}^*	t_{bl}	n^*	n	n_{bl}^*	n_{bl}
100	3.264	3.264	0.000	0.000	1.422	1.422	0.000	0.000
95	3.306	3.306	0.000	0.000	1.513	1.513	0.000	0.000
90	3.359	3.359	0.000	0.000	1.619	1.619	0.000	0.000
85	3.425	3.425	0.000	0.001	1.743	1.743	0.000	0.000
80	3.509	3.509	0.000	0.002	1.891	1.891	0.000	0.001
75	3.619	3.618	0.000	0.003	2.071	2.071	0.000	0.002
70	3.766	3.764	0.001	0.007	2.297	2.296	0.000	0.004
65	3.967	3.963	0.001	0.015	2.588	2.585	0.001	0.010
60	4.250	4.241	0.004	0.034	2.977	2.969	0.003	0.024
55	4.666	4.641	0.012	0.082	3.519	3.497	0.009	0.062
50	5.298	5.228	0.035	0.199	4.308	4.244	0.029	0.162
45	6.281	6.087	0.114	0.491	5.499	5.311	0.100	0.428
40	7.787	7.290	0.379	1.178	7.275	6.768	0.354	1.093
35	9.825	8.780	1.224	2.613	9.601	8.516	1.196	2.535
30	11.788	10.282	3.382	5.101	11.744	10.195	3.369	5.058
25	12.791	11.464	7.218	8.601	12.788	11.447	7.217	8.588
20	12.989	12.219	12.011	12.786	12.989	12.218	12.011	12.785

This work was partially supported by the Bialystok University of Technology under grants S/WI/4/03 and W/WI/7/03.

References

[1] Akyildiz I.F. 1988. 'Mean Value Analysis for Blocking Queuing Networks'. *IEEE Transaction on Software Engineering* 14(4), pp. 418-428.

[2] Balsamo S., de Nito Persone V., Onvural R. 2001. 'Analysis of Queueing Networks with Blocking'. *Kluwer Academic Publishers*.

[3] Balsamo S., de Nito Persone V., Inverardi P. 2003. 'A review on queueing network models with finite capacity queues for software architectures performance predication', *Performance Evaluation* 51(2-4), pp. 269-288.

254

[4] Boucherie R.J., van Dijk N.M. 1997. 'On the arrival theorem for product form queueing networks with blocking', *Performance Evaluation* 29(3), pp. 155-176.

[5] Clo M.C. 1998. 'MVA for product-form cyclic queueing networks with blocking'. *Annals of Operations Research* 79, pp. 83-96.

[6] Economou A., Fakinos D. 1998. 'Product form stationary distributions for queueing networks with blocking and rerouting', *Queueing Systems* 30(3/4), pp. 251-260.

[7] Gomez-Corral A. 2002. 'A Tandem Queue with Blocking and Markovian Arrival Process, *Queueing Systems* 41(4), pp. 343-370.

[8] Harrison P.G. 2003. 'A new blocking problem from Java-based schedulers', *Performance Evaluation* 51(2-4), pp. 229-246.

[9] Kaufman J.S., Rege K.M. 1996. 'Blocking in a shared resource environment with batched arrival processes', *Performance Evaluation* 24, pp. 249-263.

[10] Kouvatsos D., Awan I. 2003. 'Entropy maximization and open queueing networks with priorities and blocking'. *Performance Evaluation* 51(2-4), pp. 191-227.

[11] Martin J.B. 2002. 'Large Tandem Queueing Networks with Blocking', *Queueing Systems* 41(1/2), pp. 45-72.]

[12] Morrison J.A. 1996. 'Blocking probabilities for multiple class batched arrivals to a shared resource, *Performance Evaluation* 25, pp. 131-150.

[13] Oniszczuk W. 2003. 'Blocking and Delay Factors in Computer Information Systems'. *Computer Information Systems and Industrial Management Applications, BUFM Press*, pp. 282-288.

[14] Onvural R. 1990. 'Survey of closed queuing networks with blocking'. *Computer Survey* 22(2), pp. 83-121.

[15] Perros H.G. 1994. 'Queuing Networks with Blocking. Exact and Approximate Solution'. *Oxford University Press*.

[16] Pinsky E., Conway A.D. 1996. 'Mean-value analysis of multi-facility blocking models with state-dependent arrivals', *Performance Evaluation* 24, pp. 303-309.

[17] Ramesh S., Perros H.G. 2000. 'A two-level queueing network model with blocking and non-blocking messages'. *Annals of Operations Research* 93(1/4), pp. 357-372.

[18] Sereno M. 1999. 'Mean value analysis of product form solution queueing networks with repetitive service blocking'. *Performance Evaluation* 36-37, pp. 19-33.

[19] Strelen J.Ch., Bärk B., Becker J., Jonas V. 1998. 'Analysis of queueing networks with blocking using a new aggregation technique'. *Annals of Operations Research* 79, pp. 121-142.

[20] Tolio T., Gershwin S.B. 1998. 'Throughput estimation in cyclic queueing networks with blocking'. *Annals of Operations Research* 79, pp. 207-229.

PART III

Artificial Intelligence-Oriented Trends and Applications

Genetic BDD-oriented Pattern Classifiers

Witold Pedrycz

Dept of Electrical & Computer Eng., University of Alberta, Edmonton, Canada, *pedrycz@ee.ualberta.ca* and Systems Research Institute, Polish Academy of Sciences, 01-447 Warsaw, Poland

Zenon A. Sosnowski

Department of Computer Science, Technical University of Bialystok, Bialystok, Poland, *zenon@ii.pb.bialystok.pl*

Abstract: In this study, we introduce a BDD – based pattern classifier. The essence of the proposed approach lies in a binarization of continuous data representoin of an original classification data in the form of a binary decision diagram (BDD). The resulting BDD helps compress the data, reveal the most essential binary features and complete classification. It is shown that such BDDs can serve as a digital blueprint of the underlying classifiers.

Keywords: decision rules, Binary Decision Diagrams, Genetic Algorithms, discretization, granulation, classifier

1 Introduction

The BDD (Binary Decision Digram) [1,2] is used in a wide range of areas [3] including large fault trees analysis [4]. The objective of this paper is to introduce BDD – based pattern classifier. In conjunction to the discussion of the BDD architecture and the ensuing development, we will be presenting an illustrative example. The example itself involves a relatively large dataset so all essential points of the BDD classifier can be demonstrated in great detail. The data set of interest concerns several makes of cars and is available from the Turing Institute [5]. It involves 4 classes of vehicles described by 18 features listed in Table 1.

In this paper, we follow a standard design methodology used in pattern classifiers that is we randomly divide the data set into a certain training and testing subset; the training portion involves 60% of the total set.

No	ATTRIBUTES	DESCRIPTION
0	COMPACTNESS	(average perim)**2/area
1	CIRCULARITY	(average radius)**2/area
2	DISTANCE CIRCULARITY	area/(av.distance from border)**2
3	RADIUS RATIO	(max.rad-min.rad)/av.radius
4	PR.AXIS ASPECT RATIO	(minor axis)/(major axis)
5	MAX.LENGTH ASPECT RATIO	(length perp. max length)/(max length)
6	SCATTER RATIO	(inertia about minor axis)/(inertia about major axis)
7	ELONGATEDNESS	area/(shrink width)**2
8	PR.AXIS RECTANGULARITY	area/(pr.axis length*pr.axis width)
9	MAX.LENGTH RECTANGULARITY	area/(max.length*length perp. to this)
10	SCALED VARIANCE ALONG MAJOR AXIS	(2nd order moment about minor axis)/area
11	SCALED VARIANCE ALONG MINOR AXIS	(2nd order moment about major axis)/area
12	SCALED RADIUS OF GYRATION	(mavar+mivar)/area
13	SKEWNESS ABOUT MAJOR AXIS	(3rd order moment about major axis)/sigma_min**3
14	SKEWNESS ABOUT MINOR AXIS	(3rd order moment about minor axis)/sigma_maj**3
15	KURTOSIS ABOUT MINOR AXIS	(4th order moment about major axis)/sigma_min**4
16	KURTOSIS ABOUT MAJOR AXIS	(4th order moment about minor axis)/sigma_maj**4
17	HOLLOWS RATIO	(area of hollows)/(area of bounding polygon)

Table 1. Attributes of AUTO dataset and their description; here sigma_maj**2 is the variance computed along the major axis and sigma_min**2 is the variance along the minor axis, while area of hollows = area of bounding poly-area of object.

We adhere to the following notation. The patterns are treated as a m-dimensional vectors in $\mathbf{R}^m$, namely $\mathbf{x}(1)$, $\mathbf{x}(2),\ldots,$ $\mathbf{x}(N)$ where"N" denotes a size of the data set. Moreover, we are concerned with "c" classes, that is ω_1, ω_2, ..., ω_c.

The paper is organized in the following manner. First, we briefly review the essence of BDDs as representation structures aimed at describing binary data (Section 2). As BDDs operate on binary (two-valued) variables, we develop a binarization procedure based on the use of genetic optimization (Section3). In Section 4, we present an overall development process along with some illustrative examples. Concluding observatioons are covereed in Section 5.

2   Binary Decision Diagrams (BDD) as representation structures of binary data

The concept of BDDs was introduced in the realm of digital system design as an important vehicle of an efficient representation of logic (Boolean) functions. Here we briefly recall the generic concept. Let us consider "*n*" binary variables, namely the variables assuming values in {0,1}. A BDD is a directed acyclic graph that describes an algorithm for the computation (determination) of a Boolean function *f*. The vertices of the BDD are called inner nodes or sinks (terminal nodes). Each sink is labeled by a certain Boolean constant (that is 0 or 1). Each inner node is labeled by a Boolean variable and has two outgoing edges, a THEN-edge (or 1-edge) and ELSE-edge (0-edge). A computation path for an input $b = (b_1, b_2, \ldots, b_n)$ starts at the unique source node. At an inner node with label x_i the b_i-edge is chosen. This is iterated until the sink has been reached. The label of the sink is just the value $f(b)$. More formally we can define BDD as follows.

Definition . A BDD is a directed acyclic graph representing a Boolean function. It can be uniquely defined as a tuple, $\mathbf{BDD} = (\mathbf{\Phi}, \mathbf{V}, \mathbf{E}, \{0,1\})$, where $\mathbf{\Phi}$ is the function node (root), $\mathbf{V}$ is the set of internal nodes, $\mathbf{E}$ is a set of edges, and $\mathbf{0}$, $\mathbf{1}$ are the terminal nodes.

As an example, Figure 1 illustrates a representation of the function $f(x_1,x_2,x_3)$ defined by teh truth table given on the left, for a special case where the graph is actually a tree. Each inner note is labeled by a variable and has edges directed towards two children: THEN-edge (shown as T) corresponding to the case where the variable is assigned to 1, and ELSE-edge (shown as E) corresponding to the case where the variable is assigned to 0. Each terminal note is labeled 1 or 0. For a given assignment to the variables, the value yielded by the function is determined by tracing a path from the root to a terminal node, following the edges indicated by the values assigned to the variables. The function value is then given by the terminal node label. Due to the way the edges are ordered in this figure, the values of the terminal nodes, read from left to right, match those in the truth table , read top to bottom.

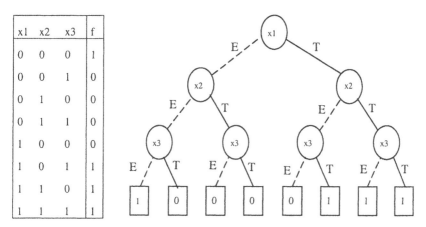

x1	x2	x3	f
0	0	0	1
0	0	1	0
0	1	0	0
0	1	1	0
1	0	0	0
1	0	1	1
1	1	0	1
1	1	1	1

Figure 1. Truth Table and Decision Tree Representations of a Boolean Function. A dashed (solid) tree branch denotes the case where the decision variable is 0 (1).

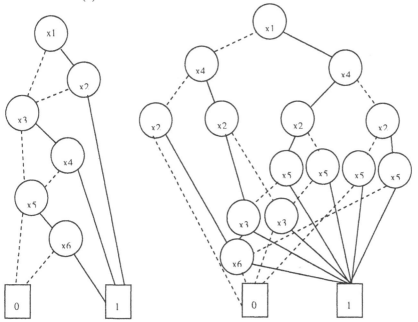

Figure 2. OBDD Representation of a Single Function for Two Different Variable Orderings.

It is known that the form and size of the BDD is very sensitive to the variable order. A random, or carelessly chosen variable order will frequently result in an exponential size of the BDD. For example, Figure 2 shows two BDD representation of the function denoted by the Boolean expression $x1 \cdot x4 + x2 \cdot x5 + x3 \cdot x6$, where $\cdot$ denotes the AND operation and the $+$ denotes the OR operation. For the case on the left, the variables are ordered $x1 < x2 < x3 < x4 < x5 < x6$, while for the case on the right they are ordered $x1 < x4 < x2 < x5 < x3 < x6$.

Many variable ordering heuristics have been proposed. Most of these ideas depend on a fundamental operation, *adjacent variable swapping* [6]. One of the most efficient algorithms, *sifting*, was proposed by Rudell [7].

3 A genetic binarization of data

As BDDs operate in binary environment (viz. the framework of binary data), it is essential to convert continuous data (features) into their binary representatives. Obviously, such a process is not unique and may invoke a number of interesting and potentially promising alternatives. No matter how we proceed, it seems to be a clear objective: we would like to divide the range of each continuous variable into two intervals so that the derived intervals are as homogeneous as possible with respect to the class allocation to each of these intervals. Ideally, one should have elements (patterns) belonging to a single class fully allocated to a single interval. As we are concerned with the binarization of the features, one has to determine "n" ($n <= m$) optimal points of binarization. It is allowed to split a particular feature for more then two intervals, as some binarization points concern the same feature. Interestingly, the problem is of combinatorial nature and as such could be handled by genetic optimization. In what follows we discuss the details on how the GA is structured . In particular, this concerns problem representation conveyed in the form of some chromosome and a way how the optimization is guided through a certain fitness function.

Chromosome representation. The chromosome is constructed as $2*n$-dimensional vector consisting of a sequence of binarization points $((i_1,s_1), (i_2,s_2), ..., (i_n,s_n))$, where i_j is the attribute number, and s_j is the binarization point of the i_j-th feature.

Fitness function. A fitness function to be minimize represents the number of conflict in the dataset.. The calculation the number of conflicts is based on the binary representation of data points which is performed by the mapping

$$f : R^{n+1} -> \{0,1\}^n \times R$$

defined as

$$f(x^k_{i1}, x^k_{i2}, ..., x^k_{in}, \omega^k) = (b^k_1, b^k_2, ..., b^k_n, \omega^k)$$

where

$$b_j = \begin{cases} 0 & x_{ij} < s_{ij} \\ 1 & otherwise \end{cases}$$

We say that two data points are in conflict if they belong to the different decision class but their binary representation is equal. Such situations can be captured by the fitness function assuming the form

$$fit : \{0,1\}^n \times R \to N$$

where

$$fit = \sum_{k=2}^{N} g(b_1^k, b_2^k, ..., b_n^k, \omega^k)$$

and

$$g(b_1^k, b_2^k, ..., b_n^k, \omega^k) = \begin{cases} 1 & iff \quad \underset{j}{\exists} \ (1 \le j < k) : [\overset{n}{\underset{i=1}{\forall}} \ b_i^j = b_i^k \wedge \omega^j \ne \omega^k] \\ 0 & otherwise \end{cases}$$

The results of the GA binarization (discretization) for the experimental data are shown in Table 2. This table shows the split points taken as a simple average. Which contrast the genetically optimized split points with a very basic strategy.

Point No	Attribute No	MIN	MAX	Medium split point	GA split point
1	2	40	112	76	50.3055
2	12	109	268	188.5	151.2036
3	5	2	55	28.5	7.6693
4	0	73	119	96	103.7397
5	11	184	1018	601	468.0225
6	9	118	188	153	137.0857
7	17	181	211	196	188.0424
8	15	0	41	20.5	22.7929
9	11	184	1018	601	266.4064
10	16	176	206	191	177.5681

Table 2. The results of the GA binarization.

In all experiments, we used a standard GA with the following parameters: population 200, mutation 0.1, crossover 0.7. These values are a result of some experimentation and they pretty much coincide with the typical values uncountered in the literature. Subsequently the obtained values of the fitness function (best individual and average population) are shown in Table 3.

Iter.	Min	Max	Average	Standard deviation
00	221	380	315.14	29.745
50	199	374	265.79	43.162
100	194	390	262.56	52.985
150	186	374	258.38	54.771
200	186	375	256.94	56.519
250	179	372	255.01	57.047
300	179	380	252.07	57.588
350	173	393	251.72	58.35
400	156	373	250.88	58.754
450	156	404	249.21	58.783
500	156	367	248.76	59.12

Table 3. The values of the fitness function (shown are the best individual and an average fitness for the entire population).

In comparison to a simple equal-split strategy we get far worse results as again illustrated in Table 4.

Experiment no.	GA split point	Medium split point
1	169	290
2	165	287
3	156	277
4	162	277
5	162	277
Average	162,8	281,6
Standard deviation	4,764452	6,387488

Table 4. Number of conflicts for the GA split point and uniform split point; note a substantial improvement provided by the genetic optimization.

4 The overall design methodology of BDD classifiers and experimental results

The design of the BDD classifiers consists of two main phases

- Optimal binarization of continuous features

- Minimization of BDDs using one of the existing minimization techniques (those are standard in digital system design so we will not cover them in this study)

Each class is described by a separate BDD, so for "c" classes we end up with "c" BDDs.

The performance of BDD for the class 2 is summarized in Table 5. Each path of the BDD corresponds to the decision rule, which is described by the sequence of binary variables listed starting from the top of the tree. The use of the classifier concerns traversing the diagram for a given vector of binary features. We count the number of the most activated paths that are also the shortest. The performance of the classification rules on testing set is described by number of properly classified cases.

Rule description	Classification rate of the rule
8 variables	
16 –0 -9 15 -11 -5 -12 2	5
9 variables	
16 0 9 11 5 12 17 11 2	27
16 –0 -9 15 -11 5 17 11 2	0
16 –0 -9 –15 -11 -5 -12 -17 -11	0
10 variables	
16 –0 -9 –15 -11 5 -12 17 11 2	4
16 –0 -9 –15 -11 -5 12 17 -11 2	1
16 –0 -9 –15 -11 -5 12 -17 11 2	1
16 –0 -9 –15 -11 -5 -12 -17 11 2	1
16 –0 9 15 -11 -5 12 17 11 2	0
16 –0 -9 -15 11 5 12 17 11 2	0

Table 5. The performance of BDD for the class 2.

To obtain reliable and stable results as well as to avoid any potential experimental bias, we divided the data set into the training (60%) and testing set (40%) and repeated the experiment 5 times (a rotation method).

To compare the results of genetic-based BDD classification, we take into consideration the results of classification obtained when exploiting fuzzy context-based clusters [8]. As summarized in Table 6 some general observation can be derived that hold over the series of experiments conducted so far. It becomes apparent that the genetic-based BDD classification performs better on the testing set (the results on training set are worst). Note, however, that the size of decision trees based on fuzzy context-based cluster is much higher comparing the ones being generated with the proposed method.

Experiment no.	No of nodes	Error on Training (%)	Error on Testing (%)
1	67	29,13	36,98
2	66	28,94	32,54
3	85	25,2	35,2
4	85	25,59	36,69
5	85	25,59	36,09
Average	77,6	26,89	35,5
Standard diversion	10,13903	1,965719	1,789288
context-based clustering			
Average	495,2	8,5	36,4
Standard deviation	62,94	0,9	1,81

Tab. 6. Classification results of the genetically optimized BDDs.

The relevance of particular attributes from the auto data set is shown in Table 7. This table is based on statistics for 5 decision trees. All of the trees were built on the base of 10 attributes selected by GA. The columns of this table correspond to the number of attributes while its rows denote the frequency of the selection of particular attribute by GA. It is easy to notice that there are two dominant attributes, i.e., 11 and 5 that appear in the decision trees 8 and 7 times respectively. Obviously, one should not make too general projections that should not go far beyond this particular data set.

Exper. no	Attribute no																	
	0	1	2	3	4	5	6	7	8	9	10	11	12	13	14	15	16	17
1	1	2				2		1				1	1					2
2	1			1	1	1		2		1		1		1				1
3	1		1			2				1		2					1	1
4	1				1	1		1		1		2		1		1	1	
5	1				1	1		1		1		2		1		1	1	
Σ	5	2	1	1	3	7	0	5	0	4	0	8	1	3	0	2	3	4

Table 7. The distribution of the attributes in decision rules reflecting their relevance.

The resulting rules sorted with respect to the number of properly classified cases (for the training set) are gathered in Table 8.

Class 2			
Rule no	Number of variables	Classification rate (training)	Classification rate (testing)
2	9	45	27
1	8	10	5
4	9	9	0
3	9	6	0
7	10	6	4
9	10	5	1
10	10	3	1
5	10	2	0
6	10	1	0
8	10	1	1

Table 8. The resulting rules the class 2.

The compression rate calculated as the number of rules divided by the number of objects in training set is shown in Table 9. It is worth noting that when we consider only 50% of the best rules from each class, the compression rate is less then 3% while the classification error rises only slightly from 35.5% to 36.7 %. The resulting trees are very small and easy to analyze by the human expert.

Experiment no.	No of rules	Compression rate (%)
1	20	3,94
2	25	4,92
3	34	6,69
4	33	6,50
5	33	6,50
Average	29	5,71
Standard deviation	6,20	1,22

Table 9. Values of the compression rate versus the number of rules (reported are 5 experiments).

5   Conclusions

We have dealt with the genetic BDD-oriented design of pattern classification and showed how BDDs can be used in the granulation (binarization) of the attributes encountered in the problem. This granulation is carried out for all attributes at once through a genetic algorithm. It has been found through the series of experiments that this approach outperforms other of designing decision rules methods (including decision trees based on fuzzy context based clustering) in terms of more compact BDD and higher classification accuracy.

Acknowledgment

Support from the Natural Science and Engineering Research Council of Canada (NSERC) is gratefully acknowledged. The second author gratefully acknowledges support from the Technical University of Bialystok (grant W/WI/8/02).

References

[1]   Akers B., "Binary decision digrams", *IEEE Trans. Comput.*, **C-27**(6), pp.509-16, 1978.

[2]   Wegener I., "BDDs – design, analysis, complexity, and applicartions", *Discrete Applied Mathematics*, **138**, pp. 229-251, 2004.

[3]   Byrant R., "Symbolic Boolean manipulation with ordered binaty digrams", *ACM Comput. Surv.*, **24**, pp. 293-318, 1992.

[4]   Jung W.S., Han S. H., and Ha J., "A fast BDD algorithm for large coherent fault trees analysis", *Reliability Engineering & System Safety*, **85**, pp. 369-374, 2004.

[5]   Siebert J.P., "Vehicle recognition using rule-based methods", *Turing Institute Research Memorandum, TIRM-87-017* (March 1987).

[6]   Ishiura N., Sawada H., and Yajima S., "Minimization of binary decision diagrams based on exchanges of variables", In *Proceedings of the International Conference on Computer-Aided Design*, pp. 472-475, Santa Clara, CA, November 1991.

[7]   Rudell R., Dynamic variable ordering for ordered binary decision diagrams,In *Proceedings of the International Conference on Computer-Aided Design*, pp. 42-47, Santa Clara, CA, November 1993.

[8]   Pedrycz W., Sosnowski Z.A., "Designing Decision Trees with the Use of Fuzzy Granulation", *IEEE Transactions on Systems, Man, and Cybernetics – Part A*, **30**, pp. 151-159, 2000.

A fuzzy way to evaluate the qualitative attributes in bank lending creditworthiness

Gisella Facchinetti - Giovanni Mastroleo

Faculty of Economics, University of Modena and Reggio Emilia, Italy
facchinetti@unimore.it, mastroleo@unimore.it

Abstract:
In this paper we address bank evaluation of clients in lending credit, based on qualitative attributes. Till now, the banks have dodged to face this part of the lending credit. There are several reasons for this. One is the impossibility of using a statistical approach; the variables are linguistic attributes, not numbers. Another one, which we think really serious, is the difficulty of fixing which qualitative attributes are important. Every bank uses a personal contact with the client, the experts have not a unique behaviour. Here we present a sketch of our work, performed with an Italian bank, in which a fuzzy approach is used. In particular, we have used two different methods: a fuzzy expert system and a fuzzy cluster method.

Keywords: bank creditworthiness, qualitative attribute, fuzzy expert system, fuzzy cluster

1   Introduction

In this paper we address how one bank may evaluate clients in lending credit procedure basing oneself on their qualitative attributes.

All banks have always recognized that lending credit is based on two aspects, one quantitative, one qualitative. Historically, only the first has been treated in a systematic way. The literature is rich of researchs that use instruments of statistical and econometric type. Recently, the soft computing instruments have brought a new impulse into this area and several interesting results have been obtained using neural and fuzzy approaches. ([3-6]). Every bank has always treated the second aspect, the qualitative one, in a private mode. No research is available about the codification of this problem. The banks avoid the codification of this part in lending credit. There are several reasons for this lack. One is the impossibility of using a statistical approach; the variables are linguistic attributes, not numbers. Another, we think really serious, is the difficulty of fixing which are the qualitative attributes the experts regard to be important. Every bank uses a personal contact with the client. All credit officers have their own methods of evaluating the client's qualitative attributes and therefore any information is available in the bank's archives.

Recently, for several reasons, some Italian banks have decided to address this problem. One of these banks has constructed a questionnaire including several evaluations about the client's qualitative attributes. They have proposed this questionnaire to their officials with regard to the monitoring problem. The replies to this questionnaire contain information on clients current position: "Good Position" and "Bad Position". As they use an expert system for the evaluation of the quantitative attributes, they were interested in a similar idea for the qualitative ones. Because of the several joint works we have had with banks in landing credit problems, they contact us with this new problem. Immediately we understand that this new problem is very interesting even from the point of view of research as no papers are present in this field. We discuss for a long time with them about the possible instruments we may use to evaluate the questionaire results. We agree that a weighted average is not the best method for a final evaluation, inter alia, because they have no idea of which would be the correct weight to use. We propose two different possibilities based on fuzzy logic. The motivation is very natural. Fuzzy logic is able to "compute with word", as L. A. Zadeh says, and the variables of the problem are words, not numbers.

Here we present a sketch of the two ideas that are: a fuzzy expert system and a fuzzy cluster method. The first one is the natural evolution of expert system they know, the second one is due to their interest to have a rating method. The two methods produce about the same results. Notice that these are the results of the qualitative information only. The complete evaluation needs of the mix of qualitative and quantitative data, so we are sure that the addition of quantitative information can only to improve the final results. The misclassified cases are the 15,7%. We have checked these cases and, for the 96% of them, they are cases in which the input data are typical of Good client but the actual situation is of Bad position and vice versa. We have some clients with the same expert judgement that are in different classes. So we can say that the two methods show a good performance to discriminate the two classes of clients. The second method offers a rating with two clusters, Good and Bad client, but even a rating with four clusters, GoodGood, Good, Bad, BadBad.

2 Bank's evaluation of client's creditworthiness

The phase concerning the bank lending risk evaluation is one of the most important but also the most difficult in credit activity. One way to estimate client reliability is to assign a value (either a number or a judgement) which represents the risk level. One of these possible values is client solvency analysis. This is comprehensive of both the moral qualities and the means of the client. The credit file has to supply a photograph of the firm, but it is influenced both by the way in which this is done and by the quality of the persons who are involved in credit lending. The criteria of analysis used by banks are of two types: static-patrimonial and dynamic-profitability criteria. These criteria are based on economic and financial characteristics of the firm requesting credit, but evaluation of the validity of the programs that show an assumed income capacity is fundamental. In this respect, a lot of qualitative aspects must be considered — more precisely, the aspects connected with the technical and organizing characteristics of firm and the market and logistic opportunities. In fact these two aspects contribute to determine the future of the firm and may help the bank to know the firm's economic and financial prospects.

All these aspects are present in every lending credit request, but this complex of researches is not developed in the same way. Every bank has different procedures that reflect the bank's internal situation, such as bank dimension or organizing complexity but the same procedure may depend on the characteristics of the client, such as his economic activity or his dimension and organization. In any case, the procedure consists of two phases: one quantitative, one qualitative. Mixing the two analysis results produces the final evaluation. Many researches and many different methods have been proposed to approach the quantitative valuation. These methods are mostly of statistical, econometric and probabilistic type.(see [8],[11]). Recently, "soft computing" techniques have entered the credit world, producing interesting results.

3   Qualitative analysis: an Italian case

The qualitative aspects of a firm requesting credit, are useful in the corporate case, but have particular relevance for the small business. In this situation, book-values are poorly reliable, often having fiscal origins. This suggests that it is better to use qualitative-competitive analysis than the traditional budget to decide a firm's creditworthiness.

No research or methods have been proposed for qualitative valuation. This is due to the fact that, till now, the banks have avoided to codify this aspect. There are various reasons for this. One is the impossibility of quantifing the results; the variables are linguistic attributes, not numbers. Another, we think really serious, is the difficulty of standardizing a procedure able to evaluate the qualitative attributes. Every bank uses a personal contact with the client. All credit officers have their own methods for evaluating the client's qualitative attributes. Therefore, at the end, any information is available in bank archives.

Since we have had many opportunity to work toghether with banks on clients creditworthiness, an Italian bank, which decided to study a method for qualitative evaluation of their clients, ask us to begin a joint work with them. The bank has already devised a questionnaire which incorporated several questions about the client's qualitative attributes. The questionnaire was proposed to their officials with regard to the monitoring problem. The replies contain information on clients actual position, "Good Position" and "Bad Position".

A first analysis shows to us that the submitted questionaire is too wide and, in several case, the questions are ill-posed. Then we face the problem of how to evaluate the replies to those questionnaires. The simplest way is the typical approach connected with a sort of weighted average, like in social statistics studies, but the bank does not know what are the correct weights to use. As they have an expert system for qualitative evaluations, they was very happy to test a fuzzy approach. We proposed two different possibilities: a fuzzy expert system and a fuzzy cluster method. Here we present a sketch of the two ideas.

4   The two fuzzy methods

The reason for using fuzzy logic as a basic instrument is very natural. Fuzzy logic is able to "compute with words", as Professor Zadeh says, and the variables of the problem are judgements expressed in a linguistic way, not numbers.

One of the most fascinating and useful features of fuzzy models is their ability to be both linguistically tractable and mathematically sound. In fact, many investigations ([10],[14]) have established that any sufficiently regular mapping from inputs to outputs could be approximated with any degree of accuracy by fuzzy systems maintaining linguistic interpretability. Formally speaking, it is possible to demonstrate that: given a normed space $(X, \| . \|_p)$ $p \in R^+$ and $f \in C_K^0$, with K a compact of X, $\forall \varepsilon > 0$ a fuzzy system exists with an input-output relationship F such that $\| f - F \| < \varepsilon$, where $\| . \|_p$ is the Lebesgue norm of some order p.

Fuzzy modelling schemes exist and generate extremely smooth approximation of target functions. The Mamdani systems are certainly the most common and were the first fuzzy models for which the universal approximation property was proved.

The essential steps for a fuzzy system design are: (i) identifying the problem and choosing the type of fuzzy system which best suits the requirement of the problem, (ii) definition of the input and output variables, their fuzzy values and their membership function (fuzzification of input and output), (iii) definition of the control rules and the translation of these into a fuzzy relation, (iv) treatment of any input information to choose the fuzzy inference method, (v) translation of the fuzzy output in a crisp value (defuzzification methods), (vi) tuning the fuzzy system for validation of the results. ([9], [13]).

The problems of fuzzification and construction of blocks of fuzzy rules are treated in several ways. Here we use the interview with experts of the problem. This method does not use the past history of the problem and permits a real contact with the experts that may allow into the study all the experience matured in years of work in that field.

The fuzzy cluster approach is a data-mining method, which lives on the past data. Here we have input-output data, but we use only the first ones as we leave free the number of clusters the data produce. Mathematical tools (see chapter 7) produce that for these data the optimal number of clusters are two and four. Owing to the bank's request we show only the case of two clusters.

The two methods we present, are able to discriminate Good and the Bad clients.

5   The bank questionnaire

The analysis areas deal with several aspects of the firm situation.

- The activity of the firm.
- The ownership structure (independent firm or belonging to a group).
- The characteristic of the markets in which it works.
- Its position in the market.
- The critical factors of sector success/ weakness.
- Management evaluation.
- Presence of risk factors in the past or in the present.
- The explicative factors of the actual economic-financial position.

Looking at this list, some remarks can be made. Some evaluations may be considered objective while others are subjective. For example, the "firm's position in the market" is an objective aspect as it derives from information that are measurable. "Management evaluation" is a subjective aspect. It deals with a valuation based on reputation, image, notoriety and credibility of owners and management.

Owing to the bank's request for privacy, we cannot show the complete questionnaire that contains more than sixty questions. We show the thirty-five variables of the expert systems, which are obtained by an aggregation of the initial inputs, done earlier in the process. This aggregation was decided with the bank itself. The work of aggregation is due to the fact that some variables were considered redundant and already considered in other information. In the next we present the meaning of inputs (varxx), the intermediate variables (intxx) and the output, present in system picture (figure 1).

var01	Cohesion level and goal unitariness.
var02	Contracting capacity, experience, flexibility and expertise of the decisor.
var03	Undertaker risk propensity.
var04	Number of release signals in the firm's management.
var05	Resources drag.
var06	Decisor morality and will to meet his obligations.
var07	High or irregular standard of living.
var08	Reluctance in the budget presentation.
var09	Insufficient clearness and entirety in the information supplied.
var10	Insufficient caution in budget valuation.
var11	Distribution activity and client assistance.
var12	Image and quality of the product in the market.
var13	Efficiency and capacity of production and procurement.
var14	Price competitiveness.
var15	Marketing with one or few clients or channel of trade.
var16	Geographic typology of the channel of trade.
var17	Level of the life cycle of the firm's products.
var18	Firm's competitiveness in the market.
var19	Membership and position in a group.
var20	Tenure years of the present shareholder.
var21	Firm manager characteristics.
var22	Years of relations with the bank.
var23	Owners' typology.
var24	Problems connected with the generational transfer.
var25	Stopping of the financial underwriting on behalf of the control group or the owners.
var26	Dependence on one or few suppliers.
var27	Redundancies.
var28	Legal or fiscal controversy.
var29	Difficulty and delay in cashing credits.
var30	Reduction of the guarantee capital.
var31	Delay in payment of hires, taxes, and suppliers.
var32	Past crisis, delay in paying a debt, etc.
var33	Firm in economic difficulties.
var34	Financial reorganization or office closure.
var35	Firm belonging to a group which is in financial reorganization.
int01	Other risk factors
int02	Capability
int03	Marketing Capability
int04	Produttivity Capability
int05	Clients Characteristics
int06	Decisors Profile
int07	Ownership Characteristics
int08	Historic Characteristics

int09	Behaviour of Decisors
int10	Managerial behaviour of Decisors
int11	Informations on Behaviour
int12	Aggregated judgement of firm
int13	Decisors Behaviour
int14	Risk Factors
int15	Marketing Strenght
int16	Complex of informations about firm
int17	Competitivity Position
int18	Ownership
int19	Risks
int20	Risk Situations
int21	Crisis Situations
int22	Ownership situation
int23	Firm Evaluation
output	Total Evaluation

6   The fuzzy system and results

The complexity of the problem and the high number of variables create a lot of intermediate variables, which collect together few variables in groups that have a significant meaning. As you see, the system (figure 1), is built by two macro-groups: all the information on the firm and the risk factors. The two partial outputs produce the final evaluation. This choice is due to the fact that, for the bank, the risk factors have a greater importance than the firm evaluation. The final rules-block takes into account this bank decision.

As example in Figure 2 we shaw some details about var 01 = Cohesion Level, var 02 = Decisor Capacity, var 03 = Risk Propensity and the rules block that generates intermediate variable int 06 = Decisor Profile.

In figure 3, the first rules block shows the aggregation int 09 = Decisor Behaviour = f (int06,int10), where int 06 = Decisor Profile and int 10 = Managerial behaviour of Decisors.

The second is relative to int11=Behaviour Information =g (var08,var09,var10), with var08 = Insufficient Caution, var09 = Insufficient clearness, var10 = Reluctance. The third is relative to Int 13 = Decisor = h (int9,int11), with int 09 = Decisor Behaviour, int11=Behaviour Information. The last rules block (Figure 4) is relative to the partial final evaluation int 23 = Firm Evaluation that depends by int 12 = Aggregate Judgement of Firm and int 18 = Ownership. The last is the fuzzification of the partial output Firm Evaluation Its range is [0,1] and has eight linguistic attributes.

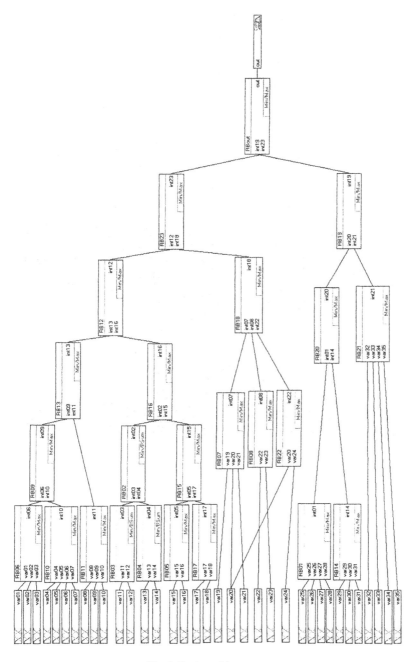

Fig. 1. Design of the system

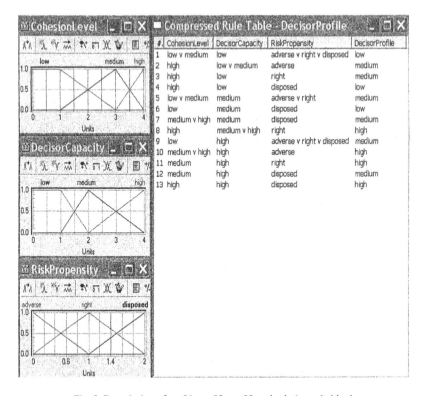

Fig. 2. Description of var01, var02, var03 and relative rule block

#.	DecisorProfile	MarBehavDecisors	DecisorBehaviour
1	low	low	very_low
2	low	medium	low
3	low	high	medium
4	medium	low	low
5	medium	medium	medium
6	medium	high	high
7	high	low	medium
8	high	medium	high
9	high	high	very_high

#.	BehaviourInform	DecisorBehaviour	Decisor
1	low	very_low	very_low
2	medium v high	very_low	low
3	low	medium	low
4	medium	medium	medium_low
5	high	medium	medium_high
6	low	high	medium_high
7	medium v high	high	high
8	low v medium	very_high	high
9	high	very_high	very_high

#.	InsuffCaution	InsuffClearness	Reluctance	BehaviourInform
1	low_caution	low_clearness	reluctance	low
2	low_caution	clearness	reluctance	medium
3	low_caution	low_clearness	availability	low
4	caution	low_clearness	availability	medium
5	low_caution	clearness	availability	medium
6	caution	clearness	availability	high

Fig. 3. Rule block of int09, int11 and int13

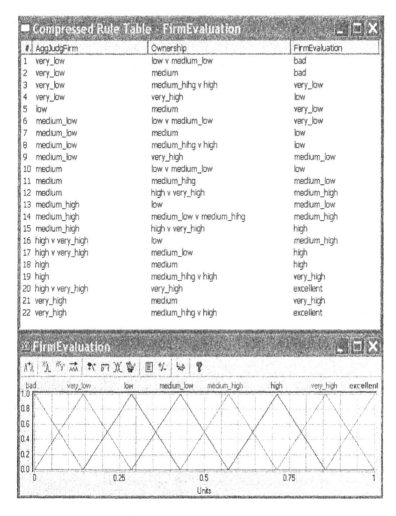

Fig. 4. Rule block of int12, int18 and int23 (FirmEvaluation) with layout

We tested the system using as input values the results obtained by the questionnaires proposed to the bank officials. The bank give us data of 287 positions, 171 "in Good Position"(G), 116 in "Bad Position" (B). To decide what is the best cut-off point, we used the classical method of the cumulated frequencies. The results are presented in table 1, where four columns are shown. The first one contains the valuation intervals, the second one, for every interval, contains the cumulate percentages of "Good Position", the third one the analogous values for the "Bad Positions" and the fourth contains the difference between the bad and the good cumulated percentage.

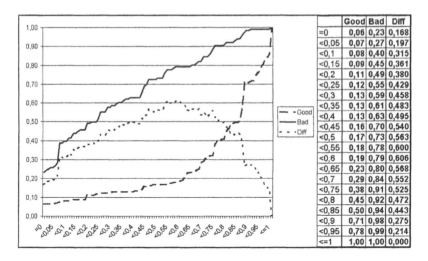

	Good	Bad	Diff
=0	0,06	0,23	0,168
<0,05	0,07	0,27	0,197
<0,1	0,08	0,40	0,315
<0,15	0,09	0,45	0,361
<0,2	0,11	0,49	0,380
<0,25	0,12	0,55	0,429
<0,3	0,13	0,59	0,458
<0,35	0,13	0,61	0,483
<0,4	0,13	0,63	0,495
<0,45	0,16	0,70	0,540
<0,5	0,17	0,73	0,563
<0,55	0,18	0,78	0,600
<0,6	0,19	0,79	0,606
<0,65	0,23	0,80	0,568
<0,7	0,29	0,84	0,552
<0,75	0,38	0,91	0,525
<0,8	0,45	0,92	0,472
<0,85	0,50	0,94	0,443
<0,9	0,71	0,98	0,275
<0,95	0,78	0,99	0,214
<=1	1,00	1,00	0,000

Tab. 1. Cumulate Percentage

The fourth column is calculated in order to evaluate the cut-off threshold by which we minimise the number of firm misclassified. The table shows that the optimal point between 0,55 and 0,50. A more detailed table shows that it is 0,58. This value is the one that shows the maximum discriminant level of the system. Fixed the cut-off point, we have studied the misclassified cases. If we indicate with G', the clients labelled by the system in a "Good Position" and with B' the ones in "Bad Position", in Table 2 the fourth and fifth rows and second column show the percentage of all clients who are indicated in a "Good Position" and are recognized by the system and the same for the clients in a "Bad position".

	Good and Bad correct	Good and Bad incorrect
G'/G	146/171	25/171
B'/B	93/116	23/116
G'/G %	86%	14%
B'/B %	81%	19%

Tab. 2. System performance

We have analyzed who are the 48 clients misclassified. Few of them, about 4%, have evaluations in a narrow neighbourhood of the cut-off level. Little changes in the analysts replayes carry to correct evaluations. The remaining part have the same evaluation of clients correctly classified, but they were in different classes. As always happens, the best way to understand what happens in the misclassified situations, is to go back in the system tree and to look at the intermediate variables. They produce the same results. So we go back more and we have analized all the inputs. They were, in practice, the same. Small differences were present in some input, but in these cases no other method would be able to classify them in the right position. The comment we have done with the bank was that there are two possibilities. Or the firms were really identically in the expert judgement or the experts do not work well, when they edit the questionaire.

7   The fuzzy cluster method

The second method is due to a request of the bank to have a rating procedure. We propose a fuzzy clustering approach. The primary objective of clustering is to partition a given data set into so-called homogeneous goups (clusters). "Homogeneous" indicates that all points in the same group are close to each other and are not close to points in other groups. In hard (crisp) clustering every object belongs to one and only one cluster. Very often, this crisp partition produces a number very high of clusters. If we let that, every object belongs to every cluster with a different membership function, we works in a fuzzy cluster contest. One of the most frequently used fuzzy cluster algorithms is the Fuzzy C-Mean (FCM) (Bezdek J.C. 1981). This algorithm is a generalization of Basic ISODATA one, called hard c-means (Duda R.- Hart P. 1973). Fuzzy clustering allows feature vectors to have membership of multiple clusters, each to varying degrees. Membership functions can be interpreted as the degrees of typicality of degrees of sharing. The fuzzy c-means method aims to minimise an objective function. The standard objective function is

$$J_m(U,v) = \sum_{j=1}^{n} \sum_{i=1}^{c} (u_{ij})^m \left\| x_j - v_i \right\|^2 \tag{1}$$

where $u_{ij} \in [0,1]$, $\sum_{i=1}^{c} u_{ij} = 1, 0 < \sum_{j=1}^{n} u_{ij} < n$, $U = (u_{ij})$, is the partition matrix

of dimension (c,n), which elements are the membership value of every data x_j to each cluster i.

$$v_i = \frac{\sum_{j=1}^{n} (u_{ij})^m x_j}{\sum_{j=1}^{n} (u_{ij})^m}, \text{ is the centroid of cluster } i \tag{2}$$

$\| \ \|$ is the Euclidean norm, c is the number of clusters, $m \in [1.+\infty)$ is the fuzzifier. The fuzzifier m determines the level of cluster fuzziness. If $m \rightarrow +\infty$ the partitions becomes more and more fuzzy. For $m=1$, the memberships u_{ij} converge to 0 or 1, and we have a crisp partitioning. In the absence of experimentation or domain knowledge, m is commonly set to 2. This algorithm has in its internal formulation the number c of cluster we desire, so it seems that FCM is an input-output data classifier. In reality the individuation of c is obtained earlier in the process by the contemporary maximization of the partition coefficient and minimization of the partition entropy [1]. The bank data produce that the optimal value of c are 2 or 4. Here we present the case of $c=2$, Good and Bad position. In the next figure (Figure 5) we show the two sets. There are few cases of misclassification. They are the same ones misclassified by the expert system. This method provides a great deal of information. It also enables to understand who is the typical client in a Good (Bad) position; he realizes the maximum level of membership function in the relative cluster , he is the centroid.

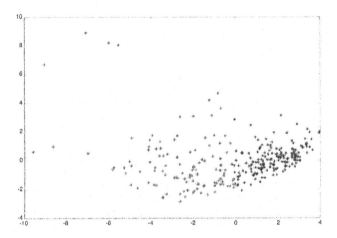

Fig. 5. Dark colour=Good Clients, Pale colour= Bad Clients

8   Conclusion

This paper is the first attempt to address the problem of qualitative analysis in bank lending. No other results are present in literature and we are very lucky to find a bank that had the idea to formalize this problem.

Scientific research in modelling and simulation needs new techniques to deal with new complex problems, where good theoretical models are lacking. Approximate solutions are needed to deal with systems where classical methods are insufficient.

Tolerance for imprecision, vagueness and uncertainty is a part of reality which cannot be avoided. We are at the beginning of this research and it is our intention to continue the study, combining the two methods proposed.

9 Reference

[1] Bezdek J.C., "Pattern recognition with fuzzy objectivefunction algorithm", Plenum New York, 1981.

[2] Duda R.- Hart P., "Pattern classification and scene analysis" Wiley, New York, 1973.

[3] Facchinetti G. - Bordoni S. - Mastroleo G., "Bank Creditworthiness using Fuzzy Systems: A Comparison with a Classical Analysis Tecnique" Risk Assessment and Management in Technology, Environment and Finance. Ruan, Mario Fedrizzi and Janusz Kacprzyk Editors, pp. 472-486, Springer Verlag Press, 2000.

[4] Facchinetti G. - Mastroleo G., "A Comparison between a Score Card and a Fuzzy Approach for Granting Personal Credit" Proceedings of Third Spanish-Italian Meeting on Financial Mathematics, Bilbao 2000.

[5] Facchinetti G. - Cosma S. - Mastroleo G. - Ferretti R., "A fuzzy credit rating approach for small firm creditworthiness evaluation in bank lending. An Italian case." Proceedings of ICSC 2001, Methods & Applications (CIMA 2001) Bangor, U.K. June 19-22, 2001.

[6] Facchinetti G. - Giove S. - Mastroleo G.," Fuzzy expert systems and data mining for bank credit rating" Proceedings of IV Meeting Italo Spagnolo di Matematica Finanziaria ed Attuariale, pp. 303-311, Alghero 2001.

[8] Gulden R, Rosignoli C, Salcioli G., "L'adozione di sistemi basati sulla conoscenza nell'area fidi degli enti creditizi" in Il Risparmio, n.2, 1994.

[9] Kasabov N.K., "Foundations of Neural Networks, Fuzzy Systems, and Knowledge Engineering" MIT Press, 1996.

[10] Kosko, B., "Fuzzy Systems as Universal Approximators" Proc. IEEE Int. Conf. On Fuzzy Systems, pp. 1153-1162, 1992.

[11] Ruozi R., "Sull'attendibilità dei bilanci e sulla loro attitudine ai fini di previsione delle insolvenze" in Bancaria, n.1, 1974.

[13] von Altrock C., "Fuzzy Logic and neurofuzzy applications in business and finance." Prentice Hall, 1997.

[14] Wang L., "Fuzzy systems are universal approximators" Proc. Of Int. Conf. On Fuzzy Engineering, pp. 471-496, 1992.

Multidimensional Systems, Signals, Circuits, and Repetitive Processes: Theory, Applications, and Future Trends

K. Galkowski*, A. Kummert**

*Institute of Control and Computation Engineering, University of Zielona Gora, Podgorna Str. 50, 65-246 Zielona Gora, Poland,
Gerhard Mercator Guest Professor, Electrical, Information and Media Engineering, University of Wuppertal, e-mail: galkowsk@uni-wuppertal.de
**Faculty of Electrical, Information and Media Engineering, University of Wuppertal, Rainer-Gruenter-Str. 21, 42119 Wuppertal, Germany,
e-mail: kummert@uni-wuppertal.de

Abstract:
In this overview the basics and recent results in multidimensional systems and repetitive processes theory and applications together with future trends are concisely revisited.

Keywords: *multidimensional systems, repetitive processes.*

1   Introduction

The past two to three decades, in particular, have seen a continually growing interest in so-called two-dimensional (2D) or, more generally, multi-dimensional (nD) systems. This is clearly related to the wide variety of applications of both practical and/or theoretical interest. The key unique feature of an nD system is that the plant or process dynamics (input, output and state variables) depend on more than one indeterminate and hence information is propagated in many independent directions.

Many physical processes have a clear nD structure. Also, the nD approach is frequently used as an analysis tool to assist, or in some cases enable, the solution of a wide variety of problems. A key point is that the applications areas for nD systems theory/engineering can be found within the general areas of Circuits, Control, and Signal Processing (and many others). An obvious approach to, for example, the control related analysis of nD systems, particularly at the conceptual level where some degree of similarity is often apparent, is to simply extend standard, i.e. 1D, techniques. This approach is, in general, incorrect since many common 1D techniques do not generalise. Also, there are many nD systems phenomena, which have no 1D systems counterparts.

Despite the diversity of applications areas, a very large volume of literature exists on basic nD systems research and is continually being added to, see e.g. [6, 25, 26, 28, 32]. This often requires mathematical tools outside those required in standard (1D) linear systems theory. Space limitations prevent a comprehensive treatment of these techniques. Instead we give a summary of the main ones placing emphasis on where fundamental/essential differences with the 1D case arise.

At an "abstract" level nD systems theory sets out to examine the same basic questions as 1D theory, e.g. controllability, observability, causality, construction of state space models (realisation theory), stability and stabilisation, feedback control, passivity. The basic reason why generalising 1D results (generally) fails is due to strong mathematical difficulties with the analysis tools employed. Also, as already noted, there are many key issues associated with nD, systems, which have no 1D counterparts.

Consider now the 2D/nD systems case where transfer function representations are to be used as the analysis base. Then difficulties immediately arise here due to the complexity of the underlying ring structure, i.e. functions in two or more indeterminates where the underlying ring does not have a division algorithm. The existence of a division algorithm for Euclidean rings forms the basis for the algorithmic derivation of many canonical forms and solution techniques at the heart of 1D systems theory, e.g. the Smith form and the solution of 1D polynomial equations. Furthermore, nD nonnegative polynomials cannot be always written as a sum of squares of polynomials, which also prevents in some cases the application of 1D techniques [40].

In the 1D case, coprimeness of polynomial matrices is a key analysis tool; see e.g. [31]. There are three forms of coprimeness for an nD polynomial matrix, termed factor, minor and zero respectively. These are all equivalent in the 1D case, but for the 2D case only minor and factor coprimeness are equivalent. For the nD case none of these concepts are equivalent ([31]).

As a simple example in the 2D case, consider the polynomials $(z_1 + 1)(z_2 + 1)$ and $z_1 z_2 + 2z_2 + 1$. These two polynomials are factor coprime but have a common zero at (-1, -1). It is also straightforward to see that zeros of a two-variate polynomial are not isolated points. Obviously for the first polynomial every pair of the form of $(z_1, -1), z_1 \in C$ or $(-1, z_2), z_2 \in C$ is a polynomial zero. Also, the investigation of the stability of 2D linear systems (and also nD linear systems) is greatly influenced by this situation. In particular, the difficulty is that the numerator polynomial of the open loop can directly influence stability! This key result was first reported by Goodman [30] after a considerable volume of literature had appeared on stability tests based on 2D transfer function descriptions. As a result, it is possible for transfer functions with the same denominator but different numerators to exhibit different stability characteristics. The key point here is that such transfer functions have non-essential singularities of the second kind, which have no 1D analogues.

The a'priori information available and the modelling objectives permit the choice of different model structures to describe 2D or nD systems. As a basic starting point, these representations can be classified according to whether or not an input/output structure is included, and latent (or auxiliary) variables are included. This general area is discussed further e.g. in [45] and the relevant references. This in turn has created an extremely interesting approach to systems with contribution also to multidimensional systems, called "behavioural", or generally "algebraic", started by J. Willems and next developed also by H. Pillai, J-F. Pommaret, A.Quadrat, P. Rocha, E. Rogers, S. Sankar, G. Wood, R. Ylinen, E. Zerz, and many others.

2   State Space Models

As in the 1D case, state space models are a very important class of internal representations. In this context, the concept of the state of a system can be defined (obviously) as the memory of the system, i.e. the past and future evolutions are independent given the current state. Hence the concept of a state depends on which ordering is considered on the underlying grid. Commonly used models for systems recursive in the positive quadrant are the Roesser model ([46]) and the Fornasini-Marchesini models ([21]) in all their forms (see e.g. [42] for a generalisation of the original model in this class). Hence, the Roesser model for discrete linear 2D systems can be presented as

$$\begin{bmatrix} x^h(i+1, j) \\ x^v(i, j+1) \end{bmatrix} = A \begin{bmatrix} x^h(i, j) \\ x^v(i, j) \end{bmatrix} + Bu(i, j) \tag{1}$$

$$y(i, j) = C \begin{bmatrix} x^h(i, j) \\ x^v(i, j) \end{bmatrix} + Du(i, j) \tag{2}$$

where $x^h(i, j) \in R^{n_h}$ and $x^v(i, j) \in R^{n_v}$ are the horizontal and vertical states, respectively, $u(i, j) \in R^q$ is the system input, $y(i, j) \in R^s$ is the system output, $i, j \in Z^+$, A, B, C and D are known real constant matrices with appropriate dimensions. The boundary condition of the system is as follows:

$$x_0 = \left[x^h(0,0)^T, x^h(1,0)^T, x^h(2,0)^T \dots ; x^v(0,0)^T, x^v(0,1)^T, x^v(0,2)^T \dots \right]^T$$

The transfer function matrix of the 2D discrete-time system (Σ) can be written as

$$G(z_1, z_2) = C(I(z_1, z_2) - A)^{-1} B + D \tag{3}$$

where

$$I(z_1, z_2) = diag(z_1 I_{n_h}, z_2 I_{n_v}) \tag{4}$$

On the other hand, a 2D discrete-time system can be also described by the following Fornasini Marchesini model:

$$x(i+1, j+1) = A_1 x(i+1, j) + A_2 x(i, j+1) + B_1 u(i+1, j) + B_2 u(i, j+1)$$
$$y(i, j) = Cx(i, j) + Du(i, j) \tag{5}$$

where A_1, A_2, B_1, B_2, C and D are known real constant matrices with appropriate dimensions, and the rest of notations are the same as for the Roesser model. Then, the transfer function of the 2D discrete-time system can be written as

$$G(z_1, z_2) = C(z_1 z_2 I - z_1 A_1 - z_2 A_2)^{-1}(z_1 B_1 + z_2 B_2) + D \tag{6}$$

3   System Theoretical Features

The structure of these models (and others) has been extensively investigated. One of the most striking differences with the 1D case is the need to consider both a global, X, and a local, x, state. Basically, the global state in a diagonal line, L_k, denoted X_k, is defined as the collection of all local states along L_k. Concepts such as reachability, controllability and observability are then defined at both global and local levels and they can be quite distinct properties.

Minimality in the 1D case is completely characterised by reachability (or controllability) and observability of the state space model. This is another key area, which does not generalise from 1D to nD where only partial results are yet known. A key problem here is again related to the complicated structure of the underlying ring structure, i.e. the lack of simple methods for checking the existence of solutions of polynomial equations in more than one indeterminate.

(As noted by Cayley, there are no determinant-based conditions similar to Kramer's rule for systems of 1D linear equations). Grobner basis theory ([8] for example) may help to solve this key problem. A more detailed discussion of this problem can be found in Chapter 3.

In the 1D case, the similarity transform applied to the state vector has a key theoretical and practical role. This is again not true for nD systems where, for example, the problem of obtaining all possible state space realisations of a given state space model cannot be solved in a similar manner ([27]). Also the synthesis problem, which is at the heart of 2D/nD circuit theory and applications, has not yet been completely solved in the 2D/nD case.

Continuing, causality is a key feature of classic dynamical systems (it must be present for physical realizability). In the 1D case, the general concept of "time" imposes a natural ordering into "past", "present" and "future". Again the situation is different in the nD case due, in effect, to the fact that some of the indeterminates have a spatial rather than a temporal characteristic. Hence causality is of less relevance than in the 1D case since it is only necessary to be able to recursively perform the required computations.

Next, we give a brief overview of the developments in nD systems, which are relevant to the work reported here. The first significant work on nD systems appeared in the early 1960's in the general area of circuit analysis. There are two papers, which are widely recognized as the "starting points". First, Ozaki and Kasami (1960) [43] showed that positive real functions of two or more variables could be used in the analysis and synthesis of circuits with variable parameters. Then, in Ansell (1964) [3] showed how the same approach could be used for networks of transmission lines (distributed parameter elements and lumped reactances). This work was of particular interest to electrical engineers studying high frequency networks (micro-waves). It is also of interest to note that significant contributions to systems synthesis using 2D positive real functions was also reported by Uruski and Piekarski (1972) [49]. Also, the use of this theory in the study of transmission lines led to the suggestion that it could also be applied to the study of systems with delays.

Following these early publications, in particular, great interest was generated in the synthesis of 2D and nD positive real functions or matrices under the usual circuits restrictions of passivity, losslessness etc. Key papers in this general area include Koga and many papers since then by, for example, Youla, Saito, Scanlan and Rhodes. It is also important to note that this general area is still open in many respects.

The advances in the general area of signal/image processing have created many applications for, in particular, 2D and 3D filters. These include seismology, tomography and visual data communications applications. Early analysis/design tools were largely based on input/output descriptions in the form of multidimensional difference equations with immediate links via the multidimensional z and Fourier transforms to multidimensional transfer functions (or transfer function matrices). Design tools for multidimensional filters is an area in which much work has been done and the filters implemented - see, for example, Fettweis (1984) [10]. Also, prominent is work by Fettweis, see for example [19], on the extension of classical analogue circuit theory techniques (e.g. the Kirchoff laws, passivity) together with wave digital filters to digital applications, which is a subject of thew further sections.

Another field for nD systems theory are processes modelled by partial differential and/or difference equations. Interesting applications reported to date include river pollution modelling, [22].

4 Realization Theory

The crucial problem of constructing state-space realizations of 2D/nD linear systems from input-output data – often is given in the form of a 2D/nD transfer function description. Here, the basic philosophy followed arises from the following quotation by Fornasini (1991) [23] "The unquestioned success of the estimation and regulation procedures in 1D theory mainly relies on state space methods that allow for efficient and explicit synthesis algorithms. Along the same lines, it is expected that the introduction of state space models that depend on two independent variables will eventually display concrete applications of rich body of 2D theory" .

The problem of constructing state-space realizations for 2D/nD linear systems is much more complicated than for 1D, linear systems and, amongst others, this is due to the complexity of the underlying multivariate polynomial ring. This general area has been the subject of much research effort over the years (leading to a number of competitive methods) but, in general, it is still an open research problem.

A second motivation for the general approach to be employed here is taken from Youla and Pickel (1984) [52]: "Some of the most impressive accomplishments in circuits and systems have been obtained by in-depth exploitation of the properties of elementary polynomial matrices. ... Algorithms for the construction of such matrices are, therefore, of both theoretical and practical importance" . Based on this underlying idea, Galkowski (2002) has developed the so-called Elementary Operations Algorithm (EOA), which is a systematic method for constructing a range of state-space realizations for 2D systems. Note also that the possibility of achieving various equivalent state-space realizations is of particular interest for 2D/nD systems since, as mentioned, unlike the 1D linear systems case, the similarity transform does not provide all possible realizations.

5 Theory and Application of Multidimensional Circuits

Multidimensional circuits [5, 17, 35, 36, 37, 38, 39, 40] (as a significant part of systems theory) gained considerable attention during the last decades due to a great variety of application in image processing, geophysics, medical imaging, and virtual reality.

The primary signals occurring in classical one-dimensional (1D) electrical circuits are voltage and current which are, in the case of lumped elements, functions of time. Such networks obey Kirchhoff's laws and are well investigated systems. In this context there exists a one to one correspondence between voltages and currents in a physical sense and the signals used in graphs on model level. Nevertheless, the graph theoretical based network theory also would be possible without any physical meaning as a mathematical well defined building of axioms and theorems. On this level, the restriction to one independent variable can be overcome by considering all signals in such generalized networks to be dependent of several variables, $t_1, \ldots, t_n$, where n is the dimensionality of the problem. In order to be in accordance with 1D circuit theory, such signals still will be called voltage and current, however, need not necessarily represent such quantities in a physical sense. Working on such a graph theoretic level, Kirchhoff's laws still can be maintained (see Fig. 1).

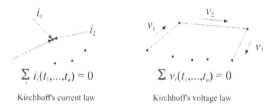

$$\sum_i i_i(t_1,\ldots,t_n) = 0 \qquad \sum_i v_i(t_1,\ldots,t_n) = 0$$

Kirchhoff's current law   Kirchhoff's voltage law

Fig. 1: Kirchhoff's laws still apply in the nD case

Furthermore, building elements can be ideal lines, constant building elements like ideal transformer, gyrators, circulators, and real resistors. Also two different types of reactive building elements exist, called inductance and capacitance, which are nD generalisations of the corresponding 1D elements, i.e. voltage and current at such a one-port are related via a first order derivative. However, in the nD case, a partial derivative with respect to one of the independent variables $t_1, \ldots, t_n$ is performed, see Fig.2.

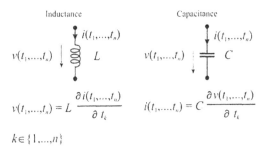

$$v(t_1,\ldots,t_n) = L \frac{\partial\, i(t_1,\ldots,t_n)}{\partial\, t_k} \qquad i(t_1,\ldots,t_n) = C \frac{\partial\, v(t_1,\ldots,t_n)}{\partial\, t_k}$$

$$k \in \{1,\ldots,n\}$$

Fig. 2: Two different types of reactive building elements

In other words, multidimensional networks are Kirchhoff circuits in the classical sense, with the exception that reactive building elements (inductances and capacitances) can differ in the variable t_k to which respect the partial derivative is performed.

Next, to each variable t_k we associate a complex frequency variable (Laplace variable), p_k, $k = 1,\ldots,n$. For the steady state case we can introduce the complex calculus, where the relation between complex amplitudes of voltage and current is described via a complex impedance, see Fig. 3.

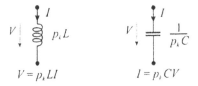

$$V = p_k LI \qquad\qquad I = p_k CV$$

Fig. 3: Steady state relations

Obviously, a reactive element is characterized by

- the value of the building element: L or C, respectively

- the type of complex frequency variable: p_k

An example for a two-dimensional ($n = 2$) circuit is given in Fig. 4, where $e(t_1,\ldots,t_n)$ acts as input signal and $v(t_1,\ldots,t_n)$ (voltage over R_2) acts as output signal of a linear 2D system.

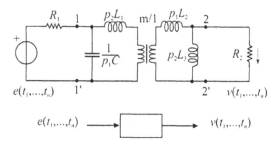

Fig. 4: Example for a 2D circuit

In general, an nD multiport (see Fig. 5) is described via the associated impedance matrix $Z(p_1,\ldots,p_n)$ or the scattering matrix $S(p_1,\ldots,p_n)$ which now are rational matrices in n independent frequency variables $p_1,\ldots,p_n$.

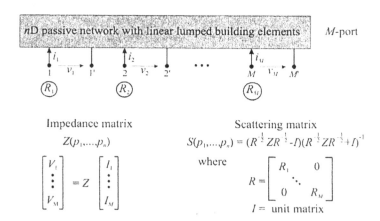

Fig. 5: nD multiport

In case of passive building elements the overall passivity of the network is guaranteed. The latter is strongly related to the stability of such a system.

Passivity itself is defined as

$$\text{Re} \sum_{i=1}^{M} V_i I_i^* \geq 0 \quad \text{for} \quad \text{Re} \, p_k \geq 0, \ k = 1,\ldots,n \tag{7}$$

In this case, the scattering matrix obeys the equation

$$I - S^* \left(p_1,\ldots,p_n \right) S \left(p_1,\ldots,p_n \right) \geq 0 \quad \text{for} \quad \text{Re} \, p_k \geq 0, \ k = 1,\ldots,n \tag{8}$$

In other words, passivity leads to stability in a Lyapunov type sense. This aspect is of greatest interest in the context of the design of nD systems, since structural passivity guarantees stability of the resulting system. Furthermore, lossless systems form a very important subclass of passive systems. In such special cases the scattering matrix additional obeys the property

$$S^* \left(j\omega_1,\ldots,j\omega_n \right) S \left(j\omega_1,\ldots,j\omega_n \right) = I, \omega_k \in R, k = 1,\ldots,n. \tag{9}$$

In the case of real networks this property is equivalent to

$$S^T \left(-p_1,\ldots,-p_n \right) S \left(p_1,\ldots,p_n \right) = I \tag{10}$$

For simplicity of notation, let us restrict our attention to real circuits in the following, although all results also can be generalized to the complex case.

Stability in particular depends on the denominator polynomial of the scattering matrix $S \left(p_1,\ldots,p_n \right)$. In contrast to 1D systems theory, different classes of Hurwitz polynomials have to be discussed in the nD case [5, 11, 15, 16]. The class appearing as denominator of scattering matrices of passive circuits is called "scattering Hurwitz polynomial" and obeys the following properties.

An n-variable real polynomial is called scattering Hurwitz, if

- $g \left(p_1,\ldots,p_n \right) \neq 0 \quad \text{for} \quad \text{Re} \, p_k > 0, \ k = 1,\ldots,n$,

- $g \left(p_1,\ldots,p_n \right)$ and $g \left(-p_1,\ldots,-p_n \right)$ are relatively prime.

Following the above discussion, there might be the impression that the concept of nD circuits is only of academic importance since such systems cannot be realised in a physical sense by using classical electrical building elements. However, such a conclusion is not true, nD circuits serve as reference networks for the design of stable and robust nD discrete systems by using bilinear transform. Such a procedure is well known from 1D filter design and can be generalized to the nD case. To be more specific, let $S_{ij} \left(p_1,\ldots,p_n \right)$ be an element of the scattering matrix of a passive circuit, by using the bilinear transform

$$p_k = \frac{1}{T_k} \frac{z_k + 1}{z_k - 1}, \quad k = 1, \ldots, n,$$

(11)

we obtain

$$H\left(z_1, \ldots, z_n\right) = S_{ij}\left(\frac{1}{T_1} \frac{z_1 + 1}{z_1 - 1}, \ldots, \frac{1}{T_n} \frac{z_n + 1}{z_n - 1}\right),$$

(12)

where $H\left(z_1, \ldots, z_n\right)$ can be used as transfer function of a stable nD discrete system. A more sophisticated procedure to use this concept implicitly is the wave digital filter approach [1, 9, 12], where the structure and building elements of the nD reference circuit are transformed into a signal flow graph of a discrete system whose transfer behaviour is again described by $H\left(z_1, \ldots, z_n\right)$ defined in (12). The advantage of the wave digital filter approach can be seen in the property that synthesis of $H\left(z_1, \ldots, z_n\right)$ is done automatically in a way that the resulting discrete system is not only stable under ideal linear conditions but also if nonlinear effects like quantization and overflow are taken into account.

As outlined above, nD circuits can be used for modeling partial differential equations which are derived from real situations in physics. The latter aspect is of great importance since only passive systems can be comprised. The integration of such partial differential equations can be accomplished by deriving the associate wave digital filter [13, 18, 20, 24, 50]. In future this aspect will be of great importance since even nonlinear cases can be covered by considering nonlinear inductances, capacitances, and resistors.

Finally, multidimensional networks can be used to generate stable nD polynomials [41]. Assume any nD circuit consisting of passive building elements, then for any nonnegative choice of the values of these building elements, i.e. $R_i, L_i, C_i \in R$, the denominator of the associated scattering matrix is a stable polynomial in $\left(p_1, \ldots, p_n\right)$ and after using the bilinear transform (11) a "discrete" stable polynomial in $\left(z_1, \ldots, z_n\right)$ can be derived.

6   Repetitive Processes

In contrast to the 1D case, it is possible to consider models with a so-called mixed structure. For example, Kaczorek (1994) [33] has studied systems described by state space models, which are discrete in one direction and continuous in the other.

Such models have obviously close links with linear repetitive processes, which have numerous practical applications, Rogers and Owens (1992) [47]. The essential unique feature of a linear repetitive process is a series of sweeps, or passes, through a set of dynamics defined over a fixed finite duration known as the pass length. On each pass, an output, termed the pass length, is produced which acts as a forcing function on, and hence contributes to, the next pass profile. Practical examples include long-wall coal cutting and metal rolling, Smyth (1992) [48], and algorithmic examples include classes of so-called iterative learning control schemes, see e.g. [2], and iterative solution algorithms for classes of non-linear dynamic optimal control problems based on the maximum principle Roberts (2000) [44].

The state space model of the differential linear repetitive processes considered here has the following form over $0 \le t \le \alpha$, $k \ge 0$,

$$\dot{x}_{k+1}(t) = Ax_{k+1}(t) + Bu_{k+1}(t) + B_0 y_k(t)$$
$$y_{k+1}(t) = Cx_{k+1}(t) + Du_{k+1}(t) + D_0 y_k(t)$$
(13)

Here on pass k, $x_k(t)$ is the $n \times 1$ state vector, $y_k(t)$ is the $m \times 1$ pass profile vector, and $u_k(t)$ is the $l \times 1$ vector of control inputs.

To complete the process description, it is necessary to specify the 'initial conditions' – termed the boundary conditions here, i.e. the state initial vector on each pass and the initial pass profile. Here no loss of generality arises from assuming $x_{k+1}(0) = d_{k+1}, : k \ge 0$ and $y_0(t) = f(t)$, where d_{k+1} is an $n \times 1$ vector with known constant entries and $f(t)$ is an $m \times 1$ vector whose entries are known functions of t. Such a model is clearly a continuous discrete linear 2D system but it is also possible to define the discrete linear repetitive process clearly resembling the standard discrete 2D system. Following Rogers and Owens [29] the state-space model of a discrete linear repetitive process has the following form over $0 \le p \le \alpha$, $k \ge 0$

$$x_{k+1}(p+1) = Ax_{k+1}(p) + Bu_{k+1}(p) + B_0 y_k(p)$$
$$y_{k+1}(p) = Cx_{k+1}(p) + Du_{k+1}(p) + D_0 y_k(p)$$
(14)

where on pass $k, x_k(p)$ is the $n \times 1$ state vector, $y_k(p)$ is the $m \times 1$ vector pass profile, and $u_k(p)$ is the $l \times 1$ vector of control inputs.

To complete the process description, it is necessary to specify the 'initial conditions' - termed the boundary conditions here, i.e. the state initial vector on each pass and the initial pass profile. Here no loss of generality arises from assuming $x_{k+1}(0) = d_{k+1}$, $k \geq 0$ and $y_0(p) = f(p)$ where d_{k+1} is an $n \times 1$ vector with known constant entries and $f(p)$ is an $m \times 1$ vector whose entries are known functions of p.

Comparing this process with a discrete linear 2D system of the Roesser form we easily see that (14) can be transformed to the form of (1), see e.g. [29], and then

$$x_{k+1}(p) \to x^h(i,j); y_k(p) \to x^v(i,j)$$

$$A \to A_{11}, B_0 \to A_{12}, C \to A_{21}, D_0 \to A_{22}$$

The discrete repetitive process dynamics can be highlighted by the folowing figure, which describes the role of the two-dimensional information updating in the system.

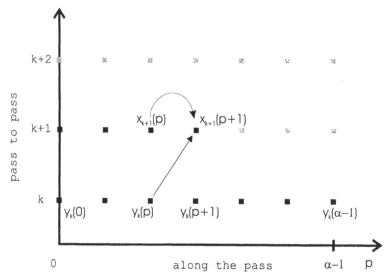

Fig.6: State dynamics

7   Stability and Stabilisation

A great practical, as well, as theoretical interest for all system classes are stability analysis and appropriate stabilising controller design. Now, we revisit concisely base notions and methods. Following e.g. Kaczorek [32] remind the asymptotic stability definition.

Definition 1 The 2-D linear discrete-time system is said to be asymptotically stable if

$$\lim_{i,j \to \infty} \|x(i,j)\| = 0 \tag{15}$$

under zero input $u(i,j) \equiv 0$ and the boundary condition such that

$$\sup_j \|x^h(0,j)\| < \infty \text{ and } \sup_i \|x^v(i,0)\| < \infty,$$

where

$$x(i,j) = \left[x^h(i,j)^T, \quad x^v(i,j)^T \right]^T$$

It is well known that the asymptotic stability of 2D systems [32] can be characterised in the spectral form by the following lemma.

Lemma 1 The 2D system is asymptotically stable if and only if the characteristic polynomial has no zeros in the domain

$$\{(z_1, z_2) : |z_1| \geq 1 \text{ and } |z_2| \geq 1\}, \text{ that is,}$$

$$C(z_1, z_2) = \det[I(z_1, z_2) - A] \neq 0 \text{ if } |z_1| \geq 1 \text{ and } |z_2| \geq 1.$$

It is however a troublesome task to provide the effective tests for stability checking in this way. A very efficient approach is based on the Lyapunov theory and exploits the so called Linear Matrix Inequalities (LMI) [7], which can be solved in the well developed, easily accessible toolboxes as e.g. under Matlab and Scilab and many other solvers. The following theorem [29] provides an easy sufficiency test for asymptotic stability of the 2D linear system or the so-called stability along the pass of the discrete linear 2D system.

Theorem 1 [29] The 2D system is asymptotically stable if there exist matrices $P > 0$ and $Q > 0$ satisfying the following LMI:

$$\begin{bmatrix} \hat{A}_1^T P \hat{A}_1 + Q - P & \hat{A}_1^T P \hat{A}_2 \\ \hat{A}_2^T P \hat{A}_1 & \hat{A}_2^T P \hat{A}_2 - Q \end{bmatrix} < 0 \tag{16}$$

where

$$\hat{A}_1 = \begin{bmatrix} A_{11} & A_{12} \\ 0 & 0 \end{bmatrix}, \ \hat{A}_2 = \begin{bmatrix} 0 & 0 \\ A_{21} & A_{22} \end{bmatrix} \tag{17}$$

In terms of the design of control schemes for 2D systems, it has become clear that the most powerful control action comes from feedback action. For the Roesser model it is of the form

$$u(i,j) = Kx(i,j) = \begin{bmatrix} K_1 & K_2 \end{bmatrix} \begin{bmatrix} x^h(i,j) \\ x^v(i,j) \end{bmatrix} \tag{18}$$

where K is an appropriately dimensioned matrix to be designed. Next, introduce the matrices

$$\hat{B}_1 = \begin{bmatrix} B_1 \\ 0 \end{bmatrix}, \ \hat{B}_2 = \begin{bmatrix} 0 \\ B_2 \end{bmatrix}, \tag{19}$$

then we have the following result.

Theorem 3 [29] The 2D system is asymptotically stabilisable by a state feedback of the form (18) if there exist matrices $Y > 0, Z$ and N such that the following LMI holds

$$\begin{bmatrix} -Y+Z & 0 & Y\hat{A}_1^T + N^T\hat{B}_1^T \\ 0 & -Z & Y\hat{A}_2^T + N^T\hat{B}_2^T \\ \hat{A}_1 Y + \hat{B}_1 N & \hat{A}_2 Y + \hat{B}_2 N & -Y \end{bmatrix} < 0 \tag{20}$$

If the conditions are satisfied, then a stabilizing control is given by (18) with

$$K = NY^{-1}. \tag{21}$$

It is important to note that LMI methods, despite some level of conservativeness introduced due to providing only sufficient conditions for most multidimensional problems, are very efficient in handling many practically motivated cases, as e.g. with a model uncertainty, i.e. with no full information on the system [29].

8 Conclusions and Future Trends

Multidimensional systems recently found many applications to solve or assist numerous important practically and theoretically problems. Finally, we mention a few particularly interesting subareas for further work:

1. Continuous and hybrid /continuous discrete/ systems and circuits, e.g. repetitive processes, including multidimensional /e.g. plane/ repetitive processes,

2. Nonlinear systems via Volterra operators and multidimensional system methods,

3. Algebraic approach to multidimensional systems, including fractional, complex and quaternionic methods,

4. Probabilistic multidimensional systems,

5. Systems and circuits with switched dynamics /time and space variant/,

6. Delay effects, and many, many others,

7. Circuits as reference network for nD digital filters,

8. Circuits as models for partial differential equations,

9. Derivation of stable polynomials by means of nD circuits.

9 References

[1]   Aggarwal J. K., "Principles of multidimensional wave digital filtering", Digital Signal Processing, Ed. Fettweis A., 262-282, Point Lobo Press, Hollywood, 1979.

[2]   Amann N., Owens D.H., Rogers E., "Predictive optimal iterative learning control", Int. J. Control, Vol. 69, No. 2, 203-226, 1998.

[3]   Ansell H.G., "On certain two-variable generalizations of circuits theory, with applications to network of transmission lines and lumped reactances", IEEE Trans. on Circuits and Systems, Vol. CAS-11, 214-223, 1964.

[4]   Basu S., Fettweis A., "On the factorization of scattering transfer matrices of multidimensional lossless two-ports", IEEE Trans. on Circuits and Sytems, Vol. CAS-32, 925-934, 1985.

[5]   Basu S., Fettweis A., "New results on stable multidimensional polynomials-Part II: Discrete case", IEEE Trans. on Circuits ans Systems, Vol. 34, No. 11, 1264-1274, 1987.

[6]   Bose N.K. (Ed.), Buchberger B. (Ed.), Guiver J.P. (Ed.), "Multidimensional Systems Theory and Applications", Kluwer Academic Pub., 2004.

[7]   Boyd S., Ghaoui L. E., Feron E., and Balakrishnan V., "Linear Matrix Inequalities In System And Control Theory", vol. 15 of *SIAM studies in applied mathematics*. SIAM, Philadelphia, 1994.

[8]   Buchberger B., "Ein algorithmishes kriterium fur die losbarkeit eines algebraishen gleichungsystems", Aeq. Math., Vol. 4, 374-383, 1970.

[9]   Fettweis A., "Multidimensional wave digital filters", European Conf. Circuit Theory and Design, Vol. II, 409-416, 1976.

[10]   Fettweis A., "Multidimensional circuits and systems", in Proc. IEEE Int. Symp. on Circuits and Systems, Vol. 3, 951-957, 1984.

[11]   Fettweis A., "Some properties of scattering Hurwitz polynomials", Archiv für Elektronik und Übertragungstechnik, Vol. 38, 171-176, 1984.

[12]   Fettweis A., "Wave digital filters: Theory and practice", (invited paper) Proc. of the IEEE, Vol. 74, No. 2, 270-327, 1986.

[13]   Fettweis A., "Discrete passive modeling of physical systems described by PDEs", European Signal Proceeding Conference, Vol. 1, 55-62, 1992.

[14]   Fettweis A., "Simulation of hydromechanical partial differential equations by discrete passive dy-namical systems", In Kimura H. et al Eds. Recent Advances in Mathematical Theory of Systems, Control and Signal Processing II, MITA Press, 489-494, 1992.

[15]   Fettweis A., Basu S., "New results on multidimensional Hurwitz polynomials", ISCAS, Vol. 3, 1359-1362, 1985.

[16]   Fettweis A., Basu S., "New results on stable multidimensional polynomials-Part I": Continuous case", IEEE Trans. on Circuits ans Systems, Vol. 34, No. 10, 1221-1232, 1987.

[17]   Fettweis A., Linnenberg G., "An extension of the maximum-modulus principle for application to multidimensional networks", Archiv für Elektronik und Übertragungstechnik, Vol. 38, 131-135, 1984.

[18]   Fettweis A., Nitsche G., "Numerical integration of partial differential equations by means of multidimensional wave digital filters", IEEE International Symposium on Circuits and Systems, Vol. 2, 954-957, 1990.

[19]   Fettweis A., Nitsche G., "Numerical integration of partial differential equations using principles of multidimensional wave digital filters", Journal of VLSI Signal Processing, vol. 3, 7-24, 1991.

[20]   Fettweis A., Seraji G. A., "New results in numerically integrating PDEs by the wave digital approach", IEEE International Symposium on Circuits and Systems, Vol. 5, 17-20, 1999.

300

[21] Fornasini E., Marchesini G. "Doubly-indexed dynamical systems", Math. Syst. Theory, Vol. 12, 59-72, 1978.

[22] Fornasini E., "A 2-D systems approach to river pollution modelling, Multi-dimensional Systems and Signal Processing, Vol. 2, 233-265, 1991.

[23] Fornasini E., Zampieri S., "A note on the state space realization of 2D FIR transfer functions", Systems & Control Letters, Vol. 16, 117-122, 1991.

[24] Fries M., "Numerical integration of Euler flow by means of multidimensional wave digital principles", Dissertation, Ruhr-Universität Bochum, 1995.

[25] Gałkowski K., Vinnikov V., (Ed.), "International Journal of Control, spec. issue", 2004, Vol. 77, no 9.

[26] Gałkowski K., Longman R. W., Rogers E., (Ed.), "International Journal of Applied Mathematics and Computer Science: Special Issue: Multidimensional Systems nD and Iterative Learning Control", 2003, Vol. 13, no 1.

[27] Galkowski K., "State-space Realizations of Linear 2-D Systems with Extensions to the General nD (n>2) Case", vol. 263 of Lecture Notes in Control and Information Sciences. Springer, London, 2002.

[28] Galkowski K., Wood J., Eds., "Multidimensional Signals, Circuits and Systems", Taylor & Francis, 2001.

[29] Galkowski K., Rogers E., Xu S., Lam J. and Owens D. H., "LMIs-A fundamental tool in analysis and controller design for discrete linear repetitive processes", IEEE Transactions on Circuits and Systems I: Fundamental Theory and Application, 49(6), pp. 768-778, 2002.

[30] Goodman D,. "Some stability properties of two-dimensional linear shift-invariant filters", IEEE Trans. on Circuits and Systems, Vol. CAS 24, 201-208, 1977.

[31] Johnson D.S., Rogers E., Pugh A.C., Hayton G.E., Owens D.H., "A polynomial Matrix theory for a certain class of 2-D linear systems", Linear Algebra and Its Applications, no.241-243, pp 669-703, 1996.

[32] Kaczorek, T., "Linear Control Systems", Research Studies Press LTD, (distributed by John Wiley & Sons Inc), 1993.

[33] Kaczorek T., "2-D continuous-discrete linear systems", in Proc. Tenth Int. Conf. on System Eng. ICSE'94, Vol. 1, 550-557, 1994.

[34] Kailath T., "Linear Systems", Prentice-Hall, Englewood Cliffs, N.Y., 1980.

[35] Kummert A., "Synthesis of two-dimensional lossless m-ports with prescribed scattering matrix", Circuits, Systems, and Signal Processing , Vol. 8, No. 1, 97-119, 1989.

[36] Kummert A., "On the number of frequency-dependent building elements of multidimensional lossless networks", Archiv für Elektronik und Übertragungstechnik, Vol. 43, No. 4, 237-240, 1989.

[37] Kummert A., "Synthesis of 3-D lossless first-order one-ports with lumped elements", IEEE Trans. on Circuits and Systems, Vol. CAS-36, No. 11, 1445-1449, 1989.

[38] Kummert A., "Synthesis of two-dimensional passive one-ports with lumped elements, Signal Processing, Scattering and Operator Theory, and Numerical Methods", Eds. Kaashoek M. A., van Schuppen J. H., Ran A. C. M., International Symposium on Mathematical Theory of Networks and Systems, 1989, Vol. III, 99-106. Birkhäuser, Boston, 1990.

[39] Kummert A., "The synthesis of two-dimensional passive n-ports containing lumped elements", Multidimensional Systems and Signal Processing , Vol. 1, No. 4, 351-362, 1990.

[40] Kummert A., "On the synthesis of multidimensional reactance multiports", IEEE Trans. on Circuits and Systems, Vol. CAS-38, No. 6, 637-642, 1991.

[41] Kummert A., "2-D stable polynomials with parameter-dependent coefficients: Generalisations and results", IEEE Transactions on Circuits and Systems, Vol. 49, No. 6, pp. 725-731, 2002.

[42] Kurek J.E., "The general state-space model for a two-dimensional digital systems", IEEE Trans. on Automatic Control, Vol. AC-30, 345-354, 1985.

[43] Ozaki H., Kasami T., "Positive real functions of several variables and their applications to variable networks", IRE Trans. on Circuit Theory, Vol. 7, 251-260, 1960.

[44] Roberts P.D., "Numerical investigations of a stability theorem arising from the 2-dimensional analysis of an iterative optimal control algorithm", Multidimensional Systems and Signal Processing, Vol. 11, No. 1/2, 109-124, 2000.

[45] Rocha P., "Structure and Representations for 2-D Systems", PhD Thesis, University of Groningen, The Netherlands, 1990.

[46] Roesser R., "A discrete state space model for linear image processing", IEEE Trans. Automatic Control, vol. 20, pp. 1-10, 1975.

[47] Rogers E., Owens D.H., "Stability analysis for linear repetitive processes", Lecture Notes in Control and Information Sciences, 175, Ed. Thoma M., Wyner W., Springer Verlag, Berlin, 1992.

[48] Smyth K., "Computer aided analysis for linear repetitive processes", PhD Thesis, University of Strathclyde, Glasgow, UK, 1992.

[49] Uruski M., Piekarski M., "Synthesis of a network containing a cascade of commensurate transmissions lines and lumped elements", Proc. IEEE, Vol. 119, No. 2, 153-159, 1972.

[50] Vollmer M., An approach to automatic generation of wave digital stzructures from PDEs, IEEE International Symposium on Circuits and Systems, 2004.

[51] Youla D.C., Gnavi G. Notes on n dimensional systems, IEEE Trans on Circuits and Systems, Vol. CAS-26, No. 2, 105-111, 1979.

[52]   Youla D.C., Pickel P.F., "The Quillen-Suslin theorem and the structure of n-dimensional elementary polynomial matrices", IEEE Trans. on Circuits and Systems Vol. CAS-31(6):513-518, 1984.

[53]   Zak S. H., Lee E. B., Lu W. S., "Realizations of 2-D filters and time delay systems", IEEE Trans on Circuits and Systems, Vol. CAS-33, No. 12, 1241-1244, 1986.

Modelling using probabilistic algorithms

Anna BOROWSKA, Wiktor DAŃKO, Joanna KARBOWSKA-CHILIŃSKA

Technical University of Bialystok
address, e-mail: anbor@ii.pb.bialystok.pl, danko@ii.pb.bialystok.pl, asia@chilan.com

Abstract: Markov chains are typical tools for modelling real stochastic processes. The present paper suggest to use an equivalent model of Iterative Probabilistic Algorithms, interpreted in a finite structure. The Probabilistic Algorithms model gives the possibility of modelling subprocesses and obtaining the algorithm modelling the whole process as an (algorithmic) composition of algorithms modelling subprocesses. The typical parametres (the transition matrix of the algorithm, average number of steps,...) can be determined without experiments and compared to results of the statistical analysis of computer simulations.

Keywords: probabilistic algorithm, Markov chain, probabilistic model

1   Introduction

The aim of the paper is to discuss the possibility of modelling real stochastic processes by means of Iterative Probabilistic Algorithms (cf. [1,2,4,7,8]), interpreted in a finite structure.

Iterative probabilistic algorithms are equivalent to Finite Markov Chains (cf. [5,6]), therefore one can use them in all those situations, where Markov chain model is suitable.

Iterative Probabilistic Algorithms are especially useful in the cases, where the modeled process can be considered as a composition of several subprocesses related in a probabilistic and/or algorithmic way. The advantage of Probabilistic Algorithms model consists in the possibility of modelling subprocesses and obtaining the algorithm modelling the whole process as an (algorithmic) composition of algorithms modelling subprocesses. One can say, that the use of Probabilistic Algorithms model enables us to realize the structural programming strategy.

In this work is analyzed an example modelling a (simplified version of) a real situation. First, its description is transformed into a Probabilistic Algorithm model. Next, we shall use this algorithm to simulate the real process and investigate its behaviour (probabilities of passing from a state to another one, average number of steps, ...) by means of the standard statistical methods (cf. Appendix 2).

On the other hand, one can determine these statistical parameters without experiments; the transition matrix of the algorithm, average number of steps, ..., can be established in a theoretical way by means of algebraic methods (cf. Appendix 1 and [4,8]).

If the parameters determined by means of experiments and parameters obtained by the theoretical analysis of the algorithm differ essentially, we suggest to improve generators of pseudorandom objects in implemented version of the algorithm.

2 Iterative probabilistic algorithms

Let L be a first order language containing a countable set $X = \{x, y, ...\}$ of individual variables, a set $F = \{f, g, ...\}$ of function symbols, a set $R = \{=, r, s, ...\}$ of predicate symbols and a set $C = \{c, d, ...\}$ of constant symbols.

Let $\Im = <A, F, R, C>$ be a structure for L, where A is a finite u-element universe. By a valuation of variables from the set $X^h = \{x_1, ..., x_h\}$ we shall understand any mapping $\varpi : X^h \to A$. The set of all valuations of variables from X^h we shall denote by W_h.

We shall use an abstract programming language L_p being an extension of L. Probabilistic programs of L_p are understood as iterative programs using typical program constructions:

$x := a;$

begin ... end,

if ... then ... else ...,

while ... do ...
and two probabilistic constructions:

$x := random,$

either$_p$ ... or ...
interpreted as follows: the first construction corresponds to a random generation of a value of the variable and the first part of the second one is chosen with the probability p and the other with the probability (1-p).

The probability distribution corresponding to random generation of elements in assignments of the form $x := random$ will be denoted by ρ :

$$\rho : A \rightarrow [0,1], \quad \sum_{i=1}^{u} \rho(a_i) = 1,$$

By a probabilistic structure for L_p we shall understand the pair $< \Im, \rho >$ and denote by $\Im_\rho$.

We shall assume that each possible valuation of the program variables is assumed to appear with a probability. Thus one can speak about (sub)distributions of probabilities μ defined on the set W_h of valuations:

$$\mu : W_h \rightarrow [0,1], \quad \sum_{i=1}^{n} \mu(\{\varpi_i\}) \leq 1,$$

where $n = u^h$.

Denote by M_h the set of all such subdistributions. Since $A = \{a_1, \ldots, a_n\}$ and $X^h = \{x_1, \ldots, x_h\}$, then W_h consists of $n = u^h$ elements, $W_h = \{\varpi_1, \ldots, \varpi_n\}$. Thus each distribution μ can be represented as a n-element vector $\mu = [\mu_1, \ldots, \mu_n]$, where $\mu_i = \mu(\varpi_i)$, $i = 1, \ldots, n$.

A probabilistic program P is interpreted in the structure $< \Im, \rho >$ as a (total) mapping transforming input subdistributions into output subdistributions:

$$P_{< \Im, \rho >} : M_h \rightarrow M_h.$$

In this case $P_{< \Im, \rho >}(\mu)$ will denote the output subdistribution realized by the program P in the structure $< \Im, \rho >$ with the initial subdistribution μ. The notion of probabilistic program realization can be illustrated as follows:

$$
\begin{array}{ccc}
\varpi_1 & \xrightarrow{\ \mu_1\ } & \\
& \cdots & K \\
\varpi_n & \xrightarrow{\ \mu_n\ } &
\end{array}
\quad
\begin{array}{ccc}
& \xrightarrow{\ \mu_1'\ } & \varpi_1 \\
& \cdots & \\
& \xrightarrow{\ \mu_n'\ } & \varpi_n
\end{array}
$$

The following lemma (cf. [4]) gives an algebraic method of determining, for a given program and an input subdistribution, the corresponding output subdistribution, and therefore can be treated as an (algebraic) method of defining the semantics of iterative probabilistic algorithms computations.

There are many (equivalent) methods of defining the semantics of probabilistic programs computations (e.g., cf. [5]). This (algebraic) approach seems to be the most useful for our purposes.

Lemma

Let $< \mathfrak{I}, \rho >$ be a structure for L_p with the universe $A = \{a_1, \ldots, a_n\}$. For every program $P(x_1, \ldots, x_h)$ we can construct, in an effective way, a $n \times n$ matrix $P = [p_{i,j}]_{i,j=1,\ldots,n}$, such that for every vectors $\mu = [\mu_i]_{i=1,\ldots,n}$, $\mu' = [\mu'_j]_{j=1,\ldots,n} = P_{< \mathfrak{I}, \rho >}(\mu)$, the following holds:

$$\mu' = \mu \circ P$$

Moreover, an element p_{ij} of P corresponds to the probability that ϖ_j is the output valuation after computation of P, provided that the valuation ϖ_i appears as the input valuation with the probability 1.

Construction of the matrix P for a given program P is briefly described in Appendix 1 (cf. also e.g. [9]).

Example

Let us consider a program K of the form:

K: *while x=0 do*

K_1:   *either$_{(1/2)}$ x:=0; or x:=random;*

This algorithm contains one variable which takes values from the 2-element universe $A = \{0,1\}$. Since one instruction of this program is a probabilistic assignment, than we must give a probability distribution for it; let $\rho = [p, 1-p]$).

Now we shall determine output probability distribution for the input distribution $\mu = [p_1, p_2]$.

First, according to the method presented in Appendix 1 we get the following transition matrix for our program:

$$K = \begin{bmatrix} 0 & 1 \\ 0 & 1 \end{bmatrix}.$$

Using this matrix and the input probability μ distribution we can determine the following output probability distribution: $\mu' = [0, p_1 + p_2]$.

3   Algorithmic modelling of probabilistic processes

In this section we shall illustrate the use of a probabilistic algorithm to investigate a real situation. Suppose that there is a small warehouse of agricultural machines in town. This warehouse employ only one attendant, because in the same time there are only six machines in the building. On the basis of contract two producers supply machines and two consumers receive them. First producer send his product twice as frequently than second one. In one deliver first producer can supply two machines and second one provide four machines. Second consumer may take two products twice as frequently than first consumer, which take four products during one visit in the warehouse. Certainly the attendant can not serve two people in the same time.

Let us consider the case where, for example, in the warehouse there are four machines and the second producer want deliver products (four pieces). This delivery is destined to fail because one can have only six machines in the warehouse.

We shall now describe this situation in terms o probabilistic algorithms.

By P_1, P_2, K_1, K_2 we shall denote producers and consumers respectively. The variable M will describe the current state of the warehouse and F will be used to denote the number of unsuccessful transaction. The values of the variable P_K will belong to the set $\{P_1, P_2, K_1, K_2\}$. This variable will describe the person actually served by the attendant.

For readability of the text of the algorithm we decide to modify (to diminish) the capacity of the warehouse and the size of delivers.: we shall consider a warehouse with the capacity of only three machines. Each deliver of P_1 and P_2 include one and two machines respectively. K_1 takes two machines and K_2 takes one machine during one visit in the warehouse.

Before we construct an algorithm describing this situation, let us denote by *P1* the following subprogram:

P1:   *if* P_K = P_1 *then if* $M \leq 2$ *then* $M := M+1$ *else* $F := F+1$;

This program models the behaviour of the first producer. The test $M \leq 2$ verifies whether it is possible to transfer products to the warehouse.

Similarly, the following program *K2*, corresponding to the second consumer, can be written as follows:

K2:   *if* P_K = K_2 *then if* $M \geq 1$ *then* $M := M-1$ *else* $F := F+1$;

The subprogram

R: P_K:= *random* $\{P_1, P_2, K_1, K_2\}$;

realizes the choice of a client (a producer or a consumer) which actually visits the warehouse (in such a model problems like deadlock do not occur).

To define this precisely, it is necessary to define the probabilities p_{P_1}, p_{P_2}, p_{K_1}, p_{K_2} such that $p_{P_1} + p_{P_2} + p_{K_1} + p_{K_2} = 1$.

We shall use in the example the following values of the random distribution ρ :

$p_{P_1} = 1/3, p_{P_2} = 1/6, p_{K_1} = 1/6, p_{K_2} = 1/3$.

One step of the cooperation among producers, consumer and attendant of the warehouse, can be describing by the following algorithm:

N: $\quad begin$

$\qquad$ P_K:= $random$ {P_1, P_2, K_1, K_2};

$\qquad$ if P_K = P_1 $then$ if M ≤ 2 $then$ M := M + 1 $\quad else$ F := F + 1;

$\qquad$ if P_K = P_2 $then$ if M ≤ 1 $\quad then$ M := M + 2 $else$ F := F + 1;

$\qquad$ if P_K = K_1 $then$ if M ≥ 2 $\quad then$ M := M - 2 $else$ F := F + 1;

$\qquad$ if P_K = K_2 $then$ if M ≥ 1 $\quad then$ M := M - 1 $\quad else$ F := F + 1;

$\qquad end$;

The iteration of the cooperation process leads to the following probabilistic program P:

P: $\quad while$ F ≤ 2 do

$\qquad begin$

$\qquad$ P_K:= $random$ {P_1, P_2, K_1, K_2};

$\qquad$ if P_K = P_1 $then$ if M ≤ 2 $then$ M := M + 1 $else$ F := F + 1;

$\qquad$ if P_K = P_2 $then$ if M ≤ 1 $then$ M := M + 2 $else$ F := F + 1;

$\qquad$ if P_K = K_1 $then$ if M ≥ 2 $then$ M := M - 2 $else$ F := F + 1;

$\qquad$ If P_K = K_2 $then$ if M ≥ 1 $then$ M := M - 1 $else$ F := F + 1;

$\qquad end$;

The set of all possible valuations of the program variables M, P_K, F can be represented by means of $n = 49$ states. For example, the states (valuations) can be enumerated as follows:

$\qquad v_1$: $\quad$ M=0, PK = P_1, F = 0,

$\qquad v_2$: $\quad$ M=1, PK = P_1, F = 0,

$\qquad v_3$: $\quad$ M=2, PK = P_1, F = 0,

$\qquad v_4$: $\quad$ M=3, PK = P_1, F = 0,

$\qquad v_5$: $\quad$ M=0, PK = P_1, F = 1,

$\qquad v_6$: $\quad$ M=1, PK = P_1, F = 1,

$\qquad v_7$: $\quad$ M=2, PK = P_1, F = 1,

$\qquad v_8$: $\quad$ M=3, PK = P_1, F = 1,

$\qquad v_9$: $\quad$ M=0, PK = P_1, F = 2,

.

.

.

$v_{47}:$ M=2, PK = K$_2$, F = 2,

$v_{48}:$ M=3, PK = K$_2$, F = 2,

v_{49} ,   , F = 3.

Now, we shall use this probabilistic algorithm to determine statistical parameters related to the described situation. To each of subprocesses we shall assign its transition matrix (according to the rules given in Appendix 1).
One can check, that for the subprogram *P1* we obtain the following matrix P1:

In a similar way we can construct matrices P2, K1, K2 for the modules P2, K1, K2. The matrix corresponding to the subprogram *N* repeated during the realization of the loop, can be simply obtained from matrices R, P1, P2, K1, K2.

The matrix below corresponds to the situation after the first repetition of the subprogram *N* during the realization of the loop *"while ... "* , i.e., we give the matrix for the program *if* F ≤ 2 *then N* :

```
0 1/3 0 0 0 0 0 0 0 0 0 0 0 2/6 0 0 0 0 0 0 0 0 0 0 0 2/6 0 0 0 0 0 0 0 0 0 0 1/3 0 0 0 0 0 0 0 0
0 0 1/3 0 0 0 0 0 0 0 0 0 0 0 2/6 0 0 0 0 0 0 0 0 0 0 0 2/6 0 0 0 0 0 0 0 0 0 1/3 0 0 0 0 0 0 0 0
0 0 0 1/3 0 0 0 0 0 0 0 0 0 0 0 2/6 0 0 0 0 0 2/6 0 0 0 0 0 0 0 0 0 0 1/3 0 0 0 0 0 0 0 0 0 0 0
0 0 0 0 1/3 0 0 0 0 0 0 0 0 0 0 0 2/6 0 0 0 0 0 2/6 0 0 0 0 0 0 0 0 0 0 1/3 0 0 0 0 0 0 0 0 0 0
0 0 0 0 0 1/3 0 0 0 0 0 0 0 0 0 0 0 2/6 0 0 0 0 0 0 0 0 0 2/6 0 0 0 0 0 0 1/3 0 0 0 0 0 0 0 0 0
0 0 0 0 0 0 1/3 0 0 0 0 0 0 0 0 0 0 0 2/6 0 0 0 0 0 2/6 0 0 0 0 0 0 0 0 0 0 1/3 0 0 0 0 0 0 0 0
0 0 0 0 0 0 0 1/3 0 0 0 0 0 0 0 0 0 0 0 2/6 0 0 0 0 0 2/6 0 0 0 0 0 0 0 0 0 0 0 0 0 0 0 0 0 1/2
0 0 0 0 0 0 0 0 1/3 0 0 0 0 0 0 0 0 0 0 0 2/6 0 0 0 0 0 0 0 0 0 0 0 0 0 0 0 0 0 1/3 0 0 2/6
0 0 0 0 0 0 0 0 0 1/3 0 0 0 0 0 0 0 0 0 0 0 2/6 0 0 0 0 0 0 0 0 0 0 0 0 0 0 0 0 1/3 0 2/6 1/2
0 0 0 0 0 0 0 0 0 0 0 0 0 0 0 0 0 0 0 0 0 0 0 0 2/6 0 0 0 0 0 0 0 0 0 0 0 0 0 1/3 0 1/2
1/3 0 0 0 0 0 0 0 0 0 0 2/6 0 0 0 0 0 0 0 0 0 0 0 2/6 0 0 0 0 0 0 1/3 0 0 0 0 0 0 0 0 0 0
0 0 1/3 0 0 0 0 0 0 0 0 0 2/6 0 0 0 0 0 0 0 2/6 0 0 0 0 0 0 0 0 1/3 0 0 0 0 0 0 0 0 0 0 0
0 0 0 1/3 0 0 0 0 0 0 0 0 2/6 0 0 0 0 0 0 0 2/6 0 0 0 0 0 0 0 0 1/3 0 0 0 0 0 0 0 0 0 0 0
0 0 0 0 1/3 0 0 0 0 0 0 0 2/6 0 0 0 0 0 0 0 0 0 0 2/6 0 0 0 0 0 0 1/3 0 0 0 0 0 0 0 0 0 0
0 0 0 0 0 1/3 0 0 0 0 0 0 2/6 0 0 0 0 0 0 0 0 0 0 2/6 0 0 0 0 0 0 1/3 0 0 0 0 0 0 0 0 0 0
0 0 0 0 0 0 1/3 0 0 0 0 0 0 0 0 0 0 0 0 2/6 0 0 0 0 0 0 0 0 0 0 0 0 0 0 0 0 0 0 0 0 1/2
0 0 0 0 0 0 0 1/3 0 0 0 0 0 0 0 0 0 0 0 2/6 0 0 0 0 0 0 0 0 0 0 0 0 0 0 1/3 0 0 2/6
0 0 0 0 0 0 0 0 1/3 0 0 0 0 0 0 0 0 0 0 0 2/6 0 0 0 0 0 0 0 0 0 1/3 0 0 2/6
0 0 0 0 0 0 0 0 0 0 0 0 0 0 0 0 0 0 0 0 0 0 0 0 2/6 0 0 0 0 0 0 0 0 0 0 0 1/3 0 1/2
1/3 0 0 0 0 0 0 0 0 0 0 2/6 0 0 0 0 0 0 0 0 0 0 0 2/6 0 0 0 0 0 0 1/3 0 0 0 0 0 0 0 0 0 0
0 1/3 0 0 0 0 0 0 0 0 0 0 2/6 0 0 0 0 0 0 0 0 0 0 2/6 0 0 0 0 0 0 1/3 0 0 0 0 0 0 0 0 0 0
0 0 1/3 0 0 0 0 0 0 0 0 0 2/6 0 0 0 0 0 2/6 0 0 0 0 0 0 0 0 0 1/3 0 0 0 0 0 0 0 0 0 0
0 0 0 1/3 0 0 0 0 0 0 0 0 0 2/6 0 0 0 0 0 0 0 0 0 0 0 2/6 0 0 0 0 1/3 0 0 0 0 0 0 0 0 0 0
0 0 0 0 1/3 0 0 0 0 0 0 0 0 2/6 0 0 0 0 0 0 0 2/6 0 0 0 0 0 0 0 0 1/3 0 0 0 0 0 0 0 0 0 0
0 0 0 0 0 1/3 0 0 0 0 0 0 0 0 0 0 0 0 0 2/6 0 0 0 0 0 0 0 0 0 0 0 0 0 0 0 0 0 0 0 0 1/2
0 0 0 0 0 0 1/3 0 0 0 0 0 0 0 0 0 0 0 2/6 0 0 0 0 0 0 0 0 0 0 1/3 0 0 2/6
0 0 0 0 0 0 0 1/3 0 0 0 0 0 0 0 0 0 0 2/6 0 0 0 0 0 0 0 0 0 1/3 0 0 2/6
0 0 0 0 0 0 0 0 0 0 0 0 0 0 0 0 0 0 0 0 0 0 0 0 2/6 0 0 0 0 0 0 0 0 0 0 1/3 0 1/2
1/3 0 0 0 0 0 0 0 0 0 0 2/6 0 0 0 0 0 0 0 0 0 0 2/6 0 0 0 0 0 1/3 0 0 0 0 0 0 0 0 0 0
0 1/3 0 0 0 0 0 0 0 0 0 0 2/6 0 0 0 0 0 0 0 0 0 0 2/6 0 0 0 0 0 1/3 0 0 0 0 0 0 0 0 0 0
0 0 1/3 0 0 0 0 0 0 0 0 0 2/6 0 0 0 0 0 2/6 0 0 0 0 0 0 0 1/3 0 0 0 0 0 0 0 0 0 0
0 0 0 1/3 0 0 0 0 0 0 0 0 2/6 0 0 0 0 0 0 0 0 0 0 0 0 2/6 0 0 0 1/3 0 0 0 0 0 0 0 0 0 0
0 0 0 0 1/3 0 0 0 0 0 0 0 2/6 0 0 0 0 0 0 0 2/6 0 0 0 0 0 0 0 0 1/3 0 0 0 0 0 0 0 0 0 0
0 0 0 0 0 1/3 0 0 0 0 0 0 0 0 0 0 0 0 2/6 0 0 0 0 0 0 0 0 0 0 0 0 0 0 0 0 0 0 0 0 1/2
0 0 0 0 0 0 1/3 0 0 0 0 0 0 0 0 0 2/6 0 0 0 0 0 0 0 0 0 0 1/3 0 0 2/6
0 0 0 0 0 0 0 1/3 0 0 0 0 0 0 0 0 2/6 0 0 0 0 0 0 0 0 0 1/3 0 0 2/6
0 0 0 0 0 0 0 0 0 0 0 0 0 0 0 0 0 0 0 0 0 0 0 2/6 0 0 0 0 0 0 0 0 0 1/3 0 1/2
0 0 0 0 0 0 0 0 0 0 0 0 0 0 0 0 0 0 0 0 0 0 0 0 0 0 0 0 0 0 0 0 0 0 0 0 0 0 0 0 0 0 1
```

The matrix P, for the whole algorithm P, can be obtained by means of the rule [W] of Appendix 1, where it is described the matrix construction for the loop instruction *"while"*.

The matrix P corresponding to the whole algorithm P is surprisingly simple. All positions of the last column are equal to 1; all remaining positions are equal to 0:

$$
\begin{array}{cccc}
1 & 2 & \cdots & 48 \quad 49
\end{array}
$$
$$
\begin{bmatrix}
0 & 0 & \cdots & 0 & 1 \\
0 & 0 & \cdots & 0 & 1 \\
\cdots & \cdots & \cdots & \cdots & \cdots \\
0 & 0 & \cdots & 0 & 1 \\
0 & 0 & \cdots & 0 & 1
\end{bmatrix}
$$

We shall determine the average number of steps of program P. This value is described by the formula (cf. [9]).

$$AT = (I - K)^{-1} * e$$

where I is identify $(n-1) \times (n-1)$-matrix, e is one-column matrix of ones and K denotes the following modification of the matrix P; the rows and columns related to states not being final are rejected (the set of final states of our example consists of the state 49 only).

The above formula enables us to determine the average number of visits of the customers and producers. For example, for the first producer if we start from a state satisfying M=0, F=0 then the average number of steps of the process is equals to 8,7475.

This result, concerning the average number of visits of the producers and customers suggest that the capacity of the warehouse is too small.

To find an optimal size of the warehouse (depending, e.g., on the actual maximal sizes of delivers) we can prepare an array, of average numbers of steps of the algorithm, for different values of the capacity of the varehouse (different maximal values of the variable M):

size M	M=3	M=4	M=5	M=6	M=7	M=8
Average number of steps	8,7475	...	...	...	...	...

Since our example is not of practical use, we will not analyse this matrix and do not determine its remaining positions.

4   Final remarks

As we have mentioned, the considered model is rather simple and has a character of an academic example. On the other hand, it is easy to modify this model to be close to a real situation, e.g., by augmenting the numbers related to the control (the maximal content of the warehouse and the number of admissible failures).

The most important problem concerns the dimensions of matrices appearing in our considerations. However, in many professional products related to algorithms of linear algebra "sufficiently great" matrices are admissible. Each problem solvable in terms of a Markov chain model is also solvable in terms of probabilistic algorithms modelling.

By means of probabilistic programs we can model another aspects of relations among producers, consumers and capacity of storehouse. For example, if we assume that the machines are not anonymous, and are represented by the number of a producer, then we can model preferences of the consumers:

- instead of the integer variable M ranging over the set of values $\{0,1,2\}$ we shall use a variable S from the set of values $\{\varnothing,\{1\},\{2\},\{1,1\},\{1,2\},\{2,2\}\}$ (the values are sets with repeated elements),

- if the preferences of the first consumer are the following: only machines made by the second producer are admissible then this reaction can be modeled by the algorithm:

if S = {2} *or* S = {1,2} *or* S = {2,2} *then*

  begin

  K1 := 2

  if S = {2} *then* S := $\varnothing$

  else

    if S = {1,2} *then* S := {1}

    else if S = {2,2} *then* S := {2}

  end

It is aesy to modify this algorithm in order to realize a less restrictive strategy, e.g., he takes a machine of first producer if two last visits in the storehouse are not successful (the storehouse does not contain machines of the second producer).

In a similar way another preferences of consumers can be modelled.

At the end, let us notice that the above examples show, that modules of producers/consumers may contain fragments corresponding to "learning procedures".

5 References

[1] Borowska A., "Implementation of Algorithm Determining Probabilities of Behaves Probabilistic Algorithms", MSc thesis, Technical University of Białystok, Białystok 2002;

[2] Borowska A., "Determining of Probabilities of Transitions in the Probabilistic Algorithms", MSc thesis, University of Białystok, Bialystok 1999;

[3] Borowska A., Dańko W., Karbowska-Chilińska J., "Probabilistic Algorithms as a Tool for Modelling Stochastic Processes", Proceedings of the conference CISIM 2004, 14-16 June 2004, Ełk; Poland, vol I, pp 380-389.

[4] Dańko W., "The Set of Probabilistic Algorithmic Formulas Valid in a Finite Structure is Decidable with Respect to its Diagram", Fundamenta Informaticae, vol. 19 (3-4), pp. 417-431, 1993;

[5] Feldman Y., Harell D.,"A probabilistic dynamic logic", ACM Journal of Comp., 1982

[6] Feller W., "An Introduction to Probability Theory", PWN, Warsaw 1977;

[7] Iosifescu M., "Finite Markov Processes and Their Applications", John Wiley & Sons, New York, London 1988;

[8] Karbowska J., "Probabilistic Iterative Algorithms with Continuous Time Parameter", Proceedings of the conference CISIM 2003, 26-28 June, 2003, Ełk; Poland, pp 133-140.

[9] Koszelew J., "The Methods for Verification Properties of Probabilistic Programs", Ph. D. thesis IPI PAN, Warsaw 2000.

6 Appendix 1 (Construction of the transition matrix for a given program)

In this section we will present construction of the matrix P for a given program P.

This one is defined inductively (with respect to the number of program constructions). Thus we will begin from constructions for the most elementary programs of the form: $x := a$; and $x := random$;:

[DA] Let the program P be of the form $x_r := t$ $(r = 1, \ldots, h)$, where t is a term. The matrix $P = [p_{ij}]_{i,j=1,\ldots,n}$, where $n = u^h$ we define in the following way:

$$p_{ij} = \begin{cases} 1 & \text{iff } [x_r := t]_{<\Im,\rho>}(\varpi_i) = \varpi_j \\ 0 & \text{iff } [x_r := t]_{<\Im,\rho>}(\varpi_i) \neq \varpi_j \end{cases}$$

[PA] If the program P is of the form $x_r := random$ $(r=1,\ldots,h)$, then the matrix P is as follow:

$$p_{ij} = \begin{cases} \rho(\varpi_j(x_r)) & \text{iff } \left(\forall_{\substack{s=1,\ldots,h \\ s \neq r}} \varpi_i(x_s) = \varpi_j(x_s) \right), \text{where} \\ 0 & \text{otherwise} \end{cases}$$

ρ - is a probability distribution corresponding to random generation of elements from universe A.

[F] To formulate the other definitions briefly we first define the matrix of the program of the form: $while \neg\gamma \ do \ x:=x$; (we will be denote it by $[\gamma?]$ and the matrix corresponding to it we will by denote by $I_{[\gamma?]}$). Thus:

$$a_{ij} = \begin{cases} 1 & \text{iff } i = j \text{ and } \Im,\varpi_i \models \gamma \\ 0 & \text{otherwise} \end{cases}$$

[C]   If P is of the form: *begin P_1; P_2 end* and P_1, P_2 are matrix corresponding to the subprograms P_1 and P_2, then P is defined by:

$$P=P_1{}^{\circ}P_2$$

[DB]   If the program P is a branching of the form: *if γ then P_1 else P_2;* then the matrix for it is following:

$$P=I_{[\gamma?]}{}^{\circ}P_1+I_{[\neg\gamma?]}{}^{\circ}P_2$$

[NB]   For construction of probabilistic branching of the form *either$_p$ P_1 or P_2*, we define matrix P on following way:

$$P=p\cdot P_1+(1-p)\cdot P_2$$

[W]   If P is a program of the form *while γ do P_1*, then we shall use the following equation

$$(I-I_{[\gamma?]}{}^{\circ}P_1){}^{\circ}P=I_{[\neg\gamma?]}.$$

motivated by the equivalence of the programs

while γ do P_1,

begin if γ then P_1 else begin P_1; while γ do P_1 end .

If the determinant of the matrix $(I-I_{[\gamma?]}{}^{\circ}P_1)$ is different from 0 then the matrix P can be determined immediatelely (this is the case of the example considered in Section 2); otherwise, we need a more complicated technique described in [1,2,4,8].

7   Appendix 2 (Results of the experiments)

The algorithm P, considered in the Section 2, has been implemented in Pascal and realized several (33000) times.

Our analysis was restricted to the case of the average number of steps (for each computation the number of steps is established and the average value was detrermined). This "experimental" average number of steps is equal to 8.7492. The corresponding "theoretical" average number of steps, described by the expression quoted in Section 2 is equal to 8.7475.

For our "academic" example of Section 2, the difference between experimental and theoretical results seems to be not essential. However, for models of real situations, each noticable difference should be analysed. Those differencies can be caused by:

- errors of numerical computations of "theoretical" values,

- low quality of generators of pseudorandom objects in implemented version of the algorithm.

The "numerical" errors, in the case of algorithms of linear algebra, are rather small; the observed errors are rather caused by low quality of used generators of pseudorandom objects.

Therefore, in the case, where the errors seems to be to great, we suggest to improve (or change) pseudorandom generators.

Fuzzy Parametric Integral Equations System in modelling of polygonal potential boundary problems described by the Laplace equation

Eugeniusz Zieniuk, Andrzej Kuzelewski

University of Bialystok, Faculty of Mathematics and Physics,
Institute of Computer Science, Sosnowa 64, 15-887 Bialystok, Poland
e-mail: ezieniuk@ii.uwb.edu.pl, akuzel@ii.uwb.edu.pl

Abstract: The following paper presents an application of the fuzzy Parametric Integral Equations System (PIES) for solving potential boundary problems in polygonal domains with uncertainly defined boundary geometry and boundary conditions. The proposed method is based on the PIES and ordered fuzzy numbers. The boundary geometry is created using a small number of control points and modelled by parametric linear functions. Neither the boundary nor the domain discretization is required to process the algorithm.

Keywords: Parametric Integral Equations System, interval arithmetic, ordered fuzzy numbers, boundary problems

1 Introduction

The traditional methods of modelling of boundary problems do not consider a problem of measurement errors (such as an instrumental error, an error of a method, etc.). In effect, the results obtained from the computer simulation can significantly deviate from real values. In general, the measured values can be treated as numbers belong to a certain interval. Therefore, the simulation process requires particular methods of boundary problems modelling, which should consider interval nature of the measurements.

One of the widely used methods in solving boundary problems is the Boundary Element Method (BEM) [1]. The Fuzzy Boundary Element Method (FBEM) [2] is an extension of the BEM considering uncertain nature of measurements. However, the FBEM inherits from the BEM a few significant disadvantages (such as discontinuity at the points of segments join, a big number of nodes required to define boundary geometry precisely, a process of boundary discretization).

The fuzzy Parametric Integral Equations System (PIES) [3] is an alternative method, free from the above-mentioned disadvantages. The fuzzy PIES was elaborated as an extension of the PIES [4] in order to effective solving of not sharply defined boundary problems. The algorithm allows approximately define both boundary geometry and boundary conditions – using ordered fuzzy numbers [5]. The fuzzy PIES was created as a result of modification of the mathematical theory describing the traditional PIES by the ordered fuzzy numbers theory [5] and the Kaucher complete interval arithmetic [6].

The former experiments on applying the fuzzy PIES present, that it inherits the advantages of the PIES, such as effectiveness, high accuracy of results and easiness of modelling of boundary problems. An application of the fuzzy PIES to solving potential problems described by the Laplace equation in polygonal domains with uncertainly defined boundary geometry is presented in [7].

The aim of this paper is to propose an application of the fuzzy PIES (formulated for the Laplace equation) to solving boundary problems in polygonal domains with both boundary conditions and boundary geometry uncertainly defined. The numerical algorithm and solution of an example problem is presented.

2 Definition of boundary geometry and boundary conditions

Uncertainly defined polygonal domains in boundary problems can be approximately described using parametric linear functions. The boundary geometry Ω described using the above-mentioned functions is presented in fig. 1a.

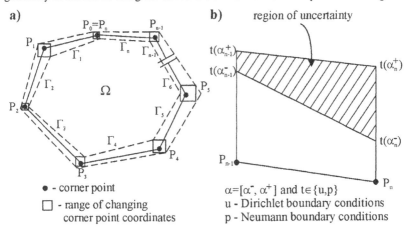

Fig. 1. Definition of: a) domain Ω using corner points, b) boundary conditions

The boundary functions are approximated using global base functions [8] (Chebyshev polynomials). The coefficients of these functions are interval values considering uncertain nature of boundary conditions (fig. 1b).

Each function $\Gamma_k(s)$, $k = 1, 2, ..., n$ (fig. 1a) can be described by the following function:

$$\Gamma_k(s) = a_k \underline{s} + b_k, \qquad 0 \le \underline{s} \le 1. \tag{1}$$

Effectiveness of a such way is connected with a small number of the corner points, which define the boundary geometry, and absence of both boundary and domain discretization.

2.1 The fuzzy Parametric Integral Equations System

The PIES modified by an application of the ordered fuzzy numbers theory and the Kaucher complete interval arithmetic are used in order to solve boundary problems. Following [3] the fuzzy PIES is defined by the below relation:

$$\frac{1}{2}\hat{u}_l(s_1) = \sum_{j=1}^{n} J_j \int_{s_{j-1}^{-(+)}}^{s_j^{-(+)}} \left\{ \overline{U}_{lj}^*(s_1,s)\hat{p}_j(s) - \overline{P}_{lj}^*(s_1,s)\hat{u}_j(s) \right\} ds,$$

$$l = 1,2...n, \qquad s_{j-1}^{-(+)} \le s \le s_j^{-(+)} \tag{2}$$

where $\hat{u}_l(s_1), \hat{p}_j(s), \hat{u}_j(s)$ are fuzzy functions:

$$\hat{u}_l(s_1) = [u_\lambda^-(s_1), u_\lambda^+(s_1)], \qquad \hat{p}_j(s) = [p_\lambda^-(s), p_\lambda^+(s)],$$

$$\hat{u}_j(s) = [u_\lambda^-(s), u_\lambda^+(s)], \qquad 0 \le \lambda \le 1.$$

The integrands in the equation (2) are presented by the following relations [3]:

$$\overline{U}_{lj}^*(s_1,s) = \frac{1}{2\pi}\ln\frac{1}{\left[\eta_1^2 + \eta_2^2\right]^{0.5}}, \quad \overline{P}_{lj}^*(s_1,s) = \frac{1}{2\pi}\frac{\eta_1 n_1 + \eta_2 n_2}{\eta_1^2 + \eta_2^2} \tag{3}$$

where $\eta_1 = \Gamma_l^{(1)}(s_1) - \Gamma_j^{(1)}(s)$ and $\eta_2 = \Gamma_l^{(2)}(s_1) - \Gamma_j^{(2)}(s)$. The functions $\Gamma_l^{(i)}, i = 1,2$ are defined by (1).

The expressions (3) are called *a fuzzy boundary fundamental solution* and *a fuzzy boundary singular solution* respectively [3] similar to non-fuzzy solutions.

Solution in a domain is obtained from an integral identity [9]:

$$u(x) = \sum_{j=1}^{n} J_j \int_{s_{j-1}}^{s_j} \left\{ \overline{U}_j^*(x,s)p_j(s) - \overline{P}_j^*(x,s)u_j(s) \right\} ds, \tag{4}$$

The integrands $\hat{U}_j^*, \hat{P}_j^*$ are presented by the following formulas:

$$\hat{\bar{U}}_j^*(x,s) = \frac{1}{2\pi} \ln \frac{1}{\left[\ddot{r}_1^2 + \ddot{r}_2^2\right]^{0.5}},$$

$$\hat{\bar{P}}_j^*(x,s) = \frac{1}{2\pi} \frac{\ddot{r}_1 n_1^{(j)}(s) + \ddot{r}_2 n_2^{(j)}(s)}{\ddot{r}_1^2 + \ddot{r}_2^2}, \tag{5}$$

where: $\ddot{r}_1 = x_1 - \Gamma_j^{(1)}(s)$ and $\ddot{r}_2 = x_2 - \Gamma_j^{(2)}(s)$.

The expressions (5) are called *a fuzzy fundamental solution in the domain* and *a fuzzy singular solution in the domain* respectively [9].

2.2 Solution of the fuzzy PIES

The pseudospectral method (PM) [10] is applied to solving the fuzzy PIES (3). Interval nature of the coefficients approximating the boundary functions $\hat{u}_j(s)$ and $\hat{p}_j(s)$ [8] is taken into account as well. An approximation of the boundary functions is described by the following relations:

$$\hat{p}_j(s) = \sum_{p=0}^{M} p_j^p T_j^p(s), \quad \hat{u}_j(s) = \sum_{p=0}^{M} u_j^p T_j^p(s), \tag{6}$$

where:

$$\hat{p}_j(s) = [p_\lambda^-(s), p_\lambda^+(s)], \quad \hat{u}_j(s) = [u_\lambda^-(s), u_\lambda^+(s)], \quad 0 \leq \lambda \leq 1$$

$$\left.\begin{array}{l} u_j^p = [u^-, u^+]_j^p \\ p_j^p = [p^-, p^+]_j^p \end{array}\right\} \quad - \text{ are unknown interval coefficients,}$$

M – is a number of the coefficients in the segment,

$T_j^p(s)$ – are global base functions in the particular curve (Chebyshev polynomials).

After substituting (6) to (2) the following relation is obtained:

$$\frac{1}{2}\hat{u}_l(s_1) = \sum_{j=1}^{n}\sum_{p=0}^{M} p_j^p \int_{s_{j-1}^{-(+)}}^{s_j^{-(+)}} \bar{U}^*(s_1,s)T_j^p(s)J_j(s)ds -$$

$$-\sum_{j=1}^{n}\sum_{p=0}^{M} u_j^p \int_{s_{j-1}^{-(+)}}^{s_j^{-(+)}} \bar{P}^*(s_1,s)T_j^p(s)J_j(s)ds, \tag{7}$$

where the interval coefficients p_j^p and u_j^p are extracted from the integrals.

After substituting the collocation points to (7) an algebraic equations system according to the unknown interval coefficients is obtained.

It is possible to reduce the equation (7) to the below relation:

$$Hu = Gp, \tag{8}$$

where both the column matrices u and p contain interval coefficients of the approximating boundary functions. Taking into account the boundary conditions, the equation (8) can be transformed into the linear algebraic equations system with the asymmetrical interval coefficients matrix:

$$A_\lambda X_\lambda = F_\lambda, \qquad X_\lambda = \begin{Bmatrix} p \\ u \end{Bmatrix}_\lambda, \quad 0 \le \lambda \le 1, \tag{9}$$

where the X vector contains unknown interval coefficients of the approximating boundary functions and the F vector depends on the given boundary conditions.

3 Outline of the extended interval arithmetic

The ordered fuzzy numbers [5] and the Kaucher complete interval arithmetic [6,11] are used in order to create and solve the fuzzy PIES. The set of directed intervals D is the equivalent of the set of all ordered pairs of the real numbers $\{[\alpha, \beta] \mid \alpha, \beta \in \Re\}$ [11]. The first endpoint of the interval $a \in D$ is denoted by a^-, and the second by a^+, therefore $a = [a^-, a^+]$. The interval a is *proper* if $a^- \le a^+$, *degenerate* if $a^- = a^+$, and *improper* if $a^- \ge a^+$. The set of all proper intervals is denoted by $I(\Re)$, the set of degenerate intervals by $\Re$, and the set of improper intervals is $\overline{I(\Re)}$ [11].

The extended arithmetic for direct intervals can be described by standard interval operations (such as interval addition, interval multiplication, etc.) and component-wise operations presented by:

- inverse (opposition)

    $\mathrm{opp}(a) = [a^-, a^+],$

- dualization

    $\mathrm{dual}(a) = [a^-, a^+].$

There are numerical methods of solving an interval algebraic equations system that can be used [11–13]. One of the easiest but very effective algorithms is the interval Gauss elimination method [13]. Combination of this method with the algorithm of iterative increasing accuracy and the Kaucher complete interval arithmetic is applied to the experiments.

4   Numerical test

In the experiments we have assumed that the membership function $\lambda = 0$, therefore it is a particular event of the fuzzy PIES.

A potential problem of an hexagon shape is given to consider (fig. 2a). The boundary conditions and the boundary geometry are interval values. The boundary geometry is created by six corner points. Each of them is described by an interval value in two dimensions x_1 and x_2. The coordinates of the points are presented in tab. 1.

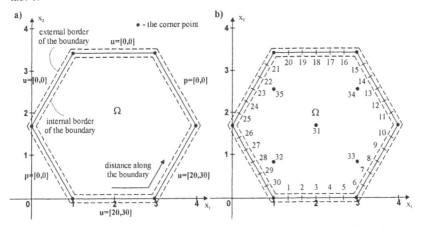

Fig. 2. a) Uncertainly defined boundary geometry, b) The points of the solution

No. of a point	Coordinates			
	x_1^-	x_1^+	x_2^-	x_2^+
P_0	0.95	1.05	-0.05	0.05
P_1	2.95	3.05	-0.05	0.05
P_2	3.95	4.05	1.68205	1.78205
P_3	2.95	3.05	3.4141	3.5141
P_4	0.95	1.05	3.4141	3.5141
P_5	-0.05	0.05	1.68205	1.78205

Table 1. Coordinates of the corner points

The solution in the domain (tab. 2) and on the boundary (tab. 3) is obtained in the points from fig. 2b.

No. of	Coordinates		Potential	
a point	x_1	x_2	u^-	u^+
31	2	1.73205	9.96295	15
32	1	0.86602	11.9843	18.0059
33	3	0.86602	17.5648	27.1269
34	3	2.59807	7.90809	12.0237
35	1	2.59807	1.86827	3.65286

Table 2. The results of experiments in the domain

No. of	Potential		Potential derivative	
a point	u^-	u^+	p^-	p^+
1	20	30	9.6522	15.4212
2	20	30	6.70959	10.7096
3	20	30	5.36902	8.55878
4	20	30	4.59423	7.3155
5	20	30	3.34895	5.32651
6	20	30	3.32114	5.37117
7	20	30	4.5621	7.37548
8	20	30	5.33979	8.62588
9	20	30	6.68637	10.7691
10	20	30	9.63395	15.4519
11	15.8722	23.8109	0	0
12	12.8084	19.2211	0	0
13	10.0128	15.0307	0	0
14	7.21567	10.8345	0	0
15	4.14701	6.22722	0	0
16	0	0	-15.5647	-9.65215
17	0	0	-10.7829	-6.70977
18	0	0	-8.6128	-5.36926
19	0	0	-7.37307	-4.59438
20	0	0	-5.38228	-3.34889
21	0	0	-5.39505	-3.3211
22	0	0	-7.3938	-4.56225
23	0	0	-8.63376	-5.34003
24	0	0	-10.7613	-6.68655
25	0	0	-15.4227	-9.63391
26	4.12613	6.20198	0	0
27	7.186	10.8079	0	0
28	9.97962	15.0082	0	0
29	12.7771	19.2062	0	0
30	15.8486	23.8049	0	0

Table 3. The results of experiments on the boundary

324

The considered potential problem has been solved for mid-point boundary values and mid-point boundary geometry to compare interval results with deterministic ones. The boundary values are described by:

$$u = \frac{1}{2}\left(u^- + u^+\right), \quad p = \frac{1}{2}\left(p^- + p^+\right),$$

and boundary geometry is presented by the following relation:

$$(x_1, x_2)_i = \left(\frac{1}{2}\left(x_1^- + x_1^+\right), \frac{1}{2}\left(x_2^- + x_2^+\right)\right)_i,$$

where i – a number of a corner point.

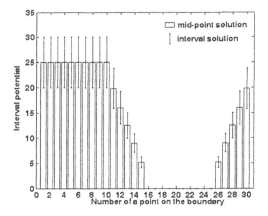

Fig. 3. The interval solution – potential ($\hat{u}$)

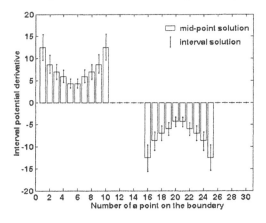

Fig. 4. The interval solution – potential derivative ($\hat{p}$)

The figures 3 and 4 present the solutions from the tab. 3 and for the mid-point potential problem for their better visualization. The former presents the potential while the latter depicts the potential derivative.

The points of the solution are presented in order to compare interval results with deterministic ones. It is necessary to notice that the solution of the fuzzy PIES is continuous, therefore it allows to obtain result in any point of domain (or boundary) without approximation or interpolation process. The corner points are used only to define boundary geometry.

5 Conclusions

The numerical test shows that the fuzzy PIES is a powerful tool for effective solving uncertainly defined boundary problems with polygonal boundary geometry modelled using parametric linear functions.

Accuracy of the interval algebraic equations system solution considerably influences on the accuracy of obtained numerical results. The Gauss elimination is one of the easiest and effective methods of solving algebraic equations systems.

Application of the fuzzy PIES allows decrease a number of numerical experiments concerning modelled boundary problems in comparison to traditional, non-fuzzy methods. Including both boundary geometry and boundary conditions errors (arising from uncertain define of boundary problem) in experiments is also possible.

An advantage of the fuzzy PIES is easiness of boundary problems modelling – boundary geometry is created using a small number of corner points. Moreover, the amount of computational data is considerably reduced in contrast to the traditional methods.

In the authors' opinion, the proposed method is able to produce satisfactory results for other shapes of segments; however, it needs more detailed experiments.

References

[1]   Brebbia C., Telles J. C. F., Wrobel L. C., "Boundary Element Techniques – Theory and Applications in Engineering", Springer–Verlag, Berlin, Heidelberg, New York, Tokyo, 1984.

[2]   Burczynski T., Skrzypczyk J., "Fuzzy aspects of the boundary element method", Engineering Analysis with Boundary Elements 19, pp. 209-216, 1997.

326

[3]   Zieniuk E., "New idea of solving fuzzy boundary problems", Informatyka teoretyczna. Metody analizy informacji niekompletnej i rozproszonej, Politechnika Bialostocka, X lat Instytutu Informatyki, Bialystok , pp. 182-192, 2000 (in polish).

[4]   Zieniuk E., "Bézier curves in the modification of boundary integral equations (BIE) for potential boundary-values problems", International Journal of Solids and Structures 40, pp. 2301-2320, 2003.

[5]   Kosinski W., Prokopowicz P., Slezak D., "Ordered Fuzzy Numbers", Bulletin of the Polish Academy of Sciences, Mathematics 51, pp. 329-341, 2003.

[6]   Kaucher E., "Interval analysis in the extended interval space I$\Re$", Computing Suppl. 2, pp. 33-49, 1980.

[7]   Zieniuk E., Kuzelewski A., "Simulation of fuzzy boundary problems using PIES in polygonal domains modelled by Laplace equation", X Warsztaty PTSK „Symulacja w Badaniach i Rozwoju" Zakopane, pp. 439-446, 2003 (in polish).

[8]   Zieniuk E., "Potential problems with polygonal boundaries by a BEM with parametric linear functions", Engineering Analysis with Boundary Elements 25, pp. 185-190, 2001.

[9]   Zieniuk E., "A new integral identity for potential polygonal domain problems described by parametric linear functions", Engineering Analysis with Boundary Elements 26, pp. 897-904, 2002.

[10] Gottlieb D., Orszag S. A., "Numerical analysis of spectral methods", SIAM, Philadelphia 1977.

[11] Markov S., "An iterative method for algebraic solution to interval equations", Applied Numerical Mathematics 30, pp. 225-239, 1999.

[12] Shary S. P., "Algebraic approach to the interval linear static identification, tolerance and control problems", Reliable Computing 1, pp. 3-33, 1996.

[13] Neumaier A., "Interval Methods for System of Equations", Cambridge University Press, Cambridge, New York, Port Chester, Melbourne, Sydney 1990.

From Integrated Circuits Technology to Silicon Grey Matter: Hardware Implementation of Artificial Neural Networks

Kurosh Madani

Intelligence in Instrumentation and Systems Laboratory (I²S / JE 2353), Sénart Institute of Technology - University Paris-XII, Avenue Pierre Point, 77127 Lieusaint, France

Abstract: A very large number of works concerning the area of Artificial Neural Networks deal with implementation of these models as software but also hardware solutions. However, hardware implementations of these models and issued solutions have essentially concerned the execution speed aspects. Today, a new question becomes unavoidable: taking into account the actual computers operation speeds (exceeding several Giga-operations per second), the specific hardware implementation of Artificial Neural Networks is it still an pertinent subject? This paper deals with two main goals. The first one is related to ANN's hardware implementation showing how theoretical bases of ANNs could lead to electronic implementation of these intelligent techniques. The second aim of the paper is to discuss the above formulated question through learning plasticity and robustness of ANN hardware implementations.

Keywords: artificial neural networks, hardware implementation, global perturbation immunity, structural robustness, learning plasticity

1 Introduction

Over past decades, new approaches based on Artificial Neural Networks (ANN) have been proposed to solve problems related to optimization, modeling, decision making, classification, data mining or nonlinear functions (behavior) approximation. Inspired from biological nervous systems and brain structure, ANNs could be seen as information processing systems, which allow the elaboration of many original techniques covering a large field of applications ([1] to [14]). The most popular properties of these models are their learning and generalization capabilities (extrapolation of learned tasks to unknown or unlearned situation). However, they own other nameless but very appealing properties. One of these additional attractive features is their natural parallelism. In fact, by analogy to the natural systems, artificial neural information processing could be organized in parallel (simultaneous) way. Beside the operation speed improvement, this point leads to operation redundancy making such processing robust. Another very enticing attribute of such artificial systems is their distributive information storage. In fact, contrary to conventional computational algorithms (or machines) where the information storage is performed by using addressable memory cells (registers, etc.), in neural system the information is coded and stored in synaptic links (synaptic weights). This second feature makes such artificial systems immune to information misplace. Finally, together, these two properties lead to global perturbation immunity and robustness of artificial neural network based solution.

A very large number of works concerning the area of ANNs deal with implementation of these models as software but also hardware solutions. Especially digital and analogue implementations of ANNs as CMOS integrated circuits show several attractive features [1]. However, hardware implementations of these models and issued solutions have essentially concerned the execution speed dilemma. Today, a new question becomes unavoidable: taking into account the actual computers operation speeds (exceeding several Giga-operations per second), the specific hardware implementation of Artificial Neural Networks is it still an pertinent subject?

This paper deals with two main goals. The first one is related to ANN's hardware implementation showing how theoretical bases of ANNs could lead to electronic implementation of these intelligent techniques. The second aim of the paper is to discuss the above formulated question through learning plasticity and robustness of ANN hardware implementations.

Section 2 reminds artificial neural model operation principles and the learning paradigm. In section 3 a simple hardware implementation approach based on usual electronic devices will be introduced analyzed and discussed. Section 4 will be dedicated to more sophisticated models and their hardware implementations. An analog and a digital implementation will be presented. Section 5 will consider learning plasticity and robustness of ANN hardware implementation on the basis of one of the neural circuits introduced in section 4. The simultaneous effects of two global perturbations will be analyzed: temperature and voltage supply perturbations. Experimental results will be reported and discussed. Finally, in Section 6, a discussion will shed light on the above-formulated question.

2 Neural Models and Learning Paradigm

Much is still unknown about how the brain trains itself to process information, so theories abound. It is admitted that in the biological systems (human brain), a typical neuron collects signals from others through a host of fine structures called *dendrites*. Figure 1 shows a simplified bloc diagram of biological neural system comparing it to the artificial neuron.

The neuron sends out spikes of electrical activity through a long, thin stand known as an *axon*, which splits into thousands of branches. At the end of each branch, a structure called a *synapse* converts the activity from the axon into electrical effects that inhibit or excite activity from the axon into electrical effects that inhibit or excite activity in the connected neurons. When a neuron receives excitatory input that is sufficiently large compared with its inhibitory input, it sends a spike of electrical activity down its axon. Learning occurs by changing the effectiveness of the synapses so that the influence of one neuron on another changes.

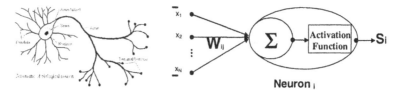

Fig.1. *Biological neuron representative scheme (left) and artificial neuron simplified bloc-diagrams (right).*

Inspired from biological neuron, artificial neuron reproduces a simplified functionality of that complex biological neuron. The neuron's operation could be seen as following: a neuron updates its output from weighted inputs received from all neurons connected to that neuron. The decision to update or not the actual state of the neuron is performed thank to the "decision function" depending to activity of those connected neurons. Let us consider a neuron with its state denoted by x_i (as it is shown in figure 1) connected to M other neurons, and let x_j represent the state (response) of the j-th neuron interconnected to that neuron with $j \in \{1, \cdots, M\}$. Let W_{ij} be the weight (called also, synaptic weight) between j-th and i-th neurons.

In this case, the activity of all connected neurons to the i-th neuron, formalized through the "synaptic potential" of that neuron, is defined by relation (1). Fall back on its synaptic potential (and sometimes to other control parameters), the neuron's decision function will putout (decide) the new state of the neuron according to the relation (2). One of the most commonly used decision functions is the "sigmoidal" function given by relation (3) where η is a control parameter acting on decision strictness or softness, called also "learning rate".

$$V_i = \sum_{j=1}^{j=M} W_{ij} . x_j \qquad (1)$$

$$S_i = F(x_i , V_i) = F\left(x_i , \sum_{j=1}^{j=M} W_{ij} . x_j \right) \qquad (2)$$

$$F(x) = \frac{1}{1 + e^{-\frac{x}{\eta}}} \qquad (3)$$

2.1 From Artificial Neuron to Neural Network

An artificial neural network (ANN) is an information-processing paradigm inspired by the densely interconnected, parallel structure of the mammalian brain information processes. Artificial neural networks are collections of mathematical models that emulate some of the observed properties of biological nervous systems and draw on the analogies of adaptive biological learning. The key element of the ANN paradigm is the novel structure of the information processing system. It is supposed to be composed of a large number of highly interconnected processing elements that are analogous to neurons and are tied together with weighted connections that are analogous to synapses. However, a large number of proposed architectures involve a limited number of neurons. Figure 2 compares a simplified biological neural network's scheme with an artificial neural network's bloc-diagram.

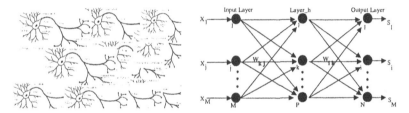

Fig.2. *Biological neural system (left) and artificial neural network (right) simplified bloc-diagrams*

Biologically, neural networks are constructed in a three dimensional way from microscopic cells. These neurons seem capable of nearly unrestricted interconnections. This is not true in any artificial network. Artificial neural networks are the simple clustering of the primitive artificial neurons. This clustering occurs by creating layers, which are then connected to one another. How these layers connect may also vary. Basically, all artificial neural networks have a similar structure of topology. Some of the neurons interface the real world to receive its inputs and other neurons provide the real world with the network's outputs. All the rest of the neurons are hidden form view. In general, the input layer consists of neurons that receive input form the external environment. The output layer consists of neurons that communicate the output of the system to the user or external environment. There are usually a number of hidden layers between these two layers. When the input layer receives the input its neurons produce output, which becomes input to the other layers of the system. The process continues until a certain condition is satisfied or until the output layer is invoked and fires their output to the external environment.

To model how an ANN operates, let us consider, as example, a 3 layers standard neural network, including an input layer, a hidden layer and an output layer, conformably to the figure 2. Let us suppose that the input layer includes M neurons, the hidden layer includes P neurons and the output layer includes N neurons. Let $X = (x_1, ..., x_j, ..., x_M)^T$ represents the input vectors, with $j \in \{1, \cdots, M\}$, $H = (H_1, ..., H_k, ..., H_P)^T$ represents the hidden layer's output with $k \in \{1, \cdots, P\}$ and $S = (S_1, ..., S_i, ..., S_N)^T$ the output vector with $i \in \{1, \cdots, N\}$. Let us note W_{kj}^H and W_{ik}^S synaptic matrixes elements, corresponding to input-hidden layers and hidden-output layers respectively. Neurons are supposed to have a non-linear decision function (activation function) F(.). V_k^H and V_i^S, defined by relation (4), will represent the synaptic potential vectors components of hidden and output neurons, respectively (e.g. vectors V^H and V^S components). Taking into account such considerations, the k-th hidden and the i-th output neurons outputs will be given by relations (5).

$$V_k^H = \sum_{j=1}^{j=M} W_{kj}^H . x_j \quad \text{and} \quad V_i^S = \sum_{k=1}^{k=P} W_{ik}^S . h_k \qquad (4)$$

$$H_k = F(V_k^H) \text{ and } S_i = F(V_i^S) \qquad (5)$$

2.2   Artificial Learning and Its Interpretation as "Feature-Space" Fashioning

Learning in biological systems involves creation, modification and adjustment of synaptic connections between the neurons. This could be assumed for ANNs as well. Learning typically occurs by example through training, or exposure to a set of input/output data (called also, learning database) where the training algorithm (learning rule) iteratively adjusts the connection weights (synaptic weights). These synaptic weights store the knowledge necessary to solve specific problems. The strength of connection between the neurons is stored as a weight-value for the specific connection. The system learns new knowledge by adjusting these connection weights. The learning process could be performed in "on-line" or in "off-line" mode. In the off-line learning methods, once the systems enters into the operation mode, its weights are fixed and do not change any more. Most of the networks are of the off-line learning type. In on-line or real time learning, when the system is in operating mode (recall), it continues to learn while being used as a decision tool. This type of learning needs a more complex design structure.

The learning ability of a neural network is determined by its architecture (network's topology, artificial neurons nature) and by the algorithmic method

332

chosen for training (called also, "learning rule"). In a general way, learning mechanisms (learning processes) could be categorized in two classes: "supervised learning" ([15], [16], [18]) and "unsupervised learning" ([15], [17]).

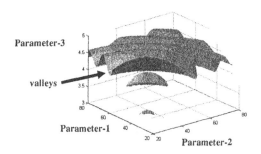

Fig.3. *Example of a 3-dimenssionnal feature-space representation relationship learning involving three parameters (Dr. Jian-Feng Feng, Cambridge Univ. - UK).*

The supervised learning works on reinforcement from the outside. The connections among the neurons in the hidden layer are randomly arranged, then reshuffled according to the used learning rule in order to solving the problem. In general an "error" (or "cost") based criterion is used to determine when stop the learning process: the goal is to minimize that error. It is called supervised learning, because it requires a teacher. The teacher may be a training set of data or an observer who grades the performance of the network results (from which the network's output error is obtained). In the case where the unsupervised learning procedure is applied to adjust the ANN's behavior, the hidden neurons must find a way to organize themselves without help from the outside. In this approach, no sample outputs are provided to the network against which it can measure its predictive performance for a given vector of inputs. In general, a "distance" based criterion is used assembling the most resembling data. After a learning process, the neural network acts as some non-linear function identifier minimizing the output errors. If G (.) is the learned transfer function (or input-output relationship), then the considered neural network realizes S = G (X), where S denotes the output vector and X the input one.

Such artificial learning could be interpreted as some kind of "feature-space" fashioning (sculpture). In fact, referring to the ANN multi-layer representation of figure 2, the input vector dimensionality defines an M-dimensional feature space where input-output relation (learned by neural network) will appear as some hyper volume. So, the learning process could be seen as some action which handles the shape of such hyper volume. The hyper volume resulting from the learning process is characterized by a number of "attractors", called also "valleys", in corresponding M-dimensional feature-space. These attractors are interpreted as stable states resulting from (created by) the learning procedure to which the learned the artificial neural network's behavior tends to converge. In other words, the M-dimensional hyper volume could be seen as artificial neural net knowledge's geometrical representation and attractors in that M-dimensional space could be interpreted as stable learned knowledge of the artificial system. Figure 3 gives an example of 3-dimenssional case involving three parameters.

3 A Simple illustration of ANN Implementation

Referring to analogy between natural and artificial neurons and above presented discussion concerning "artificial learning" and its interpretation in term of "feature-space" fashioning let us illustrate by a simple example how one can use electronic basic devices to implement such artificial structures. Before beginning the illustration through a simple example, let us remind some key-points broadcasted from previous sections:

- artificial neuron could be seen as decision (threshold) device deciding its new state from weighted integration of other neurons connected to this neuron.

- knowledge is stored (learned) thank to "synaptic weights" associated to connections between neurons.

- modification of "synaptic weights" related to a pair of neurons modifies information (state) transmission rate between these two neurons privileging some of possible states of neurons among others.

Let us now consider the behavior in a 2-D feature-space of a pair of simple binary neurons interconnected to each other by associated synapses. In this case each neuron could take two states corresponding to its "excitation" or "inhibition", coded as "1" and "0" respectively. A simple purpose to implement such a binary neuron with a threshold based activation function (decision) is to use "invertors" as neurons. Concerning the synaptic connection, a resistor could be used. Figure 4 illustrates this simple electronic implementation. One can remark that the resistors values modification will result in a current modification modifying the state transition capability of one of these neurons comparing to the other one. So, considering for example the excitation state "1", the associated feature-space will include two attractors.

If the resistors values are equals, then any one among these two possible attractors is favorite. But if resistors are of different values (one more or less resistive that the other), then one of the two inverters will be excited more frequently that the other (see figure 5). So, the modification of synaptic weights performed here by resistors values adjustment results in a new fashioning of the feature-space

334

geometry uplifting one of the two stable states making it an attractor comparing to the other one.

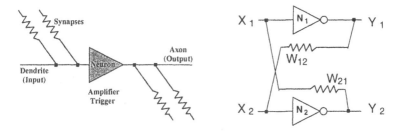

Fig.4. *Simple electronic implementation example showing analogy between natural and artificial (left) and two neurons and their synaptic connections (right). Synaptic weights are realized by adjustable resistors and neurons by invertors.*

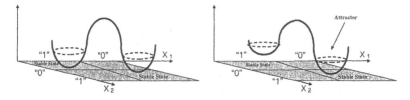

Fig.5. *Learning and attractors behavior in feature-space representation for the example of Fig.4 showing stable states before learning where resistors have the same values (left) and creation of an favorite attractor after performing the learning procedure modifying resistors values.*

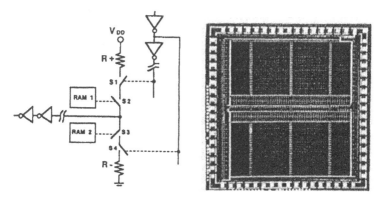

Fig.6. *Neurons and digitally programmable learning implementation scheme (left) and a microphotograph of the neural network chip for template matching (right). (H. P. Graf & L.D. Jackel from AT&T Bell Labs.)*

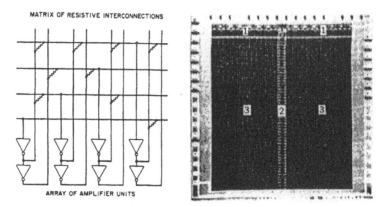

Fig.7. *Schematic of an associative memory (left) and a microphotograph of the corresponding neural chip (right). (H. P. Graf & L.D. Jackel from AT&T Bell Labs.).*

Several implementations have been realized using above-mentioned concept ([19] and [20]). Figure 6 shows an electronic neural network with digitally programmable synaptic weights. Synaptic weights are realized by fixed value resistors and their excitatory or inhibitory actions are activated by programmable switches performing the networks learning. Figure 7 illustrates an associative memory (content addressable memory) and the corresponding neural chip designed and realized by Graf and Jackel from AT&T Bell Laboratories. The main advantage of these kind of implementation is related to their implementation simplicity. However, their main disappointment comes from the learning plainness of such implementations.

4 Advanced Models and Their Hardware Implementation: a Digital and an Analog Electronic Implementation Examples

Previous section pointed up a simple way to implement ANN models showing neural circuits examples designed and realized on the above-mentioned principle. If model simplicity of the above-illustrated examples could provide an advantage for implementation issues of these circuits, on the other hand, the same simplicity represents their main limitations. In fact, the learning mechanism simplicity in those implementations doesn't allow a fine fashioning of the feature space.

In the present section two more sophisticated hardware implementations are presented. The first one, IBM ZISC-036, implements kernel based ANN as RCE (Restricted Coulomb Energy) or RBF (Radial Basis Functions) models. The

336

second one implements the synchronous Boltzmann Machine which is a probabilistic ANN model.

4.1 Kernel Based ANNs and Their IBM ZISC-036 Digital Implementation

4.1.1 Kernel Based ANNs

This kind of neural models belong to the class of "evolutionary" learning strategy based ANN ([15], [21], [22] and [23]). That means that the neural network's structure is completed during the learning process. Generally, such kind of ANNs includes three layers: an input layer, a hidden layer and an output layer. Figure 3 represents the bloc-diagram of such neural net. The number of neurons in input layer corresponds to the processed patterns dimensionality e.g. to the problem's feature space dimension. Figure 8 shows the bloc diagram of such kind of ANN and a simple example of the learning mechanism when the feature space is a 2-D space.

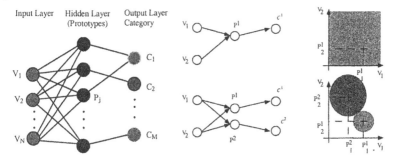

Fig.8. *Radial Basis Functions based ANN's bloc-diagram (left). Example of learning process in 2-D feature space (right).*

The output layer represents a set of categories associated to the input data. Connections between hidden and output layers are established dynamically during the learning phase. It is the hidden layer which is modified during the learning phase. A neuron from hidden layer is characterized by its "centre" representing a point in an N dimensional space (if the input vector is an N-D vector) and some decision function, called also neuron's "Region Of Influence" (ROI). ROI is a kernel function, defining some "action shape" for neurons in treated problem's feature space. In this way, a new learning pattern is characterized by a point and an influence field (shape) in the problem's N-D feature space. In the other words, the solution is mapped thank to learning examples in problem's N-D feature space. The goal of the learning phase is to partition the input space associating prototypes with a categories and an influence field, a part of the input space around the prototype where generalization is possible. When a prototype is memorized, ROI of neighbouring neurons are adjusted to avoid conflict between neurons and related categories. The neural network's response is obtained from relation (7) where C_j represents a "category", $V = [V_1 \quad V_2 \quad ... \quad V_N]^T$ is the input vector, $P^j = [p_1^j \quad p_2^j \quad ... \quad p_N^j]^T$ represents the j-th "prototype" memorized (learned) thanks to creation of the neuron j in the hidden layer, and λ_j the ROI associated to this neuron (neuron j). F(.) is the neuron's activation (decision) function which is a radial basis function (a Gaussian function for example).

$$C_j = F\big(dist\big(V, P^j\big)\big) \quad If \quad dist\big(V, P^j\big) \le \lambda_j$$
$$C_j = 0 \qquad\qquad\qquad If \quad dist\big(V, P^j\big) > \lambda_j \qquad (7)$$

$$dist = \sqrt[n]{\sum_i \left| V_i - p_i^j \right|^n} \qquad (8)$$

$$\text{with} \quad \sum_i \left| V_i - p_i^j \right| \le \left(\sum_i \big(V_i - p_i^j\big)^2 \right)^{\frac{1}{2}} \le \max_i \left| V_i - p_i^j \right| \qquad (9)$$

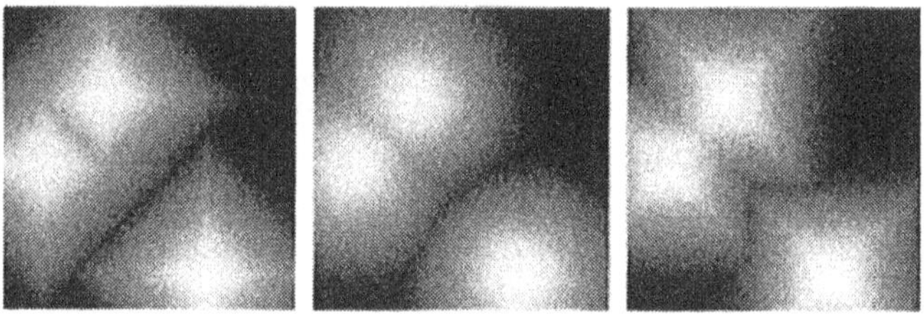

(a)   (b)   (c)

Fig.9. *Examples of neurons and related region of influence representations in a 2-D feature space obtained using Ll (a), Euclidean (b and LSUP(c) distance metrics, respectively.*

The choice of the distance calculation (choice of the used norm) is one of the main parameters in the case of the RCE-KNN like neural models (and derived approaches). The most usual function used to evaluate the distance between two patterns is the Minkowski function expressed by relation (8), where V_i is the i-th component of the input vector and p_i^j the i-th component of the j-th memorized pattern (learned pattern). Manhattan distance ($n = 1$, called also L1 norm) and Euclidean distance ($n = 2$) are particular cases of the Minkowski function and the most applied distance evaluation criterions. One can write relation (9). Figure 9 illustrates neurons and related region of influence (shape) for each kind of above-presented distances.

338

4.1.2 IBM ZISC-036 Neuro-Processor

The IBM ZISC-036 ([15], [21], [22], [23], [24] and [25]) is a parallel neural processor based on the RCE and KNN algorithms. Each chip is capable of performing up to 250 000 recognitions per second. Thanks to the integration of an incremental learning algorithm, this circuit is very easy to program in order to develop applications; a very few number of functions (about ten functions) are necessary to control it. Each ZISC-036 like neuron implements two kinds of distance metrics called L1 and LSUP respectively. Relations (10) and (11) define the above-mentioned distance metrics were P_i represents the memorized prototype and V_i is the input pattern. The first one (L1) corresponds to a polyhedral volume influence field and the second (LSUP) to a hyper-cubical influence field. ZISC-036 implements two learning rules implemented as two distinguished operational modes of the circuit. The first one, called "ROI" (Region Of Influence) corresponds to the usual feature space mapping, described in the previous subsection. The only difference comes from the distance metrics: usage of L1 and LSUP instead the Euclidean distance. The second one, called "KNN" (K Nearest Neighbors) operation mode, is based on the WTA (Winner Takes All) strategy. Figure 10 illustrates a simple learning example for each mode in the caser of a 2-D feature space mapping.

$$\text{L1: } dist = \sum_{i=0}^{n} |V_i - P_i| \qquad (10)$$

$$\text{LSUP: } dist = \max_{i=0...n} |V_i - P_i| \qquad (11)$$

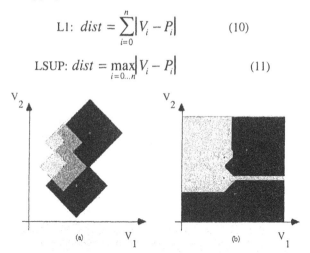

Fig.10. *Example of input feature space mapping (learning) in a 2-D space using ROI and 1-NN modes. Distance metrics L1 Radial Basis Functions based ANN's bloc-diagram (left). Example of learning process in 2-D feature space (right).*

Figure 11 gives the ZISC-036 chip's bloc diagram as well as the neuron's architecture. A 16 bit data bus handles input vectors as well as other data transfers (such as category and distance), and chip controls. Within the chip, controlled access to various data in the network is performed through a 6-bit address bus.

ZISC-036 is composed of 36 neurons. This chip is fully cascadable which allows the use of as many neurons as the user needs (a PCI board is available with a 684 neurons). A neuron is an element, which is able to:

- memorize a prototype (64 components coded on 8 bits), the associated category (14 bits), an influence field (14 bits) and a context (7 bits),
- compute the distance, based on the selected norm (norm L1 given by relation or LSUP) between its memorized prototype and the input vector (the distance is coded on fourteen bits),
- compare the computed distance with the influence fields,
- communicate with other neurons (in order to find the minimum distance, category, etc.),
- adjust its influence field (during learning phase).

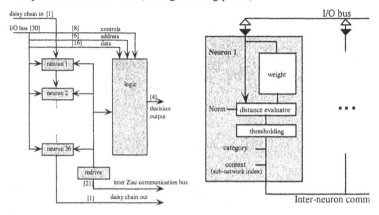

Fig.11. *IBM ZISC-036 chip's bloc diagram (left) and the architecture of a ZISC-036 like neuron (right).*

Two kinds of registers hold information in ZISC-O36 architecture: global registers and neuron registers. Global registers hold information for the device or for the full network (when several devices are cascaded). There are four global registers implemented in ZISC-036: a 16-bits Control & Status Register (CSR), a 8-bits Global Context Register (GCR), a 14-bits Min. Influence Field register (MIF) and a 14-bits Max. Influence Field register (MAF). Neuron registers hold local data for each neuron. Each neuron includes five neuron registers: Neuron Weight Register (NWR), which is a 64-by-8 bytes register, a 8-bits Neuron Context Register (NCR), Category register (CAT), Distance register (DIST) and Neuron Actual Influence Field register (NAIF). The last three registers are both 14-bites registers. Association of a context to neurons is an interesting concept, which allows the network to be divided in several subsets of neurons. Global Context Register (GCR) and Neuron Context Register (NCR) hold information relative to such subdivision at network and neuron levels respectively. Up to 127 contexts can be defined.

4.2 About Synchronous Boltzmann Machine Neural Model

4.2.1 Synchronous Boltzmann Machine Model

Synchronous Boltzmann Machine [26] belongs to the class of stochastic neural models. That means that the neurons decision function (activation function) is a probabilistic function deciphering the state transition probability. So, the neuron state updating is performed randomly with respect to the neuron's state transition probability.

In the Synchronous Boltzmann Machine model, by opposition to the asynchronous model [27], neurones update their states simultaneously. Let u_i be the i-the neurone of the network, x_i^n be the *neurone state* of u_i at instant n (which may have values 1 or 0) and w_{ij} the weight between the neurone u_i and the neuron u_j connected to this neurone, with $n \in \{1, 2, ..., N-1, N\}$. Let V_i^n be the *action potential* of u_i at instant n, which is computed according to relation (1). Then the state of the neurone u_i at discrete time step (n+1) is tossed at random with the probability given by relation (12), where T is a positive control parameter, called also "Boltzmann parameter" or "Boltzmann temperature" by analogy to the absolute temperature of Boltzmann's model in statistical physics.

$$P\left(X_i^{n+1} = 0\right) = \frac{1}{1 + \exp\left(\frac{V_i^n}{T}\right)} \qquad (12)$$

$$\Delta W_{ij} = \frac{\eta}{T}\left(p_{ij}^+ - p_{ij}^-\right) \qquad (13)$$

The learning rule is based on an indicator called "the concurrence" p_{ij} which represents the number of neurons in hidden layers having the same states. The weight update process (learning process) is repeatedly performed for all the pattern associations, and for each of them, it consists in a two phases learning procedure: a clamped phase and a free phase. During the clamped phase, a pattern from the learning database and the corresponding correct network's output are imposed on both input and output neurones while the hidden neurones are left free. In this configuration, a first indicator called "clamped concurrence" p_{ij}^+ is computed. Whereas during the free phase, the input pattern is presented to the input neurones while the output and hidden neurones are left free. As for the clamped phase, the "free concurrence" p_{ij}^- is computed. The weights are updated according to the generalized gradient rule given by relation (13), where η is a positive parameter and T is the control parameter mentioned previously. One can remark that the Boltzmann parameter (T) appears as a key parameter of this neural model.

4.2.2   Mixed Analog/Digital Electronic Implementation

[11] has investigated an analogue implementation of this neural model leading to an integrated circuit (MBA2 chip) including 32 Boltzmann stochastic neurons and [28] had realised a mixed digital/analogue synaptic circuit (MBA11 chip), including 16 synapses for a mixed digital/analogue implementation of the whole network. The electronic board realised by [28] includes two main integrated circuits : MBAT2 chip and MBAT11 chip. The prototype includes two MBAT11 synaptic chips, one MBAT2 neurone circuit and some standard control logic. The neurone cell includes :

- a cellular Automaton Random Number generator. This bloc (C.A.R.N.) performs random numbers according to a uniform probability low,

- a Current to voltage Converter (C.V.C.) with a T parameter input that performs some voltage representation of the $\frac{V_i^n}{T}$ quantity,

- a Boltzmann parameter control bloc (B.T.C.B. represented in figure 12),

- a Sigmoidal Function Bloc (S.F.B.), performing $f\left(V_i^n\right)$ operation, realizing a hyperbolic tangent (th (.)) witch gives a good approximation of relation (2) of this paper,

- a compactor circuit that compares $f\left(V_i^n\right)$ (S.F.B. bloc's output) to C.A.R.N. bloc's output and decide the neurone state changing.

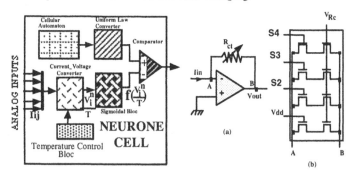

Fig.12. *Bloc diagram of a neurone cell of the MBAT2 chip as it has been described by [11] (left) and a) Boltzmann Temperature parameter Control Bloc circuit.(b) R_{ct} resistor's realisation (right).*

Each neurone cell of the MBAT2 chip performs following operations : it collects and add up synaptic currents ; then converts the total synaptic current into a voltage ; computes the potential action and gives a voltage representation of the $f\left(V_i^n\right)$; at the same time a random number distributed according into the uniform probability low is generated (as a voltage) by C.A.R.N. circuit of the neurone cell ; finally, the generated random voltage is compared to the proportional voltage representation of the $f\left(V_i^n\right)$ performing the neurone state updating ([11], [28], [29]).

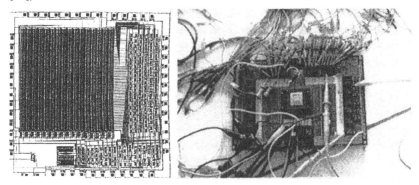

Fig.13. *Layout schematic of the MBAT2 chip as it has been designed, described and presented by P. Garda and E. Belhaire in [11] (left) and a photograph of the functional board including 32 neurons and corresponding electronic environment.*

Figure 12 reproduce the bloc diagram of a neurone cell and the B.T.C.B. circuit (Boltzmann Temperature parameter Control Bloc) of the MBAT2 chip. Figure 13 represents the layout schematic of the neural chip MBA2 and issued board with it's functional electronic environment. Of course the increased complexity inherent to this implementation is firstly due to Boltzmann Machine model's relative complexity. But it should also be noted that the described electronic implementation is able to perform much more sophisticated tasks with an increased learning versatility, making it more "generalist" than the previous strongly dedicated electronic neural networks implementations.

5 Learning Plasticity and Robustness

All implementations (analogue or mixed digital/analogue) of A.N.N. have been supposed to be working in ideal conditions (without perturbations) : natural analogy between the biological systems and implementation of such models made suppose these implementations to be as robust as biological systems. However, reliability and robustness are among key points for success of A.N.N. based approaches and their effective application in industrial world : especially, when a hardware implementation of such models is needed. Of course, numerous research works have pointed out the tolerance and the robustness of A.N.N. models when the perturbation is a local one : by "local perturbation" we identify the case where one or a few neurones of the networks are faulty but the major of them operate correctly [30]. Even if these studies show some structural robustness of ANN models comparing to classical computing systems, several points concerning such studies remain unrealistic.

One of these points concerns the fact that all of these studies are based on inhibition of a relatively small number of neurones (or synapses) of the network (other neurones or synapses of the neural network are supposed to operate perfectly). In the real world, a circuit or a system operates interacting in a global manner with it's environment, and so, it will be subject to some global perturbation. The global perturbation means that a large number (or all) of system's modules (neurones or synapses) operate out of their nominal (or correct) mode. Another point is related to the fact that these works don't take into account any physical parameter of environment in which the neural network will operate : only mathematical structure (in a large number of cases, a graphs theory based analysis) is considered. As example, in the case of a thermal perturbation, all neurones of the neural network will be influenced by some temperature gradient. So in such case, some global perturbation will affect each unit (neurone) of the system : all neurones work but don't operate correctly. Even if natural tendency consists to consider that redundancy of operation units and distributed nature of the encoded information in synapses will lead to some system robustness, it is basic to evaluate impacts of such global perturbations on system's operation capabilities (learning capability, synaptic activity, etc.). Unfortunately, very few works have been interested in the behaviour modelling and analysis of analogue implementation of neural networks or in their limitations [8] [9] [10] [30] [31].

We have scrutinised the behaviour analysis of the synchronous Boltzmann Machine implementation with both thermal and electrical (supply voltage) perturbations ([31], [32], [33]). The raison of our interest on Boltzmann Machine results, on the one hand, from the availability of an electronic implementation of the synchronous model from [11] and [28], and on the other hand, from the availability of a learning example with experimental results reported by [28] and [29], useful to confirm our investigations.

5.1   Experimental Protocol and Instrumentation

As it has been mentioned in previously, two global effects have been focused as perturbations disturbing the neural circuit's behaviour: ambient temperature variation and supply voltage failure. To evaluate learning plasticity of the implemented stochastic neural network an experimental protocol, based on the XOR learning paradigm, has been created. This experimental protocol is built on the basis of the XOR paradigm learning by the Boltzmann Machine's electronic

344

implementation (described previously) in globally disturbed conditions. Concretely, that means that the above described MBA2 neural circuit based prototype board learns the XOR function table under thermal and electrical variations. Inspired from [14], the implemented neural network performing the XOR operation is shown in figure 14. In this scheme 6 neurons are needed. The input layer includes two neurons corresponding to 2-dimensionnal input vector: taking values (0,0), (0,1), (1,0) and (1,1). The hidden layer includes three neurons: two of them are free neurons and the 3-th one is a clamped neuron with it's state set up to "1" (always active neuron). Finally, the output layer contains one neuron corresponding to output XOR states (taking values in binary ensamble).

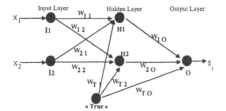

Synaptic Weights	Value	Synaptic Weights	Value
W_{11}	-9	W_{T2}	-5
W_{12}	2	W_{TO}	1
W_{21}	10	W_{1O}	-11
W_{22}	-3	W_{2O}	-13
W_{T1}	7		

Fig.14. *Implemented XOR paradigm conformably to Alspector&al. from Bellcore (right) and synaptic weights indicative values after learning.*

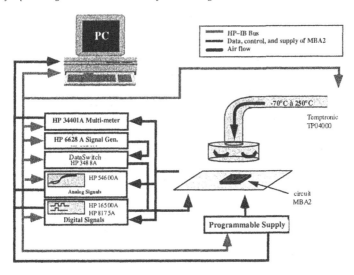

Fig.15. *Experimental chain with programmable global constraints on supply voltage and on the circuit's ambient temperature.*

The thermal perturbations constraint the circuit to work out of nominal temperature (supposed to be 22°C). Disturbed environment is realized thank to an industrial thermal conditioner "Temptronix TPO4000" able to compel the circuits global temperature from -75°C to 250°C with 0.2°C precision. The range of temperature variation concerning the experiment has been fixed from 0°C to 50°C.

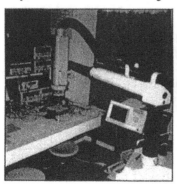 

Fig.16. *Photographs showing experimental protocol realization.*

Figure 15 shows bloc diagram of experimental chain including a set of HP-IB based instruments, a programmable voltage supply, and a temperature conditioner Temptronix TPO4000. All instrumental chain is controlled by a PC. Figure 16 reproduces a global view of the experimental set and a zoomed view of the neural circuit and the thermal conditioner .

5.2   Experimental Results

The first experimental results concern Boltzmann parameter "T" and it's deviation with thermal and electrical disturbances. In fact, this key parameter of Boltzmann Machine's neural model interferes directly in neurons activity (decision function) and in learning procedure control and issued performances (learning convergence speed for example).

For that, the experimental protocol has been organized as following: the circuit learns the XOR state table under nominal conditions (22°C ambient temperature and 5V standard supply voltage required for all standard CMOS technology). To evaluate learning plasticity of the implemented stochastic neural network's learning procedure has been disturbed by varying temperature in above-indicated range and scaring the supply voltage in 20% of it's nominal value (a variation from 4 to 6 volts). Concretely, that means that the above described MBA2 neural circuit based prototype board learns the XOR function table under thermal and electrical variations. In these conditions, Boltzmann parameters "T" has been hold in such a way that the learning performances remain the same as those obtained in nominal conditions. Figure 17 represents Boltzmann parameters "T" versus ambient temperature and supply voltage variations. This result shows that neurons

346

could adapt their activity to compensate global constraints in such a way that the system conserve it's nominal learning performances.

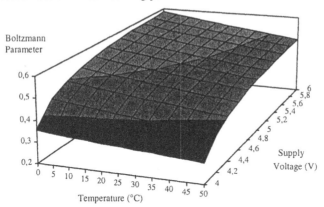

Fig.17. *Boltzmann parameters "T" versus ambient temperature and supply voltage variations.*

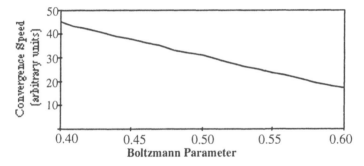

Fig.18. *Learning convergence speed versus Boltzmann paramete.*

Form these results one can reconstruct the neural network's behaviour with respect to the learning convergence speed (figure 18). This figure shows that the learning convergence speed will be affected by the global action of considered perturbations. However, the global learning performances remain truthful performing correct learning of XOR state table.

The second results concerns learning plasticity showing synaptic weights adaptive nature. In fact, directly related to the stochastic learning rule mentioned in previous sections, Boltzmann parameter "T" variation versus ambient temperature and supply voltage variations could be used to reconstruct the above-used neural network's synaptic weights behaviour. Figure 19 shows synaptic weights variations with Boltzmann parameter's evolution. From this information and the Boltzmann parameter's behaviour with ambient temperature and supply voltage, it is possible to construct synaptic values variations with respect to the ambient temperature and supply voltages disturbances. Figure 20 gives the obtained synaptic dynamics versus the above-mentioned global perturbation conditions. This figure shows the learning plasticity of the ANN electronic implementation highlighting the robustness of such implementations comparing to conventional electronic systems.

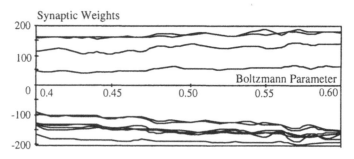

Fig.19. *Synaptic weights behaviour versus Boltzmann parameter's variations* .

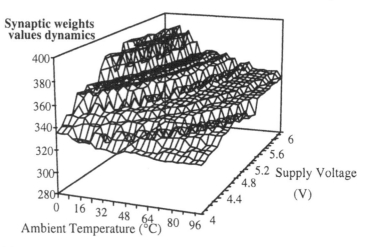

Fig.20. *Synaptic weights values dynamics evolution, after the learning phase, as a function of both ambient temperature and supply voltage variation*

6   Discussion and Conclusion

Starting from the statement that the very large number of works dealing with ANNs hardware implementations have essentially concerned the execution speed enhancement aspects, today, a new question becomes unavoidable: taking into account the actual computers operation speeds (exceeding several Giga-operations per second), the specific hardware implementation of Artificial Neural Networks is it still an pertinent subject?

To answer this relevant question two main goals have absorbed the basic attention in the present paper. The first one was related to ANN's hardware implementation showing how theoretical bases of ANNs could lead to electronic implementation of these intelligent techniques. Concerning this first aspect, firstly a simple approach to ANN hardware implementation has been presented and analysed. Then, a more sophisticated hardware implementation show implementation capability of complex models. The second aim was to flaunt, through learning plasticity, the robustness of ANN hardware implementations. The analysis concerned the learning plasticity under two global perturbations disturbing thermal and electrical nominal conditions. The neural circuit's functionalities out of nominal operation conditions have been explored showing the functional robustness of such electronic implementations.

Taking into account the above presented works and given out results, the above formulated question could be argued positively, concluding on actuality and effectiveness of ANNs hardware implementation issue. Several arguments push to allow in such confident statement.

The first one concerns electronic implementation convenience. In fact, the wide diversity of ANNs hardware implementations, from the simplest to the most sophisticated, show achievability of a hardware solution to most of ANN models and issued structures. The second one is the intrinsic parallelism of such implementations. Indeed, beside the operation speed improvement, this feature of ANN hardware implementations leads to operation redundancy making such circuitry robust. Another strong argument for their structural and operational robustness is related to their distributive information storage capability. As a matter of fact, by coding and storing information in synaptic weights such electronic systems benefit from information misplace immunity. Moreover, their learning plasticity make them be used in hostile environment and conditions.

Finally, an additional argument is related to reliability aspects. In fact, beside the operational and storage plasticity (make such electronic implementations much more robust than the conventional ones), their natural parallelism makes them operate with a high global operation speed but with an individually low cadence leading to material stress reduction and so, to the to reliability enhancement. For that let consider as example the case of a standard VLSI technology (for example a CMOS 0.1 μm to 0.2 μm technology). In such technology, a conventional standard microprocessor (as Pentum, Celeron, etc.) operating in the operation speed range of a couple of Giga hertz (2 to 4 GHz) corresponds to approximately 10 to 15 watts power dissipation requirements. An increase doubling-up the operation speed will result to a significant growth of power dissipation requirement and decrease exponentially the circuit's reliability. In the case of a neural massively parallel implementation (for example the ZISC-036 of IBM) individual operating speed at neuron's level remains low (less than 100 MHz) but it's massively parallel nature makes it reach execution performances comparable to the fastest sequencial computers. Contrary to the conventional circuits, in this case no notable incidence on reliability should be observed: on the one hand, because of feeble material stress in such low speeds and on the other hand, because of structural robustness of such hardware implementation compensating the reliability degradation due to the number of circuits (per chip) elevation.

7 References

[1] C.A. Mead, "Analogue VLSI and neural systems", Addison Wesley 1989.

[2] R.F. Lyon and C.A. Mead, " An Analog electronic cochlea". IEEE transactions on Acoustic, Speech and signal Processing, Vol. 36, N°7, pp. 1119- 1134, 1988.

[3] L. Jackel, "Electronic neural networks". In NATO ARW, Neuro-algorithms, architecture and applications, Les Arcs, 1989.

[4] M. Chiaberge, L. M. Reyneri, "Cintia : A Neuro-Fuzzy Real-Time Controller for Law-Power Embedded Systems", IEEE Micro Vol. 15, pp. 40-47, June 1995.

[5] Bazoon M., Stacey D. A., and Cui C., 'A hierarchical artificial neural network system for the classification of cervical cells', IEEE Int. Conf. On Neural Networks, Orlando, July 1994.

[6] G. Mercier, K. Madani, "CMAC Real-Time Adaptive Control Implementation on a DSP Based Card", , From Natural to Artificial Neural Computation, LNCS Vol. 930, Springer Verlag, pp.1114-1120, 1995.

[7] K. Madani, P. Garda, E. Belhaire, F. Devos, Two Analog Counters for Neural Network Implementation, IEEE Journal of Solid-State Circuits, VOL. 26, N° 7, JULY 1991, pp. 966-974.

[8] J.L. Wyatt and D.L. Standley, "Circuit design criteria for stable lateral inhibition neural networks "In IEEE International Symposium Circuits and systems, IEEE pp 997-1000, June 1988.

[9] M.A. Sivilotti, M.R. Emerling, and C.A.Mead, "VLSI Architectures for implementation of Neural Network". In AIP conference Proceedings on Neural Network for computing, J.S. DENKER, American Institute of physic, Snowbird, UTAH pp408-413, 1986.

[10] M.Verleysen and P. Jespers, " precision of sum-of-product in Analog Neural Network". In Proceedings of the first International workshop on Microelectronics for Neural Networks, Dortmund, RFA, June 1990.

350

[11] P. Garda E. Belhaire, An Analog chip set with digital I/O for synchronous Boltzmann Machine, VLSI for Artificial Intelligence and Neural Network, Kluwer Academic, J.G.Delgado-frias and W.R. Moore, BOSTON, 1990.

[12] P. Lalanne, J.C. Rodier, H. Richard, P. Chavel, E. Belhaire, K. Madani, P. Garda, 2-D optical generator of updating probabilities for VLSI implementation of Boltzmann Machines, International Journal of Optical Computing, Vol. 1, pp. 25-30, 1990.

[13] R David, E. Williams, G. De Trémiolles, P. Tannhof, Description and Practical Uses of IBM ZISC-036, VI-DYNN'98 - Virtual Intelligence - Dynamic Neural Networks Stockholm - Sweden - June 22-26, 1998.

[14] J. Alspector, B. Gupta, R.B. Allen, performance of a stochastic learning microchip, Neural Information Processing Systems, Ed. David Touretzky, Morgan-Kaufmann, pp; 748-760, 1989.

[15] M.A. Arbib (ed.), "Handbook of Brain Theory and Neural Networks" 2ed. M.I.T. Press. 2003.

[16] S. Hebb, The Organization of Behaviour, Wiley and Sons, New-York, U.S.A., 1949.

[17] T. Kohonen, Self-Organization and Associative Memory, Springer-Verlag, Germany, 1984.

[18] D. Rumelhart, G. Hinton, R. Williams, Learning Internal Representations by Error Propagation", Rumelhart D., McClelland J., "Parallel Distributed Processing: Explorations in the Microstructure of Cognition", I & II, MIT Press, Cambridge MA, 1986.

[19] H.P. Graf, L.D. Jackel, Analog electronic Neural Network Circuits, IEEE Circuit & Devices Magazine July 1989, pp.44-49.

[20] H.P. Graf, L.D. Jackel, W.E. Hubbard, VLSI implementation of a Neural Network model, Computer, IEEE 1988, pp.34-41.

[21] M. Bogdan, H. Speakman, W. Rosenstiel, Kobold : A neural Coprocessor for Back-propagation with on-line learning, Proc. NeuroMicro 94, Torino, Italy, pp. 110-117.

[22] Reyneri L.M., 1995. Weighted Radial Basis Functions for Improved Pattern Recognition and Signal Processing. Neural Processing Letters, Vol. 2, No. 3, pp 2-6, May 1995.

[23] Trémiolles G., Madani K., Tannhof P., 1996. A New Approach to Radial Basis Function's like Artificial Neural Networks. In NeuroFuzzy'96, IEEE European Workshop, Vol. 6 N° 2, pp 735-745, April 16 to 18, Prague, Czech Republic, 1996.

[24] De Tremiolles G. I., " Contribution to the theoretical study of neuromimetic models and to their experimental validation: use in industrial applications" (Contribution à l'étude théorique des modèles neuromimétiques et à leur validation expérimentale: mise en œuvre d'applications industrielles), Ph.D. thesis report, University Paris XII, 05 March 1998.

[25] Madani K., Tremiolles G., Tanhoff P., 2003 - a. Image processing using RBF like neural networks: A ZISC-036 based fully parallel implementation solving real world

and real complexity industrial problems. In *Journal of Applied Intelligence N°18, 2003, Kluwer Academic Publishers, pp. 195-231.*

[26] R. Azencott, "Synchronous Boltzmann Machines and their learning algorithms". In NATO ARW, Springer-Verlag, les arcs, February 1989.

[27] G.E. Hinton and T.J. Sejnowski, "learning in Boltzmann machines ".In Cognitive 85, PARIS, PP 283-290, 1985.

[28] V. Lafargue, "Contribution à la réalisation électronique de Réseaux de Neurones formels: Intégration mixte de l'apprentissage des machines de Boltzmann "; Ph. D. Report, thèse de doctorat en science de l'université PARIS XI, Orsay, January 1993.

[29] E. Belhaire, "Contribution à la réalisation électronique de réseaux de Neurones Formels : Intégration Analogique d'une machine de BOLTZMANN" ; Ph.D. report, thèse de doctorat en science de l'université Paris XI, Orsay February 1992.

[30] J.J. Hopfield,"Neurons with graded response have collective computational properties like those of two state neurones". Proceedings of the national Academy of science of U.S.A., vol 81 pp 3088-3092, 1984.

[31] K. Madani, I.Berechet, G. De Tremiolles, Analysis of limitations in Analog Implementation of stochastic Artificial Neural Network V, Orlando, Floride, U.S.A., 4 - 8 April 1994.

[32] K. Madani, G. De Tremiolles, Global Perturbation Effects Analysis in a CMOS Analogue Implementation of Synchronous Boltzmann Machine, 3-rd. International Workshop on Thermal Investigations of Integrated Circuits and Microstructures, IEEE-CNRS, Cannes - Côte d'Azur, September 21 - 23, 1997.

[33] K. Madani, G. De Tremiolles, Effects of Global Perturbations on Learning Capability in a CMOS Analogue Implementation of Synchronous Boltzmann Machine, Lecture Notes in Computer Science – Biological and Artificial Computation : From Neuroscience to Technology, Edited by : Jose Mira, Roberto M. Diaz and Joan Cabestany - Springer Verlag Berlin Heidelberg 1999, N°ISBN : 3-540-66069-0, pp. 107-116.

A Tiny Flat-island in a Huge Lake – How can we search for it if completely flatland elsewhere?

Akira Imada

Brest State Technical University

Moskowskaja 267, 224017 Brest, Belarus

Abstract:

In the background of this paper, lies a simulation of an associative memory model with spiking neurons. We want, however, to put the issue aside for a while, since we came across a problem, very simple but extremely difficult one, when we explored a fitness landscape – a weight configuration space of high dimensionality where weight solutions are supposed to look like peaks. In the landscape, the location of one of those peaks is already known. This is called the Hebbian peak – a weight configuration in which two neurons are wired when they both fire. We guess many other peaks exist though we have not found any yet so far. During we searched for such solutions, we observed that the fitness landscape was almost everywhere completely flatland of altitude zero except for the Hebbian peak which shows a peculiar shape like a-tiny-flat-island-in-a-huge-lake. In such circumstances how could we search for other peaks? This paper is a call for challenges to the problem.

Keywords: Associative Memory, Spiking Neuron, Evolutionary Computations, Fitness Landscape, Needle in Haystack, Random Hill-climbing, Baldwin Effect, Artificial Immune System.

1 Introduction

Assume a black-box which has N inputs and one output, and the output tells us the degree to how good is the input configuration. When we search for a solution to a problem which is expressed by N parameters, we can regard the black box as such a problem; the set of N inputs as a candidate solution; and the output as how fit does the candidate solution to the problem, that is, fitness value. Usually, the distribution of these fitness values gives us a gradient information, namely, it gradually approaches to the highest value, whichever it might be local or global maximum value. In general, we search for the solution using this gradient information. However, if we think of a situation where only exactly one configuration is good and all the others are bad. When, specifically, the inputs are N binary numbers and just one configuration out of those 2^{N-1} is fitness 1 while all the others are of fitness 0, which we call a search for a needle in a haystack. How could we locate the solution without any gradient information?

With the goal being a realization of associative memory by a neural network with spiking neurons, we explored the weight space of a neural network in which some weight configurations are assumed to give the network a function of associative memory. Hyper-planes defined on those spaces are sometimes called fitness landscapes when we fictitiously plot a measure of goodness, or equivalently, a fitness value on all the possible points of configuration assuming altitude of the hyper-plane constructs a landscape, and hence the location of peaks implies the solution of our problem. In our experiment of associative memory, when we were exploring the fitness landscape to try to find those peaks exhaustively, we noticed that the landscape was a very unusual one. That is, the landscape is everywhere a flat-land of fitness 0 except for one peak and the shape of the peak is more like a mesa than a peak. The top is not a pin-point due to a synaptic plasticity of the neural network and the sidewall is very steep. Therefore, evolutionary computations which usually recombine points on the hyper-plane as candidate solutions selecting those points which perform better than others, would not work in this fitness landscape of almost everywhere flat-land of fitness 0. This reminds us a classical but a seminal experiment by Hinton & Nowlan [1] which was proposed to find a peak like a needle in a haystack.

In short, assuming that we have many peaks in a huge landscape of almost everywhere completely flatland in which only a few of the peaks are already known, our goal is to find a computational method that has a capability to search for those unknown peaks by employing an information of already known peaks.

In the following three sections, we describe Associative Memory, Fitness Landscape, and Hinton & Nowlan's experiment more in detail. Then we propose a test-function and some results of exploring it.

2 Associative Memory

How does anyone stop thinking of something? Accidentally, accidental thoughts, all thoughts are accidental. – From "Key to Rebecca" by Ken Follett.

Associative memory is a memory system in which we can store information and recall it later from its partial and/or imperfect stimuli. Information is stored as a number of stable states with a domain of attraction around each of the stable states. If the system starts with any stimulus within the domain it will converge to the attractor following a trajectory, hopefully a short one. This models human memory in the sense that, e.g., we can recognize our friend's face even without meeting for a long time, or we can recall a song immediately after listening to a very beginning part of the song. Hopfield [2] proposed a fully connected neural network model of associative memory in which a set of patterns is stored distributedly among neurons as attractors. Since then the model had been fairly well studied for more than a decade, and we now know it is not so practical, partly due to its small storage capacity, and we study another model using spiking neurons instead of the McCulloch-Pitts [3] neurons which construct the Hopfield model, with the goal being to overcome those problems and, more importantly, to look for more biologically plausible models of human memory.

Some regions in our brain such as neo-cortex or hippocampus are said to be made up of two categories of neurons, that is, pyramidal cells and inter-neurons. Typically, the pyramidal cells communicate with each other via excitatory synapses (positive influences), while inter-neurons send signals to pyramidal cells via inhibitory synapses (negative influences). As Wilson [4] wrote in his book, Marr [5] was one of the first to propose this hippo-campal model involving both recurrent excitation via Hebbian [6] synapses and inhibition. In his book, Wilson [4] wrote that a single neuron which emits spike train when it receives an external stimulus $P(t)$ could be modeled by

$$\frac{dR(t)}{dt} = \frac{1}{r}(-R(t) + S(P(t)))$$

where Wilson [4] proposed to employ, among many alternatives, Naka-Rushton function [7]:

$$S(P) = \begin{cases} M \cdot P^n / (\sigma^n + P^n) & \text{if } P \geq 0 \\ 0 & \text{if } P < 0, \end{cases}$$

M and σ are called *saturation* and *semi-saturation constant*, respectively, and n is an integer parameter for its graph to fit a phenomenon. Here we assume N pyramidal cells and implicit number of inter-neurons. We simulate these pyramidal cells by spiking neurons which interact with each other using electric current via plastic synapses. Pyramidal cells are also interacted by inter-neurons by global inhibition.

To be more specific, stimuli to one pyramidal cell are given from all the other pyramidal cells via synaptic strength, as well as inter-neuron cells whose number is reduced to only one here for the sake of simplicity.

The synaptic strength from pyramidal cell j to i is denoted as w_{ij} and all the inhibitory synapses from inter-neuron are assumed to have a value g. Then stimulus to the i-th pyramidal cell p_i is described as

$$P_i = \left(\sum_{j=1}^{N} w_{ij} \cdot R_j - g \cdot G \right)_+^2$$

where $(\cdot)_+$ means that we use the value if and only if inside the parentheses is positive and zero otherwise. Following Wilson [4], we experimented with $\sigma = 10$, $M = 100$, and $n=2$ in the above Naka-Rushton equation. Thus, our equation of spiking ratio of the i-th pyramidal cell R_i with the spiking ratio of the inter-neuron G is given as

$$\tau_R \frac{dR_i}{dt} = -R_i + \frac{100 \left(\sum_{j=1}^{N} w_{ij} R_j - 0.1 G \right)_+^2}{100 + \left(\sum_{j=1}^{N} w_{ij} R_j - 0.1 G \right)_+^2}$$

$$\tau_G \frac{dG}{dt} = -G - 0.07 \sum_{j=1}^{N} R_i$$

where, both τ_R and τ_G are to be set to 10. Note that w_{ii} $(i = 1, ..., N)$ should be set to all zero. In order to encode N-bit binary patterns using N spiking neurons, we use *firing-rate* of a neuron within certain time window which expresses binary number according to whether the rate exceeds a threshold or not. In what he calls *CA3 network* in his book, Wilson [4] employed 256 pyramidal cells so that these cells represent a pattern constructed by 16×16 array of pixels. The network also incorporates one inter-neuron cell to provide pyramidal cells a feedback inhibition. The task of the network is to recognize four given patterns from its noisy input. Each of the four patterns is represented by 32 active cells plus other 224 quiet cells. Network has learned to recognize these four patterns by modifying the synapses according to the following what might be called Hebb's [6] rule .

$$w_{ij} = k \cdot sgn(R_i - 0.5M) \cdot sgn(R_j - 0.5M),$$

where k is set to 0.016, M is a saturation level in the Naka-Rashton equation, and $sgn(x)$ is equal to 1 if $x>0$ and 0 otherwise. The equation is called Hebb's rule in the sense that w_{ij} will be modified if and only if both the neuron i and j should be activated. Also note that equation of Hebb's rule above is applied only if the previous value of w_{ij} is 0, otherwise, w_{ij} will remain intact.

A noisy input of a pattern is constructed by randomly picking up about one-third of the active cells of the selected pattern with adding them other 20 quiet cells, also chosen at random, after turning them active. Then one of these four patterns is given to the network, that is, network starts the dynamics with the pattern as the initial configuration of its neurons' state. Network updates the state according to a series of N differential equations above. The dynamics is observed during a total of 100 ms (assuming step of dt of dr/dt to be 1 ms), with the noisy input being continued to be fed for the first 20 ms.

3   Fitness Landscape

The hill on the south side of the town sloped steeply to the river, here. On the west there was a long ridge which fell gently to the plain. - From "Pillar of the Earth" - by Ken Follett.

The concept of the fitness landscape was first introduced by Wright [8] to study biological evolutionary processes. Since then, this concept has been used not only in evolutionary biology but also in chemistry, physics, computer science and so on.

In chemistry, for example, a molecule can be represented as a string of N letters with each letter being chosen from an alphabet of size k (see Macken et al. [10]) Twenty amino acids (k=20) for proteins or four nucleotides (k=4) for nucleic acids can be considered as examples of the alphabet. The k^N possible combinations of the letters construct a configuration space of the string. Then, for example, the free energy of RNA folding into secondary structures (see Fontana et al. [11]) or the ability of peptides to bind to a particular substrate to catalyze a specific reaction (see Maynard Smith [12]) is assigned as a fitness value to each configuration.

In physics, the Hamiltonian energy of Ising spins defines a fitness landscape on the configuration space of N spins, where each spin takes the value either 1 or -1 (k=2). Bray and Moore [9] argued about the number and distribution of meta-stable states (local optima) of the Hamiltonian energies.

To explore these fitness landscapes, we need a rule by which a point in the space moves to one of its neighbors. Then, consecutive movements of a point to the neighbors form a *walk* on the landscape. Macken et al. [10] used *random point mutation* that changes a single letter in the string to specify neighbors of the string. Then, by sampling points along an *"evolutionary walk"* in which point moves to the *firstly found fitter neighbor*, they studied the statistical properties of the landscape defined by the chemical affinity of antibody for antigen in immune response.

Weinberger [14] used two different walks: *"gradient walk"* in which the walker steps to the *best* of its neighbors and *"random adaptive walk"* in which the next step is chosen *at random* from the set of better neighbors, to investigate the Kauffman's NK landscape [13] which is a model formulated in more general form.

We extend the concept of the discrete fitness landscape to a continuous one. Namely, a capability of a fully-connected neural network to store a set of bipolar patterns (each bit is either 1 or -1) as associative memory assigns fitness on the configuration space of real-valued synaptic weight configuration space ($k = \infty$). A walker moves to its neighboring point determined by Gaussian random mutation.

4 A Needle in a Haystack

One day I'd cooked soba. Great! I tried teuchi udon the next day and it was also great. It is really easy to make such delicious dishes just from flour or buckwheat flour. The main thing is sauce, however. It is either tasty or not. Nothing in between. - Edward Venskovich (Personal Communication).

The problem Hinton & Nowlan [1] proposed is to search for only one configuration of 20 bits of one and zero, that is, the search space is made up of 2^{20} points all of which except for one point are assigned fitness 0. Only exactly one points, say, (11111111111100000000000) is assigned fitness 1. That is why this is called *search for a needle in a haystack*. See Fig. 1 bellow.

Fig. 1 A fictitious sketch of fitness landscape of a needle in a haystack.

It seems impossible to solve this if we use a simple genetic algorithm, since usually it recombines two genotypes whose phenotypes are a little better than others, and in our circumstance almost all genotypes perform equally badly. Any hill-climbing would not seem to work. Hinton & Nowlan [1], however, exploited *lifetime learning* of each individual. That is, chromosome is made up of genes of which about 25% are "1", 25% are "0", and the rest of the 50% are "?". Within one generation all the "?"' position are assigned either "1" or "0" at random and fitness is evaluated, which is called *lifetime learning* of each individual. Each individual repeats the learning 1000 times in its lifetime. If it reaches the point of fitness 1 at the n-th trial, then the *degree to which learning succeeded* is calculated as

$$1 + 19 \cdot (1000 - n)/1000.$$

Hinton & Nowlan's model is a sort of Gedanken-experiment to study how the *lifetime learning* affects an evolution, that is, the *Baldwin effect*. The location of the unique solution (whose fitness is 1, while all others' are 0) is assumed to be known before a run, though it is not of the case in real world problems.

5 A Tiny Flat Island in a Huge Lake

It's Spring Cleaning time again ... for my brain. Below, a cluster of random follow-ups, postscripts and observations to tide you over until the spring weather actually turns spring-like. - David Pogue from New York Times 10th Apr. 2003.

Hinton & Nowlan's experiment is valid under an assumption, as they wrote, *"genotype can recognize when it has achieved the perfect fitness during its lifetime learning."* This usually does not hold when it is applied to solve a real world problem. If the phenotype recognizes that it reaches the solution, all we need is to check its genotype to know the parameter configuration which gives the phenotype to achieve its goal. As such, no need for a further computation. Without such an assumption, on the other hand, we could not explore this specific fitness landscape searching for the goal.

For example, see Fig. 2. This is the peak we observed in the fitness landscape during our simulation of associative memory with spiking neurons. The plot shows a trace of random downhill walker from a point on the top region of the Hebbian peak. As shown in the Figure, the peak has a completely flat and wide region in the top area, which implies a synaptic plasticity. And take a look also at side wall of the peak, we find it really steep. It's more like a tiny flat island in a huge lake than a hill or peak in a more or less ragged landscape.

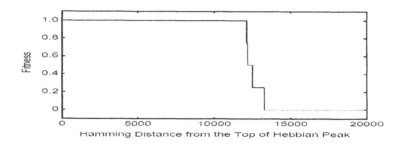

Fig. 2 A trace of a downhill walk from the top of the Hebbian peak.

To simplify the problem, we proposed a test function.

Test-function 1 (**A Tiny Flat Island in a Huge Lake**) *Assuming an n-dimensional hypercube all of whose coordinate x_i (i=1, ...,n) lies [-1,1], find an algorithm to locate a point in the region A whose coordinates all lie [0, a] (a ≤ 1).*

The goal is to search for a hypercube in the n-dimensional Euclidean space. This is essentially equivalent to the Hinton & Nowlan's a-needle-in-a-haystack when we set $n=20$ and $a=1$, and also those continuous-valued coordinates are considered to be binary strings by regarding all the positive components as "1" and negative ones as "0". If necessary, we can make the needle tinier by decreasing the value of a, that is, the complexity of the search are controlled by changing a and n.

6　Experiment

6.1　A Needle in a Haystack

We retried the Hinton & Nowlan's experiment. However, we were obliged to modify it, because when individuals of 20 chromosomes with "0" "1" and "?" created at random, they usually do not reach fitness 1 even with 1000 times of lifetime learning. Hence, we create individuals one by one at random and each time we make it learn 1000 times, and if it reaches the fitness 1 we put it in the population of the first generation, and this is repeated until those individuals fill the population. In other words, a run starts with a population of individuals who are within 1000 steps from the needle. An example run shows we have to try a total of 118,499 times randomly to obtain such a population of 100 individuals, though those numbers depend on the length of chromosome.

From an application view point, it would sound peculiar if we start an evolution with this population, since we can get the solution from any individual in this first population. All of the individuals have already reached the needle (solution) via the lifetime learning. No need to try further evolution.

From an artificial evolution view point, on the other hand, it would be interesting to observe the further evolution starting with this population, if we assume the "?" genes are not replaced with either "0" or "1" but remain intact when the individual reaches the needle. This is what is called "Baldwin Effect". If, on the other hand, lifetime learning modifies some genes, it is called "Lamarckian Inheritance". Fig. 3 shows how the degree-to-which-learning-succeeded defined in Section 4 evolves in a run.

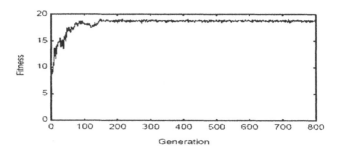

Fig. 3 An evolution of search for "a needle in a haystack" from the experiment of Hinton & Nowlan.

The number of "?" genes decreases as the evolution proceeds, but the final individuals still have those "?" genes. In the run shown in Fig. 3, chromosomes in the first generation have an average of 10.2 those "?" genes. Then as evolution proceeds the number decreases and eventually in the generation 12,000, where all chromosomes have converged to the same one, they have 6 "?" genes (Transition of the number is not shown in the figure). Those genes have something to do with an evolution of *"learnability"*. It is, however, beyond the topic of this paper.

6.2   A Tiny Flat Island in a Huge Lake

Thus, we now know that although the Hinton & Nowlan's experiment is elegant method to see lifetime learning enhances the genetic search, that is, the Baldwin effect works in our evolutionary computations, while in reality we have not found so far an algorithm to solve this type of a needle hidden in a haystack.

Then we proposed a test-function in the previous Section, and here we show results of applying both a *simple random search* (not even a random hill-climbing), and the *lifetime learning* (the one proposed by Hinton & Nowlan but only within one generation) to the test-function.

6.2.1   Simple random search

We set $a=1$ and study if a randomly created chromosome with length n will be in the domain A or not, that is to say, a random search looking for points in A. The result is that, as n becomes large, search becomes more and more difficult, and eventually when $n=20$ we cannot find any such point within a reasonable time, say, in 24 hours. No wander Hinton & Nowlan adopted the chromosome of length 20! In Fig. 4 how many chromosomes were on A out of 10,000 randomly created ones is shown.

362

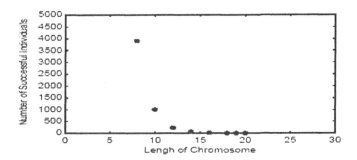

Fig. 4   Number of individuals who happens to be in a point in the target region A out of randomly created 10,000 individuals.

6.2.2   Lifetime learning

Here we also created a chromosome at random one by one, but we study if each of them reaches the domain A after 1000 times of learning. In Fig. 5 we plot how many chromosomes we have to create until we find those individuals who reach the goal within 1000 times of lifetime learning. We see the results are a little better than the random search.

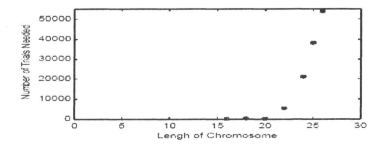

Fig. 5 Average Number of random individuals needed to find a one who succeeded in reaching the target via 1000 times of lifetime learning.

These results suggest that the Baldwin effect - effect of learning during each individual's lifetime becomes hard exponentially as the dimension increases.

6 Summary & Future Works

We came across a very difficult problem when we explore a fitness landscape. The landscape was a very unusual one: everywhere low flat land of fitness zero except for a strange shaped peak – like a tiny flat island in a huge lake. The lake is too huge to get a bird's eye view of the whole lake and we have never been able to see other islands. To approach this problem we have proposed in this paper a test function which is a simplified version of our problem and we can easily control the difficulty of the problem with the structure being essentially the same. This landscape reminds us of the Hinton & Nowlan's classical experiment of searching for a needle in a haystack in which individual's lifetime learning was employed. We made an experiment to learn if this what might be called a Baldwin effect works in our evolution in PC and we have found that the lifetime learning also somehow works in the proposed test-function if we compare it to a simple random search. However, we still doubt more or less if we can apply the Baldwin effect as it is to a real world problem. So, this paper is a call for challenge proposals of the methods to solve our test-function. In short, not so short though, in a huge landscape of almost everywhere completely flat-land, assuming we have many peaks only a few of which we know, our goal is to find a computational method that can search for those unknown peaks, by employing an information of those already known peaks. As a candidate of these methods, we now thinking of *anomaly detection by artificial immune system*.

Our concern here is if we regard the points which belongs to A as *non-self*, while all the other points as *self*. Then can a Negative Selection Algorithm (see e.g. [16]), for example, detect these *non-selves* as anomaly? On the contrary, if we regard points in A as *self*, then can a Positive Selection Algorithm (see e.g., [17]) distinguish them from *other non-selves*? Or, a clonal selection can detect those points as anomalies? These await for our exploration.

2 References

[1] G. E. Hinton and S. J. Nowlan (1987) "How Learning can Guide Evolution." Complex Systems, 1, pp. 495--502.

[2] J. J. Hopfield (1982) "Neural Networks and Physical Systems with Emergent Collective Computational Abilities." Proceedings of the National Academy of Sciences, USA 79, pp. 2554-2558.

[3] W. S. McCulloch and W. Pitts (1943) "A Logical Calculus of Ideas Immanent in Nervous Activity." Bulletin of Mathematical Biophysics, 5, pp. 115--113.

[4] H. R. Wilson (1999) "Spikes, Decisions, and Actions: The Dynamical Foundations of Neuroscience." Oxford University Press.

[5] D. Marr (1971) "A Theory for Archicortex." Philosophical Transactions of the Royal Society of London, B262, pp. 23—81.

[6] D. O. Hebb (1949) "The Organization of Behavior." Wiley.

[7] K. I. Naka and W. A. Rushton (1966) "S-potentials from Colour Units in the Retina of Fish." Journal of Physiology, 185, pp. 584--599.

[8] S. Wright (1932) "The Roles of Mutation, Inbreeding, Crossbreeding and Selection in Evolution." Proceedings of the 6th International Congress of Genetics, pp. 56--366.

[9] A. Bray, and M. Moore (1980) "Metastable States in Spin Glasses." Journal of Physics C: Solid State Physics 13, pp. L469--L476.

[10] C. Macken, P. Hagan, and A. Perelson (1991) "Evolutionary Walks on Rugged Landscapes." SIAM Journal of Applied Mathematics 51, pp. 799--827.

[11] W. Fontana, and P. Schuster (1987) "A Computer Model of Evolutionary Optimization." Biophysical Chemistry 26, pp123--147.

[12] J. Maynard Smith, J. (1970) Natural Selection and the Concept of a Protein Space. Nature 225. pp563--564.

[13] S. A. Kauffman, S. A. (1993) "The origin of Order: Self-organization and Selection in Evolution." Oxford University Press.

[14] E. D. Weinberger, E. D. (1990) "Correlated and Uncorrelated Fitness Landscapes and How to Tell the Difference." Biological Cybernetics 63, pp. 325--336.

[15] Kwee-Bo Sim and Dong-Wook Lee (2003) "Modeling of Positive Selection for the Development of a Computer Immune System and a Self-Recognition Algorithm." International Journal of Control, Automation, and Systems Vol. 1, No. 4, pp. 453—458.

[16] S. Forrest, A. S. Perelson, L. Allen, and R. Cherukuri, (1994) "Self-nonself discrimination in a computer." Proceedings of the IEEE Symposium on Research in Security and Privacy, pp. 202-212.

[17] J. Kim and P. Bentley (2001) "Investigating the roles of Negative Selection and Clonal Selection in an Artificial Immune System for Network Intrusion Detection." Technical Report, Department of Computer Science, London.

A Soft Computing Based Approach Using Signal-To-Image Conversion for Computer Aided Medical Diagnosis (CAMD)

Amine Chohra, Nadia Kanaoui, and V. Amarger

Intelligence in Instrumentations and Systems Laboratory (I²S / JE 2353) Sénart Institute of Technology - University Paris-XII, Avenue Pierre Point, 77127 Lieusaint, France, {chohra, amarger}@univ-paris12.fr

Abstract: Dealing with expert (human) knowledge consideration, Computer Aided Medical Diagnosis (CAMD) dilemma is one of the most interesting, but also one of the most difficult problems. Among difficulties contributing to challenging nature of this problem, one can mention the need of fine classification and decision tasks. In this paper, we present a new approach founded on an hybrid scheme, multiple model approach for reliable CAMD, including a signal-to-image converter, a Neural Network (NN) based classifier and a fuzzy decider. This new concept has been used to design a computer aided medical diagnostic tool able to assert auditory pathologies based on Brainstem Auditory Evoked Potentials (BAEP) based biomedical tests, which provides an effective measure of the integrity of the auditory pathway.

Keywords: Computer Aided Medical Diagnosis (CAMD), image processing, analysis and interpretation of biomedical signals, pattern recognition, classification, neural networks, fuzzy decision-making.

1 Introduction

Computer Aided Medical Diagnosis (CAMD) is an attractive area leading to future promising applications in biomedical domain. However, dealing with expert (human) knowledge consideration, the computer aided medical diagnosis dilemma is one of most interesting, but also one of the most difficult problems. Among difficulties contributing to challenging nature of this problem, one can mention the need of pertinent information (indicators) and fine classification.

Several approaches have been developed in order to analyze biomedical signals: electrocardiogram signals [1] and particularly Brainstem Auditory Evoked Potentials (BAEP) [2], [3]. The approach developed by [2] is based on fuzzy sets for identification and particularly in BAEP analysis. A cross-correlation with a priori information have been used in a pattern recognition approach [3].

Over past decades, Neural Networks (NN) and related techniques show many attractive features in solution of wide class of problems [4] such as classification, expert knowledge modeling, and decision-making [5], [6], [7], [8], [9], [10].

This paper deals with soft computing based pattern classification of images obtained from biomedical tests issued signals and particularly from BAEP signals. The aim of this paper is to suggest a promising approach which consists of transforming biomedical signals in images to be processed afterwards using NN for pattern recognition (classification) and fuzzy logic for the decision-making. In fact, such approach take advantage from features which are unreachable from unidimensional signal (time dependent waveform). More, it allows to use image-like representation and processing, which offers benefit of a reacher information representation (than the signal related one).

Section 2, processing of biomedical signals, and particularly BAEP, as images is developed. Section 3, a soft computing (implying NN and fuzzy logic) based image processing approach for BAEP analysis and interpretation is suggested. Section 4, the implementation of the suggested approach and the obtained results are detailed. Finally, in Section 5, a discussion dealing with the suggested approach and how it relates to some other works is given.

2 Biomedical Signals-To-Images Conversion

Traditionally, biomedical signals are processed using signal processing approaches, mainly based on peak and wave identification approaches and pattern recognition approaches, such as in [1], [2], [3]. The main problem is then to identify pertinent parameters (to which depends the studied phenomenon). This task is not trivial, because the time (or frequency) is not always the variable that points up the studied phenomena's features (behavior, etc...). Contrary to a time or frequency (signal) based representation, the image based one, taking benefit from it's 2-D nature, offers advantage a reacher representation allowing to take into account more complex features (objects, information, etc...).

2.1 Brainstem Auditory Evoked Potential (BAEP)

BAEP based clinical tests provide an effective measure of the auditory pathway up to the upper brainstem level. It is based on analysis of "Evoked Potentials", which are electrical response caused by the brief stimulation of a sense system. In fact, the stimulus triggers a number of neurophysiologic responses along the auditory pathway. An action potential is conducted along the eight nerve, the brainstem and finally to the brain. A few times after the initial stimulation, the signal evokes a response in the brain area where sounds are interpreted. The right picture of Figure 1 (extracted from [11]) represents two critical cases of such BAEP: first one corresponds to a healthy patient and second to a an auditory disorder pathology.

Usually, the experts diagnose the pathology using a surface of 50 estimations called "Temporal Dynamic of the Cerebral" trunk (TDC). Figure 1 shows an example of BAEP based clinical test principle and typically obtained signals.

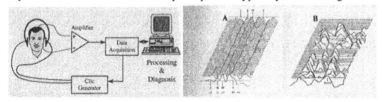

Fig. 1. BAEP based clinical test chain (left) and examples of obtained TDC Surfaces showing healthy (A) and auditory disorder (B) cases respectively (right).

2.2 BAEP Signals-to-Image Conversion

In this work, the BAEP signals are transformed in images to be processed and analyzed. Indeed, each image is built of 86 BAEP signals where each BAEP signal is sampled and represented by 51 points. The conversion of BAEP signals to representative issued images is performed thanks to conventional thresholding interpolation techniques [12]. Consequently, each resulting image is represented in a matrix of 86 lines by 51 columns. Thus, the used image database is built of 206 images such as: 38 images represent Retro-Cochlear-Patients, 77 images represent Endo-Cochlear-Patients, and 91 images represent Normal-Cochlear-Patients.

3 Suggested Soft Computing Based Image Processing Approach

General bloc diagram of the suggested processing chain is depicted in Figure 2. As one can remark in this figure, our approach includes 3 processing stages: Signal-to-Image converter stage, NN classification stage and Fuzzy decider. The input of the Signal-to-Image converter is a BAEP signal and it's output corresponds to an image based representation of this input. The obtained image is then processed (classified) by the second stage. Outputs of this stage are a set of diagnosis related categories (classes). The mission of the last stage is to state the final diagnosis. Figure 3 gives bloc diagram of classification and decision chain.

As it could be seen, the implemented classification strategy is based on a multiple neural networks structure. It includes two neural classifiers. The first one operates on the basis of a local pattern recognition. So, a first classification, based on local indicators in image, leads to a first diagnosis (local diagnosis). The second classifier operates on the basis of a global pattern recognition taking into account whole image. These two classification results are then used by the Fuzzy decider to decide of the most appropriated final diagnosis.

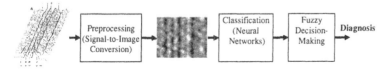

Fig. 2. Soft Computing based image processing approach synopsis.

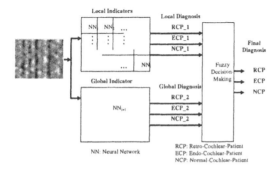

Fig. 3. Classification and decision processing chain.

4 Implementation and Results

In this work, the suggested multiple model approach to medical diagnosis from classification of BAEP signals converted in images is mainly based on soft computing implying NN classification [8], [13] and Fuzzy decision-making. Indeed, the efficiency of this classification emerges from the two classification ways: several NN for local sub-images resulting in the local indicators, and one NN for the global image resulting in the global indicator.

4.1 Neural Network Classifiers

The results presented in Figure 4 correspond to the local classification built of 20 feedforward Neural Networks, local indicators (NN1, ..., NNi, ..., NN20), since the image is divided in 20 areas of 10x20 pixels, where each area is classified by a Neural Network built of 3 layers: 200 input neurons (input layer), 241 sigmoïdal hidden neurons (hidden layer), and 3 sigmoïdal output neurons (output layer).

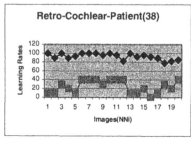
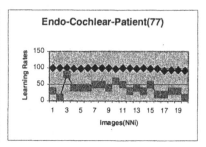

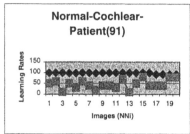

Fig. 4. Local NN classification results (Local Indicators): black curves represent learning base results while gray curves represent generalization base results.

The NN1, ..., NNi, ..., NN20 classifiers are trained using the supervised gradient back propagation paradigm from the training set (learning base). The weights are adjusted from a random weight initialization between [-1, +1] with the learning rate $\eta = 0.1$ and momentum = 0.8. This classifier yields convergence to the tolerance $E_T = 0.0001$ in well under the cycle number CN = 5000.

The results presented in Table 1 correspond to the global classification built of one (01) Neural Network, global indicator (NN21), where all the image, 80x50 pixels, is classified by one (01) Neural Network, where in each area the mean of 10x20 pixels constitute an input component. Thus, NN21 is built of 3 layers: 20 input neurons (input layer), 23 sigmoïdal hidden neurons (hidden layer), and 3 sigmoïdal output neurons (output layer).

	Rétro-Cochlear-Patient (38 images)	Endo-Cochlear-Patient (77 images)	Normal-Cochlear-Patient (91 images)
Learning Base (Training Set)	100.0000 % over 28	95.5000 % over 67	100.0000 % over 81
Test Base	80.0000 % over 10	20.0000 % over 10	60.0000 % over 10

Tab. 1. Global Neural Network classification results (Global Indicator).

The NN21 classifier is trained using the supervised gradient back propagation paradigm from the training set (learning base). The weights are adjusted from a random weight initialization between [-1, +1] with the learning rate $\eta = 0.1$ and momentum = 0.8. This classifier yields convergence to the tolerance $E_T = 0.0001$ in well under the cycle number CN = 5000.

4.2   Fuzzy Decision-Making System

In order to exploit the expert (human) knowledge [14], the Fuzzy decision-making system, developed in this Section, is based on Mamdani's fuzzy inference must be able to decide of the appropriate diagnosis among Retro-Cochlear-Patient (O_{RCP}), Endo-Cochlear-Patient (O_{ECP}), and Normal-Cochlear-Patient (O_{NCP}). The *Fuzzy Decision-Making System* is suggested to the decision-making help to the diagnosis, i.e., to select the appropriate diagnosis for each patient among Retro-Cochlear-Patient (O_{RCP}), Endo-Cochlear-Patient (O_{ECP}), and Normal-Cochlear-Patient (O_{NCP}).

The input parameters are RCP_1, ECP_1, NCP_1, RCP_2, ECP_2, and NCP_2. These inputs are obtained from neural networks, i.e., scaled from 0 to 1. Then, the membership functions of these inputs have been defined for the RCP, ECP, and NCP parameters as shown in Figure 5, where Far (F), and Near (N) are the fuzzy variables. Thus, the input vector is then the vector $\mathbf{I}$ = [RCP_1, ECP_1, NCP_1, RCP_2, ECP_2, NCP_2]. For each input, this *Fuzzy Decision-Making System* must be able to select the appropriate diagnosis.

The *Fuzzy Decision-Making System* is used to capture the decision-making behavior of a human expert while giving the appropriate diagnosis [10], i.e., it must mimic the input/output mapping of this human expert. Indeed, the latter has formulated his knowledge in a linguistic form which provides an explanation to give an appropriate diagnosis.

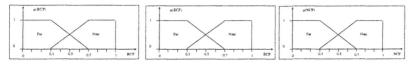

Fig. 5. Retro-Cochlear-Patient (RCP), Endo-Cochlear-Patient (ECP), Normal-Cochlear-Patient (NCP) membership functions.

To mimic this diagnosis, the fuzzy linguistic formulation is used and a set of fuzzy rules are then established. Thus, these fuzzy rules are used to incorporate this human expert knowledge in the suggested *Fuzzy Decision-Making System*, illustrated in Figure 6, where the vectors Fuzzy RCP_1, Fuzzy ECP_1, Fuzzy NCP_1, Fuzzy RCP_2, Fuzzy ECP_2, and Fuzzy NCP_2, represent the fuzzy vectors of the input values RCP_1, ECP_1, NCP_1, RCP_2, ECP_2, NCP_2, respectively ; while $\tilde{\mathbf{O}}$ represent the fuzzy vector of the output Oj which is a component of the vector $\mathbf{O}$ = [O_{RCP}, O_{ECP}, O_{NCP}] where O_{RCP}, O_{ECP}, O_{NCP} are Retro-Cochlear-Patient, Endo-Cochlear-Patient, and Normal-Cochlear-Patient.

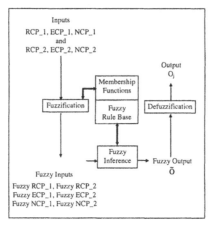

Fig. 6. Fuzzy Decision-Making System.

The operation of the fuzzification calculates the degrees for each evaluated parameter (input) belonging to the three membership functions, e.g., for RCP_1 this operation calculates {μ_F(RCP_1), μ_N(RCP_1)} with μ_F(RCP_1) and μ_N(RCP_1) the membership degrees of fuzzy sets F and N, respectively.

The fuzzy rule base is built of 2^6 = 64 rules deduced from the six (06) inputs where each input has three (02) fuzzy variables. Thus, established fuzzy rules are:

If(RCP_1 is F and ECP_1 is F and NCP_1 is F and RCP_2 is F and ECP_2 is F and NCP_2 is F) *Then* $\tilde{\mathbf{O}}$ = [$\mu(O_{RCP})$, $\mu(O_{ECP})$, $\mu(O_{NCP})$],
If(RCP_1 is F and ECP_1 is F and NCP_1 is F and RCP_2 is F and ECP_2 is F and NCP_2 is N) *Then* $\tilde{\mathbf{O}}$ = [$\mu(O_{RCP})$, $\mu(O_{ECP})$, $\mu(O_{NCP})$],

...

If(RCP_1 is N and ECP_1 is N and NCP_1 is N and RCP_2 is N and ECP_2 is N and NCP_2 is F) *Then* $\tilde{\mathbf{O}}$ = [$\mu(O_{RCP})$, $\mu(O_{ECP})$, $\mu(O_{NCP})$],
If(RCP_1 is N and ECP_1 is N and NCP_1 is N and RCP_2 is N and ECP_2 is N and NCP_2 is N) *Then* $\tilde{\mathbf{O}}$ = [$\mu(O_{RCP})$, $\mu(O_{ECP})$, $\mu(O_{NCP})$].   (1)

In this fuzzy rule base, the fuzzy decision-making vector $\tilde{\mathbf{O}}$ is expressed by:

$$\tilde{\mathbf{O}} = [\; \mu_{(RCP\_1m, ECP\_1m, NCP\_1m, RCP\_2m, ECP\_2m, NCP\_2m)}(O_{RCP}),$$
$$\mu_{(RCP\_1m, ECP\_1m, NCP\_1m, RCP\_2m, ECP\_2m, NCP\_2m)}(O_{ECP}),$$
$$\mu_{(RCP\_1m, ECP\_1m, NCP\_1m, RCP\_2m, ECP\_2m, NCP\_2m)}(O_{NCP}) \;] \qquad (2)$$

where $\mu_{(RCP\_1m,\ ECP\_1m,\ NCP\_1m,\ RCP\_2m,\ ECP\_2m,\ NCP\_2m)}(O_j)$ represents the membership function degree of O_j with m = 1 or 2. The fuzzy inference is achieved by the Min and Max operations. Thus, for each specific decision-making situation, the values of inputs are mapped to the discrete intervals to form the fuzzy sets:

$$\text{Fuzzy RCP\_1} = \{\mu_1(RCP\_1),\ \mu_2(RCP\_1)\},$$
$$\text{Fuzzy ECP\_1} = \{\mu_1(ECP\_1),\ \mu_2(ECP\_1)\},$$
$$\text{Fuzzy NCP\_1} = \{\mu_1(NCP\_1),\ \mu_2(NCP\_1)\},$$
$$\text{Fuzzy RCP\_2} = \{\mu_1(RCP\_2),\ \mu_2(RCP\_2)\},$$
$$\text{Fuzzy ECP\_2} = \{\mu_1(ECP\_2),\ \mu_2(ECP\_2)\},$$
$$\text{Fuzzy NCP\_2} = \{\mu_1(NCP\_2),\ \mu_2(NCP\_2)\},\tag{3}$$

where for instance $\mu_m(RCP\_1)$, with m = 1 or 2, are the membership function degrees of the input RCP_1. With this description, one can have $2^6 = 64$ possible conditions corresponding to sixty four (64) fuzzy rules. Then, the level of certainty of each condition μ_1, μ_2, ..., μ_{64} can be found using the Min operation:

$\mu_{cond}(RCP\_11,\ ECP\_11,\ NCP\_11,\ RCP\_21,\ ECP\_21,\ NCP\_21) = MIN(\mu_1(RCP\_1),$
$\mu_1(ECP\_1),\ \mu_1(NCP\_1),\ \mu_1(RCP\_2),\ \mu_1(ECP\_2),\ \mu_1(NCP\_2)) = \mu_1$,
$\mu_{cond}(RCP\_11,\ ECP\_11,\ NCP\_11,\ RCP\_21,\ ECP\_21,\ NCP\_22) = MIN(\mu_1(RCP\_1),$
$\mu_1(ECP\_1),\ \mu_1(NCP\_1),\ \mu_1(RCP\_2),\ \mu_1(ECP\_2),\ \mu_2(NCP\_2)) = \mu_2$,
...
$\mu_{cond}(RCP\_12,\ ECP\_12,\ NCP\_12,\ RCP\_22,\ ECP\_22,\ NCP\_22) = MIN(\mu_2(RCP\_1),$
$\mu_2(ECP\_1),\ \mu_2(NCP\_1),\ \mu_2(RCP\_2),\ \mu_2(ECP\_2),\ \mu_2(NCP\_2)) = \mu_{64}$, $\qquad(4)$

where cond represents the fuzzy set of conditions which is written as follows:

$$\text{cond} = \{\ \mu_1, \mu_2, ..., \mu_{64}\ \}.\tag{5}$$

Each possible condition is associated with a decision-making situation O_j. Then, certainty of each situation is obtained by Max and Min operations as follows:

$\mu_{ORCP} = MAX\{\ MIN(\mu_1,\ \mu_{(RCP\_11,\ ECP\_11,\ NCP\_11,\ RCP\_21,\ ECP\_21,\ NCP\_21)}(O_{RCP})),$
$MIN(\mu_2,\ \mu_{(RCP\_11,\ ECP\_11,\ NCP\_11,\ RCP\_21,\ ECP\_21,\ NCP\_22)}(O_{RCP})),$
...
$MIN(\mu_{64},\ \mu_{(RCP\_12,\ ECP\_12,\ NCP\_12,\ RCP\_22,\ ECP\_22,\ NCP\_22)}(O_{RCP}))\ \}$,
$\mu_{OECP} = MAX\{\ MIN(\mu_1,\ \mu_{(RCP\_11,\ ECP\_11,\ NCP\_11,\ RCP\_21,\ ECP\_21,\ NCP\_21)}(O_{ECP})),$
$MIN(\mu_2,\ \mu_{(RCP\_11,\ ECP\_11,\ NCP\_11,\ RCP\_21,\ ECP\_21,\ NCP\_22)}(O_{ECP})),$
...
$MIN(\mu_{64},\ \mu_{(RCP\_12,\ ECP\_12,\ NCP\_12,\ RCP\_22,\ ECP\_22,\ NCP\_22)}(O_{ECP}))\ \}$,
$\mu_{ONCP} = MAX\{\ MIN(\mu_1,\ \mu_{(RCP\_11,\ ECP\_11,\ NCP\_11,\ RCP\_21,\ ECP\_21,\ NCP\_21)}(O_{NCP})),$
$MIN(\mu_2,\ \mu_{(RCP\_11,\ ECP\_11,\ NCP\_11,\ RCP\_21,\ ECP\_21,\ NCP\_22)}(O_{NCP})),$
...
$MIN(\mu_{64},\ \mu_{(RCP\_12,\ ECP\_12,\ NCP\_12,\ RCP\_22,\ ECP\_22,\ NCP\_22)}(O_{NCP}))\ \}$. $\qquad(6)$

Collection of situations forms final fuzzy decision-making situation vector $\tilde{O}$:

$$\tilde{O} = \{\ \mu_{ORCP}(O_{RCP}),\ \mu_{OECP}(O_{ECP}),\ \mu_{ONCP}(O_{NCP})\ \}\tag{7}$$

The Max operation is used for the defuzzification process to give the final decision-making situation O_j :

$$O_j = \text{Max}\{ \mu_{ORCP}, \mu_{OECP}, \mu_{ONCP} \} \tag{8}$$

5 Discussion and Conclusion

In this paper, a promising soft computing (implying NN and fuzzy logic) image processing aproach for the biomedical signal analysis and interpretation, and particularly for BAEP signals, is suggested in order to take advantage from features which are unreachable from unidimentional signal (time dependent waveform). Based on a hybrid scheme, multiple model approach, the aim of the suggested approach is to develop an efficient tool for a reliable CAMD.

For this purpose, at first a processing view of biomedical signals is developed. That consists to a Signal-to-Image conversion which opens a large opportunity to beneficiate of more information than if seen and processed as signals. Second, a multiple model approach to medical diagnosis is developed from classification of BAEP signals converted in images. Indeed, this multiple model approach is mainly based on NN classification and Fuzzy decision-making stage. More, the efficiency of this classification emerges from the two classification ways: several NN for local sub-images resulting in the local indicators, and one NN for the global image resulting in the global indicator. The obtained results from NN classification represent the first step of results which will be significantly enhanced by the Fuzzy decision-making exploiting the expert (human) knowledge. The Fuzzy decision-making system based on Mamdani's fuzzy inference must be able to decide of the appropriate diagnosis among Retro-Cochlear-Patient (O_{RCP}), Endo-Cochlear-Patient (O_{ECP}), and Normal-Cochlear-Patient (O_{NCP}). Thus, once this Fuzzy part implemented, the multiple model approach built of NN and Fuzzy decision-making is expected to be an efficient approach for a reliable CAMD.

With regard to other approaches [1], [2], [3], the suggested BAEP signal analysis and interpretation approach for a reliable CAMD exploits the two main advantages from its Signal-to-Image conversion and multiple model approach [15]. An interesting alternative for future works could be, on the one hand, the investigation in other neural networks for classification such as fuzzy neural networks or radial basis function networks [10], [16], and on the other hand the generalization of suggested approach to a larger field of applications such as fault detection and diagnosis in industrial plants [17].

Acknowledgments

Authors would like to thank Prof. Kurosh Madani for his scientific supervision concerning the present work, his helps and useful discussions.

References

[1] Wolf A., Hall Barbosa C., Monteiro E. C., and Vellasco M., 'Multiple MLP Neural Networks Applied on the Determination of Segment Limits in ECG Signals', 7th International Work-Conf. on Artificial and Natural NN, Proc. Part II, Mao, Menorca, Spain, June 2003, LNCS 2687, Springer-Verlag Berlin Heidelberg, pp. 607-614, 2003.

[2] Piater J. H., Stuchlik F., von Specht H., and Mühler R. (1995): Fuzzy Sets for Feature Identification in Biomedical Signals with Self-Assessment of Reliability: An Adaptable Algorithm Modeling Human Procedure in BAEP Analysis. Computers and Biomedical Research 28, pp. 335-353, Academic Press.

[3] Vannier E., Adam O., and Motsch J.-F., 'Objective detection of brainstem auditory evoked potentials with a priori information from higher presentation levels', Artificial Intelligence in Medicine, 25, pp. 283-301, 2002.

[4] Widrow B. and Lehr M. A., '30 years of adaptive neural networks: perceptron, madaline, and backpropagation', Proc. of IEEE, Vol. 78, pp. 1415-1441, 1990.

[5] Bazoon M., Stacey D. A., and Cui C., 'A hierarchical artificial neural network system for the classification of cervical cells', IEEE Int. Conf. On NN, Orlando, July 1994.

[6] Goonatilake S. and Khebbal S., 'Intelligent Hybrid Systems', John Wiley & Sons, 1995.

[7] Jordan M. I. and Xu L., 'Convergence results for the EM approach to mixture of experts architectures', Neural Networks, Vol. 8, No. 9, pp. 1409-1431, 1995.

[8] Haykin S., 'Neural Networks: A Comprehensive Foundation', International Edition, Second Edition, Prentice-Hall, 1999.

[9] Zhang G. P., 'Neural networks for classification: a survey', IEEE Trans. on Systems, Man, and Cybernetics – Part C: Applic. and Reviews, Vol. 30, no. 4, pp. 451-462, 2000.

[10] Azouaoui O. and Chohra A., 'Soft computing based pattern classifiers for the obstacle avoidance behavior of Intelligent Autonomous Vehicles (IAV)', *Int. J. of Applied Intelligence*, Kluwer Academic Publishers, Vol. 16, No. 3, pp. 249-271, 2002.

[11] Motsh J. F., 'La dynamique temporelle du tronc cérébral: receuil, extraction, et analyse optimale des potentiels évoqués auditifs du tronc cérébral', PhD Thesis, Paris-XII University, 1987.

[12] Gonzalez R. C., and Woods R. E., 'Digital Image Processing', Prentice-Hall, 2002.

[13] Egmont-Petersen M., De Ridder D., and Handels H., 'Image processing with neural networks – a review', Pattern Recongnition, 35, pp. 2279-2301, 2002.

[14] Turban E. and Aronson J. E., 'Decision Support Systems and Intelligent Systems', Int. Edition, Sixth Edition, Prentice-Hall, 2001.

[15] Murray-Smith R. and Johansen T. A., 'Multiple Model Approaches to Modelling and Control', Taylor & Francis Publishers, 1997.

[16] Madani K., De Trémiolles G., and Tannhof P., 'Image Processing Using RBF like Neural Networks: A ZISC-036 Based Fully Parallel Implementation Solving Real World and Real Complexity Industrial Problems', *Int. J. of Applied Intelligence*, Kluwer Academic Publishers, Vol. 18, pp. 195-213, 2003.

[17] De Tremiolles G. I., 'Contribution à l'étude théorique des modèles neuromimétiques et à leur validation expérimentale: mise en œuvre d'applications industrielles', Thèse, Université Paris XII, 05 Mars 1998.

The prediction of behaviours of chaotic dynamical systems in 3D state space

M. Pankiewicz, R. Mosdorf

The University of Finance and Management in Białystok; Faculty of Engineering, Grunwaldzka Street 1, Elk, Poland; e-mail: mosdorf@wsfiz.edu.pl

Abstract: In the paper a new three-dimensional visualization technique of results of methods of prediction of chaotic time series has been analyzed. The influence of graphical presentation of attractors on the quality of forecasting results has been tested. The following methods of prediction of behaviours of chaotic dynamical systems have been considered: method of analogs, centre-of-mass-prediction method and local linear prediction method. The forecasting quality has been evaluated with using the error function and the correlation coefficient. It has been shown that 3D visualization of attractor is a necessary condition for obtaining the proper results of forecasting with using the deterministic chaos methods.

Keywords: deterministic chaos, forecasting, method of analogs, center-of-mass-prediction, local linear prediction method

1   Introduction

Forecasting the behaviors of time series is important in many different branches of science [1]. The behaviors of many real systems are chaotic. The prediction of behavior of such systems is difficult because of their unperiodic character of changes in time. In such systems the time changes are rather similar to noise [2,11].

The creation of various technique of computer visualizations of data is almost as old as an idea of programming itself [12]. During the last years the development of program visualization systems has been discussed in [12, 13]. It has been shown that data visualization is an important step in understanding of many physical processes including the chaotic processes.

In this article the selected forecasting techniques of chaotic data have been tested: method of analogs [4,6], center-of-mass prediction method (COM) [5,6], local linear prediction method [6]. The effectiveness of these methods has been analyzed. The data for analysis have been selected from various fields such as physics and economy. The low dimensional physical system and the selected indexes of Polish Capital Market have been analyzed. All analyzed systems are chaotic but the characters of changes of values of time series differ in the particular systems. The considered physical system creates in 3D phase space the attractor whose the trajectories are located in the certain pipe of irregular shape. In case of the data from the capital market the pipe defined in such a way does not exist. The correlation dimension of attractors created from capital market data is greater than correlation dimension of attractors from the physical system data.

2 The roles of analysis of behaviors of chaotic systems

Generally the analysis of behaviors of chaotic systems is based on the analysis of trajectories of system in the phase space. The trajectories of the chaotic system in the phase space do not form any single geometrical objects such as circle or tours, but form objects called strange attractors of the structure resembling fractal. The analysis starts with the attractor reconstruction. This reconstruction in certain embedding dimension has been carried out using the stroboscope coordination. In this method subsequent co-ordinates of attractor points are calculated basing on the subsequent samples between which the distance is equal to time delay τ. This time delay is a multiplication of time between the samples. For the measured data in the form of time series:

$$\left\{ x_i \right\} = \left\{ x_1, x_2, ..., x_N \right\} \tag{1}$$

the way of calculation of subsequent y_j coordinates of points of attractor has been measured as follows:

$$y_j = \left\{ x_j, x_j + \tau, ..., x_j + (D-1)\tau \right\} \tag{2}$$

where: y_j is the subsequent points of attractor, D is the dimension of the vector y_j, τ is a time delay.

The image of the attractor in D-dimensional space depends on time-delay τ. When the time-delay is too small, the attractor gets flattened and this makes the further analysis of its structure impossible. When time delay τ is too large, the attractor becomes more sophisticated. Therefore the selection of time-delay value is of great significance in the analysis of the attractor properties. For that purpose the autocorrelation function is calculated. The autocorrelation function is the normalized measure of a linear correlation between samples of time series. It is defined as follows [2]:

$$C(\tau) = \frac{1}{N-\tau} \sum_{i=0}^{N-\tau} x_i \cdot x_{i+\tau} \qquad (3)$$

where: N number of samples, x_i value of i sample.

For chaotic data the autocorrelation function rapidly decreases, while τ increases. The proper value of the time-delay τ for attractor reconstruction is determined by the condition [2]:

$$C(\tau) \approx 0.5 C(0) \qquad (4)$$

In forecasting the behaviors of chaotic time series the following relation between the last point of the attractor (y_j) and predicted point (y_{j+1}) of the attractor is searched for:

$$y_{j+1} = f(y_j). \qquad (5)$$

The function f depends on the shape of the attractor, which is a function of time delay. Very often the condition (4) does not give the proper value of time delay. It happens when time series contain a lot of noise. In this case the final verification of the proper attractor reconstruction may be done only with using the 3D visualization techniques. In our work we use the OpenGL technique for the visualization of 3D attractor.

3   Deterministic chaos prediction methods and error estimation

The method of analogs has been proposed by E. Lorenz in 1967 [4,6]. In this method the forecasted points are chosen from the previous parts of time series in such a way that expected point y_i lays on the trajectory which is close to trajectory on which there is the last point of the attractor y_j. In this method the forecasted point is calculated according to the following formula:

$$y_{j+1} = y_{i+1}, \qquad (6)$$

where y_{j+1} - forecasted point which belongs to the attractor, y_{i+1} - a next point on chosen trajectory.

In the center-of-mass prediction method (COM) the forecasted point is calculated basing on the following formula:

$$y'_{j+1} = \frac{1}{n} \sum_{k=1}^{n} y_{i+1}^{k} \tag{7}$$

where y_i^k is a n neighboring points of attractors on trajectories passing close to the last point of the attractor y_j. i – is a subsequent number of a chosen point form neighboring area, $i+1$ is a next point on chosen trajectory on which the point i lays. y'_{j+1} - forecasted point which does not belong to the attractor

In the local linear prediction method the extension of attractor trajectory is calculated according to the formula:

$$y'_{j+1} = a * y_j + b \tag{8}$$

where a and b are matrixes, y'_{j+1} - forecasted point which does not belong to the attractor.

Elements of matrixes a and b are calculated according to the formula:

$$\sum_{k=1}^{n} \| y_{i+1}^{k} - (a * y_i^k + b) \| = \min \tag{9}$$

where y_i^k is a n neighboring points of attractors on trajectories passing close to the last point of attractor y_j. i – is a subsequent number of chosen point form neighboring area, $i+1$ is a next point on a chosen trajectory on which the point i lays.

In the all methods mentioned above the quality of forecasting depends on the number of considered neighboring points.

The forecasting quality has been evaluated by error function (E) and the correlation coefficient (CC). The error function is defined as follows [9]

$$E = \frac{\sigma_{pred}}{\sigma_x} \tag{10}$$

where $\sigma_{pred} = \left\langle \left[x_{pred}(i) - x_{obs}(i) \right]^2 \right\rangle_i^{\frac{1}{2}}$, $\sigma_x = \left\langle \left[x(i) - \langle x(i) \rangle \right]^2 \right\rangle_i^{\frac{1}{2}}$

For good forecast the E is close to zero. The correlation coefficient describe the similarity between actual and predicted series. It is calculated basing on the following formula:

$$CC = \frac{\sum_{i=1}^{n}\left(x_{obs}(i)-\langle x_{obs}\rangle\right)\left(x_{pred}(i)-\langle x_{pred}\rangle\right)}{\sqrt{\sum_{i=1}^{n}\left(x_{ods}(i)-\langle x_{obs}\rangle\right)^2\left(x_{pred}(i)-\langle x_{pred}\rangle\right)^2}} \tag{11}$$

When $|CC|$ is close to 1, time series x_{obs} and x_{pred} are correlated. When the large and low values in both series appear at the same time, then $CC > 0$; but when $CC < 0$ large values in first series meet low values in other series, then. When CC is close to zero, then the time series x_{obs} and x_{pred} are not correlated.

For estimation of quality of forecasting the special computer program for visualization has been prepared [10]. The program uses the OpenGL standard. The attractors have been presented with using the 3D scene. The knowledge of system's attractor gives useful information that is necessary to predict trends in the systems. The application of methods based on chaos theory requires the proper attractor reconstruction. In Fig.1 the main window of the program has been presented. The sphere indicates the area, from which the points used in prediction procedure have been taken. Bold black line represents the predicted trajectory. The difference between the two forecasts, presented in Fig.1, lies only in value of time delay - in Fig. 1a the time delay is equal to 19 samples and in Fig. 1b it is equal to 20 samples. Analysis of 3D reconstruction of attractor allows us to indicate that in forecasting presented in Fig.1a the predicted trajectory passes parallelly to another trajectory but the predicted trajectory in Fig.1b passes across the neighbouring trajectory. Therefore the prediction showed in Fig.1b must be rejected as an incorrect one. Finally, the 3D visualization shows that even small changes of entry parameters can cause the large differences between the forecast results.

380

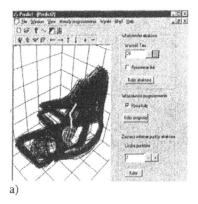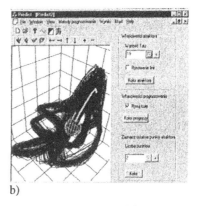

a)   b)

Figure 1. The main window of the program for 3D presentation of forecasting
chaotic systems a) τ=19, b) τ=20. The sphere shows the area for which the
neighboring points are considered.

In the application the elements of animation have been introduced. The
animation allows us to effectively identify the shape of attractor.

4   Testing the quality of forecasting in physical and economic systems

The chaotic nature of time series has been measured with using the correlation
dimension and the largest Lyapunov exponents [1,14]. The methods of prediction
were tested in the three-dimensional phase space. The 20 points of prediction
value of time series were calculated and compared with original data. The quality
of prediction was calculated with using the function E (Eq.10) and correlation
coefficient (Eq.11).

These prediction methods were applied to chaotic time series. The first data set
has been generated by chaotically departing air bubbles in water [3] (10000
samples). The other time series containing prices of shares of Polish companies:
Budimex and Okocim have been analyzed. The series of prices of Budimex shares
contained the 2375 daily observations and the series of prices of Okocim shares
contained 1190 daily observations.

The selected statistical and nonlinear characteristics of analysed series have
been summarized in Table 1. The correlation dimension has been calculated with
using the Grassberger-Procaccia method [1], and the largest Lyapunov exponent
has been calculated with using the Wolf algorithm [14]. Results of calculation

indicated that the data from the capital market are more chaotic compared with the physical system considered in the paper.

Table 1.

The statistical and the nonlinear parameters of analyzed series

Series	Samples numbers	Standard deviation	Max. value	Min. value	The largest Lyapunov Exp. [bit/sample]	Time delay [samples number]	Correlation dimension
Physical system	*10000*	*504,12*	*1439*	*833*	*0,012*	*10*	*2.1*
Budimex	*2375*	*8,70*	*51,6*	*8,1*	*0,067*	*5*	*3.6*
Okocim	*1190*	*6,82*	*42,5*	*1,46*	*0,055*	*30*	*2,3*

The examples of 3D visualization of results of forecasting have been presented in Table 2. The attractor reconstruction has been prepared from time series generated by physical system. Three methods of forecasting: analogs, centre-of-mass-prediction and local linear prediction have been used. The last two columns of Table 2 contain the values of: function E (Eq.10) and correlation coefficient CC (Eq.11).

Table 2

3D visualization of prediction methods consists of 20 samples for $\tau = 10$ (the light line represents the forecast).

The method of prediction	The visualization of prediction	E	CC
Analogs		0,291	0,962

Centre-of-mass-prediction		0,131	0,994
Local linear prediction		0,087	0,996

In Table 2 the results of 20 predictions have been marked with a light line. The black area contains the attractor trajectories. The predicted trajectory (light line) passes parallelly to another neighbouring trajectories on the attractor. The value of function E is close to value 0 for all methods under consideration that proves the high quality of forecasting. In considered cases the correlation coefficient (CC) is also high.

In Fig.2. the comparison between original data (Fig.2.a) and results of prediction has been shown. Changes of function E against the number of samples have been presented in Fig.2.b. We can notice that the prediction quality is high for all considered methods but the local linear prediction method and centre-of-mass-prediction method give us better predictions than these one resulted from the method of analogs

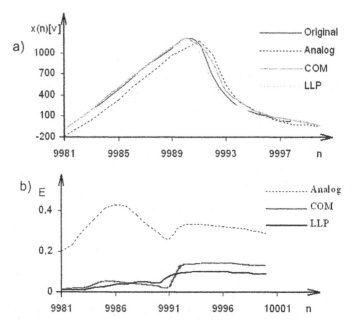

Figure 2. The forecasting evaluation of chaotic physical system. a) Comparison of original data with forecasting, b) The function E for the prediction methods: method of analogs (Analog), centre-of-mass-prediction method (COM) and local linear prediction method (LLP).

Table 3 shows the results of 3D visualization of prediction methods for the daily prices of shares of Budimex company. Three methods of forecasting: analogs, centre-of-mass-prediction and local linear prediction have been used. The last two columns of Table 3 contain the values of: function E (Eq.10) and correlation coefficient CC (Eq.11).

Table 3.

The results of prediction of prices of Budimex shares: 3D visualization of prediction methods consists of 20 samples for τ=5 (the light line represents the forecast)

The method of prediction	The visualization of prediction	E	CC
Analog		2,241	0,577
Centre-of-mass-prediction		1,878	0,230
Local linear prediction		3,021	0,592

The shape of attractor created by prices of Okocim shares seems to be less regular than the shape of attractor in the previous example. The function E gives the value larger than in the previous example. This means that the difference between the forecasting and original data increases. In the considered case the correlation coefficient has the value less than in the previous example, this means that the correlation between the forecasting and original data becomes week.

In Fig.3 the comparison between original data (Fig.3.a) and results of prediction has been shown. The changes of function E against number of samples has been presented in Fig.3b. We can notice that the quality of prediction is lower than in the previous example. The analog and centre-of-mass-prediction methods give the better prediction than the local linear prediction method.

For all considered methods, the function E increases in time (Fig. 3a), differently than it was in previous example. This means that the quality of forecasting decreases in time.

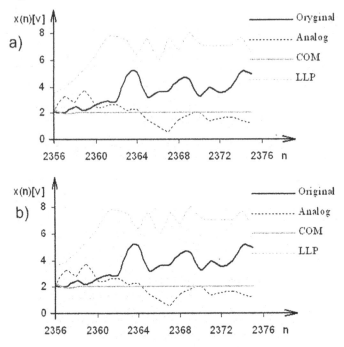

Figure 3. The forecasting evaluation of Budimex series. a) Comparison of original data with forecasting, b) The evaluation of function E, for the prediction method: method of analogs (Analog), centre-of-mass-prediction method (COM) and local linear prediction method (LLP).

Shape of attractor from daily prices of Okocim shares is similar to the shape obtained for Budimex, therefore the attractor has not been presented in the paper. In Fig.4a the comparison between original data of daily prices of Okocim shares and results of their predictions have been shown. The changes of function E against number of samples has been presented in Fig.4b. We can notice that the quality of prediction share prices is lower than the quality in considered physical system. In considered case the linear prediction method give us the better prediction than the other methods.

The function E increases in time (Fig. 4b). The value of calculated correlation coefficient ranges from 0,49 to 0,79. For all methods, the function E increases in time (Fig. 4a), differently than it was in considered physical system. This means that the quality of forecasting decreases in time.

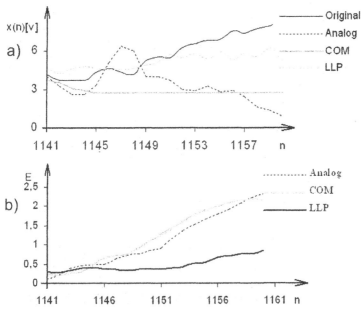

Figure 4.The forecasting evaluation of Okocim series. a) Comparison of real changes of time series with forecasting, b) The evaluation of function E, for the prediction method: method of analogs (Analog), centre-of-mass-prediction method (COM) and local linear prediction method (LLP).

The above analysis shows that forecasting of data from the capital market can be more difficult than forecasting of data from considered physical system. It can be caused by too low number of analyzed data from the capital market. According to Peters [14] we need at least 10000 stock exchange quotations to obtain reliable results. The analyzed series contain less than 3000 samples. A consequence of this can be reducing the ability of forecasting. The obtained results showed that the quality of forecasting of chaotic data depends also on the shape of attractor's trajectory in the 3D phase space.

5   Conclusion

In the paper the methods of prediction of chaotic dynamical systems behaviors based on the deterministic chaos theory have been discussed. The following methods have been considered: method of analogs, center-of-mass-prediction method and local linear prediction method. These methods are based on the geometry of the attractor. Therefore, the new 3D visualization technique has been developed in the paper. We can conclude that the graphical presentation of data series is very useful when analysing chaotic time series and evaluating whether setup parameters of forecasting are proper.

The modification of presented methods has been tested as well. We can conclude that the worst results of forecasting were obtained in case of using method of analogs with a small number of neighbouring points. The quality of forecasting increases in case of linear prediction method together with increase in the number of neighboring points.

Comparison of obtained results for different series shows that nonlinear methods of forecasting give better results for chaotic time series which create the attractors with regular shapes. For data from capital market the shapes of attractors are irregular in comparison with the shape of attractor from the data of physical system considered in the paper.

6   References

[1]   Box G. E. P., Jenkis G. M., „Analiza szeregów czasowych i prognozowanie, Wydawnictwo Naukowe PWN, Warszawa 1983.

[2]   Schuster H.G., Chaos deterministyczny – wprowadzenie, Wydawnictwo Naukowe PWN, Warszawa 1993.

[3]   Mosdorf R., Shoji M., Chaos in bubbling – nonlinear analysis and modeling, Chemical Engineering Science 58, 3837-3846, 2003.

[4]   Singh S., Multiple forecasting using local approximation, Pattern Recognition, 34, 443-445, 2001.

[5]   Reick Ch. H., Page B., Time series prediction by multivariate next neighbor methods with application to zooplankton forecasts, Mathematics and Computers in simulation 52, 289-310, 2000.

[6]   Baker G.L., Gollub J.P., Wstęp do dynamiki układów chaotycznych, Wydawnictwo Naukowe PWN, Warszawa, 1998.

[7]   Abarbanel H. D. I., Brown R., Sidorowich J. J., Tsimring L. S., The analysis of observed chaotic data in physical system, Reviews of Modern Physics, 65(4), 1331-1392, October 1993.

[8]   Little S., Ellner S., Pascual M., Kaplan D., Sauer T., Caswell H., Solow A., Detecting nonlinear dynamics in spatio-temporal systems, examples from ecological models, Physica D 96, 321-333, 1996.

[9]   Sidorowich J.J., Farmer J.D., Predicting chaotic time series, Physical Review Letters, 59(8), 1987.

[10]   Żmijkowska M., Wykorzystanie analizy fraktalnej w prognozowaniu. Praca magisterska, Politechnika Białostocka, 2003.

[11]   Sidorowich J.J., Farmer J.D., Predicting chaotic time series, Physical Review Letters, 59(8), 845-848, 1987.

[12]   Hyrskykari A., Development of Program Visualization Systems, 2nd Czech British Symposium of Visual Aspects of Man-Machine, Systems, Praha, 1993.

[13]   Szmal P., Francik J., Nowak M., Systemy wizualizacji algorytmów wspomagające badania naukowe, III Konferencja Komputery w badaniach naukowych KOWBAN, 317-322, Polanica Zdrój , 1996.

[14]   Peters E.E., Teoria chaosu a rynki kapitałowe, WIG-Press, Warszawa 1997.

Idiotypic Networks as a Metaphor for Data Analysis Algorithms

Sławomir T. Wierzchoń[*]

Bialystok Technical University, Faculty of Computer Science, 15-351 Bialystok, Poland, and

Institute of Computer Science of Polish Academy of Sciences, 01-237 Warszawa, Poland; e-mail: stw@ipipan.waw.pl

Abstract: This paper was intended as a tutorial presentation of different models used to reproduce and analyze main immune functions. An express tour over vast literature devoted to the subject is offered. The choice of corresponding bibliographic positions was motivated by their relevance in current researches, computational simplicity, and richness of behavior of the model suggested by given source of information. Particularly, some remarks on discrete models are given, and general hints concerning designing of artificial immune systems are given.

Keywords: Immune System, Artificial Immune Systems, Exploratory Data Analysis

1   Introduction

Immune algorithms, IA's for short, are representatives of still growing family of biologically inspired algorithms, like genetic algorithms, ant algorithms, particle swarm algorithms, etc. – consult [8] for extensive review of such algorithms and their applications. Shortly speaking, IA's are inspired by works on theoretical immunology and some mechanisms (described in Section 2.1) used by the natural immune system to cope with external and internal invaders. IA's are adaptive algorithms in which learning takes place by evolutionary mechanisms similar to biological evolution. Their adaptability relies on continuous generation of novel elements to handle an unpredictable and varying set of situations. Generally we distinguish population-based and network-based IA's. In this paper we focus on population-based algorithms designed for exploratory data analysis.

---

* This paper was partly supported by Białystok Technical University grant W/WI/5/04.

Most of these algorithms is based (at least conceptually) on the model proposed in the **paper** [14], although its authors recognized very soon that "the kinetic equations used in our original paper were highly idealized" ([13], p. 172). Hence, the aim of this tutorial paper is brief presentation of alternative models used in theoretical immunology with the hope, that these models will improve behavior of currently designed artificial immune systems (AIS's in brevity) for data analysis. Extended bibliography will allow an interested reader to **navigate** himself in different approaches to this subject and in common ideas used by researches to model important properties of the immune system.

2 Mathematical models of idiotypic networks

The aim of this section is **short** description of immune mechanisms important in designing computer algorithms, like clonal selection, hypersomatic mutation, tolerance, immune response, idiotypic networks and immune memory. Next we briefly review mathematical models designed to analyze these phenomena.

2.1 Basic notions from immunology

The main actors of the adaptive immune system are so-called lymphocytes, i.e. white blood cells. We distinguish lymphocytes of type B (or B-cells) and lymphocytes of type T (or T cells). Each B-cell admits about 10^5 receptors located on its surface and called antibodies (or immunoglobulin). Roughly speaking, antibodies are soluble proteins which have high affinity towards external intruders called antigens. The key portion of antigen that is recognized by the antibody is called "epitope"; it can be viewed as the identifier of that antigen. Similarly, the "paratope" is a specific region of antibody that attach to the epitope. Each type of antibody has also its own antigenic determinant called "idiotype". Real paratope and epitope are 3D molecules. If they are complementary with respect to their geometric or physico-chemical characteristics, we say that the paratope recognizes just introduced epitope; alternatively, we say that the paratope has high affinity with the epitope. To study analytically the interactions among paratopes and epitopes Perelson and Oster introduced in [24] the notion of "shape-space"[1]. If d is the number of the characteristics influencing complementarity, then a point in d-dimensional vector space, called "shape-space", represents corresponding molecules. Typically as shape space d-dimensional Euclidean (or Hamming) space is used.

---

[1] It has been observed that the idea of shape space may be misleading and produces artifacts which do not reflect any underlying biological reality – see [4]. Hence it should be used with caution.

Suppose a large number of copies of a specific, and never seen, antigen are introduced into an organism. Once a sufficient number of paratopes binds the epitopes describing just introduced antigen, so-called primary immune response occurs. It relies upon clonal expansion and somatic hypermutation. By clonal expansion we understand rapid replication of those B-cells which have a high affinity to the antigen. To "tune" molecular shapes of the paratopes characterizing produced clones to the shapes of invading epitopes, each clone is subjected very intensive mutation what leads to variation of immune response. Mutated clones with highest affinity to the antigen are subjected further expansion and cloning, while mutants with lowest affinity are removed from the organism. The process is continued until the concentration of epitopes decreases below sufficiently low threshold.

It should be noted that during primary immune response the interaction with T-cells is crucial to the dynamics of the system. These lymphocytes control the activity of B-cells and they may have excitatory or inhibitory role. A reader interested in details on how B- and T-cells cooperate is referred to e.g. [20].

A crucial effect of all these interactions is that the response to a new antigen has a bell-shaped form. There exists a minimum concentration (θ_1) of epitopes that will elicit the immune response; similarly for very high concentration of epitopes (exceeding the second threshold $\theta_2 \gg \theta_1$) the response decreases. In other words, in the immune system we observe low- and high-dose tolerance. Only medium dose of the antigen causes immune response manifested with rapid production of antibodies. In theoretical immunology the response function $f(h_i)$, representing the concentration of antibodies of i-th type, is modeled by the equation (see e.g. [25])

$$f(h_i) = \frac{h_i}{(\theta_1 + h_i)} \cdot \frac{\theta_2}{(\theta_2 + h_i)} \tag{1}$$

where h_i stands for the "field" representing the strength of influence of all epitopes present in the system on a given antibody. Usually, if m_{ij} stands for the affinity between i-th paratope and j-th epitope, x_j denotes concentration of j-th epitope, and N is the number of different types of epitopes then the field h_i is computed according to the equation

$$h_i = \sum_{j=1, \ldots, N} m_{ij} \cdot x_j \tag{2}$$

Equation (2) says that i-th antibody can be stimulated by all the epitopes present in the organism, no matter they come from antigens or other antibodies constituting given immune system. This is because a new antibody, say Ab_1, generated e.g. through somatic mutation is a new protein for the organism, and its intensive reproduction during clonal expansion causes new immune response resulting in production of antibody of other type, say Ab_2. In summary, the production of antibody Ab_i stimulates production of other types of antibodies[2] and these subsequent generations of proteins form a kind of network called by Jerne "idiotypic network" (consult [22], or [14] for details). Its characteristic feature is that it can be maintained even in the absence of antigens inducing immune response. This is due to symmetric interactions between antibodies: if Ab_i stimulates Ab_{i+1} then Ab_{i+1} stimulates production of Ab_i. Since antibody Ab_1 was induced by an antigen Ag, one of its descendants, Ab_i, must have epitope structurally similar to the epitope characterizing the Ag. It is obvious that during absence of the antigen Ag the antibody Ab_i will maintain production of other antibodies belonging to the chain $Ab_1 \rightarrow \dots \rightarrow Ab_i \dots$ called auto-catalytic loop (consult [14] or [13]). Now, if the antigen Ag enters the organism next time, its shape is "remembered" by such a loop and effective antibodies are produced almost immediately. This phenomenon is referred to as "immune memory" and fast production of effective antibodies is termed "secondary immune response".

2.2 Models of the immune networks

Many different mathematical approaches have been developed to reproduce and analyze the main immune functions. Broadly speaking we distinguish between continuous and discrete models. Ordinary differential equations are typical for the first group of models while cellular automata are commonly used in the second group. From a methodological point of view these models can be labelled as "B-models" where no distinction between free and cell-bound antibodies is made, and "AB-models" where both forms of antibodies are described. Surprisingly, both B- and AB-models lead to the same conclusions as regards the fixed point properties, (stable fixed points for dynamics are necessary for achieving tolerance in a model), [4]. Below we briefly characterize the most prominent representatives of these groups. A reader interested in other models is referred to [25], [15] and [16].

2.2.1 Continuous models

One of the first, **and most popular** among AIS community, continuous models was *"bit-string model"* proposed in [14]. It takes into account only interactions among paratopes and epitopes of antibodies and antigens represented by binary strings. The affinity m_{ij} between i-th epitope and j-th paratope is computed in a way reflecting partial matching between the two molecules. The dynamics of the system consisting of N antibody types with concentrations $\{x_1, \dots, x_N\}$ and M

---

[2] This idea was confirmed experimentally. Namely, it was observed that e.g. in the case of *polio* virus infection, Ab_2 has the internal image of *polio* antigen. It means that Ab_2 is induced by the paratope of Ab_1 rather than by its idiotype. See: Fons, U., et al., "From Jenner to Jerne: towards idiotypic vaccines". *Immunol. Rev.* **90**:93-113, 1986

antigens with concentrations $\{y_1, ..., y_M\}$ is described by the following **system of ordinary differential** equations:

$$\frac{dx_i(t)}{dt} = c \cdot \left[\sum_{j=1}^{N} m_{ji} x_i(t) x_j(t) - k_1 \sum_{j=1}^{N} m_{ij} x_i(t) x_j(t) + \sum_{j=1}^{M} m_{ji} x_i(t) y_j(t) \right] - k_2 x_i(t),$$

$$i = 1, ..., N) \tag{3}$$

The first term represents the stimulation of i-th paratope by the epitope of an antibody of type j, the second term represents the suppression of antibody of type i when its epitope is recognized by the paratope of type j, third term represents the stimulation of i-th antibody by the antigens, and the last term models the tendency of cells to die. The parameter c is a rate constant that depends on the number of collisions per unit time and the rate of antibody production stimulated by a collision. Constant k_1 represents a possible inequality between stimulation and suppression and constant k_2 represents the rate of natural death. The model was used by Bagley *et al.* [1] who studied another important concept of theoretical immunology – plasticity in an immune network. By plasticity we understand the process of removing and recruiting certain types of antibodies from/into the network. This process enables the immune system to decide which idiotypic determinants should be included/removed in/from the network without referring to an explicit fitness function. Consequently, the network is flexible and is able to modify its structure. Soon, it became obvious, [13], that the model is too simple to describe emergence of a self-asserted structure which would be able to sustain immune functions.

A prominent representative of the "*B-model*" was proposed in [9] and [10]. It was assumed that B-cells (not antibodies) interact with antigens, and this interaction determines the kinetics of the cell response. B-cells proliferate according to a log bell-shaped response function f which depends on a single field, $h_i(t)$ defined as in equation (2). In a system consisting of N different clones of B-cells, their concentrations, $x_i(t)$, $I = 1, ..., N$, vary according to the equation:

$$\frac{dx_i(t)}{dt} = \left[p \cdot f\left(h_i(t)\right) - d \right] \cdot x_i(t) + b \, , i = 1, ..., N \tag{4}$$

where p is the rate of clone proliferation, and b is the rate at which new clones are inserted into the system by the bone marrow. Here it is assumed that: (a) the occurrence of any type of B-cell paratope is equiprobable, and (b) the parameter p suffices to summarize the role of T-cells in proliferation of stimulated B-cells.

Varela and Coutinho proposed in [29] the "*second generation immune network model*" in which both B-cells and antibodies are taken into account. Their model reflects essential features of immune network and allows to study such significant functions like: recognition, memory or tolerance. In this model free antibodies and B-cells interact with each other through idiotypes. It is assumed that both a B-cell and free antibodies produced by this cell have identical idiotypes. Following [27] the affinity m_{ij}, **used in eqn. (2)**, between i-th and j-th idiotype can take only two values: "1" (indicating a threshold affinity between the corresponding idiotypes) or "0" (lack of affinity). The matrix $M = [m_{ij}]$ is said to be the *connectivity matrix*. Suppose there are N different idiotypes, and f_i (resp. b_i) stands for the concentration of antibodies (resp. B-cells) with idiotype of type i. Then the strength of influence of antibodies on i-th antibody is determined by the field $\sigma_i = \sum_{j=1,...,N} m_{ij} \cdot f_j$. The concentration of B-cells and free antibodies varies according to the differential equations

$$\frac{df_i(t)}{dt} = -k_1 \cdot \sigma_i \cdot f_i(t) - k_2 \cdot f_i(t) + k_3 \cdot mat(\sigma_i) \cdot b_i(t) \tag{5a}$$

$$\frac{db_i(t)}{dt} = -k_4 \cdot b_i(t) + k_5 \cdot prol(\sigma_i) \cdot b_i(t) + k_6 , i = 1, ..., N \tag{5b}$$

where: k_1 is the rate of neutralization of a given type of antibodies by other types of antibodies, k_2 is the rate of death of antibodies, k_3 is the rate of creation of antibodies by B-cells, k_4 is the rate of death of B-cells, k_5 is the rate of B-cells creation, and the term k_6 represents the rate of production of B-cells by the *bone marrow*. $mat(\cdot)$ and $prol(\cdot)$ – **the counterparts of the activation function defined in eqn. (1)** – are bell-shaped functions describing how B-cells mature and proliferate upon activation. In [6] these functions are modeled by the equations:

$$mat(\sigma_i) = \exp\left\{ -\left[\frac{\ln(\sigma_i / \mu_m)}{s_m} \right]^2 \right\} , \quad prol(\sigma_i) = \exp\left\{ -\left[\frac{\ln(\sigma_i / \mu_p)}{s_p} \right]^2 \right\} \tag{6}$$

where s_m, s_p, μ_m, and μ_p are parameters[3]. This model was studied in depth in [6], [3] and [21]. **Particularly, it was verified that in the model described by (5a,b) a large spectrum of long run behaviors can be observed obeying fixed point, chaotic as well as periodic and states exist. Further, it was shown in [21] that there are periodic states in which some B-cell type plays the role of switching other types to be excited. The behavior exhibited by the system hardly depends on the form of the connectivity matrix.**

2.2.2 Discrete models

The first cellular automaton model – referred to as BSP model – was proposed by De Boer, Segel and Perelson in [11]. Here each B-cell is characterized by a vector **r** in n-dimensional Euclidean space and two B-cells interact if they have complementary shapes. It was assumed that the interaction between two B-cells characterized by the idiotypes $\mathbf{r}_i$, and $\mathbf{r}_j$ is proportional to the **affinity** $m_{ij} = f(\mathbf{r}_i, \mathbf{r}_j) = \exp[-dist(\mathbf{r}_i, -\mathbf{r}_j)/c]$, where *dist* stands for the Euclidean distance, and c is a scaling factor. Note that the interaction is maximal whenever the spatial

---

[3] Precise values of these parameters and the parameters $k_1, ..., k_6$ can be found e.g. in [6]

coordinates are equal and opposite, i.e. $r_i = -r_j$. The authors observed that starting from a nearly homogenous distribution of initial population of cells, the final distribution was very **inhomogeneous**. Particularly, in 2-dimensional case formation of circular clusters of small radius was observed.

To study this model in higher dimensions, Stauffer and Weisbuch proposed in [26] a simplified version of the BSP model called BSPIII. They replaced Gaussian distribution of interactions by nearest-neighbor interactions, and they assumed that the B-cell concentrations b_i can take only three values representing the virgin ($b_i =$ 0), suppressed ($b_i = 1$) and immune ($b_i = 2$) states. With such simplifications, the authors observed a transition from stable to chaotic regimes in higher ($n > 3$) dimensions, but for lower dimensions ($n \leq 3$) the BSPIII model always evolved to stable configurations.

Zorzenon dos Santos and Bernardes studied **in [32]** another version of BSPIII with a simplified response function defined as $f(h) > 0$ if $h \in [Lo, Hi]$ and $f(h) = 0$ otherwise. The model is simulated on n-dimensional hypercubic lattice with $N = L^n$ sites, in such a way that site i interacts with $2n + 1$ sites centered at its mirror image, i.e. when $n = 2$ the cell (x, y) interacts with its mirror image $(x', y') = (L-x, L-y)$ and its four neighbors: $(L-x\pm1, L-y)$ and $(L-x, L-y\pm1)$. The field of i-th site is computed as $h_i = \sum_{j \in N(i)} b_j$, where $N(j)$ stands for the (mirror) neighborhood of i-th site. The concentration of i-th B-cell is updated according to the rule:

$$b_i(t+1) = \begin{cases} b_i(t)+1 & if \quad h_i(t) \in [Lo, Hi] \\ b_i(t)-1 & if \quad h_i(t) \notin [Lo, Hi] \end{cases} \tag{7}$$

but no change is made if it would lead to $b_i(t+1) = -1$ or $b_i(t+1) = 3$.

This model exhibits a transition from stable to chaotic regimes for $n \geq 2$, depending on the activation threshold Lo and the width of the activation interval ($Hi - Lo$). The shorter the activation interval the faster the system goes to the chaotic behavior. Moreover, it was observed that the final results are sensitive to the choice of the initial distribution of concentration of states. This distribution was defined as follows: $b_i(0) = 0$ with probability $(1 - x)$, $b_i(0) = 1$ with probability $\frac{1}{2} \cdot x$ and $b_i(0) = 2$ with probability $\frac{1}{2} \cdot x$.

Another variant of BSPIII was proposed by Bersini in [2]. Here antibodies are randomly recruited to points on a two-dimensional lattice of size $L \times L$. Only one new cell i is located randomly at each iteration at (x_i, y_i). Denote $b_i(0) > 0$ its initial concentration. Like in previous models, it is assumed that this cell exerts an affinity in a zone $Z(i, r)$ centered around its mirror image $\sim i$ with coordinates $(x_{-i}, y_{-i}) = (L - x_i, L - y_i)$, where r is a pre-specified radius. Now, the field of such an antibody is computed at iteration $t+1$ as follows:

$$h_i(t+1) = \sum_{a \in Z(a,r)} b_a(t) \cdot \xi(r - dist(\sim i, a)) \tag{8}$$

where $\xi(x) = 0$ if $x \le 0$ and $\xi(x) = x$ if $x > 0$, and $dist(\cdot, \cdot)$ stands for a distance between two cells. The concentration of the cell i evolves according to the equation (7). A cell dies, and is removed from the system, if its concentration $b_i(t)$ equals zero.

This model was carefully studied by Hart and Ross in [18]. Figure 1 shows two exemplary cells distribution after 10,000 iterations. These authors observed a number of empirical facts without their formal analysis:

(1) Tolerant and non-tolerant zones emerge that are not predetermined. A cell placed at tolerant zone can live for a long time.

(2) The zones are unsymmetrical what follows from the random nature of the system.

(3) The boundaries of zones are generally lines.

(4) The set of cells S that lie in the complementary region of any persistent cell x lying on a zone-boundary occur only around boundaries of the complementary region of x.

(5) The emergence of stable regions is dependent on the size of the recognition radius.

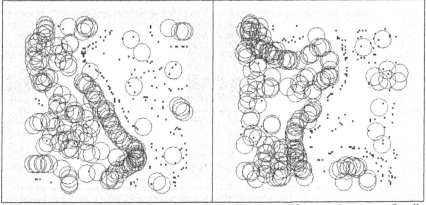

Figure 1. Stable distribution of immune cells in a self-asserted system. Small squares represent immune cells, circles – their regions of affinity. There are two slightly different modes of activity: (a) a cell can belong to its own region of affinity (left), and (b) self-stimulating cells are not allowed (right).

It seems that to explain these facts it is sufficient to note that the probability of locating new cell in i-th site equals $p = L^{-1}$, and probability of locating sufficient number of cell in the affinity region $Z(i, r)$ is governed by the binomial distribution $F_n(k)$ of obtaining k successes in n independent Bernoulli trials (the probability of success in a single trial is just p). To stimulate a virgin, or just introduced, cell i, k cells with rather high concentrations should be placed in the zone $Z(i, r)$ in relatively short period proportional to r and inversely proportional to the value $b_i(0)$. This last requirements follows from the dynamics (7): non-stimulated cell decreases its concentration by one at each iteration. Practically it means that when e.g. $b_i(0) = 10$ and $r = 10$, about 3 cells should be placed in $Z(i, r)$ within $n = 6$ subsequent iterations. Such a reasoning explains why sufficiently high values of r, $b_i(0)$, and Lo are requested to initiate the process of stable structure formation. Figure 2 illustrates different stages of such a process. Figure 3 shows that the number of cells stabilizes around a fixed value through iterations while Figure 4 shows that the process itself admits a "free-scale" nature, the probability that a cell will leave t iterations obeys the rule $P(t) \propto t^{-\tau}$, with $\tau \approx 1.78$.

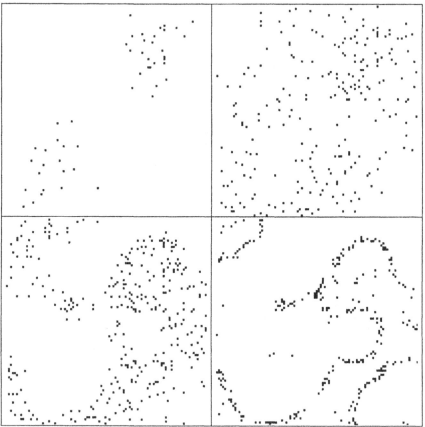

Figure 2. Snapshots of the self-assertion simulations (from upper left to lower right): after 1300, 1500, 2000 and 4000 iterations; the last structure is almost stable.

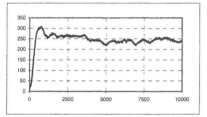
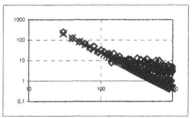

Figure 3. Number of cells in subsequent iterations.

Figure 4. Average number of cells (rhombs) living through t iterations vs. power law $P(t) = \propto t^{-\tau}$ (crosses)

A deeper insight into the impact of graph theory and more particularly the scale-free topology on immune network models can be found in [4], [5], and [28].

3 Some Hints for Designing Immune Algorithms

One of the earlier and successful applications of immune metaphors in machine learning was performed by Hunt and Cook in [19]. These authors used the idiotypic network theory mentioned in Sect. 2.1 and proposed a "generic" algorithm for constructing IA for data analysis. To calculate the stimulation of artificial cells they used a variant of equation (3). Since then, almost all authors proposing new immune clustering algorithms, like AINE or RLAIS ([12], Sect. 4.6.2), SSAIS (described in [23]), or systems introduced in [30], [31], were impressed by this idea.

Slightly different approach was used in aiNET system (consult [12] for details) which is based on clonal selection theory and freely refers to "second generation" immune systems idea introduced in [29].

The system analyzed by Gilbert and Routen in [17], and based on the "B-model", proved to be unworkable in an actual application. Carter commented the effort of these authors as follows ([7], p. 31): "Building systems that adhere closely to what is known of natural immune systems with all their innate complexity, while admirable, may in the long run prove to be less than ideal from a computational standpoint". Instead he proposed his own, rather complicated, version of immune-based pattern recognition system called "Immunos-81".

Some, very general, framework for designing biologically inspired algorithms was proposed in [12] as a three-stage procedure relying upon: (a) choosing appropriate representation for the components of the system, (b) defining a set of mechanisms to evaluate the interaction of individuals with the environment and each other, and finally (c) defining procedures of adaptation that govern the dynamics of the system. Stage (a) refers freely to the choice of appropriate "shape-space". We know however from [4] that this formalism may lead to misleading artifacts. Hence the choice should be performed very carefully. Similarly, the material from Section 2.2 shows that we have a large spectrum of models reproducing immune behavior, not only a rather idealistic model [14]. Particularly, the discrete models described briefly in Section 2.2.2 and studied intensively by statistical physicists seem to very attractive for further investigations: they are simple from a computational standpoint and they posses admit very complicated behavior.

4 References

[1] Bagley, R.J., et al. Modeling adaptive biological systems. *BioSystems* **23**: 113-138 , 1989.

[2] Bersini, H. Self-assertion vs. self-recognition: A tribute to Francisco Varela. Proc. of the 1st International Conference on Artificial Immune Systems, ICARIS'2002, University of Kent at Canterbury, 2002, pp. 107-112

[3] Bersini, H., Calenbuhr, V. Frustrated chaos in biological networks. *J. theor. Biol.*, **188**: 187-200, 1997

[4] Bonabeau, E. A simple model for the statistics of events in idiotypic networks. *BioSystems*, **39**: 25-34, 1996

[5] Burgos, J.D. Fractal representation of the immune B cell repertoire. *BioSystems*, **39**: 19-24, 1996

[6] Calenbuhr, V., Bersini, H., Stewart, J., Varela, F.J. Natural tolerance in a simple immune network. *J. theor. Biol.*, **177**: 199-213, 1995

[7] Carter, J.H. The immune system as a model for pattern recognition and classification. *J. of the American Medical Informatics Assoc.* **7**: 28-41, 2000

[8] Corne, D., Dorigo, M., Glover, F. (eds.) *New Ideas in Optimization*, McGraw-Hill 1999

[9] De Boer, R., Kevrekidis, I.G., Perelson, A.S. Immune network behavior I: from stationary states to limit cycle oscillations. *Bull. Math. Biol.* **55**: 745-780, 1993

[10] De Boer, R., Kevrekidis, I.G., Perelson, A.S. Immune network behavior I: from oscillations to chaos and stationary states. *Bull. Math. Biol.* **55**: 745-780, 1993

[11] De Boer, R., Segel, L.A., Perelson, A.S. Pattern formation in one- and two-dimensional shape space models of the immune system. *J. theor. Biol.*, **155**: 295-333, 1992

[12] De Castro, L.N., Timmis, J. *Artificial Immune Systems: A New Computational Intelligence Approach*, Springer-Verlag 2002

[13] Farmer, J.D. A Rosetta stone for connectionism. *Physica D*, **42**: 153-187, 1990

[14] Farmer, J.D., Packard, N.H., Perelson, A.S. The immune system, adaptation, and machine learning. *Physica D*, **22**:187-204, 1986

[15] Faro, J., Velasco, S. Studies on a recent class of network models of the immune system. *J. theor. Biol.*, **164**: 271-290, 1993

[16] Faro, J., Carneiro, J. Velasco, S. Further studies on the problem of immune network modelling. *J. theor. Biol.*, **184**: 405-421, 1997

[17] Gilbert, C.J., Routen, T.W. Associative memory in an immune-based system. *Proc. of 12th Nat. Conf. on Artiff. Intelligence*, AAAI Press 1994, 852-857

[18] Hart, E., Ross, P. Studies on the implications of shape-space models for idiotypic networks. In: Nicosia et. al. *ICARIS 2004*, LNCS 3239, Springer-Verlag 2004, pp. 413-426

[19] Hunt, J. Cooke, D. Learning using an artificial immune system. *J. of Network and Computer Applications.* **19**: 189-212, 1996

[20] Hofmeyr, S.A. Introduction to the immune system. In: L.A. Segel, I. Cohen (eds.) *Design Principles for the Immune System and Other Distributed Autonomous Systems*, Santa Fe Institute Studies in the Sciences of Complexity. New York: Oxford University Press 2001

[21] Itaya, S., Uezu, T. Analysis of an immune network dynamical system model with a small number of degrees of freedom. *Progress in Theoretical Physics*, **104**: 903-924, 2000

[22] Jerne N.J. Idiotypic networks and other preconceived ideas. *Immunol. Rev.* **79**: 5-25,1984

[23] Neal, M. Meta-stable memory in an artificial immune network. In: J. Timmis et al. (eds.), *ICARIS 2004*, LNCS 2787, Springer-Verlag 2003, pp. 168-180

[24] Perelson, A.S., Oster, G.F. The shape space model. *J. theor. Biol.*, **81**: 645-670, 1979

[25] Perelson, A., Weisbuch, G. Immunology for physicists. *Reviews of Modern Physics*, **69**: 1219-1265, 1977

[26] Stauffer D., Weisbuch, G. High-dimensional simulation of the\ shape-space model for the immune system. Physica A, 180: 42-52, 1992

[27] Stewart, I., Varela, F. Exploring the connectivity of the immune network. *Immunol. Rev.* **110**: 37-61, 1989

[28] Tieri, P., et al. Memory and selectivity in evolving scale-free immune networks. In: J. Timmis et al. (eds.) *ICARIS 2003*, LNCS 2787, Springer-Verlag 2003, pp. 93-101

[29] Varela, F., Coutinho, A. Second generation immune networks. *Immunol. Today*, **12**: 159-167, 1991

[30] Wierzchoń, S.T. Kużelewska, U. Stable cluster formation in an artificial immune system. Proc. of the 1st Internat. Conference on Artificial Immune Systems, ICARIS'2002, University of Kent at Canterbury, 2002, pp. 68-75

[31] Younsi, R., Wang, W. A new artificial immune system algorithm for clustering. In: Z.R. Yand et al. (eds.) *IDEAL 2004*, LNCS 3177, Springer-Verlag 2004, pp. 58-64

[32] Zorzenon dos Santos, R.M., Bernardes, A.T. The stable-chaotic transition on cellular automata used to model the immune repertoire. *Physica A*, **219**: 1-19, 1995.

Global learning of decision trees by an evolutionary algorithm [1]

Marek Krętowski, Marek Grześ

Faculty of Computer Science, Białystok Technical University, Wiejska 45a, 15-351 Białystok, Poland, *e-mail: {mkret, marekg}@ii.pb.bialystok.pl*

Abstract: In the paper, an evolutionary algorithm for global induction of decision trees is presented. In contrast to greedy, top-down approaches it searches for the whole tree at the moment. Specialised genetic operators are proposed which allow modifying both tests used in the non-terminal nodes and structure of the tree. The proposed approach was validated on both artificial and real-life datasets. Experimental results show that the proposed algorithm is able to find competitive classifiers in terms of accuracy and especially complexity.

Keywords: Data mining, decision trees, evolutionary algorithms, global induction

1   Introduction

Amount of information, which is gathered in business and scientific database systems, is growing faster and faster. Efficient analysis of huge available data becomes one of the most crucial problems in computer science. Knowledge discovery in databases (KDD) is newly emerged discipline trying to cope with this problem [9]. One of the most well known data mining techniques used in KDD process is extraction of decision trees (DT). Many induction algorithms have been proposed so far, e.g. CART [5] or C4.5 [16] (see [15] for exhausting multidisciplinary review). The advantages of the DT-based approach include among other things natural representation and ease of interpretation.

Finding the best decision tree is very difficult optimisation problem (NP-complete) [10] and therefore most of the existing DT systems use heuristic approach based on the top-down induction. Starting from the root node, which contains all feature vectors from the learning set, an optimal split is searched. If effective test is found input vectors from the considered node are divided among newly created sub-nodes and for each one the procedure is recursively called.

---

[1] This work was supported by the grant W/WI/1/02 from Białystok Technical University

Such a greedy search technique is fast and generally leads to acceptable results in typical applications. In [14] effectiveness of the top-down induction was investigated on artificial datasets with known optimal tree and near optimal solution was found in most of the cases. However, it is evident that for certain classification problems (e.g. classical "chessboard" problem [3]) top-down approach fails and more sophisticated method should be applied.

In this paper, a global approach to decision tree induction is advocated. In contrast to typical stepwise construction, in the proposed method the whole tree is searched at the time. It means simultaneous search for an optimal structure of the tree and for all tests in non-terminal nodes. As it could be expected, global tree construction is far more complicated and computationally complex problem. As a first step toward global induction limited look-ahead algorithms are proposed (e.g. APDT [17] evaluates goodness of a split based also on the degree of linear separability of sub-nodes). Another approach consists in a two-stage induction, where a greedy algorithm is applied in the first stage and then the tree is refined to be as close to optimal as possible (e.g. GTO [1] is an example of linear programming based method for optimising trees with fixed structures). In [11] Koza proposed adopting genetic programming (GP) methods for evolving LISP S-expressions corresponding to decision trees. Another GP-based system for induction of classification trees with limited oblique splits is presented in [4].

The proposed approach consists in developing a specialised evolutionary algorithm for generation of decision tree classifiers. Evolutionary algorithms (EA) are flexible optimisation techniques, which were inspired by the process of biological evolution [13]. Their main advantage over greedy search methods is their ability to avoid local optima. Several EA-based systems, which learn decision trees in the top-down manner (e.g. BTGA [7], OC1-ES [6], DDT-EA [12]), have been proposed so far. Generally, they applied evolutionary approach to the test search, especially in the form of hyper-planes.

The rest of the paper is organised as follows. In the next section, the proposed evolutionary algorithm for global induction of decision tree is presented in details. Section 3 contains experimental validation of the approach on both artificial and real-life classification problems. In the last section conclusions and possible directions of the future work are presented.

2 Evolutionary Decision Tree Learning

The proposed evolutionary algorithm follows the general framework presented in [13]. In this section, only application-specific issues are described: representation, genetic operators and the fitness function.

2.1   Representation, initialisation and termination condition

There are two the most common strategies of applying evolutionary approach to solve optimisation problems. In the first approach, the candidate solutions are encoded in the fixed-size (usually binary) chromosomes, which allow using standard genetic operators: crossover and mutation. The second approach consists in applying more sophisticated representations (e.g. variable-length) and developing specialised genetic operators.

Decision trees are complicated tree structures, in which number of nodes, type of the tests and even number of test outcomes are not known in advance. It is why the second aforementioned approach is the most adequate, especially if the whole tree is searched in one run of EA. In our system, decision trees are not especially encoded in individuals and they are represented in their actual form.

Each test in non-terminal nodes concerns only one attribute. Depending on the type of the feature used (nominal or continuous-valued) two test forms are possible. In case of a nominal attribute each value is associated with one branch. For a continuous-valued feature only typical inequality test with two outcomes is allowed ($attribute_i \leq threshold_i$). It was shown [8] that for finding the maximum of certain class of target functions it is sufficient to consider only so-called *boundary thresholds* as potential splits. A boundary threshold for the given attribute is defined as a midpoint between such a successive pair of examples in the sequence sorted by the increasing value of the attribute, that one of the examples is positive and the other is negative (Fig. 1). The above property also holds for our fitness function.

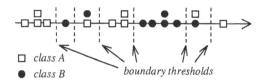

Fig. 1. The notion of the boundary threshold for the given attribute.

Hence before starting the actual evolutionary algorithm, all boundary thresholds for each continuous-valued attribute are calculated. It enables to significantly limit the number of possible spits and focus the search process. As a result the algorithm is faster and more robust.

Each individual in the initial population is generated as follows. The classical top-down algorithm is applied, but tests are chosen in a dipolar way [12]. Among feature vectors located in the considered node two objects from different classes are randomly chosen. An effective test, which separates two objects into sub-trees, is created randomly taking into account only attributes with different feature values. Recursive divisions are repeated until stopping conditions are met. Finally, the resulting tree is post-pruned based on the fitness function.

The algorithm terminates if the fitness of the best individual in the population does not improve during the fixed number of generations (default value is equal 1000), which signalises, that the algorithm converged. Additionally the maximum number of generations is specified, which allows limiting the computation time in case of a very slow convergence (default value: 10000).

2.2 Genetic operators

Two specialised and complex genetic operators are proposed: *CrossTrees* and *MutateNode*. The first one is an equivalent of the standard crossover operator. It alters two chromosomes by exchanging certain parts of input trees. There are three possible types of the exchange: two types of sub-trees exchange and exchange of only tests. At the beginning, regardless of the type, one node in each tree is randomly chosen. Then the type of exchange between trees is decided. In the system implementing the presented EA, all variants of *CrossTree* operator are equally probable. In the simplest situation, sub-trees starting from the chosen nodes are substituted (Fig. 2a). This variant is analogous to the typical crossover operator utilised in genetic programming. The second possibility consists in exchanging tests, which are associated with the chosen nodes (Fig. 2b). This type of the operator is only possible, when tests have the same number of outcomes. The last variant of the *CrossTree* seems to be the most complicated. Branches (and their sub-trees), which start from the chosen nodes are exchanged in random order (Fig. 2c). It could be observed that the last possibility is somehow redundant, because the same effect can be achieved by combining two (or more) exchanges of the first type.

It should be noted that in all variants after application of the operator, locations of input feature vectors in altered parts of the tree should be determined once again. This can lead to such a situation, where there are nodes (or even sub-trees) without any feature vectors from the learning set. As a result, empty parts of trees have to be removed.

The second operator *MutateNode* is a mutation-like one and it is applied with the given probability (default value: 0.05) to every single node of the tree. This operator can cause a modification of the test or a change of the node structure. If a non-terminal node is concerned it can be pruned to a leaf or its test can be altered. When modifying the test the following four possibilities are equally probable:

- a new threshold can be randomly chosen without changing the attribute used in the test,

- a completely new test is applied with another randomly chosen attribute and threshold,

- the current sub-tree can be replaced by a sub-tree copied from the neighbouring node (this does not apply to the root node),

- the test can be exchanged with another test taken from randomly chosen son-node (this does not apply to nodes with only leaves as sons).

If a leaf node containing feature vectors from different classes is concerned two options are possible. The leaf can be replaced by:

- a non-terminal node with a new randomly chosen test,

- a sub-tree generated according to dipolar algorithm applied for initialisation.

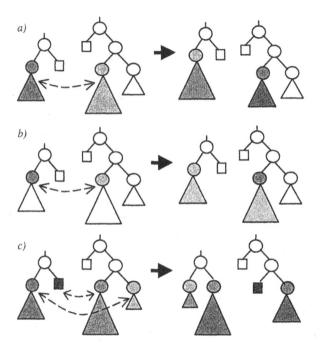

Fig. 2. CrossTree operator: *a)* exchange of sub-trees, *b)* exchange of tests in the randomly drawn nodes; the structure of sub-trees remains not changed, but input vectors can be redirected, *c)* exchange of branches in random order.

As a selection mechanism the linear ranking selection [13] is applied. Additionally, the chromosome with the highest value of the fitness function in the iteration is copied to the next population (*elitist* strategy).

2.3 Fitness function

The simplest form of the target function, which can be optimised in classification problems, concerns only the quality of reclassification. However, it is well known fact that this can lead to overspecialisation of the classifier. Introducing a complexity term allows mitigating the over-fitting problem. The fitness function, which is maximised, has the following form:

$$Fitness = Q_{Rclass} - \alpha \cdot S , \qquad (1)$$

where Q_{Rclass} is the classification quality estimated on the learning set, S is the size of the tree (number of nodes) and α - is a relative importance of the complexity term and a user supplied parameter. It seems rather obvious that there is no one optimal value of α for all datasets and this parameter can be tuned for specific problems.

3   Experimental results

In this section some preliminary experimental results are presented. First, a few artificial datasets from so-called *chessboard* domain are analysed. It is well known that such problems are difficult to solve for traditional, top-down decision tree systems. In the second group of experiments, some real life datasets taken from UCI Repository [2] are used to generate DT classifiers. Classification accuracy is estimated by running 10 times either the complete ten-fold cross-validation or by using a test set. Size of the classifier is given as a number of all nodes in the tree. Our system (described as a GDT-EA in tables) is run with default parameters mentioned earlier in the system description. The population size is set to 50. For the purpose of the comparison, results obtained by one of the most popular decision tree system - C4.5 (release 8, default parameters) [16] are also presented.

3.1   Artificial datasets

Two examples of *chessboard* training datasets are depicted in Figure 3. Decision borders are defined analytically and both training and test sets were created by using random number generator (number of feature vectors in each compartment is equal 100).

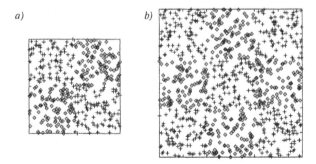

Fig. 3. Examples of *chessboard* datasets: a) 2x2, b) 3x3.

In the global approach parameter α from the fitness function can be used for finding appropriate balance between re-classification accuracy and generalisation power related to the tree complexity. In the first experiments, it is verified how GDT-EA is sensitive to the choice of α parameter (Figure 4). It can be observed that for relatively broad range of values (0.01-0.001) optimal trees were found. Further decrease of α parameter results in performance deterioration especially in terms of tree simplicity. All subsequent experiments are run with α equal 0.0025.

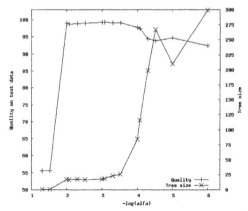

Fig. 4. Impact of α on classification quality and tree size (*chessboard* 3x3 dataset)

Results obtained by GEA-DT and by C4.5 are compared in Table 1. As it could be expected, global induction of decision tree allowed outperforming one of the most popular representatives of the top-down approach. It is especially visible for even problems, where C4.5 is able to only find trees degenerated to root nodes. It is worth to emphasise that decision trees proposed by GEA-DT were not only optimal or almost optimal in terms of the classification quality but also they were very compact.

Data set	GEA-DT		C4.5	
	Quality [%]	Size	Quality [%]	Size
2x2	99.9 ± 0.1	7.0 ± 0.0	50.0	1.0
3x3	99.1 ± 0.2	17.0 ± 0.0	98.6	23.0
4x4	97.9 ± 0.2	31.0 ± 0.0	50.0	1.0

Tab. 1. Results obtained for *chessboard* datasets.

EA-based methods are sometimes criticised as being too slow to be applied for really big datasets. In the last experiment, we try to verify how GDT-EA scales with the growth of learning set size. For this purpose a series of datasets with number of objects varying from 100 to 100000 corresponding to the chessboard 3x3 problem was prepared. In Figure 5 obtained results in terms of classification accuracy and computation time are depicted (on log scale). It should be noticed that even for the biggest dataset GDT-EA is able to find the optimal solution in reasonable time (approximately 1.5h).

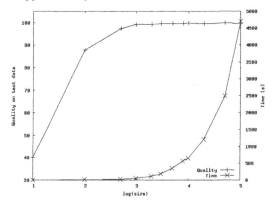

Fig. 5. Performance of GDT-EA with increasing dataset size (chessboard 3x3 domain).

3.2 Real datasets

Description of analysed real-life datasets is presented in Table 2 and results of experiments are collected in Table 3.

Name	Number of cases	Number of attributes	Number of classes
breast (bcw)	683	9	2
bupa	345	6	2
cmc	1473	9	3

Name	Number of cases	Number of attributes	Number of classes
iris	150	4	3
page-blocks	5473	10	5
pima	768	7	2
vehicle	846	18	4
wine	178	13	3

Tab. 2. Description of the real datasets.

It could be observed that results in terms of the classification quality obtained by the proposed approach and C4.5 are at least comparable. In a few domains GEA-DT performed better and in the others C4.5 was slightly more efficient. It could be also noticed that evolutionary approach was more efficient in term of the size of the classifier. Trees are significantly simpler and it is especially important in the context of understandability of discovered knowledge.

Dataset	GEA-DT		C4.5	
	Quality [%]	Size	Quality [%]	Size
breast (bcw)	95.4 ± 0.2	7.7 ± 0.1	94.9	26.0
bupa	65.6 ± 0.4	21.5 ± 0.2	64.7	44.6
cmc	54.9 ± 0.2	10.7 ± 0.2	52.2	223.8
iris	95.3 ± 0.2	8.2 ± 0.1	94.7	8.4
page-blocks	95.3 ± 0.1	8.2 ± 0.2	97.0	82.8
pima	73.8 ± 0.3	7.4 ± 0.2	74.6	40.6
vehicle	69.7 ± 0.3	29.6 ± 0.5	72.3	129.0
wine	88.1 ± 2.1	9.8 ± 0.4	85.0	9.0

Tab. 3. Results obtained for real datasets.

4   Conclusion

In the paper global approach to induction of decision trees is presented. Specialised evolutionary algorithm is proposed as an efficient search mechanism. Experimental validation shows that the proposed method is able to find accurate and very compact classifiers. Moreover, some improvement can still be obtained.

Several directions of future research exist. One of them could be more sophisticated fitness function, especially in part dealing with complexity of the classifier. We also plan to incorporate into the induction process variable misclassification costs and feature's cost, which could be especially useful in medical decision support. Another idea is an extension of the presented approach to induction of oblique trees, where not only axis-parallel tests are applied to split the data.

5   References

[1] Bennett K., "Global tree optimization: A non-greedy decision tree algorithm", Computing Science and Statistics 26, pp.156-160, 1994.

[2] Blake C., Merz C., "UCI Repository of machine learning databases" [http://www.ics.uci.edu/~mlearn/MLRepository.html] Irvine, CA: University of California, 1998.

[3] Bobrowski L. "Piecewise-linear classifiers, formal neurons and separability of the learning sets", Proc. of ICPR'96, IEEE CS Press, pp. 224-228, 1996.

[4] Bot M., Langdon W., "Application of genetic programming to induction of linear classification trees", Proc. of EuroGP, LNCS 1802, pp.247-258, 2000.

[5] Breiman L., Friedman J., Olshen R., Stone C., "Classification and Regression Trees", Wadsworth International Group, 1984.

[6] Cantu-Paz E., Kamath C., "Inducing oblique decision trees with evolutionary algorithms", IEEE Trans. on Evol. Computation 7(1), pp. 54-68, 2003.

[7] Chai B., Huang T., Zhuang X., Zhao Y., Sklansky J., "Piecewise-linear classifiers using binary tree structure and genetic algorithm", Pattern Recognition 29(11), pp. 1905-1917, 1996.

[8] Fayyad U., Irani K., "Multi-interval discretization of continuous-valued attributes for classification learning", Proc. of IJCAI'93, Morgan Kaufmann, pp. 1022-1027, 1993.

[9] Fayyad U., Piatetsky-Shapiro G., Smyth P., Uthurusamy R., (eds.) Advances in Knowledge Discovery and Data Mining, AAAI Press, 1996.

[10] Hayfil L., Rivest R., "Constructing optimal binary decision trees is NP.-complete", Information Processing Letters 5(1), pp. 15-17, 1976.

[11] Koza J., "Concept formation and decision tree induction usisng genetic programming paradigm", Proc. of PPSN 1, LNCS 496, pp. 124-128, 1991.

[12] Krętowski M., "An evolutionary algorithm for oblique decision tree induction", Proc. of ICAISC'04, Springer, LNCS 3070, pp.432-437, 2004.

[13] Michalewicz Z., "Genetic Algorithms + Data Structures = Evolution Programs", Springer, 1996.

[14] Murthy S., Salzberg S., "Decision tree induction: How effective is the greedy heuritics?", Proc. of KDD-95, 1995.

[15] Murthy S., "Automatic construction of decision trees from data: A multi-disciplinary survey", Data Mining and Know. Disc. 2, pp. 345-389, 1998.

[16] Quinlan J., "C4.5: Programs for Machine Learning", Morgan Kauf., 1993.

[17] Shah S., Sastry P., "New algorithm for learning and pruning oblique decision trees", IEEE Trans. on SMC - Part C 29(4), pp. 494-505, 1999.

Ships' domains as collision risk at sea in the evolutionary method of trajectory planning

Roman Śmierzchalski

Gdynia Maritime University; Morska str. 83; 81-225 Gdynia; Poland.

Abstract: The goal of this paper is to discuss the problem of avoiding collisions at sea from the perspective of an evolutionary process and representation in this problem the risk of collision. In an evolutionary method (EP/N Evolutionary Planer Navigator System) of generating paths of the ship in partially-known environments is presented. The evolutionary process which searches for a near-optimum trajectory in a collision situation takes into account a time parameter and the dynamic constraints, which treat to the risk of collision with meeting strange ships. The ship domain as a risk of the collision - shapes and dimensions of dynamic constrains depend on assumed safety conditions.

Keywords: ship control, evolutionary computation, modelling risk

1   Introducion

The biggest collision threat, manifesting itself, among other effects, by numerous cases of ships taking the ground, is recorded in the areas of heavy navigation traffic (harbour entrances, coastal zones, narrow sea passages: canals and straits). These areas are also characterised by frequent restricted visibility. The way the ships move there is partially controlled by formally introduced traffic separation regions. However, the execution of other marine functions, such as ferry transportation, coastal fishing, tourist services, and other activities connected with the maintenance of the navigability of water lines, result in crossing the traffic separation regions by certain craft. This creates additional collision threat. According to some sources (Dove et al. [2]), 85 per cent of collisions and singings result from human errors. Beside economical losses, accidents at sea may lead to irreversible losses in the human environment. In order to reduce this threat to the minimum, extensive works are widely carried out to develop a ship guidance system, which would guide the ship safely in complex navigational areas. The ship guidance systems were studied by Dove et al. [2]. In this work, the VTS system was used for estimating a ship trajectory along given water lines in the harbour. Burns [1] extended the problem by guiding a set of ships along a given route.

Iijima et al. [7,8] and Witt et al. [23] worked out an autonomous ship guidance system. Hayashi et al. [6] proposed a system for avoiding collision in coastal zones in which the function of an electronic map was linked with the radar operation in order to evaluate the ship's position and assess the navigational situation. Sudhendar et al. [20] formulated a list of requirements an intelligent guidance system was to comply with, and presented a review of the actual activities in this area. The author of the present paper was engaged in problems of guiding ships in collision situations. In a series of articles (Śmierzchalski [13,14,15]) this problem was formulated as a multi-criterion optimisation task. Then, the problem was solved for static and moving constraints using the decision making system. The attempt to estimate the safe trajectory using genetic algorithms was presented by Furuhashi et al. [4]. Śmierzchalski [16,17] applied in his ship guidance system a new computer technique - evolutionary algorithms. Basing on the concept of the E/PN (Evolutionary/Planner Navigator) guidance system, presented by Michalewicz et al. [11,12], Lin et al. [10], Trojanowski et al. [22] and Xiao et al. [24], a modified version of that system was prepared for solving collision problems. The present paper is a continuation of author's earlier works (Śmierzchalski [16,17,18,19]). Comparing to them, an additional parameter, the risk of the collision, was introduced to the system. The risk is modified for all met strangers targets

2 Determination of the risk collision utilising collision threat parameters area

The method of specifying CTPA (Collision Threat Parameters Area) was created by A.Lenart [9]. In the conjugate system of co-ordinates of the position (X, Y) and movement (V_x, V_y) (see Fig. 1 (a)) A.Lenart drew a relation,

The method of specifying CTPA was created by A.Lenart [9]. In the conjugate system of co-ordinates of the position (X, Y) and movement (V_x, V_y) (see Fig. 1 (a)) A.Lenart drew a relation,

$$Y = A_j X - B_j \tau \tag{1}$$

where: $A_j = \dfrac{X_j Y_j \pm D_{jCPA}\sqrt{D_j^2 - D_{jCPA}^2}}{X_j^2 - D_{jCPA}^2}$, $\quad B_j = A_j V_{Xj} - V_{Yj}$

in which Xj and Yj are the relative co-ordinates of j-th target and

$$D_j^2 = X_j^2 + Y_j^2,$$

D_{jCPA} - the distance value of the closest contact,

V_{Xj}, V_{Yj} - X and Y components of the velocity vector of the j-th target,

τ - conjugate time (e.g.12 minutes).

Equation 1 describes the locus of points for which D_{jCPA} = const in the conjugate system of co-ordinates of position (X, Y) and motion (V_x, V_y). On the other hand the locus of points in the conjugate system of co-ordinates for which the time of reaching the distance of the closest contact is constant $(T_{jCPA}$ = const) can be determined on the basis of the circle equation (2):

$$\left[X - (V_{xj} + \frac{X_j}{2T_{jCPA}})\tau \right]^2 + \left[Y - (V_{yj} + \frac{Y_j}{2T_{jCPA}})\tau \right]^2 = (\frac{D_j\tau}{2T_{jCPA}})^2 \qquad (2)$$

where the locus of points for the circle centre points lie on a straight line:

$$Y = \frac{Y_j}{X_j} X - (\frac{Y_j}{X_j}V_{xj} - V_{yj})\tau. \qquad (3)$$

It is assumed that an target B_j is dangerous, when at the moment of observation t, assuming that $D_{CPAj} = D_b$ and $T_{CPAj} = T_b$ respectively we have:

$$D_{jCPA} < D_b \text{ and } T_{jCPA} < T_b \qquad (4)$$

where: the values D_b of the safe distance and T_b - the time to reach that distance are set by the system operator (at say D_b =1Nm, T_b =20 min).

Geometrically the above condition is satisfied when the end of the vector of own ship A positioned at (V_x, V_y) in the conjugate system of co-ordinates of position and motion is found outside of the CTPA danger area. In the calculation algorithm the time of overtaking the manoeuvre of own ship and of targets was also respected. A practical realisation of visualisation of the total CTPA area determined for two targets with the proposal of the safe manoeuvre is pictured on Fig. 2. One of the drawbacks of the method presented here is that although the algorithm prescribes the manoeuvre leading out of the situation of collision created at a given time, it doesn't however assume the possibility of the appearance of new targets and does not state the moment of return of own ship to its planned course.

414

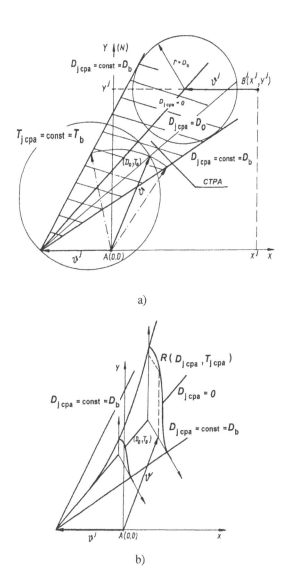

a)

b)

Fig. 1: (a) A CTPA (Collision Threat Parameters Area) area display. (b) The collision risk R

In order to evaluate the collision risk index (see Fig. 1 (b)) for one object the author suggests that the ranges of $D_{j\,cpa}$ and $T_{j\,cpa}$ values should be reduced to the real area of danger $|D_{j\,cpa}| \in (O, D_b)$ and $T_{j\,cpa} \in (0, nT_b)$ and n>1. To do this, the collision risk index was defined using the collision threat area, CTPA.

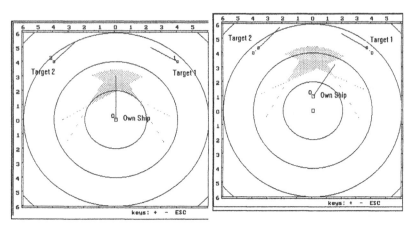

Fig. 2:   The practical realisation of CTPA area determined for two targets with the proposal of the safe manoeuvre

In this area a number of non-linear functions are defined which give the maximum closure distance and time values with relation to the assumed quantities of D_b and T_b. Such a form of the collision risk index takes into account the time-space relation, which is highly non-linear in the vicinity of the critical values of $D_{j\,cpa}$ and $T_{j\,cpa}$, for the situation of a collision danger at a given instant t. The collision risk coefficient R (5) is depended on safe distance D_b and time to safe distance T_b defined by the following relationship (5), where: $1 > R > 0$, $n > 1$, a,b,c,d values of regulate the risk coefficient.

$$\min R = \begin{bmatrix} a\,[e^{\left[\frac{D_{jcpa}}{D_b}\right]^2}]^b -0.1]\,[\frac{T_b}{T_{j\,cpa}+c} - d] & for\ D_{jcpa} < D_b,\quad T_{jcpa} < nT_b \\ 0 & for\ D_{jcpa} \geq D_b,\quad T_{jcpa} \geq nT_b \end{bmatrix} \qquad (5)$$

3   Domain estimation for approaching moving targets

A moving target representing a collision threat is configured as an area of danger, moving with the speed and at the direction (course) identified by the ARPA system. The most significant factors affecting the scale of the ship domain are the following: (1) psychological, human factors, such as: naval experience of the navigator, along with his intuition and knowledge on the navigation area, (2) physical factors, characteristic of the type of the ship, referring to its dimensions, relative speed of other approached ships, (3) physical factors, common for all ships in the area of concern, such as traffic level, hydro-meteorological conditions, etc. Goodwin E.M. [5] presented the method for estimating the area of danger on the basis of statistical data analysis. Following the maritime law regulations, the area of the object occurrence was divided into three sectors defined by the actual relative bearing to this object. Sector 1 is on the starboard side within the bearing limits of $0^0 \leq \theta \leq 112,5^0$, sector 2 is on the port side within $247^0 \leq \theta < 360^0$ and the stern sector 3 is within $122,5^0 < \theta < 247,5^0$. The dimensions of the domains were estimated on the basis of statistical data. A sample ship domain is shown in Fig. 3a. A modified domain formula, which made its modelling easier, was proposed by Davis P.V. *et al* [3] Fig. 3b. The author proposed to describe the area of danger around the object using a hexagon, whose dimensions are to be chosen experimentally.

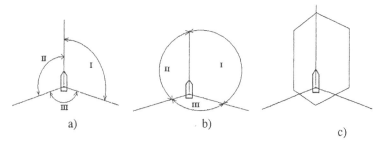

Fig. 3: Domains of objects according to a) Goodwin, b) Davis c) present work

Its manoeuvres are chosen in such a way that the restricted areas surrounding the targets and fixed obstacles are not intruded on at any time. In order to make the own ship's manoeuvres match the regulations of IML, the following assumptions were to be made when estimating the domain: (1) the area was of different structure for good and for limited visibility, (2) for good visibility, the hexagon dimensions on the port side of the target should be the largest, which in the case of course crossing will make the manoeuvre of the own ship giving way be done at a sufficient distance from the target, (3) this distance should be equal to or greater than the distance at which the target is allowed to start manoeuvres mentioned in Rule 17 a)ii). It was assumed (Fig. 4) in that the excessive approach in Sectors H,I,J,A occurs at a distance smaller than D_b , assumed here as equal to 2 nautical miles. In Sector B this distance is equal to 0,67 D_b, and in the remaining sectors it is assumed the same as in Sector B. Points M, N were selected in such a way as to be on line with the course 090°-270°, which corresponds to the ship's beam. By decreasing the distance to the excessive approach in the sectors, a hexagon-shaped domain was obtained which is dependent on actual value of D_b. assumed by the navigator. The disadvantage of this method is that D_b assumed is valid for one ship only. In the case of restricted visibility the problem of interpretation of Rule 17 is no longer valid. Rule 19 does not recognise ships with the right of way. Types and distances of the preventing action depend only on whether the target is behind the stern, in front of the bow, or on the ship beam. This regulation also recognises a conception of an excessive approach to be avoided. That means that in restricted visibility the domain should be determined using the excessive approach distance curves. In front of the bow this distance should equal at least 2 to 3 nautical miles at open sea, while in Cockroft diagram, manoeuvres at a distance larger than 4 nautical miles are recommended. Here, the crucial factor is the relative speed of the two ships approaching each other. When one ship overtakes the other, or passes it from astern, the excessive approach distance can be reduced to 2 Mm, and even less if relative speeds of the objects are not large.

4   Concept of creating hexagonal domains as the risk of collision

The assumed concept of hexagon-shaped domains around moving targets makes it possible to take into account those objects as dynamic obstacles in the evolutionary algorithm ϑEP/N++ used for estimating optimum safe trajectories. The process of creating of a hexagon-shaped area of danger – risk of collision around a given target is shown in Fig. 4(b). The lengths of the ship domain, in the bow and stern directions - parameters determining the dimension of the domain in the horizontal plane, in nautical miles (or meters), calculated from the centre of the system in the bow direction (5) and (2), (4) as well as in the stern direction (6) to its limiting value.

The appearance of a navigational constraint in the vicinity of the domain contour, or at a distance ahead on the planned passing trajectory (which depends on the navigator's experience) means the appearance of a navigational risk and its increase resulting from the decreasing distance to the detected constraint. For the ship on its course, the longitudinal dimension of the domain (its dynamical length) L_D can be evaluated using the formula [21]:

$$L_D = d_S = L \ V^{1.26} + 30 \ V + U \tag{6}$$

where: L – ship length (here, the length L of the own ship is used instead of, an unknown, length of the ship detected by the ARPA system),

V – ship speed , $V_O > V_{REL} \Rightarrow V = V_O,\ V_O < V_{REL} \Rightarrow V = V_{REL}$

V_O - own ship speed, V_{REL} - relative speed of strange ship,

U – error in estimating ship location, determined with 95% probability, U

418

$= 2M = 0.1$ Mm, M – standard quadratic error of the ship location.

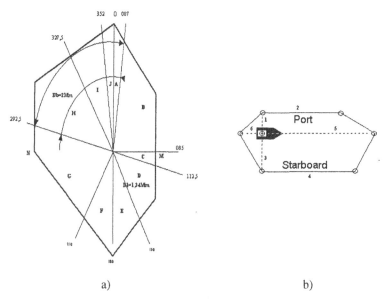

a) b)

Fig. 4: (a) Hexagon-shaped ship domain. (b) Hexagon around moving target

The level of navigational risk related to the length of the ship domain, which can be interpreted as the probability of collision with a navigational constraint in the horizontal plane, is reflected, to some extent, by the widely used in ARPA systems concept of T_{CPA} (*Time of Closest Point of Approach*), i.e. the time left to the instant when the closest point of approach, D_{CPA} is reached. With decreasing ratio between the distance from the detected navigational constraint and the ship domain length, the time T_{CPA} left for reaching D_{CPA} (T_{CPA}), decreases as well, which means the increasing risk of the navigational collision.

$$d_2 = T_{CPAo} \cdot V + U \tag{7}$$

$$d_4 = T_{CPAo} \quad V + U \tag{8}$$

where: T_{CPAo} - assumed value of T_{CPA}

After the stern, on the other hand, it is sufficient for the distance parameter equal

$$d_6 = D_b E \quad \text{or} \quad d_6 = D_b/2 \tag{9}$$

but not less than 0,5 Mm, where: E – relative speed to own speed ratio: V_{REL}/V_O

The widths of the ship domain, on the starboard or port sides - parameters determining the dimension of the domain in the horizontal plane, in nautical miles (or meters), calculated from the centre of the system in the starboard (4) or port side (5) directions of the ship to its limiting value. The equivalent of the width of the ship domain is the commonly used concept of the minimum distance D_{min} (D_{CPA}), which determines (in ARPA systems, for instance) the minimum area around the ship, which is to be kept clear by the navigator when passing another ship or a fixed navigational constraint. For the ship on its course, the lateral dimension of the domain (its dynamical width) B_D can be evaluated using the formula [21]:

$$B_D = d_3 = B \ V^{0,44} + U \qquad but \qquad d_3 > D_{CPAo}, \qquad (10)$$

where: B – ship width (here, the width B of the own ship is used instead of, an unknown, width of the ship detected by the ARPA system), D_{CPAo} - assumed value of $D_{CPA} \le D_b$

The above width of the domain is valid for the starboard side. On the port side, however, like after the stern:

$$d_l = D_{CPAo} E \qquad or \qquad d_l = D_{CPAo}/2 , \quad \text{but no less than } 0,5 \text{ Nm} \qquad (11)$$

where: E - relative speed to own ship speed ratio: V_{REL}/V_O .

5   Exemplary planning of ship trajectory

The system of evolutionary planning of the ship trajectory was tested for the numerous cases of passing fixed navigational constraints and moving targets. The analysis of cases displays the need for the introduction of an additional parameter to the evolutionary trajectory planning algorithm, namely the change of the own ship's speed along particular trajectory sections and ships' domains (see: Fig. 5). In practice, the speed was modified using an additional genetic operator: the speed mutation. A set of permissible speed values was defined as $V=\{3,6; 8,6; 13,6$ knots$\}$ from which the mutation operator could take a speed at the trajectory section of concern. Additionally, the total time of trajectory passing was added to the function of the trajectory fitness, which took into consideration changes in the own ship's speed. After this modernisation of the evolutionary process of the trajectory search, a trajectory will be looked for which, besides meeting the formerly set safety and economy conditions, will represent the shortest time needed for covering the studied distance. For this version of the algorithm, the example represents the moving targets sailing with opposite courses on the right and left sides of the own ship - a ferry, constraints having the form of islands. Here, the population consisted of 40 individuals (passage trajectories), and the changes of trajectories in the population stopped being recorded after 1000 generations. The estimated trajectories secure the passage of the ferry behind the stern of the targets on the left side. The ship's speed changed from one trajectory section to another. Initially, the ship reduced its speed to pass targets on the left

420

side, then, having sailed between the islands it increased the speed as it did not produce unacceptable nearing to target on the right side.

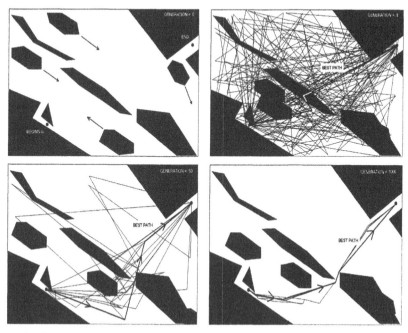

Fig. 5: Trajectory evolution for the case of approaching moving targets in the presence of static navigation constraints (population 40 trajectories).

6   Conclusions

The evolutionary system of ship trajectory planning makes it possible to steer the ship in a well known environment both with static, and dynamic navigation constraints, as well as to make adaptation corrections of the ship trajectory in order to follow unforeseeable changes in the situation at sea. The evolutionary method of determining the safe and optimum trajectory in the environment is a new approach to the problem of avoiding collisions at sea. A number of preliminary tests have made it possible to formulate the following conclusions:

- evolutionary algorithms can be effectively used for solving the problem of planning ship trajectory in areas of extensive traffic, like harbour entrances, coastal regions,

- introduction of the own ship's speed as a changing parameter makes it possible to solve the problem in a wider range. For particular trajectory sections, the actual speed is evaluated with which the ship covers this section in order to pass safely and economically all navigational constraints, both fixed and moving.

7 References

[1]   Burns RS, An Intelligent Integrated Ship Guidance System. 2nd IFAC Workshop Control Applications in Marine Systems, Genova, Italy 1992.

[2]   Dove MJ, Burns RS, Stockel CT, An Automatic Collision Avoidance and Guidance System for Marine Vehicles in Confined Waters. Journal of Navigation, Vol. 39 1986.

[3]   Davis P.V., Dove M.J., Stockel C.T., Computer Simulation of Multiship Encounters, Journal of Navigation, 1982, Vol. 35.

[4]   Furuhashi T, Nakaoka K, Uchikawa Y, A Study on Classifier System for Finding Control Knowledge of Multi-Input Systems F. Herrera, J.L.Verdegay Editors. Genetic Algorithms and Soft Computing, Phisica-Verlang 1996.

[5]   Goodwin E.M., A statistical study of ship domains, Journal of Navigation, 1975, Vol. 31.

[6]   Hayashi S, Kuwajima S, Sotooka K, Yamakazi H, Murase H, A stranding avoidance system using radar image matching: development and experiment. Journal of Navigation, Vol. 44 1991.

[7]   Iijima Y, Hayashi S, Study towards a twenty-first century intelligent ship. Journal of Navigation, Vol. 44 1991.

[8]   Iijima Y, Hagiwara, H Results of Collision Avoidance Manoeuvre Experiments Using a Knowledge-Based Autonomous Piloting System. Journal of Navigation, Vol. 47, 1994.

[9]   Lenart, A.S., Collision Threat Parameters for a New Radar Display and Plot Technique, Journal of Navigation, 1983, Vol. 36.

[10]   Lin HS, Xiao J, Michalewicz Z, Evolutionary Algorithm for Path Planning in Mobile Robot Environment. Proceeding IEEE Int. Conference of Evolutionary Computation, Orlando, Florida, 1994.

[11]   Michalewicz Z, Genetic Algorithms + Data structures = Evolution Programs. Spriger-Verlang, 3rd edition 1996 .

[12]   Michalewicz Z, Xiao J, Evaluation of Paths in Evolutionary Planner/Navigator. Proceedings of the International Workshop on Biologically Inspired Evolutionary Systems, Tokyo, Japan 1995.

[13]   Śmierzchalski R, The Application of the Dynamic Interactive Decision Analysis System to the Problem of Avoiding Collisions at the Sea (in Polish). 1st Conference "Awioniki", Jawor, Poland, 1995.

[14]   Śmierzchalski R, The Decision Support System to Design the Safe Manoeuvre Avoiding Collision at Sea. 14th International Conference Information Systems Analysis and Synthesis, Orlando, USA, 1996.

422

[15]   Śmierzchalski R, Multi-Criterion Modeling the Collision Situation at Sea for Application in Decision Support. 3rd International Symp. on Methods and Models in Automation and Robotics, Miedzyzdroje, Poland 1996.

[16]   Śmierzchalski R, Trajectory planning for ship in collision situations at sea by evolutionary computation. 4th IFAC Conference on Manoeuvring and Control of Marine, Brijuni, Creotia, 1997.

[17]   Śmierzchalski R, Dynamic Aspect in Evolutionary Computation on Example of Avoiding Collision at Sea. 4th International Symp. on Methods and Models in Automation and Robotics, Międzyzdroje, Poland 1997.

[18]   Śmierzchalski R, Evolutionary Guidance System for Ship in Collisions Situation at Sea. 3rd IFAC Conference Intelligent Autonomous Vehicle, Madrid, Spain 1997.

[19]   Śmierzchalski R, Michalewicz Z, Adaptive Modeling of a Ship Trajectory in Collision Situations. 2nd IEEE World Congress on Computational Intelligence, Alaska, USA 1998.

[20]   Sudhendar H, Grabowski M, Evolution of Intelligent Shipboard Piloting Systems: A Distributed System for the St Lawrence Seaway. Journal of Navigation, Vol. 49 1996.

[21]   Wawruch R.: System of steering ship movement. Works of Navigational Department, Gdynia Maritime Academy, Gdynia 1998.

[22]   Trojanowski K, Michalewicz Z, Planning Path of Mobil Robot (in Polish). 1st Conference Evolutionary Algorithms, Murzasichle, Poland 1998.

[23]   Witt NA, Sutton R, Miller KM, Recent Technological Advances in the Control and Guidance of Ship. Journal of Navigation Vol. 47, 1994.

[24]   Xiao J, Michalewicz Z, Zhang L, Evolutionary Planner/Navigator: Operator Performance and Self-Tuning. Proceeding IEEE Int. Conference of Evolutionary Computation, Nagoya, Japan 1996.

The work was supported by the State Committee for Science Research in Poland (grant no. 3 T11A 003 26).

Inputs' Significance Analysis with Rough Sets Theory

Izabela Rejer

University of Szczecin
Mickiewicza 64/66, Szczecin, Poland, e-mail: i_rejer@uoo.univ.szczecin.pl

Abstract: *The aim of this article is to show that a proper choice of a discretisation method is a key point in analysing the significance of attributes describing a specific real system of continuous attributes. In the second section of the article three most popular automatic discretisation methods are presented, which are next, in the third section, used for a discretisation of continuous attributes describing a system of an unemployment in Poland. The results obtained after application of these methods are compared with the results obtained with an expert method, proposed in the last part of the article.*

Keywords: *Inputs' significance, rough sets theory, discretisation methods*

1   Introduction

The most essential problem that may be encountered in the process of modelling of a real multi-dimensional system is a lack of prior knowledge about the factors determining its behaviour. Sometimes there are so many "experts" and so many different ideas about significant factors influencing the analysed system that it is extremely difficult to separate the most important ones.

One possibility of dealing with this problem is to apply in the modelling process a rough sets theory. There are two main approaches which can be used, according to this theory, in the inputs' significance analysis. Both are based on a comparison of the approximation quality of different subsets of attributes (inputs), which is calculated according to the following equation:

$$\gamma(X) = \frac{card\ Pos(X)}{card\ U} \tag{1}$$

where: card Pos(X) - cardinality of the positive regions of the concepts family X, card U - cardinality of the universe.

Approach I: First the approximation quality of the whole attributes' set is calculated. Then the attributes are one by one eliminated from the set and the quality of succeeding reduced subsets is estimated. Until both qualities (of the whole and reduced subset of attributes) are approximately the same, the last discarded attribute can be regarded as not important one.

Approach II: First the number of attributes which will be used for modelling of the analysed system is assumed. Then the approximation quality for all subsets of attributes consisted of chosen number of attributes is calculated. The subset of the biggest approximation quality is chosen for the modelling process.

Naturally when a system is described by a large number of attributes and small number of examples (what is the most common situation in the real world) only the second approach can be used.

As it has been proved a lot of times, the rough sets theory is a very powerful tool for modelling real systems of discrete attributes. For example it was successfully applied for diagnosing diseases of urinary system [1] and for calculating costs of hospital treatment [4]. However, not always attributes describing the analysed system are the discrete ones. Sometimes they are continuous and the discretisation process has to be accomplished before the application of the rough sets theory. Since there are a lot of different discretisation methods of different characteristics, the question is how to decide which one is the most suitable for a specific system?

Generally it is very difficult to give satisfactory answer for above question because it is often impossible to chose one method suitable for the whole analysed system. The reason for this is that different attributes describing the system can have different characteristics what means the discretisation method should be fitted individually to each of them.

2   Discretisation Process

There are a lot of different automatic methods used in the discretisation process. In this article only three, most commonly used, will be described. First of them is called "the equal sub-intervals method". According to this method the variation interval of an analysed attribute has to be divided into some equal sub-intervals (fig. 1a). This method is a good solution when the data are equally distributed in the whole interval but it can give negative results in other case. Figure 1b shows an example of an attribute characterised by an irregular distribution. As it can be observed, there are a lot of data in the first and last part of the interval and very rare data in the middle. If this attribute's interval is divided in the same way as the interval from the fig. 1a, then the middle sub-interval will contain very limited number of data points (fig. 1c). In most real systems intervals containing so little data are unwelcome because they lead to creation of very weakly supported rules.

Naturally, the inconvenience mentioned above can be easy eliminated by expanding the middle sub-interval like in the fig. 2d. Of course, the discretisation from the fig. 2d is not any more the example of the equal sub-intervals' method but it should be regarded as an expert method.

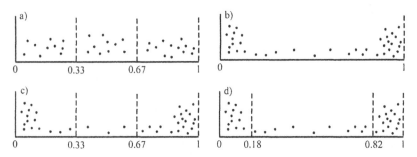

Fig. 1. The method of equal sub-intervals

The second popular automatic discretisation method is the method of equal number of data points. According to this method the whole variation interval of the attribute is divided into required number of sub-intervals containing approximately the same number of data points (fig. 2a). Mostly, this approach allows to obtain sub-intervals better fitted to the characteristic of the attribute than the method of equal sub-intervals. However sometimes, especially when it is possible to find the clear clusters in the interval, it can result in an improper discretisation. An example of mentioned situation is shown in the fig. 2. If the discretisation of the attribute from the fig. 2b is based on the assumption of equal data points in each sub-interval, the clusters existed in the data set will not be separated from each other but the margin ones will be improperly split in the middle (fig. 2c). Naturally the proper discretisation of this attribute should look like in the fig. 2d.

The third popular automatic discretisation method is the method of average values. The discretisation process carried out according to this method begins with calculation of the arithmetic average of the data points contained in the attribute's variation interval. This average defines the splitting point, which is used for partitioning of the whole interval into two sub-intervals (fig. 3a). Next, the data from the first and second sub-intervals are averaged and two next splitting points are defined. These splitting points allow to divide the previous sub-intervals into next two sub-intervals (fig. 3b). The process is continued until the required number of sub-intervals is gained. Naturally, this method allows only for splitting the whole interval into even number of sub-intervals.

Like the methods presented before, also the method of average values is not suitable for each type of attributes. For example, the application of this method to

426

the attribute shown in the fig. 2b, will split the clusters existed in the data set (fig. 3c), instead of placing each of them into separate sub-intervals (fig. 2d).

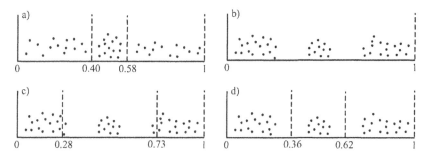

Fig. 2. The method of equal number of data points in sub-intervals

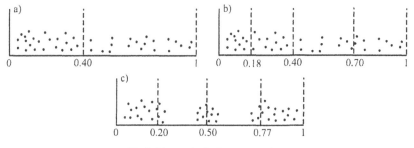

Fig.3. The method of average values

3   Case study

The influence of the discretisation method on the rough sets' skills to determine the most significant conditional attributes were analysed via a system of an unemployment in Poland in years 1992-2001. The decision attribute was the value of an unemployment rate and the conditional attributes were seven macroeconomic factors chosen on the basis of economic literature (tab. 1). The decision table contained 120 examples [5][6].

Symbol	Name	Symbol	Name
CA1	corporate income	CA5	rate of rediscount
CA2	sold production of industry	CA6	export
CA3	dollar's rate of exchange	CA7	number of inhabitants
CA4	money supply		

Tab. 1. Conditional attributes of the analysed system

Naturally, regarding the number of input variables and number of examples, the second approach to determine inputs' significance (from these presented in the section 1) had to be used. Hence, the task of the survey was set as follows: *find two attributes of the biggest importance for the analysed system.*

Since all attributes describing the system had continuous characteristics, all of them had to be discretised before the application of the rough sets theory. First the discretisation process was carried out with use of the methods described shortly in the section 2. The approximation quality of subsets containing different pairs of attributes obtained after applying in the discretisation process different discretisation methods is presented in the tab. 2. First column of the table contains numbers of attributes and three next columns - the approximation quality gained after applying succeeding methods: second column – the method of equal sub-intervals, third column – the method of intervals of equal number of data points, fourth column – the method of average values. The bold numbers inside the table underline the subsets of attributes of the best approximation quality.

No.	Method 1	Method 2	Method 3	No.	Method 1	Method 2	Method 3
1-2	0.133	0.008	0.108	3-4	0.000	0.000	0.042
1-3	0.017	0.008	0.042	3-5	0.000	0.017	0.017
1-4	0.050	0.017	0.017	3-6	0.042	0.025	0.108
1-5	0.025	0.017	0.017	3-7	0.142	0.017	0.183
1-6	0.008	0.108	0.142	4-5	**0.158**	0.050	0.117
1-7	0.017	0.017	**0.217**	4-6	0.008	0.067	0.150
2-3	0.058	0.017	0.033	4-7	0.000	0.150	0.200
2-4	0.067	0.008	0.067	5-6	0.017	0.133	0.000
2-5	0.000	0.067	0.017	5-7	0.017	0.117	0.183
2-6	0.000	0.017	0.000	6-7	0.000	**0.200**	0.183
2-7	0.025	0.183	0.183				

Tab. 2. The approximation quality of subsets containing different pairs of attributes

As it can be noticed (tab. 2), completely different pairs of attributes were pointed as the most important ones after applying different discretisation methods:

- method of equal sub-intervals: *money supply* and *rate of rediscount,*

- method of equal number of data points in sub-intervals: *export* and *number of inhabitants,*

- method of average values – *corporate income* and *number of inhabitants.*

At this stage of the analysis very important question appeared. How to decide which of three chosen subsets of attributes really contained the most significant attributes? In other words: which of these three methods was the most suitable for the examined system?

Naturally, the attributes' subsets chosen after application of different discretisation methods could not be compared on the basis of the approximation quality. The reason for this is that the approximation quality is not the absolute measure but is closely related to the values contained in the discretised decision table, which is naturally completely different in each case. Therefore, another method had to be used to compare the results obtained after the application of different discretisation methods.

In order to deal with this task, a set of neural models (10 models per each pair of attributes) was constructed. The parameters of neural networks used in the modelling process were as follows [2][3] (fig. 4):

- flow of signals: one-way;

- architecture of connections between layers: all to all;

- hidden layers: 1 hidden layer with 5 sigmoid neurons;

- output layer: 1 linear neuron;

- training method: backpropagation algorithm with momentum and changing learning rates;

- length of the training process – 20.000 epochs;

- testing method: 16-cross-fold validation.

The models' performance was compared on the basis of the mean absolute error:

$$MAE = \frac{1}{n}\sum_{i=1}^{n} |\, \hat{y}_i - y_i \,| \qquad (2)$$

where: y_i - real outputs, $\hat{y}_i$ - modelled outputs, n - number of data points.

After the training process one model per each pair of attributes (non-overfitted and characterised by the smallest mean absolute error) was chosen to the further analysis. The errors of the chosen models are presented in the tab. 3. This table shows that the most precise model was created when the method of sub-intervals of equal number of data points was applied in the discretisation process. Its error was equal to 5.15%. The models created on the basis of two other discretisation methods were less precise: 5.70% (the method of average values) and 8.25% (the method of equal sub-intervals).

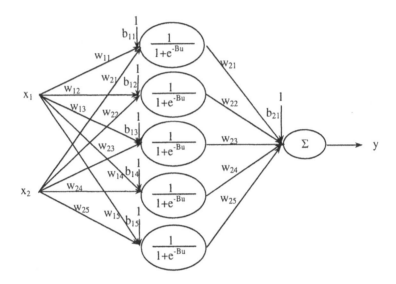

Fig. 4. A scheme of a neural network used in the modelling process

No.	Error [%]	No.	Error [%]	No.	Error [%]	No.	Error [%]
1-2	14.11	2-3	17.71	3-4	6.55	4-6	7.13
1-3	13.51	2-4	7.28	3-5	14.65	**4-7**	**2.90**
1-4	5.78	2-5	15.91	3-6	12.10	5-6	11.20
1-5	12.79	2-6	13.86	3-7	8.69	5-7	8.25
1-6	11.35	2-7	8.45	4-5	8.25	6-7	5.15
1-7	5.70						

Tab. 3. The absolute errors of neural models built on the base of all pairs of attributes

The application of the discretisation method of sub-intervals of equal number of data points allowed to gain better results than the application of the other methods. However, as it can be observed in the tab. 3, the chosen subset of attributes was not the best one. There is another pair of attributes in the tab. 3 which allowed to construct almost twice better fitted model than the pair chosen after application of the method mentioned above. Hence the question is: is it really reasonable to use rough set theory for determining inputs' significance in the systems of non-discrete attributes? As it will be shown below, the answer is affirmative but only

430

under one condition – each continuous attribute describing the analysed system has to be discretised separately according to its own characteristic. That means the discretisation process has to be carried out with the expert method.

The expert method which was used to discretise the attributes of the analysed system is based on placing the splitting lines in the discontinuous areas of the attribute's variation interval or in areas in which the slope of the data chain changes rapidly. The reason for such approach is that the discontinuous areas point to the borders of clusters existing in the data set and the slopes' changes point the areas of more (rapid areas) and less (flat areas) density. Naturally, in case of attributes which have no characteristic areas, the discretisation process can be carried out with one of the methods described in the section 2. In such case it is often of no importance which method will be used because lack of discontinuities and inflexions means that the data are equally distributed in the whole data range.

The results of the application of the expert method to discretisation of attributes describing the analysed system are shown in the fig. 5.

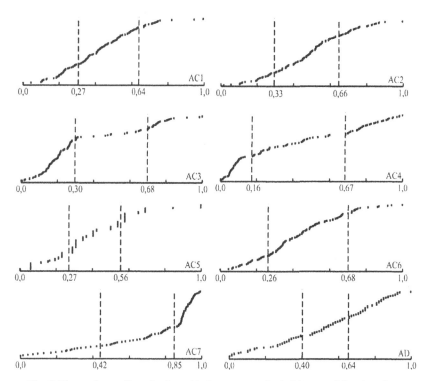

Fig. 5. The attributes discretisation with the expert method; CA – conditional attribute (numbers like in the tab. 1); DC – decision attribute

After discretisation of the attributes of the analysed system, once again the approximation quality for each subset of attributes was calculated (tab. 4). As it can be noticed the application of the expert method in the discretisation process allowed to choose the real most important attributes for the analysed system, i.e. the attributes *money supply* and *number of inhabitants*.

No.	Approximation quality	No.	Approximation quality	No.	Approximation quality	No.	Approximation quality
1-2	0.100	2-3	0.000	3-5	0.017	5-6	0.067
1-3	0.042	2-4	0.017	3-6	0.033	5-7	0.108
1-4	0.017	2-5	0.017	3-7	0.175	6-7	0.058
1-5	0.100	2-6	0.000	4-5	0.117		
1-6	0.133	2-7	0.200	4-6	0.158		
1-7	0.192	3-4	0.042	**4-7**	**0.208**		

Tab. 4. The approximation quality of the subsets containing different pairs of attributes (discretisation with the expert method)

4 Conclusion

The rough sets theory can be successfully applied in the process of determining inputs' significance not only in discrete but also in continuous systems. Naturally, before it will be applied in the system described by continuous attributes, all of them have to be discretised.

In the real world it is very difficult to find systems which attributes behave in a similar way. Normally, each attribute has its own characteristic what causes it cannot be treated in the same way as the other ones. Hence, very important is to remember that the discretisation process should not be carried out with the automatic discretisation methods. Instead of this, each continuous attribute has to be discretised separately, after careful analysis, according to its own characteristic.

5 References

[1] Czerniak J., Zarzycki H., "Application of rough sets in the presumptive diagnosis of urinary system diseases", Proceedings on 9th International Conference, ACS'2002, pp. 43-51, Kluwer Academic Publisher, London, 2003.

[2] Demuth H. Beale M., "Neural Network Toolbox User's Guide", The Math Works Inc., Natick MA USA, 2000.

432

[3] Masters T., "Practical Neural Network Recipes in C++", The Scientific-Technical Publishing House, Warsaw, 1996.

[4] Pelczar M., "Rough Sets Using for Medical Services Costs Modeling in Decision Support System", 9th International Conference, ACS'2002, Informa, Szczecin, 2002.

[5] Rejer I., "The Method of Modeling the Multi-dimensional System with Artificial Intelligence Methods on the Example of an Unemployment in Poland", The Scientific Publishing House of the Szczecin University, Szczecin, 2003.

[6] Rejer I., Piegat A., "A Method of Investigating a Significance of Input Variables in Non-Linear High-Dimensional Systems", Proceedings on 9th International Conference, ACS'2002, pp. 73-80, Kluwer Academic Publisher, London, 2002.

Semi-Markov process in performance evaluation of asynchronous processors

Wojciech Kadlubowski

Technical University of Szczecin

26 Kwietnia 10, 71-126 Szczecin, Poland

e-mail: wk@ps.pl

Abstract: A novel model of asynchronous processors for performance analysis is presented. The method of performance evaluation by Semi-Markov simulation is described.

Keywords: Simulation, asynchronous processor, Semi-Markov model

1   Introduction

There is no fixed cycle in asynchronous processors. All interactions between components are synchronised by handshaking. The state of processor is altered after each interaction. Usually trace driven simulators, in which simulation time depends on the length of benchmark, are used for performance evaluation of processors [1], [2]. The simulations have to be performed for each configuration of the processor and for each benchmark. In this method the trace of benchmark is analysed one time only. Simulation time is independent of length of the trace. Except performance evaluation, the stochastic method gives additional information about interactions between components of a processor. Researchers usually take into account an input cycle of the asynchronous processor [3], [4]. It describes average behaviour of the processor during execution of a program. There are also other important performance parameters like e.g. occupation of components. In order to get performance parameters we use a Semi-Markov process [5], which describes behaviour of asynchronous processor. For this process, steady state distribution is calculated and then performance parameter is obtained. Stochastic performance evaluation for synchronous processors is presented in [6].

2   Model of asynchronous processor

2.1   General Model

A general model of asynchronous processors consists of components whose work is synchronized by handshaking. We can consider both, superscalar and superpipeline microarchitecture (see Fig. 1). Presented pipeline includes n stages. Each stage consists of m components. It is assumed, that pipeline of length n can be split into p new pipelines (see Fig.2). . Each of p pipelines has length n_p.

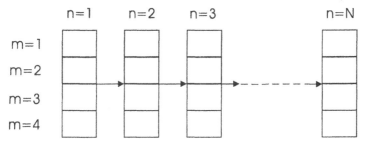

Fig.1. The model of superpipelined and superscalar processor

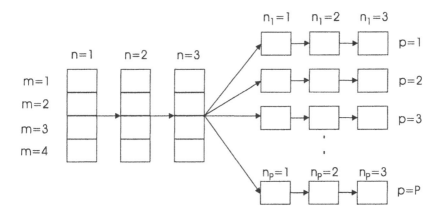

Fig.2. The model of superpipelined and superscalar processor with many execution pipes

Stages n_1-n_n represent first stages of processor (e.g. instruction fetch, instruction decode, etc.). Each of p pipelines represents functional unit of the processor (e.g. integer unit, floating point unit etc.). In-order execution of instructions is assumed.

Instruction, after completion in current stage, is sent to the next stage as soon as possible (i.e. when next stage is idle). In order to perform stochastic simulations we need to analyse particular model of the processor and create related Semi-Markov process (see [7], [8]).

2.2 Detailed Model

Detailed model depends on the delays connected with each component. The model presented in this paper is different from the one described in [7], [8]. We drop the idea of execution phases related directly to input cycle of the processor and use clocks connected with each component. When instruction enters into component, appropriate clock is set up. Setup value $k_{i\,max}$ is equal to delay of component. Clock related to given component is counted down to zero during execution of an instruction. When clocks reaches zero, instruction can move to a next component (if next one is idle), or is blocked (if next one is busy). The model presented here is more flexible than in [7], and very useful in case of calculation performance parameter other than input cycle.

The state of the model is represented by set of variables:

$$x_i, k_i, y_i, s_i$$

where

- x_i are connected with components of the processor and describe their idle or busy states. Variable x_i takes value 1 when there is an instruction in corresponding component and value 0 when the component is empty

- k_i represent execution phase of instruction in x_i and is described by related clock; $k_{i\,max}$ means delay of components

- y_i describe type of instruction in x_i

- s_i describe dependency distance of instruction in x_i from previous instruction (i.e. instruction in other components being ahead of pipeline); e.g. 0 means instruction is dependent on previous instruction, 1 instruction is dependent on second previous instruction (see [6])

The state of the model, which is defined above, allows the designer to look at the changes that occur in asynchronous processor. Processor move from one state to another when any instruction in the processor moves from one component to another one.

Number of variables x_i and k_i in the detailed model may vary, when the model with other number of components is considered. When delays connected with the components are different, then values of k_i are different as well. In every case we need to create separate Semi-Markov process.

3   Creation of Semi-Markov process

An analysis of the instruction trace can be done independently from the model of the processor (see [6], [7], [8]). The sequences of instructions are counted and sequence probabilities are calculated. Based on the processor model and instruction sequence a Semi-Markov process is constructed. This process describes behaviour of asynchronous processor. Next steady state probabilities are calculated and sojourn time for each state is estimated.

Calculation of the performance parameters consists of two parts:

- The matrices P and S, which define Semi-Markov process (see [5]), are created (P is probability matrix for Embedded Markov Chain and S describe sojourn time probabilities of the process).

- Based on steady state distributions the performance parameters for asynchronous processor are calculated:

  o   Particular states related to given performance parameter are identified (e.g. states in which occur blocking of fetch component).

  o   Probability of these states is calculated

  o   Performance parameters are calculated

For example, when we have sojourn time of every state and steady state distribution of Semi-Markov process, then we can calculate average cycle of the asynchronous processor.

4   Case study

A simple model of asynchronous processor is considered in this paragraph. There are four components which represent Instruction Fetch (IF), Instruction Decoder (ID), Functional Unit X (FU_X - execute instructions of type X) and Functional Unit Y (FU_Y execute instructions of type Y) (see [7], [8]). The component IF represents fetch stage and ID describes decode stage of the processor. Functional unit X (Y) corresponds to execution stages for instruction X (Y).

A configuration of the processor is:

$$m=1, n=2, p=2, n_{1max}=1, n_{2max}=1$$

d(IF) = 3 unit of time   d(ID) = 2 unit of time,

d(FU_X) = 5 unit of timed   d(FU_Y) = 8 unit of time

where d( ) means delay of a component

4.1 Definition of the state in the considered model

The state of the model for given delays is represented by variables:

$x_1, x_2, x_3, x_4, k_1, k_2, k_3, k_4$

where:

- x_1, x_2 are connected with fetch and decode of the processor. They can take value:

  - x - when there is an instruction of type x

  - y - when there is an instruction of type y

  - 0 - when there is no instruction in component.

In order to reduce state space, we combined (for fetch and decode) the type of instruction represented by variable y_i with occupation of components represented by x_i in one variable x_i.

- x_3, x_4 are connected with FU_X and FU_Y respectively. They can take value 1 when there is an instruction in corresponding component and value 0 when the component is empty.

- k_i represent execution phase in x_i describe by related clock; $k_{i\,max}$ means delay of components

Presented model is very simple but useful in explanation of the main idea. Much more complicated models can be constructed, as well.

For these delays the detailed model of asynchronous processor will be created. Different delay of components can introduce blocking or starving (see [7]) in interactions between them. In our example first two components (IF and ID) can suffer from blocking and instruction decoder ID can suffer from starving. The delays presented above were chosen in order to show non-trivial relation between components of the processor. In Tab.1, an example of the instruction trace is presented. We assume that asynchronous processor computes this trace in an infinite loop (i.e. after instruction i_{21} comes instruction i_0, see Fig.3.).

In Tab.2 several cycles together with related states of the processor are presented. First column includes states that correspond to model of the processor in [7]. Second column includes states of the processor for model discussed in this paper.

In next eight columns variables, that describe state of the processor, are presented. In last column sojourn time of the state is given.

instruction no.	i_0	i_1	i_2	i_3	i_4	i_5	i_6	i_7	i_8	i_9	i_{10}
instruction type	Y	y	y	x	y	x	y	X	y	x	Y
instruction no	i_{11}	i_{12}	i_{13}	i_{14}	i_{15}	i_{16}	i_{17}	i_{18}	i_{19}	i_{20}	i_{21}
instruction type	X	x	x	x	y	y	y	X	x	x	X

Tab.1. Example of instruction trace

state in old model	state in current model	x_1	k_1	x_2	k_2	x_3	k_3	x_4	k_4	τ_1
0	0	y	3	x	2	1	5	0	0	5
1	1	y	3	y	2	1	5	0	0	2
	2	y	1	0	0	1	3	1	8	1
2	3	y	3	y	2	1	2	1	7	2
	4	y	1	y	0	0	0	1	5	5
3	5	x	3	y	2	0	0	1	8	8
4	6	x	3	x	2	0	0	1	8	2
	7	x	1	0	0	x	5	1	6	1

Tab.2. The states of processor in first cycles

In Fig.3 there are four charts (IF, ID, FU_X, FU_Y) which present instruction flow in components of the processor. There is time scale at the bottom of the picture. Above it, two periods are presented. Variable c_0 and c_1 represent number connected to sojourn time in state in old model ([7], [8]), and in current model respectively. The instructions computed in components are shown as rectangles with instruction number; e.g. i_3 means the third instruction. Each rectangle denotes execution period of the instruction in a component. We have to be careful, because the rectangle does not mean the occupation of the component by the instruction. For example rectangle i_3 in the chart IF shows only the execution of instruction i_3 in fetch (execution last 3 units of time). Later this instruction stays in fetch for next 2 units due to blocking of fetch by instruction decoder. Blocking is expressed by B and starving by S. An input cycle is defined as a period between the start of execution of two consecutive instructions in fetch. A length of every input cycle can be different and is determined by timing relation between components.

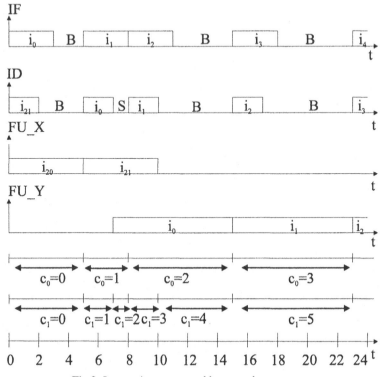

Fig.3. Instruction computed by asynchronous processor

Identification of states and instruction sequences related to them is similar to identification described in [8].

The model presented here does not work with input cycle directly. Instead, we have periods c_i (see Fig.3), which represent duration of states.

At the beginning of period $c_1=0$ we have:

- instruction i_0 enters fetch $\rightarrow x_1=y$, $k_1=k_{1max}=3$

- instruction i_{21} enters decode $\rightarrow x_2=x$, $k_2=k_{2max}=2$

- instruction i_{20} enters functional unit X $\rightarrow x_3=1$, $k_3=k_{3max}=5$

- no instruction in functional unit Y $\rightarrow x_4=0$, $k_4=0$

Execution in instruction decoder is completed (after 2 units of time), but the instruction is blocked because functional unit X is still busy (instruction i_1). After

5 units of time execution of the instruction i_{20} is completed and processor goes to next state.

At the beginning of the period $c_1=1$ we have:

- instruction i_1 enters fetch $\rightarrow x_1=y, \quad k_1=k_{1max}=3$
- instruction i_0 enters decode $\rightarrow x_2=y, \quad k_2=k_{2max}=2$
- instruction i_{21} enters functional unit X $\rightarrow x_3=1, \quad k_3=k_{3max}=5$
- no instruction in functional unit Y $\rightarrow x_4=0, \quad k_4=0$

Execution in instruction decoder is completed after 2 units of time. Then instruction moves to next component and processor enters new state.

At the beginning of the period $c_1=2$ we have:

- instruction i_1 is executed in fetch $\rightarrow x_1=y, \quad k_1=1$
- no instruction in decode $\rightarrow x_2=0, \quad k_2=0$
- instruction i_{21} is executed in functional unit X $\rightarrow x_3=1, \quad k_3=3$
- instruction i_0 enters functional unit Y $\rightarrow x_4=y, \quad k_4=k_{4max}=8$

Execution in instruction fetch is completed (after 1 unit of time), and instruction moves to next component. Processor enters next state.

At the beginning of the period $c_1=3$ we have:

- instruction i_2 enters fetch $\rightarrow x_1=y, \quad k_1=k_{1max}=3$
- instruction i_1 enters decode $\rightarrow x_2=y, \quad k_2=k_{2max}=2$
- instruction i_{21} is executed in functional unit X $\rightarrow x_3=1, \quad k_3=2$
- instruction i_0 is executed in functional unit Y $\rightarrow x_4=1, \quad k_4=7$

Execution of instruction in functional unit X is completed (after 2 units of time) and processor goes to new state.

Matrix P for Embedded Markov chain is created according to method described in [7]. In next step steady state distribution π for this chain is calculated. Then long time behavior probability φ for Semi-Markov chain can be computed according to equation (1) (see also [5]).

$$\varphi_j = \frac{\pi_j \cdot \tau_j}{\sum_{j=1}^{N} \pi_j \cdot \tau_j} \tag{1}$$

φ_j - long time behavior probability of Semi-Markov chain

π_j – steady state probability of Embedded Markov chain

τ_j - average sojourn time in state j

In Tab. 3 long time behavior probability distribution of Semi-Markov process is presented (for considered model and for given instruction trace).

φ_0	φ_1	Φ_2	φ_3	φ_4
0,0983	0,0393	0,0196	0,0393	0,0983
φ_5	φ_6	Φ_7	φ_8	φ_9
0,15573	0,0393	0,0196	0,0786	0,0196
φ_{10}	φ_{11}	φ_{12}	φ_{13}	φ_{14}
0,0786	0,0779	0,0389	0,1558	0,0389

Tab.3 Long time behavior probability distribution of Semi- Markov process

5 Conclusions

The stochastic simulation method has a small relative error comparing with trace-based simulation (see results in Tab.4 and Tab.5). Therefore we can use the first method in performance evaluation of asynchronous processors. Presented method is independent from the length of a trace. It is an important advantage, because trace-based simulation can last many hours or even several days. We are able to identify the state of an asynchronous processor based on limited sequence of instructions. An additional advantage of this method is an analysis of interactions between components of the asynchronous processor. The main goal of this paper was the explanation of the method. Therefore the presented example was very simple. However we are able to create and analyze more complicated models. We can avoid state space explosion problem by using partitioned Markov chains [6]. The processor model presented in this paper is more suitable for stochastic simulation than demonstrated in [7], [8].

	Average input cycle time (in units of time)	
Benchmark	Trace simulation	Stochastic simulation
Trace (from this paper)	4.6363	4.6385

Tab.4. Results of trace and stochastic simulation

	Blocking b in units of time					
	b=1 unit	b=2units	b=3 units	b=4 units	b=5 units	b=6 units
IF blocking - stochastic simulation	0,09755	0,07862	0	0,07864	0,09831	0
ID blocking – trace simulation	0,09803	0,07843	0	0,07843	0,09803	0
ID blocking - stochastic simulation	0,0389	0,1172	0,11793	0	0,0983	0,11797
ID blocking – trace simulation	0,03921	0,11764	0,11764	0	0,09803	0,11764

Tab.5. Probability of finding component blocked during execution of the trace

6   References

[1] F.P. Burns, A. Koelmans, A. Yakovlev – Analysing Superscalar Processor Architecture with Coloured Petri Nets, Intern. Journal SITT, 1998, p. 182-191

[2] T.D. Diep, J.P. Shen, M. Phillip, EXPROLER: A Retargetable and visualisation-based trace driven simulator, Proc. Micro-26, p. 225-235, 1993

[3] T. Nanya, TITAC-2: An asynchronous 32-bit microprocessor based on Scalable-Delay Insensitive model, University of Tokyo, 1998

[4] S.M. Burns, A. J. Martin, Performance analysis and optimisation of asynchronous circuits, in Advanced Research in VLSI Conference, Santa Cruse, CA, March 1991

[5] R. Howard, Dynamic probabilistic systems, Vol. II. Wiley & Sons 1971

[6] D.N. Noonburg, J.P. Shen A framework for statistical modelling of superscalar processor performance, Proceedings of HPCA '97, 1997

[7] W. Kadłubowski, The model of asynchronous processor for stochastic simulation method, ACS2004, Elk 2004, Poland

[8] W. Kadłubowski, Stochastic simulation in performance evaluation of asynchronous processors, ACS2004, Elk 2004, Poland

Organization of the modeling and simulation of the discrete processes

Emma Kushtina[1], Alexandre Dolgui[2], Bartlomiej Malachowski[1]

[1] Technical University of Szczecin
mkushtina@wi.ps.pl, bmalachowski@wi.ps.pl
[2] Ecole Nationale Supérieure des Mines de Saint-Etienne
dolgui@emse.fr

Abstract: In this article a methodology of queuing systems simulation models development is presented. A proper definition of simulation experiment specifications is difficult due to variety of conceptual models (ontologies) used to formulate a preliminary assumptions of a task. The proposed methodology is based on modeling using analytical methods and next, thanks to mapping principals, on translating notions from analytical model to simulation one.

Keywords: queuing systems, simulation, modeling, conceptual model, ontology, taxonomy, fundamental and procedural knowledge

1 Introduction

High accessibility and variety of simulation software gives wide capabilities of modeling and simulation of real phenomenons from different domains (telecommunication, production processes, logistics etc.). This software is invaluable tool for designing, optimisation, planning etc. The development of a simulation model requires a preliminary specification and a description of a problem from a specific domain. These assumptions highly depend on a problem domain and are described by its characteristic notions and notations. The problem description often has incoherent structure and very often, it is a simple verbal description.

High notions diversity and weak exactness of preliminary assumptions of a task create serious problems on the stage of modeling. The main issue is to correctly translate notions of a given domain to the notions and functions of specific simulation software, i.e. to a set of notions of some procedural knowledge.

Simulation packages often contains a templates library of models from different domains, however these models are usually highly simplified, unsatisfactorily flexible and they are generally delimited to the most frequent cases. On the other hand, simulation software supports very well whole classes of problems from certain subject of the mathematics, i.e. some fundamental (theoretical) knowledge, which has a specific structure and taxonomy. In this case, there usually exists an official conceptual model, mathematical engine and a notation, which allows describing of a problem very precisely (for example Kendall Notation for Queuing Systems). Thus, assumptions prepared using notions from widely known mathematical engine and its notation are much easier to translate to a set of notions used by certain simulation environment then a direct translating from imprecise notions of a domain (Figure 1). It corresponds with the transition from a set of notions of some fundamental knowledge to a set of notions of some procedural knowledge [1].

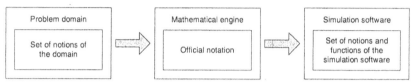

Fig. 1. Phases of the formulation of simulation experiment assumptions

Finding suitable mathematical engine, the most adequate one to describe an analyzed problem, is possible thanks to taxonomy of the mathematics. Strict hierarchy of all subjects of the mathematics helps to find a suitable mathematical engine. A good example of the taxonomic classification of the mathematics is *2000 Mathematics Subject Classification* (MSC2000) [2].

In the modeling and simulation process two main phases can be distinguished: 1) the development of the simulation model structure, 2) the creation of a mechanism which aids the identification and storing of developed models. It is obvious that the first phase is the most significant, but the second one, organized for example as a repository, is also very important, considering the need of future models utilization. Such repository is the basis of an intelligent system, which can automate research in the field of creating assumptions of simulation experiment. Realization of such repository requires adequate soft- and hardware as well as highly skilled staff.

In this article the process of simulation experiment assumptions development is presented for the class of problems, which can be modeled using queuing systems theory and simulation software ARENA from *Rockwell Software Inc.*

2   Structure of the simulation model

Simulation model assumptions are expressed in notions, which are characteristic for a given simulation package. These notions create a description language used to formulate requirements of a simulation experiment. However, the preparation of these requirements would be impossible without prior assumptions of the task from a given domain. These assumptions are hard to translate to a language (set of notions) of simulation software. Therefore, in simulation modeling an intermediate analytical model is often used, because it is much easier to simulate it using chosen simulation package.

The detailed structure of the simulation model is presented in Figure 2.

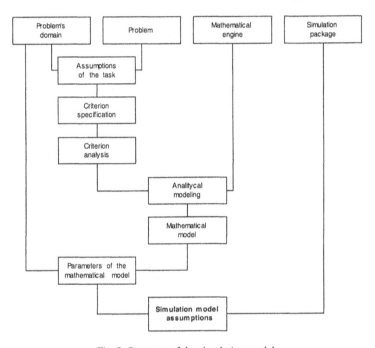

Fig. 2. Structure of the simulation model

Specification of the criterion of the model research is very important stage in the process of preparing the simulation model. When the criterion is specified it is necessary to carry out its precise analysis in order to examine its character (continuous or discrete), to find significant parameters etc. A task with a correctly analyzed criterion can be modeled using suitable mathematical engine and formulated as a criterion function. Analytical model prepared in this way, can then be easily transformed into simulation model using mapping principles. The mapping is carried out by finding direct equivalents of notions from two different conceptual models, where the first one represents some fundamental knowledge and the second one some procedural knowledge. An example of mapping of notions of Kendall Notation (notation used to describe queuing systems) into the environment of the simulation package ARENA.

3 Mapping on the example of Kendall Notation and simulation package ARENA

Kendall Notation is one of the most frequently used notations to describe queuing systems. It enables characterizing the system very precisely, its internal structure and parameters of input and output streams [3, 4].

Taxonomic hierarchy of notions classified by Kendall Notation is depicted in Figure 3.

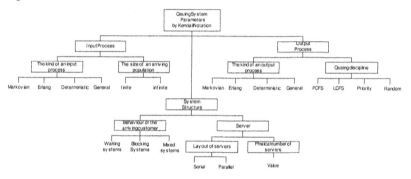

Fig. 3. Conceptual model of queuing systems according to Kendall Notation

ARENA from *Rockwell Software Inc.* is the flow oriented simulation package, designed to simulate stochastic processes. The package was developed on the basis of language SIMAN. ARENA thanks to many predefined modules, designed to build models from different domains, is suitable to simulate queuing systems. Simulation of this class of systems is obtained by certain settings of the ARENA modules. Names of the ARENA functions differ significantly from notions of the Kendall Notation. Therefore, it is necessary to detect direct equivalents of notions from two different conceptual models.

The hierarchic tree of ARENA functions used to simulate queuing systems is presented in figure 4.

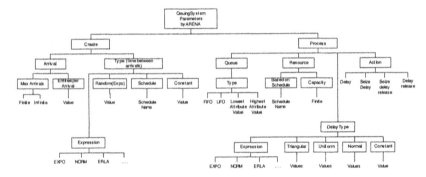

Fig. 4. Conceptual model of the ARENA functions used to simulate queuing systems

3.1 Mapping of notions related to the input stream of the queuing system

The direct equivalent of the *input stream* in the environment of ARENA is its module *Create*. By setting its parameters it is possible to model almost every configuration of the input stream, which can be expressed using Kendall Notation. All equivalents of the input stream notions are presented in Figure 5.

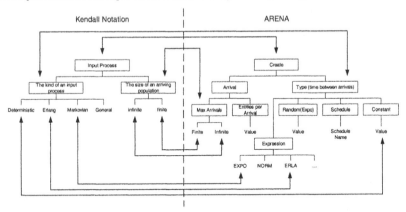

Fig. 5. Mapping of notions related to the input stream of the queuing system

448

3.2 Mapping of notions related to the queuing system's structure

Responsible for the queuing system's structure is ARENA module *Process*. It can easily simulate multi-channel queuing system with parallel servers and unlimited queue, i.e. *Waiting System* in the conceptual model of Kendal Notation. *Blocking Systems* (systems without a queue) and *Mixed Systems* (with limited queue) are impossible to direct simulation using *Process* module. In order to simulate these types of systems it is necessary to use additional modules which set certain boundaries on a queue. Impossible to direct modeling are also systems with serial layout of servers, in this case the problem can be solved by serial connection of several *Process* modules.

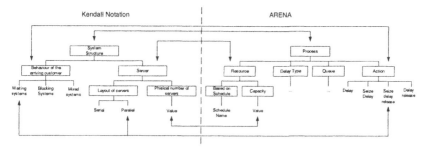

Fig. 6. Mapping of notions related to the queuing system's structure

3.3 Mapping of notions related to the output stream of the queuing system

Parameters of the output stream are set, similarly as in case of system's structure, in *Process* module of ARENA package. The mapping principles for the output stream are shown in Figure 7.

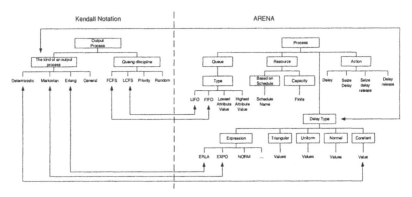

Fig. 7. Mapping of notions related to the output stream of the queuing system

4   Algorithm of the simulation model's development

The algorithm of the simulation model's development was prepared on the basis of the simulation model's structure presented in Section 2 of this article (see Figure 2). Basing on the problem definition and the queuing systems mathematical engine it is necessary to specify the most significant unit of the model, i.e. an elementary event on the input of the system. Additionally, all parameters of a stream of these events should be determined, its average intensity and the character of the inter-arrival time (stochastic or deterministic). If the input stream is stochastic it is necessary to find the probability density function of the inter-arrival times. On the input of the queuing system different events can occur and they can be classified into several classes. Occurrences of events of one class form one input stream, thus, it is important to determine parameters of every input stream of the queuing system.

Process of the elementary event definition is crucial to the model of the queuing system. Therefore, this process should be repeated many times in order to exactly analyze the given problem. It is possible that a problem, which seems to be solvable using queuing systems theory, after a detailed analysis prove to be impossible to model in this way. This process can be illustrated on the example of the office secretary. Her work consists of several kinds of jobs. These jobs flow in random time intervals and their execution last also a random time. Therefore, the work of a secretary seems to be possible to model as an open queuing system. After detailed examination of her duties it proves, that defying an elementary event (being a job to be done) and its stream is very difficult. The work of a secretary has a very uneven character. She does many kinds of jobs, sometimes very unconventional, for example: helping her principal in preparing documents, answering the phone calls, making the appointments, serving the clients, preparing the documents for the accountancy and sometimes, even preparing small meals for office employees. Some of these jobs can have higher priority and must be done immediately, some of them can be delayed. Taking all this facts into consideration it turns out that better tool to model this type of work is the Gant Chart.

On the above-mentioned example, it was justified that verification of the elementary event definition is necessary in order to develop a correct queuing system model.

The good example of a system, which can by modeled using queuing system theory, is a cashier in the bank. In the simplest case, such person does only two types of jobs. The cashier makes payments and withdrawals of the cash for the arriving customers. Thus, it is easy to distinguish two streams of events: the stream of payments and the stream of withdrawals. This gives a simple queuing system, with one server, two classes of jobs and limited input queue.

When the verification process is finished and the definition of the elementary event is correct, then, it is necessary to formulate the assumptions of the simulation experiment. These assumptions are defined using the notions and functions of ARENA. The transformation from the mathematical into the simulation model is carried out according to mapping principles presented in Section 3.

The algorithm of the simulation model development is shown in Figure 8.

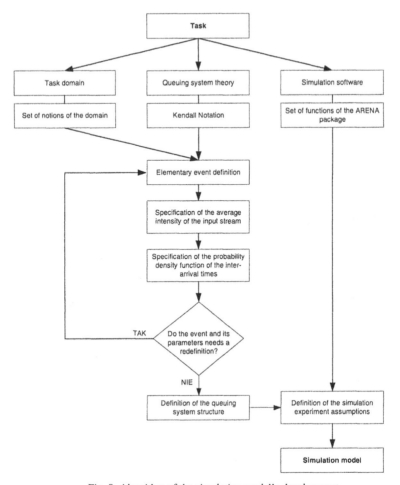

Fig. 8. Algorithm of the simulation model's development

To sum up, the algorithm of the simulation model's development proceeds in the following stages:

1. Specification of the assumptions of the task from the given domain.
2. Definition of the elementary event and parameters of the stream of these events.
3. Cyclic redefinition of the elementary event. This process is finished if there is a certainty that the problem can be solved by modeling it as a queuing system.
4. Specification of the queuing system structure.
5. Preparation of the simulation model in the ARENA environment.

5 Conclusion

The methodology of elaboration of the simulation model in the ARENA environment was presented in this article. This methodology particularly focuses on the subject of modeling the queuing systems. The proposed algorithm of queuing system elaboration is based on the simulation model structure (Section 2), which includes several different conceptual models. It creates the necessity to find the direct equivalents of notions from different conceptual models. The notions mapping principals was described in Section 3 of this article. Thanks to this principals it is possible to easily transform an analytical model, prepared using queuing systems theory and Kendall Notations, into a simulation model in the environment of the simulation package ARENA.

6 References

[1] Kushtina E., Rozewski P. (2003), "An approach to the formation of the formal description of the domain theoretical knowledge", In: Studziński J., Drelichowski L., Hryniewicz O. (Eds.), "Applications of the Computer Sciences and Operational Research in the Management". Operational Research Institute of The Polish Academy of Science, Vol. 33, pp. 29-402.

[2] "Mathematics Subject Classification", http://www.ams.org/msc/index.html

[3] Zaikin O. (2002), "Queuing Modelling of Supply Chain in Intelligent Production", Faculty of Computer Science and Information Systems – Technical University of Szczecin.

[4] Kleinrock L. (1976), "Queueing Systems", John Wiley & Sons, New York.

The Jeep Problem, searching for the best strategy with a genetic algorithm

Przemysław Klęsk

ul. Emilii Plater 96/57, 71-635 Szczecin, Poland

Abstract:
In the Jeep Problem, the goal is to maximize the distance the jeep can penetrate into the desert using a given quantity of fuel. The jeep must not take all the fuel from the base at once. The jeep is allowed to go forward, unload some fuel, and then return to its base using the fuel remaining in its tank. At the base, it may refuel and set out again. When it reaches the fuel it has stored previously, it may use it to fill up its tank. This paper describes an attempt of solving this problem (finding the best strategy for the jeep) with a genetic algorithm. Experiments with both binary and real-coded GAs were performed.

Keywords: The jeep problem, optimization, genetic algorithm

1   Introduction

A jeep on a desert is given a certain quantity of fuel, be it n containers with 1 unit of fuel each. The consumption of fuel is 1 to 1, i.e. 1 unit of fuel per 1 unit of distance. The goal of the jeep is to maximize the distance D_n it can penetrate into the desert obeying rules as follows. The jeep can fill its tank with up to 1 unit of fuel at a time and must not take any extra fuel with it. The jeep is allowed to go forward, unload some fuel, and then return to its base using the fuel remaining in its tank. At the base, it may refuel and set out again. When it reaches the fuel it has stored previously, it may use it to fill up its tank. Sometimes this problem is also called the *exploration problem* [6], [1].

Intuitively, one might guess that the jeep needs to make several preparatory runs first and set up several fueling points along the way, so that they may be used later. To achieve the best result, one must find the optimal distribution of such points plus the optimal quantities of fuel to leave at each point.

454

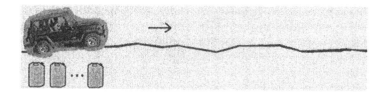

Fig. 1. Jeep with n containers of fuel on the desert.

The correct solution to the problem is as follows. For the very smallest case of $n = 0$, the jeep is not able to set out and the $D_0 = 0$. For $n = 1$, the jeep fills its tank with the single unit available and covers $D_1 = 1$ unit of distance. For $n = 2$: the jeep travels the way of $\frac{1}{3}$, leaves there $\frac{1}{3}$ of a unit of fuel, comes back to the base to refuel with the second unit, then again it travels the way of $\frac{1}{3}$, fills up the tank with $\frac{1}{3}$ left there before, and finally covers 1 more unit ending the journey at position of $D_2 = \frac{4}{3}$. Can the reader himself find now the solution for $n = 3$? How should the optimal journey for $n = 3$ proceed?

The right recursion for D_n is

$$D_0 = 0;$$

$$D_n = D_{n-1} + \frac{1}{2n-1}, \quad \text{for } n > 0. \tag{1}$$

The reasoning behind this recursion is that, when having found the solution to the problem for the case of $n - 1$ containers — i.e. knowing the optimal distribution of fueling points and quantities of fuel at those points, this solution can be used to find the solution for the greater case of n. What the jeep needs to do is simply to place 1 additional fueling point before all others, so that it can be now regarded as the new base. Then the jeep sets up the rest of fueling points, as if it was doing it for the case of $n - 1$. Therefore, the remaining points will be shifted further, relatively to the new point, but distances among them will be preserved as in the solution for $n - 1$. One should notice now that the new base needs to be crossed by the jeep $2(n - 2) + 1$ times (when traveling forth and back to fetch each of $n - 2$ containers from the original base; plus one more time when going forth on the final run using the last container). Because of this, the amount of fuel the jeep must leave at this new point is exactly equal to $(2(n - 2) + 1) / (2(n - 2) + 3)$. And the distance for the new point is therefore $1 / (2(n - 2) + 3) = 1 / (2n - 1)$, so that the jeep is able to get there, leave fuel, and return from there. Now, this explains the recursion (1). Please see also figure 2 where results for $n = 2$ and $n = 3$ are illustrated symbolically.

Let us now obtain the concise formula for D_n by rewriting it the following way:

$$D_n = D_{n-1} + \frac{1}{2n-1} = \sum_{k=1}^{n} \frac{1}{2k-1}$$

$$= 1 + \frac{1}{3} + \frac{1}{5} + \cdots + \frac{1}{2n-1}$$

$$= 1 + \frac{1}{3} + \frac{1}{5} + \cdots + \frac{1}{2n-1} + \frac{1}{2} + \frac{1}{4} + \cdots + \frac{1}{2n} - \frac{1}{2} - \frac{1}{4} - \cdots - \frac{1}{2n}$$

$$= H_{2n} - \frac{1}{2}\left(1 + \frac{1}{2} + \frac{1}{3} + \cdots + \frac{1}{n}\right)$$

$$= H_{2n} - \frac{1}{2}H_n, \quad \text{for } n > 0. \tag{2}$$

As one can see, the solution of the Jeep Problem "has something to do with" a special sum called the harmonic number, $H_n = \sum_{k=1}^{n} \frac{1}{k}$. The solutions for successive n are $0, 1, \frac{4}{3}, \frac{23}{15}, \frac{176}{105}, \frac{563}{315}, \ldots$

In a more general case not constrained to a natural n, when being given $n + \alpha$ as the quantity of fuel (with $0 \le \alpha < 1$), the solution is

$$D_{n+\alpha} = \frac{\alpha}{2n+1} + \sum_{k=1}^{n} \frac{1}{2k-1}$$

$$= \frac{\alpha}{2n+1} + \frac{1}{2}\left[\gamma + 2\ln 2 + \psi_0\left(\frac{1}{2} + n\right)\right], \quad \text{for } n > 0, \tag{3}$$

where γ is Euler-Mascheroni constant[1] and $\psi_0(z)$ the polygamma function[2]. The $\frac{1}{2}[\cdot]$ term is another way of producing the value of $H_{2n} - \frac{1}{2}H_n$, [6].

This paper describes an attempt of solving the Jeep Problem by means of a genetic algorithm. The author was trying to answer two main questions: 1. *can a genetic algorithm find the best strategy for the jeep?* — which can be understood roughly as finding the correct sequence of actions; 2. *can a genetic algorithm find the optimal quantities going with the best strategy?* — i.e. finding the right

---

[1] The Euler-Mascheroni constant is defined by the following series
$\gamma = \lim_{n \to \infty} \left(\sum_{k=1}^{n} \frac{1}{k} - \ln n\right) = \lim_{n \to \infty} (H_n - \ln n)$
$\gamma = 0.5772156649015328606065120900824024310 42\ldots$. It is not known if this constant is irrational, let alone transcendental [5].

[2] Polygamma function is given by the $(n+1)$st derivative of the logarithm of the gamma function $\Gamma(z)$, $\psi_n(z) = \frac{d^{n+1}}{dz^{n+1}} \ln \Gamma(z)$. Whereas $\Gamma(z)$ is the extension of the factorial to complex and real arguments, $\Gamma(z) = \int_0^{\infty} t^{z-1} e^{-t}\, dt$. See [7].

optimal values of distances to travel forth and back, and the optimal quantities of fuel to load or unload.

The author executed experiments with both binary and real-coded GAs. Details of genetic operations as well as results are described in the paper.

2 Representation of the jeep strategy - chromosome coding

In the Jeep Problem the strategy can be thought of as the sequence of actions, which describe the behavior of the jeep throughout the whole journey.

A single action in the strategy could be represented by the following pair *(type of action, value.*, where the *type of action* is one of: $\rightarrow$ (go forth), $\leftarrow$ (go back), $\uparrow$ (take fuel), $\downarrow$ (leave fuel); whereas the *value* denotes the length of travel or the quantity of fuel. Figure 2 shows the phenotypic representation of exemplary chromosomes, being actually the solutions for $n = 2$ and $n = 3$.

strategy for $n = 2$: $\left((\uparrow, 1), (\rightarrow, \frac{1}{3}), (\downarrow, \frac{1}{3}), (\leftarrow, \frac{1}{3}), (\uparrow, 1), (\rightarrow, \frac{1}{3}), (\uparrow, \frac{1}{3}), (\rightarrow, 1) \right)$

strategy for $n = 3$: $\big((\uparrow, 1), (\rightarrow, \frac{1}{5}), (\downarrow, \frac{3}{5}), (\leftarrow, \frac{1}{5}), (\uparrow, 1), (\rightarrow, \frac{1}{5}), (\uparrow, \frac{1}{5}), (\rightarrow, \frac{1}{3}), (\downarrow, \frac{1}{3}), (\leftarrow, \frac{1}{3}),$

$(\uparrow, \frac{1}{5}), (\leftarrow, \frac{1}{5}), (\uparrow, 1), (\rightarrow, \frac{1}{5}), (\uparrow, \frac{1}{5}), (\rightarrow, \frac{1}{3}), (\uparrow, \frac{1}{3}), (\rightarrow, 1) \big)$

Fig. 2. Phenotypic representation of chromosomes. The optimal solutions for $n = 2$ and $n = 3$.

In binary-coded chromosomes the bits related to *types of actions* were interlacing with bits related to *values*. The length of the former was always fixed to 2 bits, whereas for the latter the length was chosen depending on the size n of the problem. The greater the length dedicated to the *value* part, the greater the granularity of moving or fueling the jeep can make. Keeping in mind the harmonic number as being related to the solution, one notices that for $n = 2$ it is enough to use 2 bits for the *value,* which gives possible values: $\frac{0}{3}, \frac{1}{3}, \frac{2}{3}, \frac{3}{3}$. Further on, for $n = 3$, one can do with 4 bits[3], with possible values $\frac{0}{15}, \frac{1}{15}, \frac{2}{15}, \frac{3}{15} = \frac{1}{5}, \frac{4}{15}, \ldots, \frac{15}{15}$. Figure 5 illustrates the binary-coding of chromosomes.

---

[3] Actually, 4 would also be the next possible bit length for the *value* part, in case of $n = 2$.

As regards the real-coded chromosomes, their form is quite straightforward and corresponds strictly to the phenotypic representation, see figure 5. Genes for *type of action* and *value* interlace one after another. The *type of action* can be one of: $\{0, 1, 2, 3, 4\}$, whereas the *value* can be an arbitrary[4] real number from $[0; 1]$ interval.

For real-coded chromosomes it was necessary to introduce a small tolerance term ε when executing the journey of an artificial jeep. This was to allow the jeep to take fuel ($\uparrow$ action) from a certain neighborhood around its current position[5] x_k, i.e. from the range $(x_k - \varepsilon, x_k + \varepsilon)$. Obviously, this is not needed for the binary version, which makes the jeep travel only to discrete positions.

binary-coded chromosome: $\Big(0,0,1,1,1,0,1,0,0,1,0,1,1,0,0,1,0,1,0,0,1,1,0,1,$

$0,1,0,0,0,1,1,1,0,1,0,0,1,0,0,0,1,1,1,0,0,1,0,0 \Big)$

corresponding strategy: $\Big((\rightarrow, \frac{14}{15}), (\uparrow, \frac{6}{15}), (\uparrow, \frac{6}{15}), (\rightarrow, \frac{13}{15}), (\leftarrow, \frac{1}{15}), (\downarrow, \frac{4}{15}), (\uparrow, \frac{3}{15}), (\uparrow, \frac{4}{15}) \Big)$

Fig. 4. Exemplary binary-coded chromosome representing a jeep strategy. Bits in bold represent the types of actions: $0, 0$ — go forth; $0, 1$ — go back; $1, 0$ — take fuel; $1, 1$ — leave fuel. In the example, 4 bits were applied for each value part of an action, providing the granularity of $\frac{1}{15}$.

real-coded chromosome: $\Big(0, 0.233, 1, 0.958, 3, 0.192, 2, 0.55, 3, 0.01, 0, 0.78883, 1, 0.5, 2, 0.119 \Big)$

corresponding strategy: $\Big((\rightarrow, 0.233), (\leftarrow, 0.958), (\downarrow, 0.192), (\uparrow, 0.55), (\downarrow, 0.01), (\rightarrow, 0.78883),$

$(\leftarrow, 0.5), (\uparrow, 0.119) \Big)$

Fig. 5. Exemplary real-coded chromosome representing a jeep strategy. Genes in bold represent the types of actions: 0 — go forth; 1 — go back; 2 — take fuel; 3 — leave fuel.

How long should the chromosomes be, depending on the size n of the problem? Let's just consider here the length of the best strategy in steps, denoting it by S_n. Basing on this value the necessary chromosome length can be uniquely determined. Right is the following recursion

---

[4] Obviously, this depends on particular implementation of floating point numbers. The author was using the *double precision* floating point numbers from Java programming language, i.e. the standad 64-bit IEEE 754.

[5] k is the index of current step.

$$S_0 = 0;$$
$$S_n = S_{n-1} + 4 + 2(n-1) + 2(n-2), \quad \text{for } n > 0. \tag{4}$$

Comparing the strategy length S_n to S_{n-1}, the jeep needs: 4 additional steps to place the new fueling point — this will be the very first steps $\uparrow, \rightarrow, \downarrow, \leftarrow$; plus 2 additional steps to tank and arrive at the new fueling point on the way from the original base (this will happen for all $n-1$ remaining containers) — $\uparrow, \rightarrow$; plus 2 additional steps tank and to come back from the new fueling point on the way back to the base (this will happen for $n-2$ containers). Solving the recursion (4) one gets

$$S_n = S_{n-1} + 4 + 2(n-1) + 2(n-2) = S_{n-1} + 4n - 2$$
$$= S_{n-2} + 4(n-1) - 2 + 4n - 2$$
$$\vdots$$
$$= S_0 + 4\sum_{k=1}^{n} k - 2n = 4\frac{n+1}{2}n - 2n = 2n^2. \tag{5}$$

This means that for the Jeep Problem of size n, one must have chromosomes representing the strategies of length not shorter than $2n^2$.

Having found S_n, it is possible to assess the size of the search space the GA will tackle. E.g. for the first interesting case of $n = 2$, when using the binary-coded GA the cardinality of the search space is

$$\#\Omega = \left(\#\{\rightarrow, \leftarrow, \uparrow, \downarrow\} \right)^8 \cdot \left(\#\{(0,0),(0,1),(1,0),(1,1)\} \right)^8 = 4^8 4^8 = 4294967296, \tag{6}$$

provided that 2 bits were allocated for the *value* part of every step. For the case of $n = 3$ and with 4 bits per *value* one gets

$$\#\Omega = 4^{18} 16^{18} = 3,2451855365842672678315602057626e + 32, \tag{7}$$

which is a huge number — a huge space to search through.

As regards the real-coded GA the cardinality of search space is theoretically continuum[6]. Writing down the content of such an exemplary space for $n = 2$ it would be

---

[6] In the pure case it would be true. However, in computer implementation although very large, nevertheless it is not continuum, but discrete — keeping in mind the precision of floating-point numbers.

$$\Omega = \{\rightarrow, \leftarrow, \uparrow, \downarrow\} \times [0,1)^8 . \tag{8}$$

3 Crossover, mutation, fitness function, penalty terms

For the crossover operation, two-point crossover was applied. Two-point crossover is often recommended as having reduced susceptibility to so called: "positional bias", "hitchhikers", "endpoint effect" [4, pp. 171-173] and proving most effective in typical GAs [3, 2].

In binary-coded chromosomes the slight simplification was applied, such that the randomized crossing points could have occurred everywhere but inside *type of action* bit string. Figures 6 illustrate the version of two-point crossover that was applied respectively to binary-coded GAs.

$$\text{parent 1:} \quad \left(\boxed{0,0,} 1,1,1, \Big| 0, \boxed{1,0,} 0,1,0,1 \boxed{1,0,} 0,1,0,1 \boxed{0,0,} 1,1, \Big| 0,1 \right)$$

$$\text{parent 2:} \quad \left(\boxed{1,0,} 0,1,0, \Big| 1 \boxed{0,0,} 1,0,1,1 \boxed{0,1,} 1,1,0,1 \boxed{0,1,} 1,0, \Big| 1,1 \right)$$

$$\text{offspring 1:} \quad \left(\boxed{0,0,} 1,1,1, \Big| 1 \boxed{0,0,} 1,0,1,1 \boxed{0,1,} 1,1,0,1 \boxed{0,1,} 1,0, \Big| 0,1 \right)$$

$$\text{offspring 2:} \quad \left(\boxed{1,0,} 0,1,0, \Big| 0 \boxed{1,0,} 0,1,0,1 \boxed{1,0,} 0,1,0,1 \boxed{0,0,} 1,1, \Big| 1,1 \right)$$

Fig. 6. Illustration of two-point crossover applied to the binary-coded GA for the Jeep Problem. Type of action parts were for simplification not breakable by crossover, which is illustrated by frames around them.

As regards the mutation operation, in the binary-coded GA it was a usual flip-flop on a bit picked up at random. In the real-coded GA, the mutation was of greater importance (mainly to the *value* genes) and was done according to the following equation[7]

$$\lambda'_j = \begin{cases} \lambda_j + s(u - \lambda_j)\left(1 - \frac{g_{current}}{g_{max}}\right)^\beta, & \text{for } 0 \le s < 0.5; \\ \lambda_j + (s - 0.5)(1 - \lambda_j)\left(1 - \frac{g_{current}}{g_{max}}\right)^\beta, & \text{for } 0.5 \le s < 1, \end{cases} \tag{9}$$

---

[7] This refers only to the *value* genes. The *type of action* genes, were simply flip-flopped, since they are discrete.

where λ_j denotes the so far value of the gene under mutation selected at random location j, λ'_j is the new value after mutation, s is the random number of uniform distribution taken from $[0; 1)$ interval, l and u are respectively lower and upper bound of possible interval for a gene, and finally $g_{current}$ stands for the index of current GA generation, g_{max} stands for the maximum value of such index, while β is a heuristic exponent, usually chosen to be 2, which shapes how the generation factor $\left(1 - g_{current}/g_{max}\right)$ narrows the mutation neighborhood around λ_j as the evolution progresses[8]. This equation provides with aggressive exploration early in the evolution and concentrated sharpened exploitation in later stages [2].

In experiments, three probabilities were used: $p_{mutation}$, $p_{typeOfActionMutation}$, $p_{valueMutation}$. Therefore, setting those to e.g. $p_{mutation} = 0.3$, $p_{typeOfActionMutation} = 0.1$, $p_{valueMutation} = 0.7$ can be understood so that around 30% of the whole population is selected to undergo mutation, then, from within those 30% around 10% of genes representing the *type of action* gets mutated and around 70% of genes representing the *value* gets mutated.

The selection operation was *fitness proportionate*, i.e. typical roulette wheel selection was applied. It could be also possible to use the *rank selection* operation, which is often recommended for keeping good population diversity in early stages and preventing from the premature convergence on local optima. However, the similar effect was achieved by the mutation formula (9)[9].

The fitness function was

$$
f = \frac{x_{2n^2} + \sum_{k=2}^{2n^2} |x_k - x_{k-1}|}{\kappa \cdot \tau \cdot \omega}, \tag{10}
$$

where x_{2n^2} is the final position of jeep after the last step, the term $\sum_{k=2}^{2n^2} |x_k - x_{k-1}|$ calculates the total distance the jeep has traveled throughout its "lifetime", and κ, τ, ω represent exponential penalty terms (their meaning will be explained later).

The additional payment term — the total distance of the jeep journey, can be equally regarded as the quantity of fuel the jeep has consumed in its lifetime. In other words, being a lazy jeep did not pay.

---

[8] If $\beta = 1$, the narrowing term $\left(1 - g_{current}/g_{max}\right)^{\beta}$ would be linear.

[9] In some experiments also the mutation probabilities themselves were being extinguished along with the evolution progress using the $\left(1 - g_{current}/g_{max}\right)^{\beta}$ factor.

The penalty terms were exponential with positive arguments starting from 0, so that when a certain jeep did nothing wrong then his penalty was equal to 1. Otherwise, the penalty term increased fast punishing jeep severely. The meaning of each penalty term was as follows. κ was the penalty for the number of actions in the strategy the effective *value* of which was 0, e.g. if the jeep tried to make a traveling action but its tank was empty, or if the jeep tried to load some fuel, but there was no fuel available at its position. τ was the penalty for going to negative positions (behind the base). ω was the penalty necessary only in case of real-coded GA, and it punished the jeeps that in many steps were traveling very short distances — distances within the range of tolerance ε. Without ω it was quite interesting to discover that some jeeps in the population had developed a kind of cheating strategy consisting of many short moves, which allowed them to avoid penalty κ. For example if $\varepsilon = 0.02$ the starting sequence $(\rightarrow, 0.019), (\uparrow, 1.0)$ would make the second action successful, since the fuel containers at the base are still accessible within the ε tolerance.

4   Building blocks

Several first experiments with GA showed that the populations contained too many chromosomes with not the right interlace of moving $\{\rightarrow, \leftarrow\}$ and fueling actions $\{\uparrow, \downarrow\}$. Much computation time was lost because of this, and it took many generations in the evolution to eliminate such chromosomes. E.g. in the chromosome the sequence $(\uparrow, 0.3), (\uparrow, 0.5)$ could be just as well replaced with $(\uparrow, 0.8)$.

Because of this flaw, the author decided to introduce larger building blocks. One may notice that the optimal strategy can always be built from such three blocks:

- take fuel and go forth — $(\uparrow, \text{some value}), (\rightarrow, \text{some value})$,
- leave fuel and go back — $(\downarrow, \text{some value}), (\leftarrow, \text{some value})$,
- take fuel and go back — $(\uparrow, \text{some value}), (\leftarrow, \text{some value})$.

From now on, the chromosomes in the initial population were randomized but according to the three allowed building blocks. Also the crossover and mutation operations were adjusted to respect these building blocks.

5 Results

The tables 1 and 2 below illustrate the selected results obtained in experiments[10]. Two cases for $n = 2$ and $n = 3$ were mainly tested. These are rather small cases, but large enough to reveal the pattern for the correct best strategy to the person using the GA. Also in the sense of search space size, one could actually tell these are already very large cases, see section 2.

Columns third and forth give information about two main questions: 1. *can a genetic algorithm find the best strategy for the jeep?* 2. *can a genetic algorithm find the optimal quantities going with the best strategy?* In some experiments, the answers to these questions were 'no', 'yes' respectively. This means that the algorithm was unable to find the best strategy by itself, and only after presetting the right strategy in the chromosomes by a human, the algorithm was able to find the optimal quantities — the *value* parts of the strategy.

Column *generations executed* contains the number of generations, after which the solution was found and the GA run was stopped.

In the tables: p_c means $p_{crossover}$, p_m means $p_{mutation}$, p_{toam} means $p_{typeOfActionMutation}$, p_{vm} means $p_{valueMutation}$.

no.	GA type	was the best strategy found?	were the optimal values found?	population size	generations executed	p_c	p_m	p_{toam}	p_{vm}	bits per value	ε
1	b	yes	yes	100	17	0.8	0.2	0.1	0.3	2	-
2	b	yes	yes	100	32	0.8	0.2	0.2	0.3	2	-
3	b	yes	yes	50	75	0.9	0.1	0.2	0.8	2	-
4	b	yes	yes	50	112	0.8	0.3	0.1	0.4	2	-
5	b	yes	yes	1000	914	0.8	0.2	0.1	0.3	4	-
6	b	yes	yes	1000	1467	0.8	0.1	0.1	0.3	4	-
7	r	yes	yes	1000	385	0.9	0.9	0.3	0.9	-	0.02
8	r	yes	yes	1000	201	0.9	0.9	0.3	0.9	-	0.02
9	r	yes	yes	1000	57	0.9	0.9	0.3	0.9	-	0.02
10	r	yes	yes	1000	511	0.9	0.9	0.3	0.9	-	0.01

Tab. 1. Selected exemplary results for $n = 2$.

$$\left(\begin{array}{l} (\uparrow, 0.9822869153596993), (\rightarrow, 0.29268535330365747), (\downarrow, 0.41205049883815476), \\ (\leftarrow, 0.270454336928769), (\uparrow, 0.9861033127550701), (\rightarrow, 0.3042090189791012), \\ (\uparrow, 0.4103484363055104), (\rightarrow, 0.9971616413711467) \end{array} \right)$$

---

[10] The tables contain only selected runs of GAs, but they can be treated by the reader as the representative ones.

Fig. 8. Example of solution (effective strategy) found by a real-coded GA for $n = 2$. In this example the final position of jeep was 1.3236016767251364.

no.	GA type	was the best strategy found?	were the optimal values found?	population size	generations executed	p_c	p_m	p_{toam}	p_{vm}	bits per value	ε
1	b	yes	yes	2000	1512	0.9	0.3	0.1	0.3	4	-
2	b	yes	yes	2000	946	0.9	0.5	0.1	0.3	4	-
3	b	yes	yes	2000	2002	0.9	0.6	0.1	0.3	4	-
4	r	no	yes	5000	685	0.9	0.3	0.3	0.9	-	0.02
5	r	no	yes	5000	401	0.9	0.5	0.3	0.9	-	0.02
6	r	no	yes	5000	884	0.9	0.6	0.3	0.9	-	0.02

Tab. 2. Selected exemplary results for $n = 3$.

6 Conclusions

Although the Jeep Problem might seem like a purely mathematical riddle, such pure riddles often prove to be very good in testing the applicability of certain methods or tools, like for example genetic algorithms. The results obtained by the author were partially satisfactory and partially disappointing.

Satisfactory, in the sense that for the problem size of $n = 2$ (two containers of fuel) both binary and real-coded GAs did well and were finding the solutions (see table 1). Disappointing, in the sense that already for the problem size of $n = 3$, it became very difficult to find the solution. It required very high computational load — large population sizes and great number of generations (iterations). Eventually, for $n = 3$ the discrete binary-coded GAs managed to find both the right sequence of actions and the optimal values going with those actions. The real-coded GAs succeeded only in that second aspect, i.e. in order to find the optimal values, the right sequence of actions had to be preset for the GA, otherwise it failed (see table 2).

Further cases — for $n = 4, 5, \ldots$ were not even tested, because they imply strategy lengths of respectively $S_4 = 32$, $S_5 = 50$, and so on. Corresponding search space size are too huge.

Such half-satisfactory, half-disappointing results may be partially explained by the fact that the set of correct solutions is only a tiny fraction of the large search space (like a "needle in the hay"). In the effect, it is practically impossible for the GA to evolve generations that would contain partially good solutions. The whole chromosome must be either correct or very close to correct, or else the jeep determined by the chromosome will make a journey of little sense, e.g. by getting stuck in the middle of sequence of actions.

The better explanation however, it seems to the author, is that this very problem is of sophisticated recursive nature. Attempting to solve such problem with a typical GA, may be not a good approach. Probably, one would require rather to build some kind of recursion mechanism into the GA itself. This would mean to make the GA solve small cases first and then to combine smaller solutions into larger ones — a kind of "messy genetic algorithms", but in somewhat more recursive sense. This would probably also require introducing special crossover and mutation operations, or actually other new types of operations, e.g. an operation executing a kind of "scale and spread" of a smaller solution onto a larger one. This would mean the ability to generalize would be inside such a recursive GA itself. Whereas in the standard GA like in research hereby, it is unfortunately up to human to generalize the pattern, knowing merely that $D_1 = 1$, $D_2 = 1 + \frac{1}{3}$ and $D_3 = 1 + \frac{1}{3} + \frac{1}{5}$. Further results for $n = 4, 5, \ldots$, were beyond reasonable computation load and were not discovered.

7 References

[1] W. W. R. Ball and H. S. M. Coxeter. Mathematical Recreations and Essays. Dover, New York, USA, 13 edition, 1987.

[2] R. Bourisli and D. A. Kaminski. Solving fluid flow problems using a real-coded genetic algorithm with uniform refinement. Internet PDF document, http://raed.freewebpageorg.GAPF.pdf. Department of Mechanical, Aerospace and Nuclear Engineering, Rensselaer Polytechnic Institute, USA.

[3] L. J. Eshelman, R. A. Caruana, and J. D. Schaffer. Biases in the crossover landscape. In J. D. Schaffer, editor, Proceedings of the Third International Conference on Genetic Algorithms. Morgan Kaufmann, 1989.

[4] Melanie Mitchell. Introduction to Genetic Algorithms. The MIT Press, Cambridge, Massachusetts, USA, 1998. A Bradford Book.

[5] Eric W. Weisstein. Euler-mascheroni constant. Published by Wolfram Research, 1999. From Math World - A Wolfram Web Resource, http://mathworld.wolfram.com/Euler-MascheroniConstant.html.

[6] Eric W. Weisstein. Jeep problem. Published by Wolfram Research, 1999. From Math World - A Wolfram Web Resource, http://mathworld.wolfram.com/JeepProblem.html.

[7] Eric W. Weisstein. Polygamma function. Published by Wolfram Research, 1999. From Math World - A Wolfram Web Resource, http://mathworld.wolfram.com/PolygammaFunction.html.

Evaluation of operation and state of an object using artificial intelligence tools

Henryk Piech, Aleksandra Ptak, Marcin Machura

Technical University of Czestochowa, Institute of Mathematics and Informatics

Dabrowskiego Street, 73, 42-200 Czestochowa, Poland

e-mail: hpiech@adm. pcz.czest.pl

Abstract: An investigation of devices, phenomena, social groups or institutions characterized by some states and behaviours can include an evaluation of operation quality and obtained results. Thus, the investigation of static and dynamic operation aspects of objects is carried out

Key words: neural networks , genetic algoritms , logic and fuzzy sets

1   Main aim of researches

An exclusion of subjectivism in evaluation is not only connected with elimination of descriptions, i.e. non-deterministic elements, but also with minimization of the subjective influence in determination of weights or priorities. The artificial intelligence tools offer the possibilities of a greater objectivity of evaluation and classification of the studied object.

2   Assumptions about object characteristics modelling

One of the basic assumptions is changing in time the quantity of parameters taken into consideration in the choice of evaluation and qualification procedures. The use of fuzzy sets to illustrate this situation gives the clear picture which reflects the dynamism of changes (Figure 1).

466

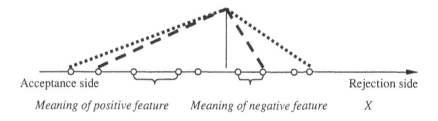

Acceptance side   Rejection side

Meaning of positive feature   *Meaning of negative feature*   *X*

Figure 1. A fuzzy model of evaluation of the object operation taking into account a chosen or changing in time set of negative and positive features

The object advantages are placed on the left side and its disadvantages on the right side of the maximum of the belonging function. This maximum means only the object existence fact, while the slopes treat files: acceptance (the left slope) and rejection (the right slope). This can be presented by means of the following notation:

$$Q = \{Z1, Z2, \ldots, Zn{:}W1, W2, \ldots, Wm\} \qquad (1)$$

The sequence layout of the positive ($\mathbf{Z}$) and negative ($\mathbf{W}$) features has only an importance in the context of dynamic characteristic investigations. The dynamic aspects will be presented as the change of degree of acceptance or rejection taking successive (addition or removal) advantages and disadvantages into consideration.

$$Q(1) = Q(0) - \Delta Q(-Zi : +Wm+1) = \{Z1, Z2, \ldots, Zi - Zi, \ldots, Zn : W1, W2, \ldots, Wm, Wm+1\} \quad (2)$$

The semantic parameters, the essences of which are presented in Figure 2, can easily be written by means of the symbolic notation.

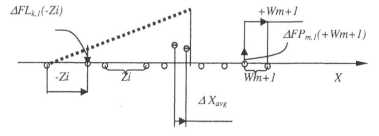

Figure 2. The correction influence of the advantages and disadvantages files on the belonging function shape, and the same on the inference element position *(Xavg)* [5,6], ΔF – belonging function increase, $L_{k,1}$, $P_{m,1}$ – the left and right slope of the belonging function after the first correction of the advantages and disadvantages files, k, m – the numbers of advantages and disadvantages respectively for which the increase of the function F is defined

The table below can illustrate the picture of dynamic changes in the object evaluation:

Increments of the belonging function	Correction No.	Change of X
$\Delta FL_{1,1}$ $\Delta FL_{2,1}$ ... * ... $\Delta FL_{n,1}$; $\Delta FP_{1,1}$ $\Delta FP_{2,1}$ ... $\Delta FP_{m,1}$ $\Delta FP_{m+1,1}$	1	$\Delta X_{avg,1}$
$\Delta FL_{1,2}$ $\Delta FL_{2,2}$ ...	2	$\Delta X_{avg,2}$
. . . .	. . . .	. . . .
$\Delta FL_{1,r}$ $\Delta FL_{2,r}$ ...	r	$\Delta X_{avg,r}$

The belonging function increments should be closely connected with real economic effects (qualitative etc.) ΔEL_i (ΔEP_j). The full economic effect can be estimated as:

$$GE = \sum_{i=1}^{n} \Delta ELi + \sum_{j=1}^{m} \Delta EPj \qquad (3)$$

where ΔEL_i and ΔEP_j are the economic effects obtained taking into account successive positive and negative characteristics.

3 Selection of weights of positive and negative characteristics using neural structure

The use of neural structures for the realization of weights selection of characteristics has a number of specific advantages, even such as a lack of the necessity of economic effects estimation for all possible combinations of positive and negative characteristics.

In the general case of Hebb's model [9] a neuron can be presented in the following way:

468

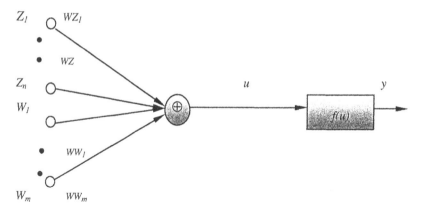

Figure 3. Neural structure.

According to Hebb's rule [9] it can be written:

$$\Delta WZ_i = \eta Z_i y \ , \ \Delta WW_i = \eta W_i y \ , \qquad (4)$$

where η is the learning coefficient.

In learning with "teacher" the output signal value y is replaced with the learning pattern d:

$$\Delta WZ_i = \eta Z_i d \ , \ \Delta WW_i = \eta W_i d \ , \qquad (5)$$

Applying Oja's modification [9] it can be written:

$$\left.\begin{array}{l} \Delta WZ_i = \eta y(Z_i - y WZ_i) \\ \Delta WW_i = \eta y(W_i - y WW_i) \end{array}\right\} (6)$$

The weight estimation model will be treated as the black box with the inputs {Z1, Z2, ..., Zn, W1 , W2 , ... , Wm } and the output y.

The data from each set are passed on the inputs and output (see Figure 4), and next the weight correction is performed by several iterations (for weight stabilization), and finally the whole process moves on to the next datasets.

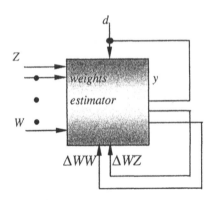

Figure 4. A model of the presynaptic weight estimator

The input number corresponding to the presence of positive and negative features should be planned with the reserve in relation to their actual number:

$$n = n + \text{reserve } n \,, \; m = m + \text{reserve } m \qquad (7)$$

These reserves can be estimated by means of prognostic methods that take into account a dynamism of the size increase of disadvantages and advantages in previous periods [9].

4 Evaluation algorithm of operation and state of the object

In general, the procedure of object evaluation includes the following stages:
- aggregation of object features with the division into advantages and disadvantages,
- specification and sequencing according to subjective criteria (e.g. ethical),
- estimation of weights with use of objective coefficients (e.g. financial),
- construction of a fuzzy model of the object evaluation,
- classification with use of centre of gravity coordinates (see Figure 2),
- determination of detailed parameters of the object evaluation.

The object evaluation can be currently conducted as the object features are increasing or decreasing. The dynamic changes in the features specification

470

require every time the realization of all procedure stages from the beginning. The model scheme for the object evaluation is presented in Figure 5.

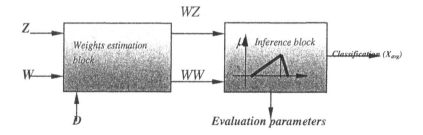

Figure 5. An evaluation model of operation and state of the object

If Xavg is negative the inference block classifies the object operation as positive, otherwise - as negative. The evaluation parameters are the percentage fraction of features in the general evaluation (see Figure 6).

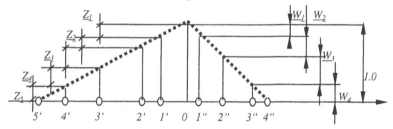

Figure 6. Evaluation parameters of the inference block $\{\underline{Z}_1, \underline{Z}_2, ...\}$ and $\{\underline{W}_1, \underline{W}_2, ...\}$

The parameters value expresses the following formula:

$$\underline{Z}_i = Z_i / \sum_{i=1}^{n} Zi \ , \quad \underline{W}_j = W_j / \sum_{j=1}^{m} Wj \qquad (8)$$

It follows that the evaluation parameters do not depend on the sequence composition of positive and negative features. Also, the classification result does not depend on the sequence arrangement of features. The inference on the positive classification occurs when satisfying the following equation:

$$\sum_{i=1}^{n} Zi > \sum_{j=1}^{m} Wj$$

The classification change follows due to appearance of the features set, on the side of the group of features that are in the "minority", with the total weight:

$$\Delta Z = \sum_{j=1}^{m} Wj - \sum_{i=1}^{n} Zi \ \ or \ \ \Delta W = \sum_{i=1}^{n} Zi - \sum_{j=1}^{m} Wj \qquad (9)$$

The new feature appearance influences each time with the decreasing the rank of remaining features of the same group (positive or negative features). This illustrates Figure 7.

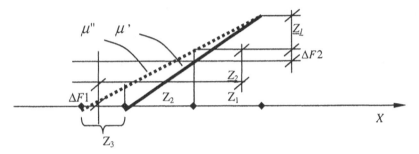

Figure 7. The influence of the introduction of the new feature on the rank of remaining features

Suppose that in the first stage there are only two positive features with the same weights Z_1, Z_2. The addition of Z_3 feature causes the evaluation parameters correction which can be defined with the help of the expression:

$$\Delta Zi = Zi \ / \sum_{j=1}^{m} Zj - Zi \ / \sum_{j=1}^{m+1} Zj \qquad (10)$$

The result of adding the successive object attributes (features) shows Figures 8, 9 and 10. Adding the successive weights causes changes that are proportional to the values of previously introduced individual weights.

472

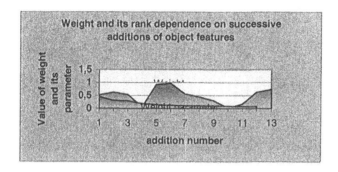

Figure 8. Dynamics of changes of weight and its rank (weight parameter) values in the process of successive additions of object attributes

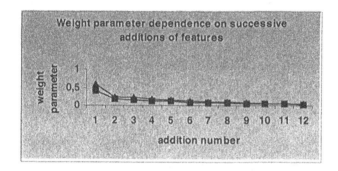

Figure 9. An example of the weight parameters value change for two selected features

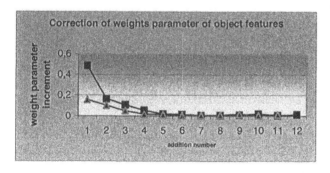

Figure 10. Increments (negative) of weight parameters for the example from Figure 9

5 QUALITY CONTROL STRATEGY ELEMENTS

The appearance of a new object feature (service) is certainly connected with economic effects. For example, positive features, as a rule, are connected with additional costs Kp_i as well as profits Zp_i resulting from them. The negative economic effect ($Zp_i - Kp_i$) can be treated as the classification of a negative feature. It happens when attributing weights to features depends exclusively or to a dominant extent on economic effects. An example of the object features set and their economic attributes with the simultaneous classification (division into disadvantages and advantages) is presented in Figure 11.

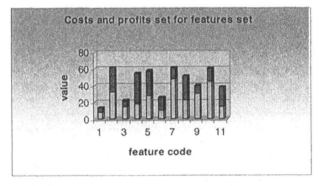

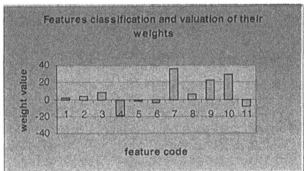

Figure 11. The structuralization of the object features set with the division into advantages and disadvantages

If non-financial factors affect the weight value then they can be taken into consideration, for example, in the following way:

$$Zi = \delta_i (Zp_i - Kp_i) + (1 - \delta_i) * Zm_i$$

$$Wk = \delta_k (Zp_k - Kp_k) + (1 - \delta_k) * Wm_k \qquad (11)$$

where Zm_i, Wm_k - the influence of non-economic factors on the weight value of an advantage and disadvantage,

δ_i - the coefficient of the economic factors share.

6 CONCLUSION

1. The influence of non-economic factors can change the feature categorization (disadvantage into advantage and vice versa). The diagrams in Figure 12 illustrate the influence ($\delta_i = 0,25$; $\delta_i=0,75$; $\delta_i=0,9$) of economic and non-economic factors on the values and categories (the result of classification) of the feature set weights.

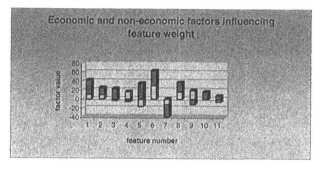

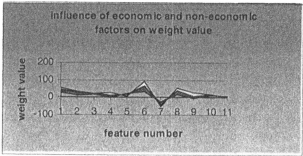

Figure 12. The dependence of the weight value on the share of economic and non-economic factors

2. The evaluation and its categorization depends on different non-economic factors that, as can be seen in Figure 12, does not radically change the feature classification although it can move its weight value towards the opposite category.

7   REFERENCES

[1]   Czogala E., Perdycz W.: Elements and methods of fuzzy sets theory. PWN, Warsaw 1985 (in Polish)

[2]   Davis L.: Genetic Algorithms and Simulated. A. Morgan Kaufmann Pub. Inc., 1988

[3]   Davis L.: Handbook of Genetic Algorithms. Nostrand Reinhold, 1991

[4]   De Groot M. H.: Optimal statistic decisions. McGraw – Hill, New York 1970

[5]   Kacprzyk J.: Fuzzy sets in system analysis. PWN, Warsaw 1986 (in Polish)

[6]   Lachwa A.: Fuzzy world of files, numbers, relations, facts, rules and decisions. Akademicka Oficyna Wydawnicza Exit, Warsaw 2001 (in Polish)

[7]   Lorayane H.: Secrets of supermemory. RAVI, Warsaw 2002 (in Polish)

[8]   Piegat A.: Fuzzy modelling and controlling. Akademicka Oficyna Wydawnicza Exit, Warsaw 2003 (in Polish)

[9]   Rutkowska D., Piliński M., Rutkowski L.: Neural networks, genetic algorithms and fuzzy systems. WN PWN, Warsaw 1997 (in Polish)

[10]   Zadeh L. A.: Fuzzy limitations calculus; design and systems; methodological problems. Ossolineum 1980 (in Polish)